PRACTICE FOR SUCCESS

SPANISH
Verb Tenses

Frank Nuessel, Ph.D.

2nd Edition

BARRON'S

All inquiries should be addressed to:
Barron's Educational Series, Inc.
250 Wireless Boulevard
Hauppauge, New York 11788
www.barronseduc.com

ISBN: 978-1-4380-0294-1

Library of Congress Control Number: 2013009630

Library of Congress Cataloging-in-Publication Data

Nuessel, Frank H.
  [Spanish verb workbook]
  Practice for success : Spanish verb tenses / Frank H. Nuessel, Ph.D., University
of Louisville.—2nd ed.
    pages cm
  Previously published as Spanish verb workbook, 2005.
  ISBN 978-1-4380-0294-1
  1. Spanish language—Verb—Handbooks, manuals, etc. I. Title.
  PC4271.N84   2013
  468.2'421—dc23   2013009630

Printed in the United States of America

9 8 7 6 5 4 3 2 1

10%
POST-CONSUMER WASTE
Paper contains a minimum
of 10% post-consumer
waste (PCW). Paper used
in this book was derived
from certified, sustainable
forestlands.

Contents

Introduction

Many people feel a sense of anxiety when starting to learn a new language. Too many conjugations! Too many uses! But verbs are crucial to the effective learning of a new language. It cannot be avoided. These feelings are normal and this book will help you to overcome these feelings very quickly.

This book is an in-depth and comprehensive manual on how to conjugate and use Spanish verbs. Its simple method is designed to help you learn the basics of Spanish verbs in an effortless way. All you need is this book, no matter at what stage of learning you find yourself. It can thus be used profitably by:

- Those who know some Spanish, but who wish to improve their knowledge of Spanish verbs in a comprehensive and intensive, but user-friendly, way.

- Students enrolled in a Spanish language course, in a high school, college, or university, who feel that they need more practice with Spanish verbs.

- Beginners of the language.

If you are a true beginner, you will find that this book makes no assumptions. You will learn about the other aspects of Spanish grammar as you work your way through it. If you are someone who already possesses some knowledge of Spanish, you will find this book particularly helpful, since it also reviews the other aspects of grammar, connecting them to the Spanish verbal system.

Thus, whether you are just beginning your study of Spanish or have had some training in the language, this book is for you. Previous knowledge has not been taken for granted in these pages; definitions and explanations are concise and clear, and examples use and reuse a core of basic vocabulary.

You should not skip any chapter, especially if you are a beginner. The book is designed to be sequential and coherent. It builds on notions and vocabulary introduced in previous chapters. By the end, you will be in a position to grasp the fundamentals of the Spanish verb system. You can also use this book as a reference manual, consulting the table of contents to guide you to the areas of Spanish verb conjugation and use for information or practice.

Finally, we ask that you consult maps of those countries where Spanish is an official language so that you can visualize these places. You will see that Spanish is truly a worldwide language.

¡Diviértete! (*Have fun!*)

How to Use This Book

This book is divided into five main parts, each consisting of a number of chapters. Part 1 covers the present indicative tenses, Part 2 covers the past indicative tenses, Part 3 the future and conditional tenses, Part 4 the subjunctive tenses, and Part 5 the imperative and the passive voice.

Overview Units

Before starting to do the exercises and activities in the chapters of a specific part, read the overview unit at the beginning, especially if you are unsure about grammatical terms or concepts. This unit explains the relevant technical terms used in each part, in a non-technical and easy-to-follow way—what is a *conjugation*, what is a verb *tense*, what is the *subjunctive*, and so on.

Conjugation Information at the Beginning of a Chapter

Each of the chapters is organized around a specific tense or problematic verb (or verbs). There are several recurring sections and features in each chapter.

In the introductory section, you are given all of the information you will need on how to conjugate verbs in a specific tense and mood. This is followed by exercises that, although they may appear mechanical, are nevertheless necessary. These are akin to scales and arpeggios in musical practice. A student will never become a good pianist or violinist without mastery over them. Correspondingly, you will need to do your exercises consistently and faithfully so as to gain mastery over Spanish verbs.

Vocabulary

Words constitute the building blocks of any language. In order to facilitate the successful completion of the exercises, we have a comprehensive Spanish-English vocabulary and English-Spanish vocabulary at the end of the book for easy reader reference.

Uses and Features

This section contains a summary of how the verb or verb tense is to be used and what its features are. Exercises focusing on usage follow. Many of these involve translating from English to Spanish. In this area of grammar, there is no better way to grasp differences in usage than by comparing how the two languages express certain things. The exercises should be pronounced aloud. It really works!

Tips, Notes, Grammar

Throughout a chapter, tips on how to use a verb, notes on aspects of grammar that are relevant to the chapter, charts introducing new vocabulary, and the like are interspersed throughout.

Crossword Puzzle

Each chapter ends with a crossword puzzle that is designed to provide an entertaining format for reinforcing what you have learned in the chapter. The clues provided will vary in nature and level of difficulty.

Vocalization

It is important to vocalize all of the exercises in each chapter. This will help you use the verbs.

1. Say each exercise aloud. In some exercises, you are asked to produce a verb form. After you have done this, make up a complete sentence (based on the vocabulary that you already know).
2. Articulate each sentence that you have to translate from English to Spanish. This will help you remember what you have done and it will give you confidence.

Back Matter

At the back of the book, you will find the answers to the exercises of all chapters and a Spanish-English and an English-Spanish vocabulary of all the words that you have been using in this book.

Part One

The Present Indicative and the Present Progressive

The Present: An Overview

What Are Verbs?

Verbs are words that indicate the action performed by the subject of a sentence. For this reason, they agree with the *person* (first, second, third) and *number* (singular or plural) of the subject.

Ella	canta
She	*sings*

↑   ↑

3rd person singular subject pronoun	3rd person singular form of verb cantar / *to sing*

Los amigos	cantan
The friends	*sing*

↑   ↑

3rd person plural subject pronoun	3rd person plural form of verb cantar / *to sing*

Infinitives and Conjugations

The *infinitive* is the form of a verb not inflected (modified) for a person or number. In English, it is commonly preceded by *to—to sing, to eat,* and so on. In a dictionary, verbs are listed in their infinitive form, the form that ends in -r.

Spanish verbs are divided into three conjugations according to their infinitive endings. A *conjugation* is the systematic arrangement of the verb forms according to tense and mood. The infinitive endings in Spanish are -ar (first conjugation), -er (second conjugation), and -ir (third conjugation).

> **TIP**
>
> The infinitive endings allow you to determine which person and number endings a verb must take when you conjugate it. Learn these now!
>
> | pagar / *to pay* | beber / *to drink* | vivir / *to live* |
> | ↑ | ↑ | ↑ |
> | first conjugation | second conjugation | third conjugation |

Tense

A verb tense indicates the time an action occurred—now (present tense), before (past tense), after (future tense).

1. Present tense:
   La <u>como</u> ahora. / *I'm eating it now.*

2. Past tense:
   La <u>comí</u> ayer. / *I ate it yesterday.*

3. Future tense:
   La <u>comeré</u> mañana. / *I will eat it tomorrow.*

Mood

Not only do verbs allow you to express the time an action took place, but they also allow you to convey the manner of thinking, point of view, etc. This aspect is known as *mood*:

1. Indicative mood = statement:
   Pedro <u>lee</u> esa novela. / *Peter is reading that novel.*

2. Imperative mood = command:
   Inés, ¡<u>lee</u> esa novela! / *Inés, read that novel!*

3. Subjunctive mood = probability:
   Es probable que Jorge <u>lea</u> esa novela. / *It is probable that George is reading that novel.*

Regular and Irregular Verbs

A *regular verb* is one that is conjugated according to a recurring pattern. A verb that is not conjugated in this way is known as *irregular*.

The Present Indicative

The present indicative, called the **presente de indicativo**, allows you to express, indicate, or refer to actions that are ongoing, permanent, or imply present time in some way. It is the most commonly used tense in everyday conversation.

The Present Progressive

The second main present tense is the present progressive, called the **presente progresivo** in Spanish. It is an alternative to the present indicative, allowing you to zero in on an ongoing action. It will be dealt with in Chapter 6.

Subject Pronouns

The subject pronouns are shown below.

Singular		Plural	
1st person	(yo) / *I*	1st person	(nosotros) / *we* (nosotras) / *we*
2nd person	(tú) / *you* (fam. sg.)	2nd person	(vosotros) / *you* (fam. pl.) (vosotras) / *you* (fam. pl.) Used in Spain.
3rd person	(él) / *he* (ella) / *she* (usted) / *you* (pol. sg.)	3rd person	(ellos) / *they* (ellas) / *they* (ustedes) / *you* (pol. pl.) General plural in Latin America.

USAGE NOTES

As you can see, there are both familiar (fam.) and polite (pol.) forms of address in Spanish. These are not to be used alternatively! If you address someone incorrectly, it might be taken as rudeness! So, be careful.

Simply put, the familiar forms are used to address people with whom you are on familiar terms: members of the family, friends, etc. If you call someone by a first name, then you are obviously on familiar terms.

Remember that the plural for the singular (sg.) forms tú (fam.) and usted (pol.) in this hemisphere is ustedes. This is the usage that you are most likely to hear unless you are in Spain. In Spain, the plural (pl.) for tú is vosotros/vosotras and the plural for usted is ustedes. In the exercises in this book, we will use the vosotros/vosotras forms, but you must remember that they are used only in Spain. The following chart illustrates this point:

Spain:	Singular		Plural
	tú	→	vosotros, vosostras
	usted	→	ustedes

Latin America:	Singular		Plural
	tú	→	ustedes
	usted	→	ustedes

Remember also that usted has the following abbreviations: Ud. and Vd. Likewise, ustedes has the following common abbreviations: Uds. and Vds.

Notice also that we have placed the first and second persons singular (yo, tú) and plural (nosotros, nosotras, vosotros, vosotras) within parentheses ( ) to call to your attention the fact that these forms are normally used for emphasis. We will follow this convention throughout the book as appropriate.

NOTE

There are three pairs of forms in this textbook: nosotros/nosotras / *we*, vosotros / vosotras / *you*, and ellos/ellas / *they*. The first form, masculine plural, may refer to men only, or to a group of men and women. The second form, feminine plural, refers only to women.

In this book, we shall abbreviate these forms as follows: nosotros/-as, vosotros/-as, and ellos/-as.

Also, note that the polite form usted / *you* may be abbreviated as Ud. or Vd. Likewise, the plural polite form ustedes / *you* may be abbreviated as Uds. or Vds. In this book, we shall use the abbreviations Ud. and Uds.

What Are Sentences?

A *sentence* is an organized sequence of words that allows you to make a statement, ask a question, express a thought, offer an opinion, etc. In writing, a sentence is easily identified because it starts with a capitalized word and ends with a period, a question mark, or an exclamation point. Remember, however, that in Spanish, you introduce a question with an "upside down" question mark: ¿. Likewise, you introduce a command with an "upside down" exclamation point: ¡.

1. Affirmative sentence:
    Él es español. / *He is Spanish.*

2. Interrogative sentence:
    ¿Quién es ese hombre? / *Who is that man?*

3. Imperative sentence:
    Margarita, ¡ven acá! / *Margarita, come here!*

Sentences have two basic parts: a *subject* and a *predicate*. A subject is "who" or "what" the sentence is about. It is often the first element in a simple sentence:

    Gloria habla español. / *Gloria speaks Spanish.*
    Ella es boliviana. / *She is Bolivian.*

But be careful! The subject is not necessarily always the first word:

    Sí, también Robérto habla español. / *Yes, Roberto also speaks Spanish.*
    No, quizás Clara no venga. / *No, perhaps Clara is not coming.*

A *predicate* is the remaining part of the sentence. It provides information about the subject. In many simple sentences, you will find it after the subject.

    Mario habla español. / *Mario speaks Spanish.*
    Él es mexicano. / *He is Mexican.*

A Note About Tense and Verb Form Names

In this book, you will learn and practice the commonly used Spanish tenses. There are 7 simple tenses and 6 compound tenses in this volume. The names of these tenses in English and Spanish follow.

Simple Tenses

English Name	Spanish Name
1. Present indicative	El presente de indicativo
2. Preterit	El pretérito
3. Imperfect indicative	El imperfecto de indicativo
4. Future	El futuro
5. Conditional	El potencial simple
6. Present subjunctive	El presente de subjuntivo
7. Imperfect subjunctive	El imperfecto de subjuntivo

Compound Tenses

English Name	Spanish Name
1. Present perfect indicative	El perfecto de indicativo
2. Pluperfect or past perfect indicative	El pluscuamperfecto de indicativo
3. Future perfect	El futuro perfecto
4. Conditional perfect	El potencial perfecto
5. Present perfect subjunctive	El perfecto de subjuntivo
6. Pluperfect or past perfect subjunctive	El pluscuamperfecto de subjuntivo

The Progressive Verb Forms

You will learn the following progressive verb forms: (1) present progressive and (2) imperfect progressive.

English Name	Spanish Name
1. Present progressive	El presente progresivo
2. Imperfect progressive	El imperfecto progresivo

Other Verb Forms

There are other verb forms in Spanish that are called non-finite forms. This means that they do not indicate the person (first, second, and third person), number (singular, plural), tense (present, past, future, conditional), or the mood (indicative, subjunctive, imperative). The following chart provides the names of these forms in English and Spanish.

English Name	Spanish Name
1. Infinitive	Infinitivo
2. Present participle	Gerundio
3. Past participle	Participio

Additional Verb Forms

There are two other verb forms. The first is the imperative or command form. The second is the passive voice.

English Name	Spanish Name
1. Imperative/Command	Imperativo/Mandato
2. Passive voice	La voz pasiva

You are now ready to start learning how to conjugate and use Spanish verbs!

Sample English Verb Conjugation

The following is a conjugation of the English verb *to speak*.

INFINITIVE: to speak
PRESENT PARTICIPLE: speaking
PAST PARTICIPLE: spoken

The Seven Simple Tenses

Tense	Tense Forms
Present Indicative	I speak, you speak, he (she, it) speaks; we speak, you speak, they speak or: I do speak, you speak, he (she, it) does speak; we do speak, you do speak, they do speak or: I am speaking, you are speaking, he (she, it) is speaking; we are speaking, you are speaking, they are speaking
Imperfect Indicative	I was speaking, you were speaking, he (she, it) was speaking; we were speaking, you were speaking, they were speaking or: I spoke, you spoke, he (she, it) spoke; we spoke, you spoke, they spoke or: I was speaking, you were speaking, he (she, it) was speaking; we were speaking, you were speaking, they were speaking
Preterit	I spoke, you spoke, he (she, it) spoke; we spoke, you spoke, they spoke or: I did speak, you did speak, he (she, it) did speak; we did speak, you did speak, they did speak
Future	I shall speak, you will speak, he (she, it) will speak we shall speak, you will speak, they will speak
Conditional	I would speak, you would speak, he (she, it) would speak; we would speak, you would speak, they would speak
Present Subjunctive	that I may speak, that you may speak, that he (she, it) may speak; that we may speak, that you may speak, that they may speak
Imperfect Subjunctive	that I might speak, that you might speak, that he (she, it) might speak that we might speak, that you might speak, that they might speak

The Six Compound Tenses

Tense	Tense Forms
Present Perfect or Past Indefinite	I have spoken, you have spoken, he (she, it) has spoken; we have spoken, you have spoken, they have spoken
Pluperfect or Past Perfect	I had spoken, you had spoken, he (she, it) had spoken; we had spoken, you had spoken, they had spoken
Future Perfect or Future Anterior	I shall have spoken, you will have spoken, he (she, it) will have spoken; we shall have spoken, you will have spoken, they will have spoken
Conditional Perfect	I would have spoken, you would have spoken, he (she, it) would have spoken; we would have spoken, you would have spoken, they would have spoken
Present Perfect Subjunctive	that I may have spoken, that you may have spoken, that he (she, it) may have spoken; that we may have spoken, that you may have spoken, that they may have spoken
Pluperfect or Past Perfect Subjunctive	that I might have spoken, that you might have spoken, that he (she, it) might have spoken; that we might have spoken, that you might have spoken, that they might have spoken

Command Forms

Imperative or Command	—speak, let him (her) speak let us speak, —speak, let them speak

What Verbs Do in Spanish

It is important to know what kind of information a Spanish verb conveys. The following list will help you to understand these important verbal functions. As you read each chapter in this book and write out the exercises, you will learn specific details relating to these roles for each verb tense.

1. The verb tells the type of action to which the verb refers, or its meaning, e.g., *to speak* / hablar, *to eat* / comer, *to live* / vivir, and so forth.

2. The theme vowel (the last vowel in the infinitive form of the verb) of the verb tells how the specific verb will be conjugated. This is indicated by the final vowel in the infinitive (the form of the verb that ends in –r, and the form that is found in a dictionary). There are three conjugation classes in Spanish: -ar, -er, and –ir. Examples of the three conjugation classes are: (1) to speak / hablar, (2) to eat / comer, and (3) to live / vivir.

3. The conjugated verb tells the tense, or the time of the action: (1) Present, (2) past, (3) future.

4. The ending of the conjugated verb tells who is speaking. It can tell if the verb is referring to one person (I, you [one person], he, she, it), or more than one person (we, you [two or more people], they).

Vos–A Regional Verb Form

The word **vos** (= *you*, familiar, singular) is a subject pronoun form that corresponds to a specific verbal suffix, or ending in the present indicative. The use of the pronoun **vos** and its corresponding second person singular verb is closely associated with the River Plate area of South America (Argentina, Paraguay, Uruguay). This pronoun is also used in other countries as well, for example, Bolivia, as well as parts of Colombia, Venezuela, Chile, and Perú. Finally, it occurs in the Central American nations of Panamá, Costa Rica, Nicaragua, El Salvador, Honduras, and Guatemala.

In simple terms, the verb forms that correspond to the subject pronoun **vos** appear in the present indicative, but there are variations from this form. The following table illustrates this usage. The stress of the **vos** forms appears on the last syllable, while the stress on the standard **tú** form falls on the next to the last syllable. The **vos** form of the verb also has a graphic accent mark on the written form of the verb to indicate a shift in the placement of the stress. In the following examples, the placement of the stress is indicated by an underline on the verb form.

Verb	Tú form, second person singular, present indicative	Vos form, second person singular, present indicative
hablar / *to speak*	hablas	hablás
comer / *to eat*	comes	comés
vivir / *to live*	vives	vivís

The Parts of Speech

English Term	Spanish Term	Definition	Examples
Verb	Verbo	A word that describes an action or a state of being	*run* / correr *be* / estar / ser
Noun	Sustantivo	A word that refers to a person, place, thing, or concept	*Mary* / María *Cuba* / Cuba *book* / libro *truth* / verdad
Adjective	Adjetivo	A word that describes a noun	*green* / verde *tall* / alto
Adverb		A word that describes an action	*clearly* / claramente *early* / temprano
Pronoun	Pronombre	A word that replaces a noun	*she* / ella [Marta = ella]
Preposition	Preposición	A word that links a noun to another word	*to* / a *in* / en
Conjunction	Conjunción	A word that joins clauses or sentences	*and* / y *when* / cuando
Interjection	Interjección	A brief exclamation of pain or surprise	*ow!* / ¡uy!

1
The Present Indicative (*el presente de indicativo*) of Regular Verbs

Uses and Features

The **presente de indicativo** / *present indicative* is used in everyday conversation to refer to actions, events, and ideas that imply the present situation or some permanent or habitual situation. Specifically, it is used:

1. To indicate an action or state of being that is taking place at the present time:
    <u>Hablo</u> con Isabel en este momento. / *I am speaking with Isabel at this moment.*
    <u>Miro</u> una telenovela ahora. / *I am watching a soap opera now.*

2. To indicate an action or state of being that is permanent or continuous:
    <u>Hablo</u> español también. / *I speak Spanish too.*
    Ella lo <u>comprende</u> todo. / *She understands everything.*

3. To emphasize something in the present time:
    Sí, ¡lo <u>comprendo</u>! / *Yes, I understand!*
    No, ¡no <u>miro</u> nada! / *No, I don't look at anything!*

4. To indicate a habitual action:
    <u>Toco</u> la guitarra todos los días. / *I play the guitar every day.*
    Los lunes, <u>limpiamos</u> la casa. / *On Mondays, we clean the house.*

5. To convey a general truth:
    Las tiendas <u>abren</u> a las siete y media. / *The stores open at 7:30 A.M.*
    Los españoles <u>trabajan</u> mucho. / *Spaniards work hard.*

6. To express an action that will occur in the near future:
    Él <u>llega</u> mañana. / *He will arrive tomorrow.*
    Dentro de poco, <u>escribo</u> un correo electrónico. / *In a little bit, I will write an e-mail.*

First Conjugation Verbs

As you learned in the preceding unit, the infinitives of regular Spanish verbs end in **-ar**, **-er**, or **-ir**. Those ending in **-ar** are first conjugation verbs. To form the present indicative of such verbs, called the **presente de indicativo**, do the following:

1. Drop the infinitive ending, -ar. This produces the "verb stem," as it is called. The verb stem contains the basic meaning of the verb.

  hablar / *to speak* → habl-

2. Add the following *endings* to the stem:

(yo)	-o
(tú)	-as
(él, ella, Ud.)	-a
(nosotros/-as)	-amos
(vosotros/-as)	-áis
(ellos/-as, Uds.)	-an

3. Here's the result:

hablar / *to speak*

Subject Pronoun	Verb Form	Meaning
(yo)	habl+o	*I speak, I am speaking, I do speak*
(tú)	habl+as	*you (fam. sg.) speak, you are speaking, you do speak*
(él, ella, Ud.)	habl+a	*he, she, you (pol. sg.) speak(s), he, she, you is/are speaking, he, she, you does/do speak*
(nosotros/-as)	habl+amos	*we speak, we are speaking, we do speak*
(vosotros/-as)	habl+áis	*you (fam. pl.) speak, you are speaking, you do speak*
(ellos/-as, Uds.)	habl+an	*they, you (pol. pl.) speak, they, you are speaking, they, you do speak*

TIP

You should note that the following endings are associated with the following verb forms in Spanish.

Person	Ending
(tú)	-s *
(nosotros/-as)	-mos
(vosotros/-as)	-is
(Uds., ellos/-as)	-n

*The preterit tense (see Chapter 7) is the one exception to this rule. It does not have an ending in -s for the tú / *you* form as you will discover.

To make a sentence negative in Spanish, just put no before the predicate (no / *no*; sí / *yes*).

Affirmative	Negative
Sí, Raquel habla español. / *Yes, Raquel speaks Spanish.*	No, Raquel <u>no</u> habla español. / *No, Rachel does not speak Spanish.*
Sí, ellos llegan mañana. / *Yes, they are arriving tomorrow.*	No, ellos <u>no</u> llegan mañana. / *No, they are not arriving tomorrow.*

TIP

Notice that the presente de indicativo is rendered by three English verb forms:

hablo   =   I speak
I am speaking
I do speak

The present tense may also be used to convey the immediate future, i.e., to an event that will take place very soon.

Hablo español esta tarde. / *I will speak Spanish this afternoon.*

USAGE NOTES

Note that the pronouns yo, tú, nosotros, nosotras, vosotros, vosotras are normally used to make an emphatic statement. In this book, we will place these forms in parentheses as a reminder that they should only be used for emphasis: (yo), (tú), (nosotros), (nosotras), (vosotros), (vosotras).

Observe the difference between the following two sentences:

Hablo español. / *I speak Spanish.* = Matter of fact statement.
Yo hablo español. / *I speak Spanish.* = Very emphatic statement (with raised voice in English).

English normally requires a subject pronoun, but in the Spanish verb system the ending tells us who is doing the speaking.

In the third person singular and plural, the subject pronouns are often used because one verb form corresponds to several possible subjects in Spanish:

Él habla. / *He speaks.*
Ella habla. / *She speaks.*
Ud. habla. / *You (pol. sg.) speak.*
Ellos hablan. / *They (men, or men and women) speak.*
Ellas hablan. / *They (women) speak.*
Uds. hablan. / *You (pol. pl. in this hemisphere, also plural of the familiar form tú) speak.*

In Spanish the -s form of the verb corresponds to tú / *you* (fam. sg.). In English the -s form of the verb of the present tense signifies the third person singular:

Spanish:

(Tú) cantas. / *You sing.*
Él canta. / *He sings.*

In Spanish, when you include yourself (yo) and at least one other person, you must use the -mos form of the verb.

Javier y yo hablamos español. / *Javier and I speak Spanish.*
Amparo, Enrique y yo hablamos inglés. / *Amparo, Enrique and I speak English.*

Common Verbs

Below are some common regular first conjugation verbs that will come in handy for basic communication.

abrazar	to embrace, to hug	hablar	to speak
acabar	to finish, to complete	hallar	to find
admirar	to admire	limpiar	to clean
andar	to walk	llamar	to call
bailar	to dance	llegar (a)	to arrive
besar	to kiss	llevar	to wear, to carry
buscar	to look for	mandar	to send
caminar	to walk	manejar	to drive
cantar	to sing	mirar	to look at, to watch
charlar	to chat	nadar	to swim
cocinar	to cook	necesitar	to need
comprar	to buy	pagar	to pay for
conjugar	to conjugate	pasar	to spend (time)
cuidar	to care for	pintar	to paint
dejar	to leave (something)	preparar	to prepare
descansar	to rest	regresar	to return
desear	to want	terminar	to complete, to finish
entrar (en)	to enter	tocar	to play (an instrument), to touch
escuchar	to listen to	tomar	to take (food)
esperar	to wait for, to hope	trabajar	to work
estudiar	to study	viajar	to travel
gastar	to spend (money)	visitar	to visit
gritar	to shout		

GRAMMAR NOTE

Certain verbs have characteristic prepositions. This means that if there is a following noun or in many cases a following infinitive, it is necessary to include this so-called characteristic preposition. In the list above, entrar (en) is one example of this type of verb. By convention, the characteristic preposition usually appears in parentheses ( ). It is used when there is a following noun: Entro en la biblioteca / I enter the library. As we progress in this book, there will be many more such verbs.

VOCABULARY NOTE

The verb acabar / to finish, to complete has the special idiomatic meaning "to have just" when used with the preposition de and an infinitive as shown below.

Acabo de estudiar.
I have just studied.

TIP

Some commonly used verbs have a preposition in their basic meaning:

buscar	*to look **for***
escuchar	*to listen **to***
esperar	*to wait **for***
pagar	*to pay **for***

It is not necessary to add an extra word for these prepositions; it is built-in!

GRAMMAR NOTE

Spanish nouns are either masculine or feminine. You can usually identify the noun's gender by the ending. If it ends in -o, the noun is (generally) masculine; if it ends in -a, it is (generally) feminine. There are exceptions to the previous rule and several commonly used nouns are among these exceptions. Also, if the word refers to people, it will be masculine or feminine if it refers to a man or a woman. Dictionaries usually indicate the gender of a noun with the following notations: (*m.*) for masculine and (*f.*) for feminine.

Masculine	*Feminine*
minut<u>o</u> / *minute*	hij<u>a</u> / *daughter*

Note the forms of the definite article ("*the*") introduced above:

el   =   with a masculine singular noun:

<u>el</u> hij<u>o</u> / *the son*

la   =   with a feminine singular noun:

<u>la</u> hij<u>a</u> / *the daughter*

NOTE

The word ¿verdad? in Spanish is used as a tag question. Its precise meaning is determined by the context as shown below.

Estudias español, ¿<u>verdad</u>? / *You study Spanish, <u>don't you?</u>*

Ellos beben café, ¿<u>verdad</u>? / *They drink coffee, <u>don't they?</u>*

EXERCISE Set 1-1

A. Supply the missing Spanish verb ending and then give the English equivalent.

EXAMPLE: *él habl_*   =   _____

   él habla   =   *he speaks, he is speaking, he does speak*

1. (yo) toc__   =   _____

2. (tú) esper__   =   _____

3. (nosotros) prepar__   =   _____

4. (ellos) llev__   =   _____

5. (vosotros) pag__   =   _____

6. (Ud.) trabaj__   =   _____

7. (ellas) mir__   =   _____

8. (Uds.) estudi__   =   _____

9. (yo) viaj__   =   _____

10. (tú) bail__   =   _____

11. (nosotras) cant__   =   _____

12. (él) compr__   =   _____

13. (ellas) habl__   =   _____

14. (Ud.) entr__   =   _____

15. (Uds.) busc__   =   _____

B. How do you say the following sentences in Spanish? Remember that sg. = singular, pl. = plural, fam. = familiar, pol. = polite. The material in parentheses tells you what verb form to use, or it provides cultural information.

1. Excuse me, do you (pol. sg.) speak English?

   _____

2. Yes, I speak English very well.

   _____

3. They do not speak Spanish very well.

_____

4. We speak Spanish a little bit.

_____

5. Rafael, you (fam. sg.) also speak Spanish, don't you?

_____

6. I do not speak Spanish, but my daughter speaks Spanish very well.

_____

7. No, it is not true. The bus is not arriving now.

_____

8. Thank you, you are very kind (pol. sg.). I do not speak Spanish well.

_____

9. Alejandro plays the cello like *Pablo Casals*[1] and Claudia paints like *Diego Velázquez*[2].

_____

10. She listens to the radio too much.

_____

11. I want to watch the bullfight[3] on TV.

_____

12. They play the piano very well.

_____

13. You (fam. sg.) are always watching television.

_____

14. You (pol. sg.) are wearing a new jacket, aren't you?

_____

15. You (pol. pl.) are waiting for the bus, aren't you?

_____

[1]Renowned Spanish cellist, 1876–1973.
[2]Renowned Spanish painter, 1599–1660.
[3]Regular afternoon program in Madrid.

Second Conjugation Verbs

Infinitives ending in -er are classified as second conjugation verbs. To form the present indicative of these verbs, do exactly the same thing you did with first conjugation verbs:

1. Drop the infinitive ending, -er. This produces the "verb stem," as it is called.
comer / *to eat* → com-

2. Add the following endings to the stem:

(yo)	-o
(tú)	-es
(él, ella, Ud.)	-e
(nosotros/-as)	-emos
(vosotros/-as)	-éis
(ellos/-as, Uds.)	-en

3. Here's the result:

comer / *to eat*

Subject Pronoun	Verb Form	Meaning
(yo)	com+o	*I eat, I am eating, I do eat*
(tú)	com+es	*you (fam. sg.) eat, you are eating, you do eat*
(él, ella, Ud.)	com+e	*he, she, you (pol. sg.) eat(s), he, she, you is/are eating, he, she, you does/do eat*
(nosotros/-as)	com+emos	*we eat, we are eating, we do eat*
(vosotros/-as)	com+éis	*you (fam. pl.) eat, you are eating, you do eat*
(ellos/-as, Uds.)	com+en	*they, you (pol. pl.) eat, they, you are eating, they, you do eat*

Common Verbs

Below are some common regular second conjugation verbs for basic communication.

aprender (a)	*to learn*	leer	*to read*
beber	*to drink*	meter (en)	*to put (into)*
comer	*to eat*	poseer	*to possess*
comprender	*to understand*	romper	*to break*
correr	*to run*	temer	*to fear*
creer	*to believe*	vender	*to sell*
deber	*ought, should, to owe*		

TIP

Note that if there are two verbs together, it is the first one that is conjugated, whereas the second one is usually an infinitive:

Juan <u>debe</u> leer. / *John must read.*
Carmen <u>necesita</u> estudiar. / *Carmen needs to study.*

GRAMMAR NOTES

Note the forms of the indefinite article ("*a/an*") introduced below:

un   =   with a masculine singular noun:
            <u>un</u> corr<u>eo</u> electrónic<u>o</u> / *an e-mail*
una =   with a feminine noun:
            un<u>a</u> amig<u>a</u> mexican<u>a</u> / *a Mexican female friend*

The plural of the indefinite article ("*a/an*") means "*some*" as shown below:

un<u>os</u> amig<u>os</u> mexican<u>os</u> / *some Mexican friends*
un<u>as</u> amig<u>as</u> mexican<u>as</u> / *some female Mexican friends*

Note: The descriptive adjective generally follows the noun and agrees with the noun also: either masculine or feminine, singular or plural. Note also that adjectives of nationality are not capitalized in Spanish.

EXERCISE Set 1-2

A. Supply the missing Spanish verb and then give the English equivalent.

EXAMPLE: *él corr__*   =   _____

                él corre   =   *he runs, he is running, he does run*

1. (yo) aprend__   =   _____

2. (tú) comprend__   =   _____

3. (nosotros) cre__   =   _____

4. (ellos) met__   =   _____

5. (vosotros) corr__   =   _____

6. (Ud.) le__   =   _____

7. (mi amiga) tem__   =   _____

8. (ellas) romp__   =   _____

9. (yo) deb__   =   _____

10. (tú) beb__   =   _____

11. (nosotras) vend__ =   _____

12. (Uds.) com__   =   _____

13. (él) aprend__   =   _____

14. (ellos) comprend__ =   _____

15. (Ud.) cre__   =   _____

B. How do you say the following things in Spanish? Note: sg. = singular, pl. = plural, fam. = familiar, pol. = polite). You do not have to translate material in parentheses; this information tells you what verb form to use, or it provides cultural information.

1. Are you (fam. sg.) reading *Don Quijote*[1]?

   _____

2. I'm not reading. I'm sending an e-mail.

   _____

3. Excuse me, are you (pol. sg.) sending an e-mail in Spanish?

   _____

4. Yes, because my friend (f.) speaks, reads and writes Spanish very well.

   _____

5. Good-bye. Do you (pol. pl.) understand?

   _____

6. I should send an e-mail in twenty minutes.

   _____

7. My friend (f.) is not selling the *SEAT*[2].

   _____

[1]Famous novel by Miguel de Cervantes, 1547–1616.
[2]Car manufactured in Spain;

8. My grandmother drinks a lot of coffee.

_____

9. I fear Spanish tests.

_____

10. My brother is selling the car.

_____

11. My sister is always breaking something.

_____

12. My Mexican friend (f.) reads *El País*[3] frequently.

_____

13. My son should read more.

_____

14. My daughter is learning to speak Spanish at the *University of Salamanca*[4].

_____

15. Do you (fam. sg.) eat a lot?

_____

[3]Major newspaper in Spain.
[4]Famous Spanish university founded in 1218 by *Alfonso IX* [1171–1230], one of the oldest universities in Europe.

Third Conjugation Verbs

Infinitives ending in -ir are called third-conjugation verbs.

1. Drop the infinitive ending, -ir. This produces the "verb stem," as it is called.
   abrir / *to open* → abr-

2. Add the following endings to the stem:

(yo)	-o
(tú)	-es
(él, ella, Ud.)	-e
(nosotros/-as)	-imos
(vosotros/-as)	-ís
(ellos/-as, Uds.)	-en

3. Here's the result:

abrir / *to open*

Subject Pronoun	Verb Form	Meaning
(yo)	abr+o	*I open, I am opening, I do open*
(tú)	abr+es	*you (fam. sg.) open, you are opening, you do open*
(él, ella, Ud.)	abr+e	*he, she, you (pol. sg.) open(s), he, she, you (pol. sg.) is/ are opening, he, she, you does/do open*
(nosotros/-as)	abr+imos	*we open, we are opening, we do open*
(vosotros/-as)	abr+ís	*you (fam. pl.) open, you are opening, you do open*
(ellos/-as, Uds.)	abr+en	*they, you (pol. pl.) open, they, you are opening, they, you do open*

Common Verbs

Below are some common regular third conjugation verbs for basic communication.

abrir	*to open*	escribir	*to write*
admitir	*to admit*	existir	*to exist*
asistir (a)	*to attend*	partir	*to leave*
cubrir	*to cover*	permitir	*to permit*
decidir	*to decide*	recibir	*to receive*
describir	*to describe*	subir (a)	*to go up, climb*
descubrir	*to discover*	sufrir	*to suffer*
discutir	*to discuss*	vivir	*to live*

GRAMMAR NOTES

Nouns in Spanish that end in a vowel are made plural by adding an -s.

Singular	Plural
amigo (m.) / *male friend*	amigos / *male friends*
amiga (f.) / *female friend*	amigas / *female friends*

Nouns in Spanish that end in a consonant are made plural by adding an -es.

Singular	Plural
animal (m.) / *animal*	animales / *animals*
universidad (f.) / *university*	universidades / *universities*

Note that nouns that end in -ión do not have the graphic accent in the plural.

Singular	Plural
nación (f.) / *nation*	naciones / *nations*

EXERCISE Set 1-3

A. Supply the missing Spanish verb and then give the English equivalent.

EXAMPLE: *él abr__*   =   _____

él abre   =   *he opens, he is opening, he does open*

1. (yo) viv__   =   _____

2. (tú) asist__   =   _____

3. (nosotros) describ__   =   _____

4. (ellos) cubr __   =   _____

5. (vosotros) sufr__   =   _____

6. (Ud.) admit __   =   _____

7. (mi amiga) discut__   =   _____

8. (ellas) viv__   =   _____

9. (yo) permit __   =   _____

10. (tú) part__   =   _____

11. (nosotras) sub__   =   _____

12. (Uds.) exist__   =   _____

13. (él) escrib__   =   _____

14. (ellos) decid__   =   _____

15. (Ud.) recib__   =   _____

B. How do you say the following things in Spanish? Note: sg. = singular, pl. = plural, fam. = familiar, pol. = polite. You do not have to translate material in parentheses; this information tells you what verb form to use, or it provides cultural information.

1. Do you (fam. sg.) receive a lot of e-mail?

_____

2. They are discussing the movie by *Luis Buñuel*[1] now.

_____

[1]Spanish film director, 1900–1983.

3. We are attending the class now.

_____

4. She leaves for (*para*) *Málaga*[2] tomorrow.

_____

5. You (pol. pl.) live nearby.

_____

6. I write, read and send a lot of e-mail.

_____

7. I need to attend class every day.

_____

8. They are describing the painting by (**de**) *Francisco de Goya*[3] now.

_____

9. Many people suffer today.

_____

10. You (fam. pl.) decide to discuss the matter.

_____

11. Marta and I open the windows.

_____

12. I discover many secrets in class.

_____

13. My husband writes like *Calderón de la Barca*[4].

_____

[2]City in Southern coastal Spain.
[3]Spanish painter, 1746–1828.
[4]Spanish dramatist, 1600–1681.

14. Do fairies exist?

_____

15. You (fam. sg.) cover the table.

_____

C. Which of the following two options, **a** or **b,** is the correct one? Say the question aloud and then say the answer out loud also. Use this and every opportunity to practice Spanish as a spoken language.

1. ¿A qué hora abren las tiendas aquí?
   - **a.** A las siete y media.
   - **b.** A las veinte.

2. ¿Llegas tarde?
   - **a.** Sí, llego tarde.
   - **b.** Sí, llegamos tarde.

3. Muchos estadounidenses ... español.
   - **a.** hablan
   - **b.** habláis

4. ¿Toca Ud. la guitarra?
   - **a.** No, no toco la guitarra.
   - **b.** Sí, tocamos la guitarra.

5. Mis amigos argentinos .... muchos periódicos.
   - **a.** leemos
   - **b.** leen

6. ¿A qué hora ... los amigos de Ignacio?
   - **a.** trabajan
   - **b.** trabajamos

7. Sí, (yo) ... muchos regalos.
   - **a.** recibe
   - **b.** recibo

8. Mis amigos ... español.
   - **a.** estudian
   - **b.** estudiamos

9. Jorge debe ... mucho.
   - **a.** estudias
   - **b.** estudiar

10. Mi amiga ... para Argentina mañana.

   a. parte
   b. partes

11. Ellos ... en Barcelona.

   a. vives
   b. viven

12. ¿Escriben Uds. muchas cartas?

   a. Sí, escribimos muchas.
   b. Sí, escribís muchas.

13. ¿Beben Uds. mucho café?

   a. No, no bebéis mucho.
   b. No, no bebemos mucho.

14. ¿Hablan Uds. español mucho?

   a. Sí, hablamos español mucho.
   b. No, no hablo español mucho.

VOCABULARY TIP

The present indicative is often used with words and expressions such as:

a esta hora	*at this time*	en este momento	*at this moment*
ahora mismo	*right now*	hoy en día	*nowadays*
ahora	*now*	mañana	*tomorrow*
cada	*every*		

Asking Questions

In written Spanish, an interrogative sentence always has an "upside down question mark" (¿) at the beginning of the sentence and a regular question mark at the end (?). The two most common methods of turning an affirmative sentence into an interrogative one are:

1. Simply put an upside down question mark (¿) at the beginning and a regular one (?) at the end in writing. In speaking, raise the tone of your voice.
   ¿Manolo habla español? / *Does Manolo speak Spanish?*

2. Put the subject at the end of the sentence, adding the appropriate dual question marks at the beginning and end in writing or raising your tone of voice when speaking.
   ¿Habla español Beatriz? / *Does Beatriz speak Spanish?*

Interrogative sentences can also be formed with interrogative adjectives and pronouns when certain information is required. Again, you must remember to use an upside down question mark (¿) at the beginning of an interrogative sentence and a regular question mark (?) at the end.

   ¿Quién habla español aquí? / *Who speaks Spanish here?*
   ¿Dónde vive José? / *Where does José live?*

> **VOCABULARY NOTE**
>
> The following question words (interrogative pronouns and adjectives) are used to ask questions. When you use these question words, you normally place the subject of the sentence at the end. Note that all of these words bear a graphic accent.
>
> | | | | |
> |---|---|---|---|
> | ¿cuál? | *which (one)?* | ¿dónde? | *where?* |
> | ¿cuáles? | *which (ones)?* | ¿por qué? | *why?* |
> | ¿cuándo? | *when?* | ¿qué? | *what?* |
> | ¿cuánto/a? | *how much?* | ¿quién? | *who? (one person)* |
> | ¿cuántos/as? | *how many?* | ¿quiénes? | *who? (more than one person)* |

Note that ¿cuánto?, ¿cuánta?, ¿cuántos?, ¿cuántas? agree with the noun they modify. This means that their endings agree in number (singular or plural) and gender (masculine or feminine) with the noun:

Masculine Singular
¿Cuánto dinero necesitas? / *How much money do you need?*

Masculine Plural
¿Cuántos libros compras? / *How many books are you buying?*

Feminine Singular
¿Cuánta leche compras? / *How much milk do you buy?*

Feminine Plural
¿Cuántas clases necesitas? / *How many classes do you need?*

Use ¿verdad? to seek approval, consent, or agreement when asking a rhetorical question.

    Amparo habla español, <u>¿verdad?</u> / *Amparo speaks Spanish, doesn't she?*
    Enrique habla muy bien, <u>¿verdad?</u> / *Henry speaks very well, doesn't he?*
    Mis amigos son muy simpáticos, <u>¿verdad?</u> / *My friends are very nice, aren't they?*

Familiar and Polite Forms of Address

Remember that in the singular, the tú form is used for familiar address (this verb form ends in -s), and the usted form for polite address (this verb form corresponds to the third person singular). Also, recall that usted has two common abbreviations: Ud. and Vd. We will use Ud. in this book.

    ¿Qué <u>necesitas</u>? / *What do you (fam. sg.) need?*
    ¿Qué <u>necesita</u> Ud.? / *What do you (pol. sg.) need?*

The ustedes form, which requires the third person plural form of the verb, is used for the plural of both tú and usted in this hemisphere. Thus, in this hemisphere, the ustedes form (abbreviated as Uds.) is the only plural form for both tú and usted.

    ¿<u>Miran</u> Uds. la televisión? / *Are you watching TV?*
    ¿Dónde <u>viven</u> Uds.? / *Where do you live?*

In Spain, the plural of tú is vosotros (all men or a group of men and women) or vosotras (all women). This usage is thus more geographically limited in its usage.

    ¿<u>Habláis</u> español mucho? / *Do you speak Spanish a lot?*
    ¿<u>Necesitáis</u> estudiar español mucho? / *Do you need to study Spanish a lot?*

Odds and Ends

Recall from the previous overview unit that subject pronouns are optional. Note that the subject pronoun "it" (plural "they") is not normally expressed when referring to things. Likewise, when referring to people, it is not necessary to repeat the third person pronoun (él, ella, Ud., ellos, ellas, Uds.) once the reference has been established in a conversation.

> <u>Abre</u> a las siete y media. / *It opens at seven thirty.*
> <u>Abren</u> a las siete y media. / *They open at seven thirty.*

The English equivalent for "Sara's friends," "my friend's guitar," etc. is rendered in Spanish with the preposition de:

> Los amigos <u>de</u> Sara necesitan café. / *Sara's friends need coffee.*
> Toco la guitarra <u>de</u> mi hija. / *I play my daughter's guitar.*

Remember: there is no 's in Spanish. You must use the preposition de / *of* to join two nouns in Spanish. <u>Mary's house</u> = la casa de María.

NOTE

The names for units of currency varies in countries where Spanish is an official language. In many cases, the unit of money is the peso, or even the U.S. dollar (dólar). The following list illustrates this point.

Argentina	peso
Bolivia	boliviano
Chile	peso chileno
Colombia	peso
Costa Rica	colón
Cuba	peso
Dominican Republic (La República Dominicana)	peso
Ecuador	peso / *U.S. dollar* (dólar)
El Salvador	quetzal / *U.S. dollar* (dólar)
Equatorial Guinea (La República de Guinea Ecuatorial)	franco
Guatemala	quetzal
Honduras	lempira
Nicaragua	córdoba
Panamá	balboa / *U.S. dollar* (dólar)
Paraguay	guaraní
Perú	nuevo sol
Spain (España)	euro
Uruguay	peso
Venezuela	bolívar

EXERCISE Set 1-4

A. Missing from each of the following sentences is the verb. The missing verbs are given to you in their infinitive forms. Put each verb, in its correct form, in each sentence according to the sense.

Verbs: comprender, escuchar, hablar, limpiar, llegar, mirar, partir, tocar, vivir.

1. Mi hermana _____ el violoncelo muy bien.

2. Mis amigos _____ para España.

3. Ahora (nosotros) _____ en México porque deseamos hablar muy bien el español.

4. En este momento, ellos _____ la televisión.

5. ¿A qué hora _____ los amigos de Pablo?

6. Cada día mi esposa y yo _____ la casa.

7. (Yo) _____ francés un poco.

8. Mi hermano siempre _____ la radio.

9. ¿ _____ (tú) el español?

B. Choose the appropriate answer to each question. You should also say the question out loud and provide the answer out loud. This will help you to remember the words.

1. ¿Dónde vives?

   a. Deseo mirar la televisión.
   b. En Sevilla.

2. ¿Miran Uds. la televisión?

   a. Sí, miráis la televisión.
   b. Sí, miramos la televisión.

3. ¿Habla Miguel español?

   a. Sí, lee y habla español.
   b. Sí, leemos y escribimos español.

4. ¿Trabaja aquí Miranda?

   a. No, no trabaja aquí.
   b. No, no trabajan aquí.

5. ¿Qué lee Mario?

   a. Lee una novela.
   b. Leo una novela.

6. ¿Cuándo llegan ellos?

   a. A las siete y media.
   b. No llegamos.

7. ¿Por qué estudian Uds. español?

   a. Deseamos hablar la lengua.
   b. Deseo hablar la lengua.

8. ¿Cuánto café bebes?

   a. Bebemos mucho.
   b. Bebo poco (little).

9. ¿Cuántos libros (books) compran Uds.?

   a. Compro los libros.
   b. Compramos muchos (many).

C. Each question is given to you in the familiar form. Change each one to the polite form. Say the question aloud.

EXAMPLE: ¿Qué bebes?
               ¿Qué bebe Ud.?

               ¿Dónde vivís? (Spain)
               ¿Dónde viven Uds.?

1. ¿Bailas el tango muy bien también?   _____

2. ¿Qué leéis en este momento? (Spain)   _____

3. ¿Qué estudias?   _____

4. ¿Por qué miras la televisión tanto (so much)? _____

5. ¿Necesitáis estudiar mucho? (Spain)   _____

D. Change the following sentences from the singular to the plural. In the first two sentences, assume you are in Spain. In the remaining three sentences, assume you are in this hemisphere.

1. Vives en Madrid.   _____

2. Ud. vive en Barcelona.   _____

3. Bebes mucho café.   _____

4. Hablas español muy bien. _____

5. Ud. canta muy bien.   _____

EXERCISE **Set 1-5**

A. Imagine that you are in a shopping center (centro commercial). Look at the pictures. Describe what the following people are buying. Use the verb comprar ("to buy"). The monetary unit in the pictures is the *euro*, the monetary unit of the European Union. The note in this chapter on names for units of currency identifies other monetary designations in countries where Spanish is an official language.

1.

el balón de fútbol

2.

el juguete

3.

el helado

4.

el teléfono

5.

la sartén

6.

el libro

1. (Nosotros) _____

2. Juan y María _____

3. (Ud.) _____

4. (Yo) _____

5. (Tú) _____

6. Ella _____

Crossword Puzzle 1

Fill in the blanks. All of the clues both vertical and horizontal are English verbal expressions that correspond to a single verb in Spanish.

Horizontales
1. you (fam. sg.) believe
3. I fear
4. I sell
6. they speak
9. we understand
10. we leave

Verticales
1. she runs
2. we study
5. they prepare
7. he breaks
8. you (Spain, fam. pl.) read

2
The Present Indicative of Stem-Changing Verbs

Stem-Changing Verbs

Stem-changing verbs have one difference from the regular verbs that we studied in the previous chapter. They have an alternation or change of the form of the vowel in their stem and this is why they are called stem-changing verbs. Recall from Chapter 1 that the stem of a verb is the form of the verb that remains after you remove the infinitive ending as shown below.

1. First conjugation verbs (-ar verbs).
   habl*ar* / *to speak* → habl-

2. Second conjugation verbs (-er verbs).
   com*er* / *to eat* → com-

3. Third conjugation verbs (-ir verbs).
   abr*ir* / *to open* → abr-

Stem-changing verbs, as just noted, have a change or alternation of the vowel in the stem. There are several patterns and we will examine each type in this chapter.

TIP

The endings of stem-changing verbs are exactly the same as those for the regular verbs that we studied in the previous chapter. The only difference is a change in the stem in certain verb forms (first, second, third person singular, and third person plural).

The best way to remember where the stem changes occur in stem-changing verbs is to remember a tried-and-true mnemonic technique. These verbs are called "shoe" verbs because the outline of where the changes occur looks like the profile of a shoe when these verbs are conjugated. We have created two profiles below to help you remember.

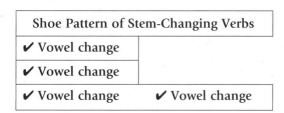

Shoe Pattern of Stem-Changing Verbs	
✔ Vowel change	
✔ Vowel change	
✔ Vowel change	✔ Vowel change

To emphasize where the stem-vowel changes and where it remains the same, we provide the following additional chart to help you see these changes. There is another important fact to remember about all stem-changing verbs: <u>The stem changes occur when the vowel in the stem receives primary stress.</u>

Location of Stem Changes in the Conjugation Format	
✔ (vowel stressed)	No Change
✔ (vowel stressed)	No Change
✔ (vowel stressed)	✔ (vowel stressed)

TIP

You will need to remember which verbs are stem-changing when you learn new verbs. Dictionaries usually list the type of stem change in parentheses after the verb entry. In the following pattern (e → ie), you will see the verb entender / *to understand* in the format of a typical dictionary entry:

  entender (ie) / *to understand*

It is important to remember which verbs change stems because not all verbs follow this pattern. For example, the verb comprender / *to understand* does not have a stem change.

Remember also that some verbs have a "characteristic preposition." In a typical dictionary entry, the verb comenzar / *to begin* would have the following format:

  comenzar (ie) (a) / *to begin*

The first parenthetical item means that this verb (ie) changes its stem (e → ie). The second parenthetical item (a) means that if there is a following infinitive, you must use the preposition a. The following example illustrates this point.

  Comienzo a estudiar. / *I'm beginning to study.*

Verbs that have the stem changes (o → ue) and (e → i) will also have similar entries. We will discuss these verbs below.

  mostrar (ue) / *to show*
  servir (i) / *to serve*

Stem-Changing Verbs (e → ie)

Now that we have established where the changes occur, we will examine the three patterns of stem-changing verbs to see how these verbs work. The first type of stem change is e → ie. Remember, these verbs change their stem in all of the forms except for nosotros /-as / *we* and vosotros/-as / *you* forms. We have highlighted the stem changes with italic type.

Remember that these changes may occur in first conjugation (-ar), second conjugation (-er), and third conjugation (-ir) verbs. The following three verbs illustrate this pattern.

cerrar (ie) / *to close*

Subject Pronoun	Verb Form	Meaning
(yo)	<u>cie</u>rr+o	*I close, I am closing, I do close*
(tú)	<u>cie</u>rr+as	*you (fam. sg.) close, you are closing, you do close*
(él, ella, Ud.)	<u>cie</u>rr+a	*he, she, you (pol. sg.) close(s), he, she, you is/are closing, he, she, you does/do close*
(nosotros/-as)	<u>ce</u>rr+amos	*we close, we are closing, we do close*
(vosotros/-as)	<u>ce</u>rr+áis	*you (fam. pl.) close, you are closing, you do close*
(ellos/-as, Uds.)	<u>cie</u>rr+an	*they, you (pol. pl.) close, they, you are closing, they, you do close*

querer (ie) / *to want*

Subject Pronoun	Verb Form	Meaning
(yo)	<u>quie</u>r+o	*I want, I am wanting, I do want*
(tú)	<u>quie</u>r+es	*you (fam. sg.) want, you are wanting, you do want*
(él, ella, Ud.)	<u>quie</u>r+e	*he, she, you (pol. sg.) want(s), he, she, you is/are wanting, he, she, you does/do want*
(nosotros/-as)	<u>que</u>r+emos	*we want, we are wanting, we do want*
(vosotros/-as)	<u>que</u>r+éis	*you (fam. pl.) want, you are wanting, you do want*
(ellos/-as, Uds.)	<u>quie</u>r+en	*they, you (pol. pl.) want, they, you are wanting, they, you do want*

sugerir (ie) / *to suggest*

Subject Pronoun	Verb Form	Meaning
(yo)	<u>sugie</u>r+o	*I suggest, I am suggesting, I do suggest*
(tú)	<u>sugie</u>r+es	*you (fam. sg.) suggest, you are suggesting, you do suggest*
(él, ella, Ud.)	<u>sugie</u>r+e	*he, she, you (pol. sg.) suggest(s), he, she, you is/are suggesting, he, she, you does/do suggest*
(nosotros/-as)	<u>suge</u>r+imos	*we suggest, we are suggesting, we do suggest*
(vosotros/-as)	<u>suge</u>r+ís	*you (fam. pl.) suggest, you are suggesting, you do suggest*
(ellos/-as, Uds.)	<u>sugie</u>r+en	*they, you (pol. pl.) suggest, they, you are suggesting, they, you do suggest*

Common Verbs

Below are some common e → ie stem-changing verbs that will come in handy for basic communication.

advertir (ie)	*to warn*	fregar (ie)	*to scrub, to wash (dishes)*
cerrar (ie)	*to close*	hervir (ie)	*to boil*
comenzar (ie) (a)	*to begin*	mentir (ie)	*to lie*
confesar (ie)	*to confess*	negar (ie)	*to deny*
consentir (ie)	*to consent*	pensar (ie) (en)	*to think (about)*
convertir (ie)	*to convert*	perder (ie)	*to lose*
defender (ie)	*to defend*	preferir (ie)	*to prefer*
empezar (ie) (a)	*to begin*	querer (ie)	*to want, to wish, to love*
encender (ie)	*to light, to turn on*	sentir (ie)	*to feel, to regret*
entender (ie)	*to understand*	sugerir (ie)	*to suggest*

TIP

Remember that it is always the <u>last</u> vowel in the stem (what is left after you remove the infinitive marker [-ar, -er, -ir]) that has a vowel change. The following examples illustrate this point. We have indicated the vowel that changes with an underline and italic type.

rec*o*rdar / *to remember* → rec*o*rd-
ent*e*nder / *to understand* → ent*e*nd-
comp*e*tir / *to compete* → comp*e*t-

NOTE

The verb pensar + an infinitive has the meaning of *"to plan"* or *"to intend."*

Pienso estudiar. / *I plan to study / I intend to study.*

GRAMMAR NOTE

Remember that when there are two verbs in a row, it is the first one that is conjugated, whereas the second one is usually an infinitive, as the examples below illustrate.

Quiero estudiar mucho. / *I want to study a lot.*
Prefiero beber café. / *I prefer to drink coffee.*

When a verb has a characteristic preposition, it goes before the infinitive:

Empiezo a fregar los platos. / *I begin to clean the plates.*

EXERCISE Set 2-1

A. Supply the missing indicative forms of the verb empezar (ie), giving the English equivalent.

EXAMPLE: él _____   =   _____

               él empieza   =   *he begins, he is beginning, he does begin*

1. (yo) _____   =   _____

2. (tú) _____   =   _____

3. (nosotros) _____   =   _____

4. (ellos) _____   =   _____

5. (vosotros) _____   =   _____

6. (Ud.) _____   =   _____

Now, supply the missing present indicative forms of the verb entender (ie), giving the English equivalent.

1. (yo) _____   =   _____

2. (Raquel y yo) _____   =   _____

3. (Uds.) _____   =   _____

4. (ellos) _____   =   _____

5. (vosotros) _____   =   _____

6. (tú) _____   =   _____

Now, supply the missing present indicative forms of the verb mentir (ie), giving the English equivalent.

1. (yo) _____   =   _____

2. (tú) _____   =   _____

3. (nosotros) _____   =   _____

4. (ellos) _____   =   _____

5. (vosotros) _____   =   _____

6. (Ud.) _____   =   _____

B. How do you say the following sentences in Spanish?

1. I am beginning to read the poetry of *Alfonsina Storni*[1].

_____

2. Do you (fam. sg.) want to read the novels of *Eduardo Mallea*[2].

_____

3. We turn on the light every night.

_____

4. Do you (pol. sg.) understand the question?

_____

5. Do you (fam. sg.) regret not reading *El túnel*[3] by (**de**) *Ernesto Sábato*[4].

_____

6. We lose our keys a lot.

_____

7. She confesses that (**que**) she watches many soap operas.

_____

8. We want to read *Mafalda*[5].

_____

9. They prefer to go to *Calle Florida*[6] in order to buy clothes.

_____

10. He suggests the book by (**de**) *Ana María Shua*[7].

_____

11. You (fam. sg.) do not lie.

_____

[1]Argentinean poet, 1892–1938.
[2]Argentinean novelist, 1903–1982.
[3]Famous Argentinean novel, 1948.
[4]Author of *El túnel*, 1911–2011.
[5]Argentinean cartoon about a mischievous little girl by Quino, pseudonym of Joaquín Salvador Lavado, 1932– .
[6]Traditional shopping area in Buenos Aires.
[7]Argentinean novelist, 1951–.

Stem-Changing Verbs (o → ue)

The second type of stem change is o → ue. Remember that these verbs change their stem in all of the forms except for nosotros/nosotras and vosotros/vosotras. These changes may occur in first conjugation (-ar), second conjugation (-er), and third conjugation (-ir) verbs. The following verbs illustrate this. We have highlighted the stem changes with italic type.

mostrar (ue) / *to show*

Subject Pronoun	Verb Form	Meaning
(yo)	m*ue*str+o	*I show, I am showing, I do show*
(tú)	m*ue*str+as	*you (fam. sg.) show, you are showing, you do show*
(él, ella, Ud.)	m*ue*str+a	*he, she, you (pol. sg.) show(s), he, she, you is/are showing, he, she, you does/do show*
(nosotros/-as)	mostr+amos	*we show, we are showing, we do show*
(vosotros/-as)	mostr+áis	*you (fam. pl.) show, you are showing, you do show*
(ellos/-as, Uds.)	m*ue*str+an	*they, you (pol. pl.) show, they, you are showing, they, you do show*

volver (ue) (a) / *to return*

Subject Pronoun	Verb Form	Meaning
(yo)	v*ue*lv+o	*I return, I am returning, I do return*
(tú)	v*ue*lv+es	*you (fam. sg.) return, you are returning, you do return*
(él, ella, Ud.)	v*ue*lv+e	*he, she, you (pol. sg.) return(s), he, she, you is/are returning, he, she, you does/do return*
(nosotros/-as)	volv+emos	*we return, we are returning, we do return*
(vosotros/-as)	volv+éis	*you (fam. pl.) return, you are returning, you do return*
(ellos/-as, Uds.)	v*ue*lv+en	*they, you (pol. pl.) return, they, you are returning, they you do return*

dormir (ue) / *to sleep*

Subject Pronoun	Verb Form	Meaning
(yo)	d*ue*rm+o	*I sleep, I am sleeping, I do sleep*
(tú)	d*ue*rm+es	*you (fam. sg.) sleep, you are sleeping, you do sleep*
(él, ella, Ud.)	d*ue*rm+e	*he, she, you (pol. sg.) sleep(s), he, she, you is/are sleeping, he, she, you does/do sleep*
(nosotros/-as)	dorm+imos	*we sleep, we are sleeping, we do sleep*
(vosotros/-as)	dorm+ís	*you (fam. pl.) sleep, you are sleeping, you do sleep*
(ellos/-as, Uds.)	d*ue*rm+en	*they, you (pol. pl.) sleep, they, you are sleeping, they, you do sleep*

Common Verbs

Below are some common o → ue stem-changing verbs that will come in handy for basic communication.

almorzar (ue)	to eat lunch	mover (ue)	to move
aprobar (ue)	to approve	poder (ue)	can, be able
colgar (ue)	to hang (up)	probar (ue)	to prove, to taste, to test
contar (ue) (con)	to count (on)	recordar (ue)	to remember
costar (ue)	to cost	resolver (ue)	to solve
devolver (ue)	to return (something)	rogar (ue)	to request, to beg
dormir (ue)	to sleep	soler (ue)	to be in the habit of
encontrar (ue)	to find	soñar (ue) (con)	to dream (of)
envolver (ue)	to wrap (up)	sonar (ue)	to ring, to sound
morder (ue)	to bite	tostar (ue)	to toast
morir (ue)	to die	volar (ue)	to fly
mostrar (ue)	to show	volver (ue) (a)	to return

NOTE

The verb volver + a + an infinitive means to ... again.

Vuelvo a estudiar. / I study again.

Stem-Changing Verbs (u → ue)

There is a single Spanish verb that has the change u → ue. Because it is a commonly used verb jugar (ue) (a) / to play (a game), it is important to learn it. We have indicated the changes with italic type.

jugar (ue) (a) / to play (a game)

Subject Pronoun	Verb Form	Meaning
(yo)	*jue*g+o	I play, I am playing, I do play
(tú)	*jue*g+as	you (fam. sg.) play, you are playing, you do play
(él, ella, Ud.)	*jue*g+a	he, she, you (pol. pl.) play(s), he, she, you is/are playing, he, she, you does/do play
(nosotros/-as)	jug+amos	we play, we are playing, we do play
(vosotros/-as)	jug+áis	you (fam. pl.) play, you are playing, you do play
(ellos/-as, Uds.)	*jue*g+an	they, you (pol. pl.) play, they, you are playing, they, you do play

Remember that jugar (ue) (a) means to play a game and tocar means to play a musical instrument or to touch. When you specify the game that you play, the name of the game is normally preceded by al, a los, or a las. The following are some common games that you may play.

jugar al ajedrez	to play chess	jugar al golf	to play golf
jugar al baloncesto	to play basketball	jugar al hockey	to play hockey
jugar al béisbol	to play baseball	jugar a un juego	to play a game
jugar al billar	to play pool	jugar a los naipes	to play cards
jugar a las damas	to play checkers	jugar al tenis	to play tennis
jugar al fútbol	to play soccer		
jugar al fútbol americano	to play football		

EXERCISE Set 2-2

A. Supply the missing indicative forms of the verb encontrar (ue), giving the English equivalent.

EXAMPLE: él _____   =   _____

él encuentra =   *he finds, he is finding, he does find*

1. (yo) _____   =   _____

2. (tú) _____   =   _____

3. (nosotras) _____   =   _____

4. (ellos) _____   =   _____

5. (Uds.) _____   =   _____

6. (Ud.) _____   =   _____

Now, supply the missing present indicative forms of the verb devolver (ue), giving the English equivalent.

1. (yo) _____   =   _____

2. (Javier y yo) _____ =   _____

3. (ellas) _____   =   _____

4. (Uds.) _____   =   _____

5. (vosotros) _____   =   _____

6. (tú) _____   =   _____

Now, supply the missing present indicative forms of the verb morir (ue), giving the English equivalent.

1. (yo) _____   =   _____

2. (tú) _____   =   _____

3. (nosotros) _____   =   _____

4. (ellos) _____   =   _____

5. (vosotros) _____   =   _____

6. (Ud.) _____   =   _____

B. How do you say the following sentences in Spanish?

1. A T-bone steak costs a lot at *La Cabaña*[1].

_____

2. You (pol. pl.) can read *El puente*[2] by (de) *Carlos Gorostiza*[3].

_____

3. She finds the car keys in the sofa.

_____

4. We are flying to *Ushuaia*[4] tomorrow.

_____

5. You (fam. sg.) dream of winning the lottery.

_____

6. They sleep late if they can.

_____

7. I hang up the phone if they are selling something.

_____

8. We are returning to *Mendoza*[5] tomorrow on *Aerolíneas Argentinas*[6].

_____

9. He remembers the essay by (de) *Domingo Faustino Sarmiento*[7].

_____

10. The telephone rings constantly.

_____

[1]Famous restaurant in Buenos Aires that serves world-famous Argentinean beef.
[2]Drama by Carlos Gorostiza, 1963.
[3]Renowned Argentinean playwright, 1920– .
[4]Southernmost town of Argentina.
[5]City south of Buenos Aires.
[6]Argentina's national airline.
[7]Argentinean essayist, 1811–1888.

Stem-Changing Verbs (e → i)

The third type of stem change is e → i. Remember that these verbs change their stem in all of the forms except for nosotros/-as and vosotros/-as. It is important to remember that the change e → i occurs only with third conjugation (-ir) verbs. We have highlighted the stem changes with italic type.

servir (i) / *to serve*

Subject Pronoun	Verb Form	Meaning
(yo)	sirv+o	*I serve, I am serving, I do serve*
(tú)	sirv+es	*you (fam. sg.) serve, you are serving, you do serve*
(él, ella, Ud.)	sirv+e	*he, she, you (pol. sg.) serve(s), he, she, you is/are serving, he, she, you does/do serve*
(nosotros/-as)	serv+imos	*we serve, we are serving, we do serve*
(vosotros/-as)	serv+ís	*you (fam. pl.) serve, you are serving, you do serve*
(ellos/-as, Uds.)	sirv+en	*they, you (pol. pl.) serve, they, you are serving, they, you do serve*

Note that some e → i verbs have a spelling change (<u>not a sound change</u>) in the stem. The changes depend upon whether the following vowel is e or i (gu spelling) or an o (g spelling). Review the introductory pronunciation and spelling guide.

seguir (i) / *to follow*

Subject Pronoun	Verb Form	Meaning
(yo)	sig+o	*I follow, I am following, I do follow*
(tú)	sigu+es	*you (fam. sg.) follow, you are following, you do follow*
(él, ella, Ud.)	sigu+e	*he, she, you (pol. sg.) follow(s), he, she, you is/are following, he, she, you does/do follow*
(nosotros/-as)	segu+imos	*we follow, we are following, we do follow*
(vosotros/-as)	segu+ís	*you (fam. pl.) follow, you are following, you do follow*
(ellos/-as, Uds.)	sigu+en	*they, you (pol. pl.) follow, they, you are following, they, you do follow*

Note that some e → i stem-changing verbs have a written accent. This is to indicate that there is no diphthong. Reír / *to laugh* and freír / *to fry* are two such verbs. We have indicated the changes with italic type.

reír / *to laugh*

Subject Pronoun	Verb Form	Meaning
(yo)	rí+o	*I laugh, I am laughing, I do laugh*
(tú)	rí+es	*you (fam. sg.) laugh, you are laughing, you do laugh*
(él, ella, Ud.)	rí+e	*he, she, you (pol. sg.) laugh(s), he, she, you is/are laughing, he, she, you does/do laugh*
(nosotros/-as)	re+ímos	*we laugh, we are laughing, we do laugh*
(vosotros/-as)	re+ís	*you (fam. pl.) laugh, you are laughing, you do laugh*
(ellos/-as, Uds.)	rí+en	*they, you (pol. pl.) laugh, they, you are laughing, they, you do laugh*

Common Verbs

Below are some common e → i stem-changing verbs that will come in handy for basic communication.

competir (i)	*to compete*	medir (i)	*to measure*
conseguir (i)	*to obtain, to get*	pedir (i)	*to ask for, to request, to order*
corregir (i)	*to correct*	reír (i)	*to laugh*
despedir (i)	*to fire*	repetir (i)	*to repeat*
elegir (i)	*to elect*	seguir (i)	*to follow*
freír (i)	*to fry*	servir (i)	*to serve*
impedir (i)	*to prevent, to hinder*		

SPELLING TIP

Verbs that end in -ger and -gir have a first person singular form (yo) as follows:

proteger / *to protect* → protejo / *I protect*
elegir / *to elect* → elijo / *I elect*

There will be more about these spelling changes in Chapter 4.

EXERCISE Set 2-3

A. Supply the missing indicative forms of the verb competir (i), giving the English equivalent.

EXAMPLE: *él* _____   =   _____

él compite   =   *he competes, he is competing, he does compete*

1. (yo) _____   =   _____

2. (tú) _____   =   _____

3. (nosotras) _____   =   _____

4. (ellos) _____   =   _____

5. (Uds.) _____   =   _____

6. (Ud.) _____   =   _____

Now, supply the missing present indicative forms of the verb medir (i), giving the English equivalent.

1. (yo) _____   =   _____

2. (ellos) _____   =   _____

3. (Lidia y yo) _____   =   _____

4. (Uds.) _____   =   _____

5. (nosotros) _____   =   _____

6. (tú) _____   =   _____

Now, supply the missing present indicative forms of the verb seguir (i), giving the English equivalent.

1. (yo) _____   =   _____

2. (Ud.) _____   =   _____

3. (nosotros) _____   =   _____

4. (ellos) _____   =   _____

5. (vosotros) _____   =   _____

6. (Joaquín y yo) _____   =   _____

B. How do you say the following sentences in Spanish?

1. They are competing for the prize.

   _____

2. The teachers need to correct the exams today.

   _____

3. I always follow the rules.

   _____

4. I ask for *churrasco*[1] in *Dora*[2].

   _____

5. When you (fam. sg.) repeat the words aloud, you remember.

   _____

6. She measures the ingredients carefully.

   _____

7. They serve excellent wine in the restaurant.

   _____

8. He fires the employees.

   _____

9. You (pol. pl.) laugh a lot.

   _____

10. They always fry the eggs here.

   _____

[1]Thick grilled steak.
[2]Well-known restaurant in downtown Buenos Aires.

EXERCISE Set 2-4

A. Missing from each of the following sentences is the verb. The missing verbs are given to you in their infinitive forms. Put each verb, in its correct form, in each sentence according to the sense.

Verbs: cerrar, competir, entender, fregar, preferir, servir, soñar (con), volar, volver.

1. (Yo) _____ estudiar en casa.

2. (Uds.) _____ la pregunta.

3. (Concepción y yo) no _____ la puerta.

4. En este momento, (él) _____ los platos.

5. ¿Con qué _____ (tú)?

6. (Yo) _____ a casa tarde.

7. (Nosotros) _____ cuando jugamos al fútbol.

8. (Ella) _____ a Mendoza en *Aerolíneas Argentinas*.

9. (Ellos) _____ una buena *parrillada*[1].

[1]A mixed grill with roast meat and sausages.

B. Which of the following two options, **a** or **b**, is the correct one? You should say the question out loud and provide the answer out loud. This will help you to remember the words.

1. ¿Pierdes tus llaves mucho?

   a. Nunca pierdo mis llaves.
   b. Siempre perdemos nuestras llaves.

2. ¿Encienden Uds. las luces cuando duermen?

   a. Sí, enciendo las luces cuando duermo.
   b. Sí, encendemos las luces cuando dormimos.

3. ¿Cierras la puerta cuando estudias?

   a. Sí, cierro la puerto cuando estudio.
   b. Sí, cerramos la puerta cuando estudiamos.

4. ¿Quieren Uds. partir para Buenos Aires ahora?

   a. No, no quiero partir.
   b. No, no queremos partir.

5. ¿Puede Marisol empezar a cocinar ahora?

   a. Sí, puedes comenzar.
   b. Sí, puede comenzar.

6. ¿Sirven bife de costilla (T-bone) aquí?

    a. No sirve.
    b. Sí, sirven bife de costilla excelente.

7. ¿Piden Uds. un buen vino cuando comen en un restaurante?

    a. Siempre pedimos un buen vino.
    b. Siempre piden un buen vino.

8. ¿Sigues la misma rutina todos los días?

    a. No, seguimos la misma rutina.
    b. Sí, siempre sigo la misma rutina.

9. ¿Prefieres estudiar o jugar al béisbol?

    a. Preferimos jugar al béisbol.
    b. Prefiero estudiar.

C. Change the following sentences from the plural to the singular. Pronounce the original sentence and then say the new sentence aloud. This will help you to remember the words and you will gain confidence by verbalizing them.

1. Volvemos a Buenos Aires.   _____

2. Almorzamos en *Güerrín*[1].   _____

3. Cerramos las puertas.   _____

4. Seguimos la misma ruta.   _____

5. Empezamos a estudiar.   _____

[1] Well-known and inexpensive restaurant in Buenos Aires.

GRAMMAR NOTE

Adverbs of manner end in -mente corresponding (in general) to the English -ly. To construct such an adverb, change the -o of an adjective to -a and then add on -mente. For all other adjectives, you just add -mente as the following examples illustrate.

    perfecto → perfecta + mente = perfectamente / *perfectly*
    fácil → fácil + mente = fácilmente / *easily*
    prudente → prudente + mente = prudentemente / *prudently*

Remember: If there is a written accent on the adjective, it also remains on the adverb.

EXERCISE Set 2-5

A. Describe the activities of the people named in this exercise. Make simple statements in the present tense using verbs that you have already learned.

1. Pilar y Carlos _____

2. Juan _____

3. Jorge y Soledad _____

4. Juana _____

5. Julián y Pedro _____

6. Hugo _____

7. Pablo _____

8. Verónica _____

9. Carmen _____

Crossword Puzzle 2

Fill in the blanks. All of the clues, both vertical and horizontal, are English verbal expressions that correspond to a single verb in Spanish.

Horizontales
2. We follow
4. We play
7. They lie
8. We fly

Verticales
1. They are closing
3. I am showing
5. You (fam. sg.) serve
6. They are eating

3

The Present Indicative of *Ser*, *Estar*, *Hay*, *Tener*, *Hacer*, *Saber*, and *Conocer*

Conjugation of *Ser*

The verb ser / *to be* is an irregular verb. Unlike the verbs that you have learned to conjugate in the first chapter, you cannot predict its forms on the basis of the infinitive. You will simply have to memorize them.

ser / to be

Subject Pronoun	Verb Form	Meaning
(yo)	soy	*I am*
(tú)	eres	*you (fam. sg.) are*
(él, ella, Ud.)	es	*he, she, you (pol. sg.) is/are*
(nosotros/-as)	somos	*we are*
(vosotros/-as)	sois	*you (fam. pl.) are*
(ellos/-as, Uds.)	son	*they, you (pol. pl.) are*

Uses of Ser

The verb ser / *to be* has a variety of uses, which we illustrate here.

Ser is used in the following situations	Examples
1. To indicate nationality.	Eperanza es cubana. / *Esperanza is Cuban.*
2. To indicate profession or vocation.	Carlos es abogado. / *Carlos is a lawyer.*
3. To indicate place of origin (with de).	Pilar es de Uruguay. / *Pilar is from Uruguay.*
4. To indicate the material from which something is made (with de).	¿De qué es la casa? / *What is the house made of?* La casa es de ladrillo. / *The house is made of brick.*
5. To indicate the time.	Es la una. / *It's one o'clock.* Son las nueve. / *It's nine o'clock.*
6. To indicate the date.	Es el dos de noviembre. / *It's November 2nd.*
7. To indicate possession (with de).	¿De quién es el libro? / *Whose book is it?* El libro es de Antonio. / *The book is Antonio's.* (Remember: There is no *'s* in Spanish.)
8. To identify basic characteristics of people or things.	Berta es simpática. / *Berta is nice.*
9. To indicate a generalization or an impersonal statement.	Es importante estudiar. / *It's important to study.*
10. To indicate the time or location of an event.	El concierto es a las nueve. / *The concert takes place at nine.*

Adjectives of Nationality

Item 3 above points out that ser / *to be* is used to indicate nationality. The following adjectives of nationality will be used throughout this book, so we are introducing them here.

americano	*American*	guatemalteco	*Guatemalan*
argentino	*Argentinean*	hondureño	*Honduran*
boliviano	*Bolivian*	mexicano	*Mexican*
chileno	*Chilean*	nicaragüense	*Nicaraguan*
colombiano	*Colombian*	panameño	*Panamanian*
costarricense	*Costa Rican*	paraguayo	*Paraguayan*
cubano	*Cuban*	peruano	*Peruvian*
dominicano	*Dominican*	puertorriqueño	*Puerto Rican*
ecuatoriano	*Ecuadorean*	salvadoreño	*Salvadoran*
español	*Spanish*	uruguayo	*Uruguayan*
estadounidense	*person from the U.S.*	venezolano	*Venezuelan*

GRAMMAR NOTE

Adjectives of nationality are not capitalized in Spanish (as they are in English). See the following example:

Elena es <u>uruguaya</u>. / *Elena is <u>Uruguayan</u>.*

GRAMMAR NOTE

There are two types of adjectives in Spanish. The first type is called limiting (definite and indefinite articles, possessive adjectives "my," "your," "his," and so forth, and demonstrative adjectives "this" and "that"; see below and Chapter 6). These go before the noun they modify as illustrated below. This is similar to English usage.

el hombre / *the man*
una mujer / *a woman*
mi esposa / *my wife*
este libro / *this book*

The other type of adjective, and the one that is of interest here, is the descriptive adjective. A descriptive adjective provides information about the noun such as size, shape, color, and nationality, to name but a few examples. Normally, these adjectives go after the noun to which they refer. This is a different pattern from English, where the descriptive adjective goes before the noun. We will use adjectives of nationality to show this pattern. We have underlined these adjectives to highlight their position relative to the noun they modify.

el hombre <u>español</u> / *the <u>Spanish</u> man*
la mujer <u>chilena</u> / *the <u>Chilean</u> woman*
los hombres <u>cubanos</u> / *the <u>Cuban</u> men*
las mujeres <u>paraguayas</u> / *the <u>Paraguayan</u> women*

Telling Time

We saw that **ser** / *to be* is used to tell time. We will now discuss this in more detail.

To ask what time it is, you say:

¿Qué hora es? / *What time is it?*

You use the verb form **es** for one o'clock.

Es la una. / *It is one o'clock.*
Es la una y cuarto. / *It's a quarter past one.*

For all other hours, you use the verb **son**.

Son las tres. / *It is three o'clock.*

To indicate time up to the half-hour, you <u>add</u> the minutes up to the half-hour as illustrated below.

Es la una y quince. / *It's one fifteen.*
Es la una y cuarto. / *It's one fifteen.*
Son las tres y veinte. / *It's three twenty.*
Son once y treinta. / *It's eleven thirty.*
Son las once y media. / *It's eleven thirty.*

To indicate the time after the half-hour, you <u>subtract</u> the minutes from the following hour as shown below.

Son las tres menos quince. / *It's two forty-five. (It's a quarter to three.)*
Son las nueve menos cuarto. / *It's eight forty-five. (It's a quarter to nine.)*
Es la una menos diez. / *It's twelve fifty (It's ten to one.)*

Another common time expression is the following:

Son las cinco en punto. / *It's five o'clock on the dot.*

Remember that in countries outside the United States there is a twenty-four-hour clock, especially for public transportation and business hours as illustrated below.

Es la una. / *It's one A.M.*
Son las trece. / *It's one P.M.*

In conversation, the twenty-four-hour clock is not used. In order to specify A.M. or P.M., the following expressions are used:

Es la una <u>de la tarde.</u> / *It's one P.M. (in the afternoon).*
Son las siete <u>de la mañana.</u> / *It's seven A.M. (in the morning).*
Son las diez <u>de la noche.</u> / *It's ten P.M. (in the evening).*

To express midnight and noon, you may say the following:

Es la medianoche. / *It's midnight.*
Es el mediodía. / *It's noon.*

Cardinal Numbers

You need to know the following cardinal numbers to tell time.

Cardinal Numbers 1-31

1	uno	9	nueve	17	diecisiete	25	veinticinco
2	dos	10	diez	18	dieciocho	26	veintiséis
3	tres	11	once	19	diecinueve	27	veintisiete
4	cuatro	12	doce	20	veinte	28	veintiocho
5	cinco	13	trece	21	veintiuno	29	veintinueve
6	seis	14	catorce	22	veintidós	30	treinta
7	siete	15	quince	23	veintitrés	31	treinta y uno
8	ocho	16	dieciséis	24	veinticuatro		

Son las doce.

Son las doce y cuarto.
Son las doce y quince.

Son las doce y media.
Son las doce y treinta.

Es la una menos cuarto de la noche.
Es la una menos quince de la noche.

Es la una.

Son las dos.

Son las tres.

Son las cuatro.

Son las ocho.

Son las ocho y diez.

Son las ocho y media.
Son las ocho y treinta.

Son las nueve menos diez.

Es el mediodía.
Son las doce.

Son las doce y cuarto.
Son las doce y quince.

Son las doce y media.
Son las doce y treinta.

Es la una menos cuarto.
Es la una menos quince.

Es la una.

Son las dos.

Son las tres.

Son las cuatro.

Son las nueve.

Son las nueve y diez.

Son las nueve y media.
Son las nueve y treinta.

Son las diez menos diez.

Descriptive Adjectives with Ser

Previously, we noted that ser / *to be* is used to indicate characteristics and qualities of a person or object. The following is a selected list of common descriptive adjectives used with ser.

Common Descriptive Adjectives Used with Ser

COLORS

amarillo	*yellow*	marrón	*brown*
anaranjado	*orange*	negro	*black*
azul	*blue*	rojo	*red*
blanco	*white*	rosado	*pink*
gris	*gray*	verde	*green*

APPEARANCE

alto,	*tall*	hermoso	*beautiful*
atractivo	*attractive*	joven	*young*
bajo	*short*	lindo	*pretty*
delgado	*slender*	moreno	*brunette*
elegante	*elegant*	pelirrojo	*red-haired*
feo	*ugly*	rubio	*blond*
gordo	*fat*	viejo	*old*

PERSONALITY

activo	*active*	mentiroso	*lying*
antipático	*unpleasant*	perezoso	*lazy*
bueno	*good*	responsable	*responsible*
cómico	*funny*	serio	*serious*
egoísta	*selfish*	simpático	*nice*
generoso	*generous*	sincero	*sincere*
inteligente	*intelligent*	tonto	*foolish*
irresponsable	*irresponsible*	trabajador	*hardworking*
malo	*bad, evil*		

Possessive Adjectives

Possessive adjectives allow you to express possession. They go <u>before</u> the noun they modify just as in English. They all agree in <u>number</u> (singular, plural). Nuestro and vuestro also agree in <u>gender</u> (masculine, feminine).

Singular		Plural	
1st person	mi / *my*	1st person	nuestro / *our*
2nd person	tu / *your* (fam. sg.)	2nd person	vuestro / *your* (fam. pl.)
3rd person	su / *his, her, your* (pol. sg.)	3rd person	su / *their, your* (pol. pl.)

TIP

Remember: <u>Possessive adjectives agree with the item possessed and **NOT** the possessor</u>. Possessive adjectives always agree in number (singular, plural). Only nuestro/-a / *our* and vuestro/-a / *your* (fam. pl.) agree in gender also. The following selected examples illustrate this point.

mi libro / *my book*
mis libros / *my books*
nuestra casa / *our house*
nuestras casas / *our houses*

Note that the subject pronoun tú / *you* (fam. sg.) has a written accent but the possessive adjective tu / *your* (fam. sg.) does not.

GRAMMAR NOTE

Note that the preposition de / *of* and the masculine singular definite article el / *the* contract to the single form del / *of the* in Spanish, as shown below.

¿<u>De</u> quién es <u>el</u> libro? / *Whose book is it?*
El libro es <u>del</u> hombre. / *It's the man's book.*

EXERCISE Set 3-1

A. Supply the missing forms of the Spanish verb ser, and then give the English equivalent.

EXAMPLE: *él* _____   =   _____

él es   =   *he is*

1. (yo) _____   =   _____

2. (tú) _____   =   _____

3. (nosotros) _____   =   _____

4. (ellos) _____   =   _____

5. (vosotros) _____   =   _____

6. (Ud.) _____   =   _____

B. Give the indicated times.

EXAMPLE: 2:45 A.M.
Son las tres menos cuarto de la mañana.
2:45 P.M.
Son las tres menos quince de la tarde.

¿Qué hora es?

1. 8:20 P.M.   _____

2. 7:30 A.M.   _____

3. 4:45 P.M.   _____

4. 10:18 A.M.   _____

5. 11:35 P.M.   _____

6. 9:00 A.M. sharp   _____

7. 2:10 P.M.   _____

8. 4:30 A.M.   _____

C. How do you say the following sentences in Spanish? You do not have to translate material in parentheses; this information tells you what verb form to use, or it provides cultural information.

1. Where are you (fam. sg.) from?

    _____

2. My wife is from Uruguay, but I am from Spain.

    _____

3. They are Uruguayan and they are nice.

    _____

4. The Spanish woman is blond.

    _____

5. What is the red pen made of? It's plastic.

    _____

6. Whose watch is it? It's Pilar's. (Remember: No 's in Spanish!)

_____

7. It is important to study Spanish today.

_____

8. Silvia is red-haired and tall.

_____

9. My home is made of wood.

_____

10. The movie is at 8 P.M.

_____

Conjugation of *Estar*

The verb **estar** / *to be* is an irregular verb. Unlike the verbs that you have learned to conjugate in the first chapter, you cannot predict its forms on the basis of the infinitive. You will simply have to memorize them. Note that there are several forms (**tú, él, ella, Ud., vosotros/vosotras,** and **ellos/-as, Uds.**) that have a written accent.

estar / *to be*

Subject Pronoun	Verb Form	Meaning
(yo)	estoy	*I am*
(tú)	estás	*you (fam. sg.) are*
(él, ella, Ud.)	está	*he, she, you (pol. pl.) is/are*
(nosotros/-as)	estamos	*we are*
(vosotros/-as)	estáis	*you (fam. pl.) are*
(ellos/-as, Uds.)	están	*they, you (pol. pl.) are*

Uses of Estar

The verb estar / *to be* has a variety of uses, which we illustrate here.

Estar is used in the following situations	Examples
1. To indicate location.	Carmen está en casa. / *Carmen is at home.*
2. To indicate health.	Roberto está enfermo. / *Robert is sick.*
3. To indicate certain conditions with some adjectives.	Mónica está preocupada. / *Mónica is worried.*
4. Estar is used in certain idiomatic expressions.	Jorge está para salir. / *Jorge is about to leave.*
5. Estar is used with present participles (gerunds) to form the present progressive tense (see Chapter 6).	Alicia está cantando. / *Alicia is singing (at this very moment).*

Descriptive Adjectives with Estar

Items 2 and 3 indicate that estar / *to be* is used with certain adjectives to indicate health and well-being. The following is a selected list of common descriptive adjectives used with estar.

HEALTH AND WELL-BEING

enfermo	*sick*	vivo	*alive*
cansado	*tired*	muerto	*dead*

OTHER ADJECTIVES WITH *ESTAR*

alegre	*happy*	enojado	*angry*
ausente	*absent*	listo para	*ready to*
casado (con)	*married*	lleno	*full*
cubierto (de)	*covered with*	sentado	*sitting*
divorciado	*divorced*	vestido (de)	*dressed (in)*

IDIOMS WITH *ESTAR*

estar de acuerdo (con)	*to be in agreement*	estar de pie	*to be standing*
estar de buen humor	*to be in a good mood*	estar seguro (de)	*to be sure (of)*
estar de mal humor	*to be in a bad mood*	estar de vacaciones	*to be on vacation*
estar de guardia	*to be on call*		

Uses of Ser and Estar

Thus far, we have looked at the specific uses of ser / *to be* and estar / *to be* in isolation. We will now see that these two verbs may be used with the same adjectives. When this happens, there is a change of meaning. The following is a list of some common adjectives with changing meanings when they are used with either ser or estar.

Adjective	With Ser	With Estar
aburrido/-a	*boring*	*bored*
bueno/-a	*good (by nature)*	*in good health*
callado/-a	*quiet*	*silent*
cansado/-a	*tiring*	*tired*
completo/-a	*exhaustive*	*not lacking anything*
despierto/-a	*alert*	*awake*
divertido/-a	*entertaining*	*amused*
listo/-a	*clever, witty*	*ready*
malo/-a	*bad, evil*	*sick*
nuevo/-a	*brand-new*	*like new*
seguro/-a	*safe (reliable), sure to happen*	*certain, sure*
verde	*green*	*ripe*
vivo/-a	*lively, bright (in color)*	*alive*

EXERCISE **Set 3-2**

A. Supply the missing forms of the Spanish verb estar, and then give the English equivalent.

EXAMPLE: *él* ____   =   _____

él está   =   *he is*

1. (tú) _____   =   _____

2. (yo) _____   =   _____

3. (nosotras) _____   =   _____

4. (ellas) _____   =   _____

5. (vosotros) _____   =   _____

6. (Uds.) _____   =   _____

B. How do you say the following sentences in Spanish?

1. I am at home now, because I am sick.

   _____

2. My husband is about to leave for Montevideo.

   _____

3. She is tired because she works a lot.

   _____

4. My sister is married to a nice man.

   _____

5. I agree with Pablo.

   _____

6. We are on vacation in Uruguay now.

   _____

7. Blanca, you (fam. sg.) are tired because you are standing so much.

   _____

8. When I study a lot, I am in a good mood because I am learning.

   _____

9. I am bored because I am not on vacation.

   _____

10. This color is very bright.

   _____

The Verb *Hay*

Uses of Hay

Hay has only one form in the present tense. The verb hay means *there is* or *there are*. Its meaning depends on the noun that follows. It is used to call attention to the presence or existence of someone or something. The following examples illustrate this point.

Hay muchas personas aquí. / *There are many persons here.*
Hay mucho dinero en el banco. / *There is a lot of money in the bank.*

There is an idiomatic expression that is used with the verb hay: hay que. It means *one must* or *it is necessary to* and it is followed by an infinitive. The following examples illustrate this point.

Hay que estudiar. / *One must study.*
Hay que dormir. / *It is necessary to sleep.*

EXERCISE Set 3-3

A. How do you say the following sentences in Spanish?

1. There are six books here.

   _____

2. There is a Uruguayan woman in the class.

   _____

3. One must be here at 8:00 A.M.

   _____

4. It is necessary to go to Montevideo.

   _____

5. There are many students in class.

   _____

Conjugation of *Tener*

The verb tener / *to have* is an irregular verb. **Tener** is a stem-changing verb. There is one exception, however. The first person singular (yo) has an irregularity. Otherwise, it follows the usual conjugation format for a stem-changing verb (e → ie) in the present indicative tense. All of the endings are regular.

tener / *to have*

Subject Pronoun	Verb Form	Meaning
(yo)	<u>teng</u>+o	*I have, I do have*
(tú)	<u>tien</u>+es	*you (fam. sg.) have, you do have*
(él, ella, Ud.)	<u>tien</u>+e	*he, she, you (pol. sg.) has/have, he, she, you does/do have*
(nosotros/-as)	ten+emos	*we have, we do have*
(vosotros/-as)	ten+éis	*you (fam. pl.) have, you are having*
(ellos/-as, Uds.)	<u>tien</u>+en	*they, you (pol. pl.) do have; they, you do have*

Tener has the basic meaning of *to have* or *to possess*. Tener also appears in many idiomatic expressions, many of which relate to bodily experiences such as experiencing hunger, thirst, cold, heat, and so forth. It should be noted that if you use the adverb *very*, you have to use the adjective mucho / *much* in Spanish. Remember that in English these expressions use the verb *to be*, whereas in Spanish you must use *to have*.

IDIOMATIC EXPRESSIONS WITH *TENER*

tener (mucha) hambre	*to be (very) hungry*	tener ganas (de)	*to feel like*
tener (mucha) sed	*to be (very) thirsty*	tener (mucho) sueño	*to be (very) sleepy*
tener (mucho) frío	*to be (very) cold*	tener razón	*to be right*
tener (mucho) calor	*to be (very) warm*	no tener razón	*to be wrong*
tener (mucho) miedo		tener vergüenza (de)	*to be ashamed (of)*
(de)	*to be (very) afraid (of)*	tener … años	*to be … years old*
tener (mucha) suerte	*to be (very) lucky*	tener que (+ infinitive)	*to have to*
tener (mucha) prisa	*to be (very much) in a hurry*		

CARDINAL NUMBERS

40	cuarenta	300	trescientos
50	cincuenta	400	cuatrocientos
60	sesenta	500	quinientos
70	setenta	600	seiscientos
80	ochenta	700	setecientos
90	noventa	800	ochocientos
100	cien, ciento	900	novecientos
200	doscientos	1,000	mil

EXERCISE Set 3-4

A. Supply the missing forms of the Spanish verb **tener**, and then give the English equivalent.

EXAMPLE: *él* _____   =   _____

          él tiene   =   *he has, he does have*

1. (ella) _____   =   _____

2. (yo) _____   =   _____

3. (tú) _____   =   _____

4. (ellas) _____   =   _____

5. (Ud.) _____   =   _____

6. (Uds.) _____   =   _____

B. How do you say the following sentences in Spanish? You do not have to translate material in parentheses; this information tells you what verb form to use, or it provides cultural information.

1. I feel like going to the (al) *Museo del Gaucho y de la Moneda*[1].

   _____

2. When I am in the casino, I am very lucky.

   _____

3. He is 50 years old.

   _____

4. She is ashamed of her actions.

   _____

5. You (pol. pl.) have to eat at *La Silenciosa*[2].

   _____

6. I am very thirsty today and I want to drink water.

   _____

[1]Excellent museum of Uruguayan *gaucho* culture and currency in Montevideo.
[2]Excellent restaurant in Montevideo.

7. When I am very hungry, I eat sausages.

_____

8. I am afraid of spiders.

_____

9. I am always in a big hurry when I have to work.

_____

10. She is very sleepy and she needs to sleep.

_____

Conjugation of *Hacer*

The verb hacer / *to do, to make* is an irregular verb. This verb has one irregular form in the first person singular (yo) of the present indicative tense. Otherwise, it follows the usual conjugation for a regular -er verb. The endings are all regular.

hacer / *to do, to make*

Subject Pronoun	Verb Form	Meaning
(yo)	<u>hag</u>+o	*I do, I am doing, I do do*
(tú)	<u>hac</u>+es	*you (fam. sg.) do, you are doing, you do do*
(él, ella, Ud.)	<u>hac</u>+e	*he, she, you (pol. sg.) does/do, he, she, you is/are doing, he, she, you does/do do*
(nosotros/-as)	<u>hac</u>+emos	*we do, we are doing, we do do*
(vosotros/-as)	<u>hac</u>+éis	*you (fam. pl.) do, you are doing, you do do*
(ellos/-as, Uds.)	<u>hac</u>+en	*they, you (pol. pl.) do, they, you are doing, they, you do do.*

Uses of Hacer

The verb hacer is used to express weather conditions. The following are common meteorological expressions with the verb hacer / *to do, to make.*

¿Qué tiempo hace?	*What's the weather like?*
Hace (muy) buen tiempo.	*It's (very) good weather.*
Hace (muy) mal tiempo.	*It's (very) bad weather.*
Hace (mucho) frío.	*It's (very) cold.*
Hace (mucho) calor.	*It's (very) hot.*
Hace (mucho) sol.	*It's (very) sunny.*
Hace (mucho) viento.	*It's (very) windy.*
Hace fresco.	*It's cool.*

The following are additional weather expressions with the verb **estar** / *to be.*

Está (muy) húmedo.	*It's (very) humid.*
Está (muy) nublado.	*It's (very) cloudy.*
Está (muy) lluvioso.	*It's (very) rainy.*

The following are additional weather expressions with other verbs.

Llueve.	*It's raining.*
Llovizna.	*It's drizzling.*
Nieva.	*It's snowing.*
Relampaguea.	*It's lightning.*
Truena.	*It's thundering.*

There are a number of important idiomatic expressions with the verb hacer. The following are a few of them.

hacer caso a	*to pay attention to*
hacer el papel de	*to play the role of*
hacer un viaje	*to take a trip*

GRAMMAR NOTE

The verb hacer / *to do, to make* may appear in a special idiomatic construction with the present tense as illustrated below. This construction indicates that a specified activity began in the past and continues into the present.

¿Cuánto tiempo hace que estudias español? / *How long have you been studying Spanish?*
Hace un año que estudio español. / *I have been studying Spanish for a year.*

The above question and answer may be expressed in a different way as seen below.

¿Desde cuándo estudias español? / *How long have you been studying Spanish?*
Estudio español desde hace un año. / *I have been studying Spanish for a year.*

Dates

Indicating days is a simple process in Spanish. You use the cardinal numbers for 2–31. For the first, however, you use the ordinal number primero / *first* to indicate the first day of the month.

¿Cuál es la fecha de hoy? / *What's today's date?*
Hoy es el primero de diciembre. / *Today is the first of December.*
Hoy es el 5 de abril. / *Today is April fifth.*
Mañana es el primero de agosto. / *Tomorrow is August 1st.*

DAYS (día, *m.*) OF THE WEEK (semana, *f.*)

lunes	*Monday*	viernes	*Friday*
martes	*Tuesday*	sábado	*Saturday*
miércoles	*Wednesday*	domingo	*Sunday*
jueves	*Thursday*		

MONTHS (mes, *m.*) OF THE YEAR (año, *m.*)

enero	*January*	julio	*July*
febrero	*February*	agosto	*August*
marzo	*March*	septiembre	*September*
abril	*April*	octubre	*October*
mayo	*May*	noviembre	*November*
junio	*June*	diciembre	*December*

SEASONS (estación, *f.*) OF THE YEAR (año, *m.*)

la primavera (*f.*)	*spring*	el otoño (*m.*)	*fall*
el verano (*m.*)	*summer*	el invierno (*m.*)	*winter*

EXERCISE Set 3-5

A. Supply the missing forms of the Spanish verb **hacer**, and then give the English equivalent.

EXAMPLE: *él* _____   =   _____

   él hace   =   *he does/makes, he is doing/making, he does do/make*

1. (tú) _____   =   _____

2. (yo) _____   =   _____

3. (nosotras) _____   =   _____

4. (ellas) _____   =   _____

5. (vosotros) _____   =   _____

6. (Uds.) _____   =   _____

B. How do you say the following sentences in Spanish?

1. How long have you (fam. sg.) been studying Spanish?

_____

2. I have been studying Spanish for an hour.

_____

3. It is cold in Montevideo in June.

_____

4. When it rains, it is cloudy.

_____

5. I pay attention to verbs when I study Spanish.

_____

6. It is hot in Montevideo in December.

_____

7. I am taking a trip to *Punta del Este*[1].

_____

8. It always snows in winter.

_____

9. It is always very good weather in June.

_____

10. It is very windy in Chicago.

_____

11. It is March 31, 2013.

_____

[1]Resort area of Uruguay.

Conjugation of *Saber*

The verb saber / *to know* is an irregular verb. This verb has one irregular form in the first person singular (yo) of the present indicative tense. Otherwise, it follows the usual conjugation for a regular -er verb. The endings are all regular.

saber / *to know*

Subject Pronoun	Verb Form	Meaning
(yo)	sé	*I know, I do know*
(tú)	sab+es	*you (fam. sg.) know, you do know*
(él, ella, Ud.)	sab+e	*he, she, you (pol. sg.) knows/know, he, she, you does/do know*
(nosotros/-as)	sab+emos	*we know, we do know*
(vosotros/-as)	sab+éis	*you (fam. pl.) know, you do know*
(ellos/-as, Uds.)	sab+en	*they, you (pol. pl.) know, they, you do know*

Uses of Saber

The verb saber/ *to know* has a variety of uses that we will illustrate here. Saber / *to know* has the basic meaning of *to know something* (information, facts, ideas, etc.) or *how to do something* (to speak Spanish, to swim, etc.).

Saber is used in the following situations	Examples
1. To indicate that you know a fact.	Marco sabe la dirección de Juana. / *Marco knows Juana's address.*
2. To indicate that you know how to do something.	Ella sabe hablar español. / *She knows how to speak Spanish.*
3. To indicate that you *know that …*	Sé que Irene está aquí. / *I know that Irene is here.*

EXERCISE Set 3-6

A. Supply the missing forms of the Spanish verb saber, and then give the English equivalent.

EXAMPLE: *él* _____   =   _____

él sabe   =   *he knows, he does know*

1. (tú) _____   =   _____

2. (yo) _____   =   _____

3. (nosotras) _____   =   _____

4. (ellas) _____   =   _____

5. (vosotros) _____   =   _____

6. (Uds.) _____   =   _____

B. How do you say the following sentences in Spanish?

1. You (fam. sg.) know how to swim well.

_____

2. She knows that (que) Raquel is here.

_____

3. I know that (que) it is necessary to sleep 8 hours.

_____

4. We know that (que) it is cold in January.

_____

5. You (pol. pl.) know that (que) I have to be in Montevideo tomorrow.

_____

6. You (fam. sg.) know today's date. (Remember: No 's in Spanish.)

_____

7. He knows that (que) I am tired.

_____

8. You (pol. sg.) know that the tango is very popular in Montevideo.

_____

9. We know that (que) *Piriápolis*[1] is in Uruguay.

_____

10. They know that (que) I am in a good mood.

_____

[1]Famous Uruguayan resort.

Conjugation of *Conocer*

The verb conocer / *to know* is an irregular verb. This verb has one irregular form in the first person singular (yo) of the present indicative tense. Otherwise, it follows the usual conjugation for a regular -er verb. The endings are all regular. See Chapter 4 for a list of additional -cer (preceded by a vowel) verbs that are conjugated like conocer / *to know*.

conocer / *to know*

Subject Pronoun	Verb Form	Meaning
(yo)	conozc+o	*I know, I do know*
(tú)	conoc+es	*you (fam. sg.) know, you do know*
(él, ella, Ud.)	conoc+e	*he, she, you (pol. sg.) knows/know, he, she, you does/do know*
(nosotros/-as)	conoc+emos	*we know, we do know*
(vosotros/-as)	conoc+éis	*you (fam. pl.) know, you do know*
(ellos/-as, Uds.)	conoc+en	*they, you (pol. pl.) know, they, you do know*

Uses of Conocer

The verb conocer / *to know* has a variety of uses that we will illustrate here. Conocer / *to know* means to know a person or to be familiar with a place.

Conocer is used in the following situations	Examples
1. To indicate that you know someone. 2. To indicate that you are familiar with something, such as a location. [1]Restaurant in Montevideo.	Conozco a Juan. / *I know John.* Gloria conoce bien Mercado del Puerto. / *Gloria is very familiar with Mercado del Puerto*[1].

GRAMMAR NOTE

In Spanish, when the direct object (the recipient of the action of the verb) refers to a person or persons, you must place the "personal a" immediately before the direct object. There is no such form in English, which means that you must remember to place it there. The following examples illustrate the "personal a."

    Quiero a Rosa. / *I love Rosa.*
    Veo a mi amigo. / *I see my friend.*

If there is a series of names, you must place the "personal a" before each name.

    Veo a Margarita y a Jesús. / *I see Margarita and Jesús.*

If you ask a question with ¿quién? / *whom?* (sg.) or ¿quiénes? / *whom?* (pl.), when it is a direct object, you must use the "personal a" as seen in the following examples.

    ¿A quién ves? / *Who(m) do you see?*
    ¿A quiénes admiras? / *Who(m) do you admire?*

You can even use the "personal a" with your pets.

    Quiero a mi perro. / *I love my dog.*

You use the "personal a" with the following verbs that have an implicit preposition.

    Miro a Juan. / *I look at John.*
    Buscas a Magdalena. / *You are looking for Magdalena.*
    Uds. esperan a Jorge. / *You are waiting for Jorge.*

Finally, you do not use the "personal a" with the verbs ser / *to be*, tener / *to have*, and hay / *there is, there are*, as illustrated in the following examples.

    Alba es doctora. / *Alba is a doctor.*
    Tengo tres hermanos. / *I have three brothers.*
    Hay muchos estudiantes aquí. / *There are many students here.*

The "personal a" is a concept that you will need to remember later in this book.

EXERCISE Set 3-7

A. Supply the missing forms of the Spanish verb **conocer**, and then give the English equivalent.

EXAMPLE: *él* _____   =   _____

   él conoce   =   *he knows, he does know*

1. (tú) _____   =   _____

2. (yo) _____   =   _____

3. (nosotras) _____   =   _____

4. (ellas) _____   =   _____

5. (vosotros) _____   =   _____

6. (Uds.) _____   =   _____

B. How do you say the following sentences in Spanish?

1. I know a good restaurant in *Punta del Este*[1].

_____

2. I know Julio Rodríguez well.

_____

3. I am familiar with the short stories of *Horacio Quiroga*[2].

_____

4. He knows the Hernández family (**los Hernández**).

_____

5. I know the city of Montevideo very well.

_____

[1]Resort area in Uruguay.
[2]Famous Uruguayan writer of suspense and horror stories, 1879–1937.

EXERCISE Set 3-8

A. How do you say the following sentences in Spanish? This set of exercises includes all of the materials in this chapter. Most of these sentences contain the English verb *to be*. ¡Ojo! (*watch out!*). There are many ways to express *to be* in Spanish.

1. I am sure that I am right.

   _____

2. I know that it is cold today.

   _____

3. I have to be here at six P.M. sharp.

   _____

4. It is necessary to be nice.

   _____

5. They are sleepy and they are tired.

   _____

6. We are Argentinean but they are Uruguayan.

   _____

7. It is 1:15 P.M.

   _____

8. I am twenty years old and I am a student.

   _____

9. Christina Aguilera is blond and pretty.

   _____

10. When it is hot, I am very thirsty.

    _____

EXERCISE Set 3-9

A. ¿Que hora es? Look at the following watches and write out the time according to the time of day.

Modelo: Son las tres y cuarto.

First, you are out during the day:

1. _____   3. _____

2. _____   4. _____

Now you are out at night:

5. _____   7. _____

6. _____   8. _____

EXERCISE Set 3-10

A. Based on the drawings, indicate what the person or persons are doing. Use the verbs that you have learned in chapters 1 to 3.

1.   María y Juan _____.

2. Yo _____.

3. Ustedes _____.

4. Ella _____.

5. Nosotros _____.

6. Tú _____.

7. Usted _____.

8. Él _____.

9. Ana y yo _____.

Crossword Puzzle 3

Fill in the blanks. The clues contain expressions that will indicate which forms of the verbs ser, estar, tener, hacer, saber, and conocer you should use.

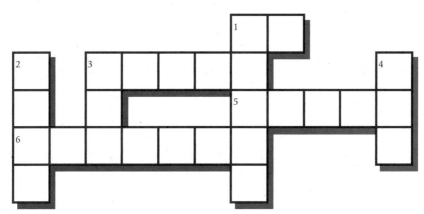

Horizontales
1. _____ el 31 de agosto.
3. (Tú) _____ la fecha.
5. (Yo) _____ que estudiar.
6. (Yo) _____ a Rosa.

Verticales
1. (Yo) _____ aquí.
2. _____ frío.
3. _____ las dos de la noche.
4. (Yo) _____ inteligente.

4

The Present Indicative of More Irregular Verbs

Irregular Verbs

We have already studied seven irregular verbs in Chapter 3. Now we will examine eight more common irregular verbs: dar / *to give*, decir / *to say/to tell*, ir (a) / *to go*, oír / *to hear*, poner / *to put, to place*, salir (de) / *to leave*, venir / *to come*, ver / *to see*. Later in this chapter, we will also see some other irregular verbs that follow certain common patterns.

dar / *to give*

Subject Pronoun	Verb Form	Meaning
(yo)	<u>d</u>+oy	*I give , I am giving, I do give*
(tú)	<u>d</u>+as	*you (fam. sg.) give, you are giving, you do give*
(él, ella, Ud.)	<u>d</u>+a	*he, she, you (pol. sg.) give(s), he, she, you is/are giving, he, she, you does/do give*
(nosotros/-as)	<u>d</u>+amos	*we give, we are giving, we do give*
(vosotros/-as)	<u>d</u>+ais	*you (fam. pl.) give, you are giving, you do give*
(ellos/-as, Uds.)	<u>d</u>+an	*they, you (pol. pl.) give, they, you are giving, they, you do give*

decir (i) / *to say, to tell*

Subject Pronoun	Verb Form	Meaning
(yo)	<u>dig</u>+o	*I say/tell, I am saying/telling, I do say/tell*
(tú)	<u>dic</u>+es	*you (fam. sg.) say/tell, you are saying/telling, you do say/tell*
(él, ella, Ud.)	<u>dic</u>+e	*he, she, you (pol. sg.) say(s)/tell(s), he, she, you is/are saying/telling, he, she, you does/do say/tell*
(nosotros/-as)	<u>dec</u>+imos	*we say/tell, we are saying/telling, we do say/tell*
(vosotros/-as)	<u>dec</u>+ís	*you (fam. pl.) say/tell, you are saying/telling, you do say/tell*
(ellos/-as, Uds.)	<u>dic</u>+en	*they, you (pol. pl.) say/tell, they, you are saying/telling, they, you do say/tell*

ir (a) / *to go*

Subject Pronoun	Verb Form	Meaning
(yo)	<u>v</u>+oy	*I go, I am going, I do go*
(tú)	<u>v</u>+as	*you (fam. sg.) go, you are going, you do go*
(él, ella, Ud.)	<u>v</u>+a	*he, she, you (pol. sg.) go(es), he, she, you is/are going, he, she, you does/do go*
(nosotros/-as)	<u>v</u>+amos	*we go, we are going, we do go*
(vosotros/-as)	<u>v</u>+ais	*you (fam. pl.) go, you are going, you do go*
(ellos/-as, Uds.)	<u>v</u>+an	*they, you (pol. pl.) go, they, you are going, they, you do go*

oír / *to hear*

Subject Pronoun	Verb Form	Meaning
(yo)	<u>oig</u>+o	*I hear, I am hearing, I do hear*
(tú)	<u>oy</u>+es	*you (fam. sg.) hear, you are hearing, you do hear*
(él, ella, Ud.)	<u>oy</u>+e	*he, she, you (pol. sg.) hear(s), he, she, you is/are hearing, he, she, you does/do hear*
(nosotros/-as)	<u>o</u>+ímos	*we hear, we are hearing, we do hear*
(vosotros/-as)	<u>o</u>+ís	*you (fam. pl.) hear, you are hearing, you do hear*
(ellos/-as, Uds.)	<u>oy</u>+en	*they, you (pol. pl.) hear, they, you are hearing, they, you do hear*

poner / *to put, to place*

Subject Pronoun	Verb Form	Meaning
(yo)	<u>pong</u>+o	*I put/place, I am putting/placing, I do put/place*
(tú)	<u>pon</u>+es	*you (fam. sg.) put/place, you are putting/placing, you do put/place*
(él, ella, Ud.)	<u>pon</u>+e	*he, she, you (pol. sg.) put(s)/place(s), he, she, you is/are putting/placing, he, she, you does/do put/place*
(nosotros/-as)	<u>pon</u>+emos	*we put/place, we are putting/placing, we do put/place*
(vosotros/-as)	<u>pon</u>+éis	*you (fam. pl.) put/place, you are putting/placing, you do put/place*
(ellos/-as, Uds.)	<u>pon</u>+en	*they, you (pol. pl.) put/place, they, you are putting/placing, they, you do put/place*

salir (de) / *to leave*

Subject Pronoun	Verb Form	Meaning
(yo)	sal**g**+o	*I leave, I am leaving, I do leave*
(tú)	sal+es	*you (fam. sg.) leave, you are leaving, you do leave*
(él, ella, Ud.)	sal+e	*he, she, you (pol. sg.) leave(s), he, she, you is/are leaving, he, she, you does/do leave*
(nosotros/-as)	sal+imos	*we leave, we are leaving, we do leave*
(vosotros/-as)	sal+ís	*you (fam. pl.) leave, you are leaving, you do leave*
(ellos/-as, Uds.)	sal+en	*they, you (pol. pl.) leave, they, you are leaving, they, you do leave*

venir / *to come*

Subject Pronoun	Verb Form	Meaning
(yo)	ven**g**+o	*I come, I am coming, I do come*
(tú)	vien+es	*you (fam. sg.) come, you are coming, you do come*
(él, ella, Ud.)	vien+e	*he, she, you (pol. sg.) come(s), he, she, you is/are coming, he, she, you does/do come*
(nosotros/-as)	ven+imos	*we come, we are coming, we do come*
(vosotros/-as)	ven+ís	*you (fam. pl.) come, you are coming, you do come*
(ellos/-as, Uds.)	vien+en	*they, you (pol. pl.) come, they, you are coming, they, you do come*

ver / *to see*

Subject Pronoun	Verb Form	Meaning
(yo)	ve+o	*I see, I am seeing, I do see*
(tú)	v+es	*you (fam. sg.) see, you are seeing, you do see*
(él, ella, Ud.)	v+e	*he, she, you (pol. sg.) see(s), he, she, you is/are seeing, he, she, you does/do see*
(nosotros/-as)	v+emos	*we see, we are seeing, we do see*
(vosotros/-as)	v+eis	*you (fam. pl.) see, you are seeing, you do see*
(ellos/-as, Uds.)	v+en	*they, you (pol. pl.) see, they, you are seeing, they, you do see*

Several of these verbs (**dar** / *to give*, **ir** / *to go*, **poner** / *to put/to place*, and **salir** / *to leave*) are used in idiomatic expressions. Following are some of the more common ones.

Idioms with Dar, Ir, Poner, and Salir

dar un paseo	*to take a walk*
dar una carcajada	*to burst out laughing*
dar igual	*to make no difference*
dar la mano	*to shake hands*
dar saltos	*to jump about*
dar voces	*to scream*
darse cuenta (de)	*to realize*
ir de compras	*to go shopping*
ir al centro	*to go downtown*
poner la mesa	*to set the table*
salir (con)	*to go out with*
salir (de)	*to leave (from a building)*

GRAMMAR NOTES

When you use the preposition a / *to* with the masculine singular definite article in Spanish, these two words contract to al / *to the*, as shown below.

> Voy al parque. / *I'm going to the park.*
> Voy al centro. / *I'm going downtown.*

The verb ir / *to go* may be used with an infinitive to indicate that you are going to do something. It is, thus, a substitute for the future as seen below.

> Voy a cantar. / *I'm going to sing.*
> Magdalena va a estudiar español. / *Magdalena is going to study Spanish.*

EXERCISE Set 4-1

A. Supply the missing indicative forms of the verb **salir**, giving the English equivalent.

EXAMPLE: *él* _____   =   _____

            él sale   =   *he leaves, he is leaving, he does leave*

1. (yo) _____   =   _____

2. (tú) _____   =   _____

3. (ella y yo) _____   =   _____

4. (ellos) _____   =   _____

5. (vosotras) _____   =   _____

6. (Ud.) _____   =   _____

Now, supply the missing present indicative forms of the verb ir, giving the English equivalent.

1. (yo) _____   = _____

2. (Isabel y yo) _____ = _____

3. (Uds.) _____   = _____

4. (ellas) _____   = _____

5. (nosotros) _____   = _____

6. (tú) _____   = _____

Now, supply the missing present indicative forms of the verb venir, giving the English equivalent.

1. (yo) _____   = _____

2. (tú) _____   = _____

3. (Ignacio y yo) _____ = _____

4. (ellos) _____   = _____

5. (vosotros) _____   = _____

6. (Uds.) _____   = _____

Now, supply the missing present indicative forms of the verb dar, giving the English equivalent.

1. (yo) _____   = _____

2. (tú) _____   = _____

3. (nosotros) _____   = _____

4. (ellos) _____   = _____

5. (vosotros) _____   = _____

6. (Uds.) _____   = _____

Now, supply the missing present indicative forms of the verb oír, giving the English equivalent.

1. (yo) _____   = _____

2. (tú) _____   = _____

3. (nosotros) _____   = _____

4. (ellas) _____   =   _____

5. (vosotros) _____   =   _____

6. (Uds.) _____   =   _____

Now, supply the missing present indicative forms of the verb decir (i), giving the English equivalent.

1. (yo) _____   =   _____

2. (tú) _____   =   _____

3. (Isabel y yo) _____   =   _____

4. (ellos) _____   =   _____

5. (vosotros) _____   =   _____

6. (Uds.) _____   =   _____

Now, supply the missing present indicative forms of the verb poner, giving the English equivalent.

1. (yo) _____   =   _____

2. (tú) _____   =   _____

3. (nosotros) _____   =   _____

4. (ellos) _____   =   _____

5. (vosotros) _____   =   _____

6. (Uds.) _____   =   _____

Now, supply the missing present indicative forms of the verb ver, giving the English equivalent.

1. (yo) _____   =   _____

2. (tú) _____   =   _____

3. (nosotros) _____   =   _____

4. (ellos) _____   =   _____

5. (vosotros) _____   =   _____

6. (Uds.) _____   =   _____

B. How do you say the following sentences in Spanish?

1. I take a walk in the park every day.

_____

2. I go out with my friends on Fridays.

_____

3. I frequently come late to the university.

_____

4. I see the *Museo de Arte Indígena*[1] now.

_____

5. I put my money in my wallet.

_____

6. I'm going to the (al) *Chaco*[2] tomorrow.

_____

7. I hear the sounds of the jungle (selva).

_____

8. I don't tell lies.

_____

[1]Museum of Indigenous Art in Asunción.
[2]Farm area in Paraguay and home to Mennonite settlers and indigenous peoples.

C. Choose the appropriate verb, **a**, **b**, or **c**, according to the meaning.

1. Cada año ... a España.

    a. doy
    b. veo
    c. voy

2. ¿Cuándo ... tu amigo? ¡Es tarde!

    a. viene
    b. dice
    c. oye

3. ¿A qué hora ... ellos de casa?

    a. ven
    b. salen
    c. dan

4. Ellos ... la mesa.

    a. vienen
    b. van
    c. ponen

5. ¿Con quién ... (tú) hoy?

    a. ves
    b. vas
    c. das

6. (Nosotros) ... al mar por las vacaciones.

    a. decimos
    b. vemos
    c. vamos

Additional Irregular Verbs

Verbs Ending in -cer Preceded by a Vowel

Verbs that end in -cer preceded by a vowel have an irregular yo form. You have already seen an example of such a verb in Chapter 3 with the verb conocer / to know. These verbs have the yo form in -zco. All other forms of the verb in the present indicative tense have regular endings. We provide an example of the verb establecer/ to establish.

establecer / to establish

Subject Pronoun	Verb Form	Meaning
(yo)	establezc+o	I establish, I am establishing, I do establish
(tú)	establec+es	you (fam. sg.) establish, you are establishing, you do establish
(él, ella, Ud.)	establec+e	he, she, you (pol. sg.) establish(es), he, she, you is/are establishing, he, she, you does/do establish
(nosotros/-as)	establec+emos	we establish, we are establishing, we do establish
(vosotros/-as)	establec+éis	you (fam. pl.) establish, you are establishing, you do establish
(ellos/-as, Uds.)	establec+en	they, you (pol. pl.) establish, they, you are establishing, they, you do establish

Common -cer Verbs Preceded by a Vowel

Below are some common -cer verbs that will come in handy for basic communication. All of these verbs have the irregular yo form in -zco.

agradecer	to thank	obedecer	to obey
aparecer	to appear	ofrecer	to offer
conocer	to know	parecer	to seem
crecer	to grow	pertenecer (a)	to belong
desaparecer	to disappear	reconocer	to recognize
establecer	to establish	yacer	to lie down
merecer	to merit, to deserve		

Verbs Ending in -ucir

Verbs that end in -ucir also have an irregular yo form. We provide the example here with the verb **conducir** / *to drive*. These verbs have the **yo** form in -zco. All other present indicative tense forms are regular.

conducir / to drive

Subject Pronoun	Verb Form	Meaning
(yo)	conduzc+o	*I drive, I am driving, I do drive*
(tú)	conduc+es	*you (fam. sg.) drive, you are driving, you do drive*
(él, ella, Ud.)	conduc+e	*he, she, you (pol. sg.) drive(s), he, she, you is/are driving, he, she, you does/do drive*
(nosotros/-as)	conduc+imos	*we drive, we are driving, we do drive*
(vosotros/-as)	conduc+ís	*you (fam. pl.) drive, you are driving, you do drive*
(ellos/-as, Uds.)	conduc+en	*they, you (pol. pl.) drive, they, you are driving, they, you do drive*

Common -ucir Verbs

Below are some common -cir verbs that will come in handy for basic communication. All of these verbs have the irregular yo form in -zco.

conducir	to drive	lucir	to light up, to display
deducir	to deduce	producir	to produce
inducir	to induce, to persuade	reducir	to reduce
introducir	to introduce	traducir	to translate

Other Irregular Verbs—Verbs Ending in -er

The following verb also has irregularities in the yo form. Other verbs listed below follow this pattern. All other present indicative tense forms are regular. We provide an example of the verb caer / *to fall*.

caer / *to fall*

Subject Pronoun	Verb Form	Meaning
(yo)	caig+o	*I fall, I am falling, I do fall*
(tú)	ca+es	*you (fam. sg.) fall, you are falling, you do fall*
(él, ella, Ud.)	ca+e	*he, she, you (pol. sg.) fall(s), he, she, you is/are falling, he, she, you does/do fall*
(nosotros/-as)	ca+emos	*we fall, we are falling, we do fall*
(vosotros/-as)	ca+éis	*you (fam. pl.) fall, you are falling, you do fall*
(ellos/-as, Uds.)	ca+en	*they, you (pol. pl.) fall, they, you are falling, they, you do fall*

Common -er Verbs

Below are some common -er verbs that will come in handy for basic communication. All of these verbs have the irregular yo form in -aigo.

atraer	*to attract*	retraer	*to bring back*
caer	*to fall*	sustraer	*to subtract*
contraer	*to contract*	traer	*to bring*

Verbs Ending in -uir

The following verbs that end in -uir have a y inserted in the stem of the first, second, and third person singular, and the third person plural. We provide an example of the verb concluir / *to conclude*.

concluir / *to conclude*

Subject Pronoun	Verb Form	Meaning
(yo)	concluy+o	*I conclude, I am concluding, I do conclude*
(tú)	concluy+es	*you (fam. sg.) conclude, you are concluding, you do conclude*
(él, ella, Ud.)	concluy+e	*he, she, you (pol. sg.) conclude(s), he, she, you is/are concluding, he, she, you does/do conclude*
(nosotros/-as)	conclu+imos	*we conclude, we are concluding, we do conclude*
(vosotros/-as)	conclu+ís	*you (fam. pl.) conclude, you are concluding, you do conclude*
(ellos/-as, Uds.)	concluy+en	*they, you (pol. pl.) conclude, they, you are concluding, they, you do conclude*

Common -uir Verbs

Below are some common -uir verbs that will come in handy for basic communication. All of these verbs have a -y- inserted in the first, second, and third person singular, and third person plural forms between the stem and the ending.

concluir	*to conclude*	huir	*to flee*
construir	*to build*	incluir	*to include*
contribuir	*to contribute*	influir	*to influence*
destruir	*to destroy*	sustituir	*to substitute*
fluir	*to flow*		

Spelling Change Verbs

There are some common verbs that undergo a spelling change according to the type of vowel that appears in the ending. When the ending vowel is -o or -a, it is preceded by a -z-. When the vowel is -e or -i, there is a -c- in the stem. In this hemisphere, the -z- and the -c- are pronounced as "s," as in the initial sound of the English word *sit*. We provide an example here of the verb convencer / *to convince*. This change occurs with verbs that end in -cer or -cir <u>when they are preceded by a consonant</u>.

Verbs Ending in -cer or -cir Preceded by a Consonant

Verbs that end in -cer or -cir, and that are preceded by a consonant, have a spelling change to -z- in the first person singular of the present indicative as illustrated below.

convencer / *to convince*

Subject Pronoun	Verb Form	Meaning
(yo)	<u>convenz</u>+o	*I convince, I am convincing, I do convince*
(tú)	<u>convenc</u>+es	*you (fam. sg.) convince, you are convincing, you do convince*
(él, ella, Ud.)	<u>convenc</u>+e	*he, she, you (pol. sg.) convince(s), he, she, you is/are convincing, he, she, you does/do convince*
(nosotros/-as)	<u>convenc</u>+emos	*we convince, we are convincing, we do convince*
(vosotros/-as)	<u>convenc</u>+éis	*you (fam. pl.) convince, you are convincing, you do convince*
(ellos/-as, Uds.)	<u>convenc</u>+en	*they, you (pol. pl.) convince, they, you are convincing, they, you do convince*

zurcir / *to mend, to darn*

Subject Pronoun	Verb Form	Meaning
(yo)	zurz+o	*I mend/darn, I am mending/darning, I do mend/darn*
(tú)	zurc+es	*you (fam. sg.) mend/darn, you are mending/darning, you do mend/darn*
(él, ella, Ud.)	zurc+e	*he, she, you (pol. sg.) mend(s)/darn(s), he, she, you is/are mending/darning, he, she, you does/do mend/darn*
(nosotros/-as)	zurc+imos	*we mend/darn, we are mending/darning, we do mend/darn*
(vosotros/-as)	zurc+ís	*you (fam. pl.) mend/darn, you are mending/darning, you do mend/darn*
(ellos/-as, Uds.)	zurc+en	*they, you (pol. pl.) mend/darn, they, you are mending/darning, they, you do mend/darn*

Common -cer *and* -cir *Verbs Preceded by a Consonant*

The following are some common verbs that have the spelling changes mentioned above. Again, these verbs are all preceded by a consonant.

convencer	*to convince*	vencer	*to conquer, to defeat*
ejercer	*to exert, to exercise*	zurcir	*to mend, to darn*
esparcir	*to scatter, to spread*		

Other Verbs with Spelling Changes

There are other common verbs that undergo a spelling change according to the type of vowel that appears in the ending. When there is a following -o or -a, there is a -j- in the stem. When the following vowel is -e or -i, there is a -g- in the stem. The -j- and the -g- are always pronounced as "h," as in the initial sound of the English word *hit*. We provide an example here of the verb escoger / *to select*.

Verbs Ending in -ger *and* -gir

For verbs that end in -ger, there is a spelling change for the sound *h* (as in *hit*). There is a spelling change to -j- before a following -o in the present indicative tense as illustrated below. Before a following -e, however, the sound *h* is spelled with a -g-.

escoger / *to select*

Subject Pronoun	Verb Form	Meaning
(yo)	escoj+o	*I select, I am selecting, I do select*
(tú)	escog+es	*you (fam. sg.) select, you are selecting, you do select*
(él, ella, Ud.)	escog+e	*he, she, you (pol. sg.) select(s), he, she, you is/are selecting, he, she, you does/do select*
(nosotros/-as)	escog+emos	*we select, we are selecting, we do select*
(vosotros/-as)	escog+éis	*you (fam. pl.) select, you are selecting, you do select*
(ellos/-as, Uds.)	escog+en	*they, you (pol. pl.) select, they, you are selecting, they, you do select*

Other -ger and -gir Verbs
The following are some common verbs that have the spelling changes mentioned above.

coger	to grasp, to seize	exigir	to demand, to require
corregir (i)	to correct	fingir	to pretend
dirigir	to direct	proteger	to protect
elegir (i)	to elect, to choose	recoger	to pick up
escoger	to select	surgir	to surge, to spur

EXERCISE Set 4-2

A. Supply the missing indicative forms of the verb ofrecer, giving the English equivalent.

EXAMPLE: él _____   =   _____

            él ofrece   =   *he offers, he is offering, he does offer*

1. (yo) _____   =   _____

2. (tú) _____   =   _____

3. (ella y yo) _____   =   _____

4. (ellos) _____   =   _____

5. (vosotras) _____   =   _____

6. (Ud.) _____   =   _____

Now, supply the missing present indicative forms of the verb producir, giving the English equivalent.

1. (yo) _____   =   _____

2. (nosotras) _____   =   _____

3. (Uds.) _____   =   _____

4. (ellas) _____   =   _____

5. (nosotros) _____   =   _____

6. (tú) _____   =   _____

Now, supply the missing present indicative forms of the verb traer, giving the English equivalent.

1. (yo) _____   =   _____

2. (Ignacio y yo) _____   =   _____

3. (Uds.) _____   =   _____

4. (ellas) _____   =   _____

5. (nosotros) _____   =   _____

6. (tú) _____   =   _____

Now, supply the missing present indicative forms of the verb incluir, giving the English equivalent.

1. (yo) _____   =   _____

2. (nosotros) _____   =   _____

3. (Uds.) _____   =   _____

4. (ellos) _____   =   _____

5. (ella) _____   =   _____

6. (tú) _____   =   _____

Now, supply the missing present indicative forms of the verb vencer, giving the English equivalent.

1. (yo) _____   =   _____

2. (Jorge y yo) _____   =   _____

3. (Uds.) _____   =   _____

4. (ellas) _____   =   _____

5. (nosotros) _____   =   _____

6. (tú) _____   =   _____

Now, supply the missing present indicative forms of the verb **proteger**, giving the English equivalent.

1. (yo) _____   =   _____

2. (nosotros) _____   =   _____

3. (Uds.) _____   =   _____

4. (ellas) _____   =   _____

5. (él) _____   =   _____

6. (tú) _____   =   _____

B. How do you say the following sentences in Spanish?

1. I know the city of Asunción well.

   _____

2. This book belongs to Carmen.

   _____

3. I'm translating poetry from Guaraní to Spanish.

   _____

4. I'm going to reduce my work hours.

   _____

5. I'm bringing my books to the office today.

   _____

6. I'm including a chapter about (**sobre**) Paraguayan literature.

   _____

7. They defeat their enemies with praise.

   _____

8. I protect my children.

   _____

C. Choose the appropriate verb, **a**, **b**, or **c**, according to the meaning.

1. (Yo) ... cuando nieva.

    a. traigo
    b. caigo
    c. atraigo

2. Ellos ... a la policía.

    a. parecen
    b. producen
    c. obedecen

3. (Tú) ... a tus amigos.

    a. esparces
    b. zurces
    c. convences

4. (Yo) ... la cosecha (crop).

    a. recojo
    b. exijo
    c. finjo

5. (Nosotros) ... del inglés al español.

    a. conducimos
    b. traducimos
    c. deducimos

6. Uds. ... de sus enemigos.

    a. influyen
    b. contribuyen
    c. huyen

Crossword Puzzle 4

Fill in the blanks. All of the clues both vertical and horizontal are English verbal expressions that correspond to a single verb in Spanish. Use the following verbs in your answers: conducir, construir, corregir, dar, decir, ir, obedecer, salir, traer.

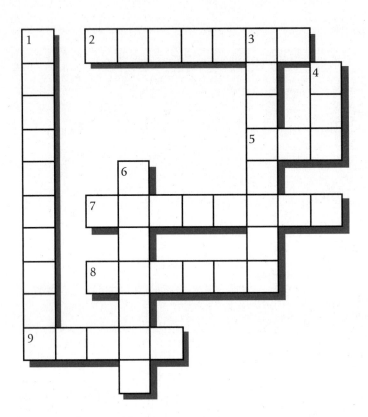

Horizontales
  2. Mis amigos y yo _____ la verdad.
  5. (Yo) _____ un paseo en el parque.
  7. (Yo) _____ a la universidad.
  8. (Yo) _____ mis libros a clase.
  9. (Yo) _____ de la universidad

Verticales
  1. (Tú) _____una casa nueva.
  3. (Yo) _____ a mis padres.
  4. (Yo) _____ a estudiar.
  6. El profesor _____ los exámenes.

5
The Present Indicative of Reflexive Verbs

Conjugation of Reflexive Verbs

A verb is reflexive when it has an identical subject and direct object, as in *She dressed herself*. The object is expressed as a reflexive pronoun. Reflexive verbs are thus conjugated in exactly the same manner as nonreflexive verbs, but with reflexive pronouns.

Here are the Spanish reflexive pronouns:

Singular		Plural	
1st person	me / *myself*	1st person	nos / *ourselves*
2nd person	te / *yourself* (fam. sg.)	2nd person	os / *yourselves* (fam. pl.)
3rd person	se / *himself, herself, yourself* (pol. sg.)	3rd person	se / *themselves, yourselves* (pol. pl.)

The following sentences exemplify typical sentences with reflexive verbs.

<u>Me</u> lav<u>o</u> por la mañana. / <u>I</u> wash <u>myself</u> in the morning.
<u>Te</u> diviert<u>es</u> en el cine. / <u>You</u> enjoy <u>yourself</u> at the movies.

NOTE

A reflexive verb is identifiable by the ending -**se** (*oneself*) attached to the infinitive.

lavar<u>se</u> / *to wash oneself*
ver<u>se</u> / *to see oneself*
divertir<u>se</u> (ie) / *to entertain onself*

Reflexive pronouns are placed in front of conjugated verbs.

Reflexive verbs are conjugated in exactly the same manner as other verbs with, of course, the addition of reflexive pronouns.

1. Drop the reflexive ending, -arse; -erse; -irse.
lavarse / *to wash oneself*
ponerse / *to put on (clothing)*
divertirse (ie) / *to entertain oneself*

2. Add the endings in the usual manner (Chapter 1).

3. Don't forget to add the reflexive pronouns.

lavarse / to wash oneself

Subject Pronoun	Reflexive Pronoun	Conjugated Verb	Meaning
(yo)	me	<u>lav</u>+o	I wash myself, I am washing myself, I do wash myself
(tú)	te	<u>lav</u>+as	you (fam. sg.) wash yourself, you are washing yourself, you do wash yourself
(él, ella, Ud.)	se	<u>lav</u>+a	he, she, you (pol. sg.) wash(es) himself/herself/ yourself, he, she, you is/are washing himself/herself/ yourself, he, she, you does/do wash himself/ herself/ yourself
(nosotros/-as)	nos	<u>lav</u>+amos	we wash ourselves, we are washing ourselves, we do wash ourselves
(vosotros/-as)	os	<u>lav</u>+áis	you (fam. pl.) wash yourselves, you are washing yourselves, you do wash yourselves
(ellos/-as, Uds.)	se	<u>lav</u>+an	they, you (pol. pl.) wash themselves/yourselves, they, you are washing themselves/ yourselves, they, you do wash themselves/ yourselves

The verb verse / to see oneself has an irregular first person singular form, as seen in Chapter 4.

verse / to see oneself

Subject Pronoun	Reflexive Pronoun	Conjugated Verb	Meaning
(yo)	me	<u>ve</u>+o	I see myself, I am seeing myself, I do see myself
(tú)	te	<u>v</u>+es	you (fam. sg.) see yourself, you are seeing yourself, you do see yourself
(él, ella, Ud.)	se	<u>v</u>+e	he, she, you (pol. sg.) see(s) himself/herself/yourself, he, she, you is/ are seeing himself/herself/yourself, he, she, you does/do see himself/herself/yourself
(nosotros/-as)	nos	<u>v</u>+emos	we see ourselves, we are seeing ourselves, we do see ourselves
(vosotros/-as)	os	<u>v</u>+eis	you (fam. pl.) see yourselves, you are seeing yourselves, you do see yourselves
(ellos/-as, Uds.)	se	<u>v</u>+en	they, you (pol. pl.) see themselves/ yourselves, they, you are seeing themselves/yourselves, they, you do see themselves/yourselves

The verb divertirse (ie) / to entertain oneself is a stem-changing verb. See Chapter 2 for a complete discussion of these verbs. Remember that the endings for stem-changing verbs are regular.

divertirse (ie) / *to entertain oneself*

Subject Pronoun	Reflexive Pronoun	Conjugated Verb	Meaning
(yo)	me	<u>divier</u>t+o	*I entertain myself, I am entertaining myself, I do entertain myself*
(tú)	te	<u>divier</u>t+es	*you (fam. sg.) entertain yourself, you are entertaining yourself, you do entertain yourself*
(él, ella, Ud.)	se	<u>divier</u>t+e	*he, she, you (pol. sg.) entertain(s) himself/herself/ yourself, he, she, you is/are entertaining himself/ herself/yourself, he, she, you does/do entertain himself/ herself/yourself*
(nosotros/-as)	nos	<u>divert</u>+imos	*we entertain ourselves, we are entertaining ourselves, we do entertain ourselves*
(vosotros/-as)	os	<u>divert</u>+ís	*you (fam. pl.) entertain yourselves, you are entertaining yourselves, you do entertain yourselves*
(ellos/-as, Uds.)	se	<u>divier</u>t+en	*they, you (pol. pl.) entertain themselves/yourselves, they, you are entertaining themselves/yourselves, they, you do entertain themselves/ yourselves*

Common Reflexive Verbs

Below are some common reflexive verbs that will come in handy for basic communication.

acordarse (ue) (de)	*to remember*	lavarse	*to wash oneself*
acostarse (ue)	*to go to bed*	levantarse	*to get up*
afeitarse	*to shave oneself*	llamarse	*to call oneself / to be named*
bañarse	*to bathe oneself*	mirarse	*to look at oneself*
cansarse	*to get tired*	peinarse	*to comb one's hair*
casarse (con)	*to get married / to marry*	ponerse (la ropa)	*to put on clothing*
cepillarse	*to brush oneself*	preocuparse (por)	*to worry (about)*
despertarse (ie)	*to wake up*	quedarse	*to remain, to stay*
desvestirse (i)	*to get undressed*	quitarse	*to take off (clothing)*
divertirse (ie)	*to entertain oneself*	secarse	*to dry oneself*
dormirse (ue)	*to fall asleep*	sentarse (ie)	*to sit down*
ducharse	*to take a shower*	sentirse (ie)	*to feel (emotions, physical well-being)*
enfermarse	*to get sick*		
enojarse	*to get angry*	verse	*to see oneself*
irse	*to go away*	vestirse (i)	*to dress oneself*

GRAMMAR NOTE

Reflexive pronouns may also be used in a construction known as the "reciprocal reflexive." It is restricted to the plural and its common English translation is "each other," or "one another." The following examples show this usage.

Mis amigos se abrazan. / *My friends embrace one another.*
Los amantes se besan. / *The lovers kiss each other.*

NOTE ON MEANING

Some verbs may have two forms: a non-reflexive version and a reflexive version. In the former case, this means that you are performing the action of the verb on someone else. In the latter version, you are performing the action on yourself. The following examples illustrate this usage. The first example in each pair is non-reflexive; the second is reflexive.

Baño a mi hijo. / *I bathe my child.*
Me baño. / *I take a bath (I bathe myself).*

Despierto a mis hijos. / *I wake up my children.*
Me despierto. / *I wake up.*

Many, but not all, reflexive verbs have these two meanings.

GRAMMAR NOTES

Certain verbs are followed directly by infinitives or by a preposition and an infinitive (see Chapter 2). With these verbs, you may place the reflexive pronoun either before the main verb (the first verb) or immediately following the infinitive and attached to it (the second verb). The following examples illustrate these two possibilities.

Before:
¿Te quieres divertir? / *Do you want to have fun?*
Uds. se pueden despertar tarde. / *You can wake up late.*

After:
¿Quieres divertirte? / *Do you want to have a good time?*
Uds. pueden despertarse tarde. / *You can wake up late.*

EXERCISE Set 5-1

A. Supply the missing indicative forms of the verb **levantarse**, giving the English equivalent.

EXAMPLE: *él* _____   =   _____

él se levanta =   *he gets up, he is getting up, he does get up*

1. (yo) _____   =   _____

2. (tú) _____   =   _____

3. (nosotros) _____   =   _____

4. (ellos) _____   =   _____

5. (vosotros) _____   =   _____

6. (Ud.) _____   =   _____

Now, supply the missing present indicative forms of the verb despertarse (ie), giving the English equivalent.

1. (yo) _____ = _____

2. (Isabel y yo) _____ = _____

3. (Uds.) _____ = _____

4. (ellos) _____ = _____

5. (nosotros) _____ = _____

6. (tú) _____ = _____

Now, supply the missing present indicative forms of the verb vestirse (i), giving the English equivalent.

1. (yo) _____ = _____

2. (tú) _____ = _____

3. (nosotros) _____ = _____

4. (ellos) _____ = _____

5. (vosotros) _____ = _____

6. (Uds.) _____ = _____

B. Choose the appropirate verb form, a, b, or c, according to the meaning.

1. Generalmente, … cuando miro la televisión.

    a. me duermo
    b. me llamo
    c. me levanto

2. Tu amigo regularmente … cuando mira una película (film).

    a. se llama
    b. se divierte
    c. se casa

3. ¿(Tú) … de todo?

    a. te despiertas
    b. te acuerdas
    c. te duermes

4. Uds. … cuando hay problemas.

    a. se duchan
    b. se peinan
    c. se enojan

5. Señora, ¿cómo ... Ud.?

    a. se llama

    b. se levanta

    c. se sienta

6. Ellos ... en el cuarto de baño todos los días.

    a. se enojan

    b. se duchan

    c. se llaman

7. (Yo) ... en el espejo.

    a. me preocupo

    b. me duermo

    c. me miro

C. How do you say the following sentences in Spanish?

1. Ana goes to bed very early.

_____

2. The author of *Raza de bronce*[1] is named *Alcides Arguedas*[2].

_____

3. Margarita wants to get married in La Paz.

_____

4. In the morning I wake up, I get up, I shower, and I get dressed.

_____

5. When I study Spanish verbs a lot, I get tired.

_____

6. After I take a bath, I dry myself.

_____

7. I feel happy when I learn Spanish verbs.

_____

8. I worry when I have a test.

_____

[1]Novel about the mistreatment of Indians in Bolivia, 1919.
[2]Famed Bolivian author, 1879–1946.

9. They fall asleep at 11 P.M.

_____

10. Guillermo looks at himself in the mirror in the morning.

_____

EXERCISE Set 5-2

A. Describe the actions in the pictures using appropriate reflexive verbs in the present tense.

1. Carlos _____

2. Juana _____

3. Luis _____

4. José _____

5. Juan _____

6. Marta y Pedro   _____

7. Raquel y Mónica   _____

8. María y Julia   _____

Crossword Puzzle 5

Fill in the blanks. All of the clues, both vertical and horizontal, are English verbal expressions that correspond to a single verb in Spanish. Use the following verbs in your answers: acostarse, afeitarse, casarse, levantarse, llamarse, preocuparse, quitarse, sentirse, verse.

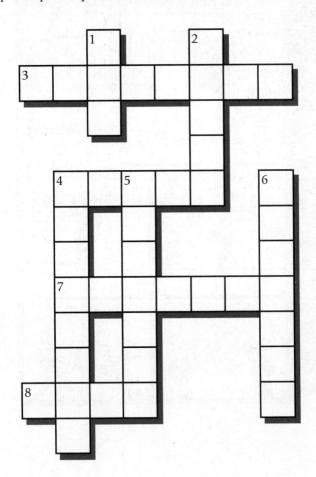

Horizontales
  3. Ud. se . . . por todo.
  4. Ella se . . . Mónica.
  7. Los hombres se . . . todos los días.
  8. Jorge se . . . con Elena.

Verticales
  1. Me . . . en el espejo.
  2. Él se . . . el sombrero.
  4. ¿A qué hora te . . . por la mañana?
  5. Ella se . . . tarde por la noche.
  6. Ellos no se . . . bien.

6

Gustar-Type Constructions and the Present Progressive (*el presente progresivo*)

Conjugation of *Gustar*

The verb gustar / *to be pleasing to, to like* is another important and very common verb. Its present indicative forms are given below. Its formation is regular, but its usage is different from the English verb *to like*. Gustar is almost always used in the third person singular or plural because of its special usage and basic meaning of *to be pleasing to*.

gustar / *to be pleasing to*

Subject Pronoun	Verb Form	Meaning
(yo)	<u>gust</u>+o	*I am pleasing to*
(tú)	<u>gust</u>+as	*you* (fam. sg.) *are pleasing to*
(él, ella, Ud.)	<u>gust</u>+a	*he, she, you* (pol. sg.) *is/are pleasing to*
(nosotros/-as)	<u>gust</u>+amos	*we are pleasing to*
(vosotros/-as)	<u>gust</u>+áis	*you* (fam. pl.) *are pleasing to*
(ellos/-as, Uds.)	<u>gust</u>+an	*they, you* (pol. pl.) *are pleasing to*

This verb allows you to express what you *like* in Spanish. It is, however, a tricky verb because it really means *to be pleasing to*.

1. In order to use it appropriately, you will first need to know the indirect object pronouns *to me, to you*, etc. We will discuss the usage of the indirect object pronouns in more detail below.

Singular		Plural	
1st person	me / *to me*	1st person	nos / *to us*
2nd person	te / *to you* (fam. sg.)	2nd person	os / *to you* (fam. pl.)
3rd person	le / *to him, to her, to you* (pol. sg.)	3rd person	les / *to them, to you* (pol. pl.)

2. The best initial learning strategy is to rephrase the English expression in your mind as shown below. Notice that the indirect object pronouns precede the verb.

English Expression	Rephrase to	Spanish Expression
↓	↓	↓
I like the book.	"To me is pleasing the book"	Me gusta el libro.
We like these books.	"To us are pleasing the books"	Nos gustan los libros.

3. If the indirect object is not a pronoun, use the preposition a before it. Note that when you are talking about someone, you will also need to use the indirect object pronoun le or les.

English Expression	Rephrase to	Spanish Expression
↓	↓	↓
Elena likes the book.	"To Elena is pleasing the book"	A Elena le gusta el libro.
My friends like those books.	"To my friends are pleasing the books"	A mis amigos les gustan los libros.

NOTE

When gustar is used with people, it means *I am attracted to*. If you want to say that you like someone, you need to use the expression caer bien a / *to like*. The following examples show this usage.

Me caes bien. / *I like you.*

Compare the above usage to the gustar expression with a person.

Me gustas. / *I am attracted to you.*

Prepositional Pronouns

You need to know another set of pronouns. These are pronouns for use after prepositions, hence their name "prepositional pronouns." These are especially useful for the gustar-type verbs we have just discussed. You will note that, except for mí / *me* and ti / *you* (fam.), the forms are just like the subject pronouns discussed in Part 1. Here the Spanish direct object pronouns are used after a preposition. Note, however, the following two prepositional pronous: conmigo / *with me*, contigo / *with you*.

Prepositional pronouns are used with third person singular (le) and third person plural (les) indirect object pronouns to clarify ambiguous forms that may mean *to him, to her, to you* (pol. sg.), *to them* (m. or f.), and *to you* (pol. pl.). When we discuss indirect object pronouns, we will see once again that it is important to know the prepositional pronouns.

Singular		Plural	
1st person	mí / *me*	1st person	nosotros / *us*
			nosotras / *us*
2nd person	ti / *you* (fam. sg.)	2nd person	vosotros / *you* (fam. pl.)
			vosotras / *you* (fam. pl.)
3rd person	él / *him*	3rd person	ellos / *them*
	ella / *her*		ellas / *them*
	Ud. / *you* (pol. sg.)		Uds. / *you* (pol. pl.)

GRAMMAR NOTE

If you use a third person indirect pronoun, you will need to include a clarifying pronominal phrase as shown below. We have underlined the clarifying phrase and the indirect object pronoun in the following examples.

A él le gusta la casa. / *He likes the house.*
A ella le gusta la casa. / *She likes the house.*
A Ud. le gusta la casa. / *You like the house.*
A ellos les gusta la casa. / *They like the house.*
A ellas les gusta la casa. / *They like the house.*
A Uds. les gusta la casa. / *You like the house.*

You may use the first- and second-person singular and plural prepositional objects with gustar-type constructions, but they are emphatic as seen in the examples below.

Me gusta leer libros. / *I like to read books.* (ordinary statement)
A mí me gusta leer libros. / *I like to read books.* (very emphatic statement)

Nos gusta Santiago. / *We like Santiago.* (ordinary statement)
A nosotros nos gusta Santiago. / *We like Santiago.* (very emphatic statement)

NOTE

If you want to make a gustar construction negative, you must place the word no immediately before the indirect object pronoun as shown below. This placement of no is true for all object pronouns (reflexive, direct, and indirect).

No me gustan los libros. / *I do not like the books.*
A ella no le gusta la casa. / *She doesn't like the house.*

GRAMMAR NOTE

Demonstrative adjectives, the words that express *this / that*, *these / those* generally appear before the noun they modify. You will need to remember a few things about them as shown here. We have indicated the agreement (number and gender) with an underline.

> est<u>e</u> lib<u>ro</u> / *this book*
> est<u>os</u> lib<u>ros</u> / *these books*
> est<u>a</u> cas<u>a</u> / *this house*
> est<u>as</u> cas<u>as</u> / *these houses*

There are two demonstrative adjectives for *that* and *those* in Spanish. To indicate *that / those* relatively near the speaker and hearer, use the forms of the demonstrative adjective **ese**.

> es<u>e</u> lib<u>ro</u> / *that book*
> es<u>os</u> lib<u>ros</u> / *those books*
> es<u>a</u> cas<u>a</u> / *that house*
> es<u>as</u> cas<u>as</u> / *those houses*

To indicate *that / those* relatively far away from the speaker and hearer, use the forms of the demonstrative adjective **aquel**. Note that the l is doubled (l → ll) in the feminine and plural forms (indicated in italic type).

> aque<u>l</u> lib<u>ro</u> / *that book*
> aque*ll*<u>os</u> lib<u>ros</u> / *those books*
> aque*ll*<u>a</u> cas<u>a</u> / *that house*
> aque*ll*<u>as</u> cas<u>as</u> / *those houses*

You may use the demonstrative forms without a following noun. In this case, they function as pronouns (*pro* means "in the place of"). When there is no following noun, it is necessary to write a graphic accent over the next to the last vowel (except for **aquél** / *that one*).

Rule of Thumb

As you can see, gustar can be confusing for anyone accustomed to the English verb *to like*. The following rule of thumb might help you to use this important verb more easily.

As the verb is often used with indirect object pronouns, just think of the pronouns as subjects; then make the verb agree with the direct object.

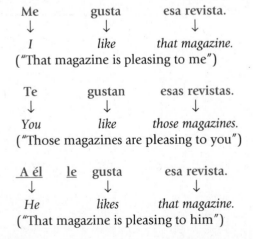

Me	gusta	esa revista.
↓	↓	↓
I	*like*	*that magazine.*

("That magazine is pleasing to me")

Te	gustan	esas revistas.
↓	↓	↓
You	*like*	*those magazines.*

("Those magazines are pleasing to you")

A <u>él</u>	<u>le</u>	gusta	esa revista.
↓		↓	↓
He		*likes*	*that magazine.*

("That magazine is pleasing to him")

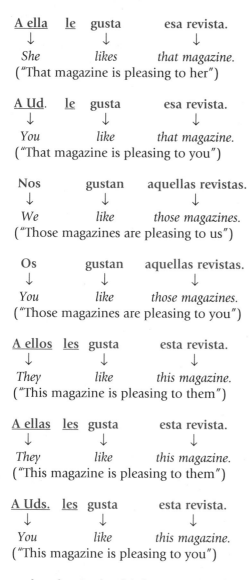

A ella   le   gusta   esa revista.
↓   ↓   ↓
She   *likes*   *that magazine.*
("That magazine is pleasing to her")

A Ud.   le   gusta   esa revista.
↓   ↓   ↓
You   *like*   *that magazine.*
("That magazine is pleasing to you")

Nos   gustan   aquellas revistas.
↓   ↓   ↓
We   *like*   *those magazines.*
("Those magazines are pleasing to us")

Os   gustan   aquellas revistas.
↓   ↓   ↓
You   *like*   *those magazines.*
("Those magazines are pleasing to you")

A ellos   les   gusta   esta revista.
↓   ↓   ↓
They   *like*   *this magazine.*
("This magazine is pleasing to them")

A ellas   les   gusta   esta revista.
↓   ↓   ↓
They   *like*   *this magazine.*
("This magazine is pleasing to them")

A Uds.   les   gusta   esta revista.
↓   ↓   ↓
You   *like*   *this magazine.*
("This magazine is pleasing to you")

Remember that in the third person singular and plural, you use a prepositional pronoun phrase and indirect object to indicate "<u>what</u> is pleasing <u>to whom</u>."

EXERCISE Set 6-1

A. Rephrase each sentence as shown, and then give its Spanish equivalent.

EXAMPLE: I like the book.
                "The book is pleasing to me" → *Me gusta el libro.*

1. I like this book.

2. My friends like that (over there) restaurant.

_____

3. You (fam. sg.) like to watch soap operas.

_____

4. We like that program.

_____

5. She likes this film.

_____

6. They like these magazines.

_____

7. He likes to visit _Antofagasta_[1].

_____

8. Rosa likes _Concepción_[2].

_____

9. Do you (pol. sg.) like Chilean food?

_____

10. They like to travel to _Punta Arenas_[3].

_____

11. I am attracted to you (fam. sg.).

_____

12. We are attracted to her.

_____

13. I like you.

_____

[1]Largest city in Northern Chile and site of two universities; also a major port.
[2]Third largest city in Chile, founded in 1515, place where Bernardo O'Higgins declared independence from Spain in 1818.
[3]Southernmost city in Chile, founded in 1843.

14. I like to go to the *Museo de Santiago*[4].

_____

15. You (pol. pl.) like to swim in the sea.

_____

[4]Museum of Santiago's history, covers the conquest period through the present.

Summary

As mentioned above, in order to use the verb gustar correctly, you must always think of what it really means.

I like the movie.

Me	gusta	la película
↓	↓	↓
To me	is pleasing	the movie

I like the movies.

Me	gustan	las películas
↓	↓	↓
To me	are pleasing	the movies

If you think that way, you will always be correct. Notice the preferred word order.

She likes the book.

A ella le	gusta	el libro
↓	↓	↓
To her	is pleasing	the book

She likes the books.

A ella le	gustan	los libros
↓	↓	↓
To her	are pleasing	the books

Other Verbs with Similar Features

The following verbs exhibit the same "grammatical behavior" of gustar / *to be pleasing to*—that is, they require frequent usage of indirect object pronouns and they may be rephrased mentally in analogous ways. The best learning strategy, once again, is to rephrase the English expression in your mind:

English Expression	Rephrase to	Spanish Expression
↓	↓	↓
My head aches.	"To me is aching the head"	Me duele la cabeza.
We need the money.	"To us is lacking the money"	Nos falta el dinero.
You (fam. sg.) *are interested in the magazines.*	"To you are interesting the magazines"	Te interesan las revistas.

The following are verbs that function like gustar / *to be pleasing to*.

agradar	*to please*	faltar	*to be lacking to, to be missing to*
apetecer	*to be appetizing, to appeal to (food)*	fascinar	*to be fascinating to*
bastar	*to be sufficient, to be enough*	importar	*to be important to*
caer bien	*to be liked, to create a good impression*	interesar	*to be interesting to*
convenir (ie)	*to suit one's interest, to be good for*	molestar	*to bother, to annoy*
doler (ue)	*to be painful, to ache*	parecer	*to seem, to appear to*
encantar	*to be enchanting to*	sobrar	*to be left over, to be in surplus*

EXERCISE Set 6-2

A. The following exercise contains verbs that function like gustar. Rephrase each sentence as shown, and then give its Spanish equivalent.

EXAMPLE: I am interested in the book.
             "The book is interesting to me" → *Me interesa el libro.*

1. Her tooth (diente) aches.

_____

2. I like you (fam. sg.).

_____

3. I need twenty *pesos*.

_____

4. I am interested in old books.

_____

5. Chilean art is important to me.

_____

6. Foolish people bother him.

_____

7. *Valdivia* is interesting to the tourists.

_____

8. It suits your (fam. sg.) interest to work hard now.

_____

B. Each question is given to you in the familiar form (singular or plural). Change each one to its corresponding polite form.

1. ¿Te gusta la literatura chilena?

_____

2. ¿Te gustan los museos de Santiago?

_____

3. ¿Te interesa ir al teatro chileno?

_____

4. ¿Te bastan 100 pesos?

_____

5. ¿Te importa leer *La Nación*?

_____

6. ¿Te conviene dormir tarde todos los días?

_____

Conjugation of *Estar*

In order to learn how to use the present progressive, called the presente progresivo, you will have to review the forms of the verb estar / *to be*. We have already learned the forms of the irregular verb estar / *to be* in Chapter 3, and we will review it here.

estar / *to be*

Subject Pronoun	Verb Form	Meaning
(yo)	estoy	*I am*
(tú)	estás	*you (fam. sg.) are*
(él, ella, Ud.)	está	*he, she, you (pol. sg.) is/are*
(nosotros/-as)	estamos	*we are*
(vosotros/-as)	estáis	*you (fam. pl.) are*
(ellos/-as, Uds.)	están	*they, you (pol. pl.) are*

The Present Progressive

The present progressive, called the presente progresivo in Spanish, is formed with the present tense of the verb estar and the present participle or the gerund of the verb, in that order.

It is very important to be aware that when we speak English, the normal verb form is the present progressive as seen below.

> What <u>are you doing</u>?
> <u>I am studying</u> Spanish.

In Spanish, however, the normal verb form is NOT the present progressive. In Spanish, the present progressive is rarely used, and when it is used, it is only to indicate what you are doing at the precise moment that you are speaking. The above interchange in English would be as follows.

> ¿Qué haces? / *What are you doing?*
> Estudio español. / *I am studying Spanish.*

When you want to know what a person is doing at the precise moment you are conversing with that person, you use the present progressive as illustrated below.

> ¿Qué <u>estás haciendo</u> ahora mismo? / *What are you doing right now?*
> <u>Estoy leyendo</u> un libro en este momento. / *I am writing a book at this moment.*

To form the present participle, or gerund, known as the gerundio in Spanish, of regular verbs:

1. Drop the infinitive ending of the verb:

hablar / *to speak*	→	habl-
comer / *to eat*	→	com-
vivir / *to live*	→	viv-

2. Add the following endings (-ando for -ar verbs; and -iendo for -er and -ir verbs) to the resulting stems:

habl+ando / *speaking*
com+iendo / *eating*
viv+iendo / *living*

hablar / *to speak*

Subject Pronoun	Estar	Present Participle	Meaning
(yo)	estoy	<u>habl</u>+ando	*I am speaking*
(tú)	estás	<u>habl</u>+ando	*you (fam. sg.) are speaking*
(él, ella, Ud.)	está	<u>habl</u>+ando	*he, she, you (pol. sg.) is/are speaking*
(nosotros/-as)	estamos	<u>habl</u>+ando	*we are speaking*
(vosotros/-as)	estáis	<u>habl</u>+ando	*you (fam. pl.) are speaking*
(ellos/-as, Uds.)	están	<u>habl</u>+ando	*they/you (pol. pl.) are speaking*

comer / *to eat*

Subject Pronoun	Estar	Present Participle	Meaning
(yo)	estoy	<u>com</u>+iendo	*I am eating*
(tú)	estás	<u>com</u>+iendo	*you (fam. sg.) are eating*
(él, ella, Ud.)	está	<u>com</u>+iendo	*he, she, you (pol. sg.) is/are eating*
(nosotros/-as)	estamos	<u>com</u>+iendo	*we are eating*
(vosotros/-as)	estáis	<u>com</u>+iendo	*you (fam. pl.) are eating*
(ellos/-as, Uds.)	están	<u>com</u>+iendo	*they/you (pol. pl.) are eating*

vivir / *to live*

Subject Pronoun	Estar	Present Participle	Meaning
(yo)	estoy	<u>viv</u>+iendo	*I am living*
(tú)	estás	<u>viv</u>+iendo	*you (fam. sg.) are living*
(él, ella, Ud.)	está	<u>viv</u>+iendo	*he, she, you (pol. sg.) is/are living*
(nosotros/-as)	estamos	<u>viv</u>+iendo	*we are living*
(vosotros/-as)	estáis	<u>viv</u>+iendo	*you (fam. pl.) are living*
(ellos/-as, Uds.)	están	<u>viv</u>+iendo	*they/you (pol. pl.) are living*

The Present Progressive of Reflexive Verbs

Reflexive verbs always use reflexive pronouns in the present progressive tense as shown below. There are, in fact, two ways of placing the reflexive pronoun. The first example shows the placement of the reflexive pronoun before the verb estar / *to be*. The second example shows the placement of the reflexive pronoun following the present participle (gerund) and attached to it. You will also note that there is a written accent over the first vowel of the present participle (gerund) ending, to indicate that the accent is retained in its original position. We indicate this with italic type in the second example.

Reflexive Pronoun Before Estar

lavarse / *to wash oneself*

Subject Pronoun	Reflexive Pronoun	Estar	Past Participle	Meaning
(yo)	me	estoy	lav+ando	*I am washing myself*
(tú)	te	estás	lav+ando	*you (fam. sg.) are washing yourself*
(él, ella, Ud.)	se	está	lav+ando	*he, she, you (pol. sg.) is/are washing himself/herself/ yourself*
(nosotros/-as)	nos	estamos	lav+ando	*we are washing ourselves*
(vosotros/-as)	os	estáis	lav+ando	*you (fam. pl.) are washing yourselves*
(ellos/-as, Uds.)	se	están	lav+ando	*they, you (pol. pl.) are washing themselves/yourselves*

Reflexive Pronoun Following and Attached to Present Participle (Gerund)

lavarse / *to wash oneself*

Subject Pronoun	Estar	Present Participle	Meaning
(yo)	estoy	lav+ándo+me	*I am washing myself*
(tú)	estás	lav+ándo+te	*you (fam. sg.) are washing yourself*
(él, ella, Ud.)	está	lav+ándo+se	*he, she, you (pol. sg.) is/are washing himself/herself/yourself*
(nosotros/-as)	estamos	lav+ándo+nos	*we are washing ourselves*
(vosotros/-as)	estáis	lav+ándo+os	*you (fam. pl.) are washing yourselves*
(ellos/-as, Uds.)	están	lav+ándo+se	*they/you (pol. pl.) are washing themselves/yourselves*

Spelling Changes in Present Participles (Gerunds)

When there is a vowel in the stem of an -er or -ir verb, you change the -i- of the present participle (gerund) ending to a -y-. The following verbs show this change. We have indicated the change in the present participle (gerund) with an underline.

atraer / *to attract*	→ atrayendo
caer / *to fall*	→ cayendo
construir / *to construct*	→ construyendo
contribuir / *to contribute*	→ contribuyendo
creer / *to believe*	→ creyendo
destruir / *to destroy*	→ destruyendo
huir / *to flee*	→ huyendo
incluir / *to include*	→ incluyendo
influir / *to influence*	→ influyendo

oír / *to hear*	→ oyendo
poseer / *to possess*	→ poseyendo
retraer / *to bring back*	→ retrayendo
sustituir / *to substitute*	→ sustituyendo
sustraer / *to subtract*	→ sustrayendo
traer / *to bring*	→ trayendo

GRAMMAR NOTES

The verb ir / *to go* has the present participle (gerund) yendo / *going*. This occurs because the complete infinitive (ir) corresponds to the verb ending (-ir). As a result, once the verb ending is removed, the -yendo addition becomes the gerund itself.

Stem-changing verbs in -ar and -er do not change their stem in the present participle (gerund) as shown below.

almorzar (ue) / *to have lunch* → almorzando / *having lunch*
pensar (ie) / *to think* → pensando / *thinking*
entender (ie) / *to understand* → entendiendo / *understanding*
volver (ue) / *to return* → volviendo / *returning*

TIP

There are a few adverbial expressions that indicate that the present progressive is an appropriate verb tense to use. The following are some of the more common expressions.

ahora mismo / *right now*
en este momento / *at this moment*

Stem Changes in Present Participles (Gerunds)

The present participle (gerund) for -ir stem-changing verbs has a vowel change in the stem. The following are the three patterns. Refer to Chapter 2 to review stem-changing verbs. The dictionary entry for this group of verbs includes a second vowel in parentheses to indicate this change as follows: dormir (ue, u) / *to sleep,* sentir (ie, i) / *to regret,* and pedir (i, i) / *to ask for/to request.*

1. Third conjugation (-ir) verbs with the stem change o → ue verbs have a change of o → u in the present participle (gerund). We have underlined the stem change in the present participle (gerund).

   dormir (ue, u) → durmiendo / *sleeping*
   morir (ue, u) → muriendo / *dying*

2. Third conjugation (-ir) verbs with the stem change e → ie verbs have a change of e → i in the present participle (gerund). We have underlined the stem change in the present participle (gerund).

   advertir (ie, i) → advirtiendo / *warning*
   consentir (ie, i) → consintiendo / *consenting*
   hervir (ie, i) → hirviendo / *boiling*
   mentir (ie, i) → mintiendo / *lying*
   preferir (ie, i) → prefiriendo / *preferring*
   sentir (ie, i) → sintiendo / *feeling*
   sugerir (ie, i) → sugiriendo / *suggesting*

3. Third conjugation (-ir) verbs with the stem change e → i verbs have a change of e → i in the present participle (gerund). We have underlined the stem change in the present participle (gerund).

      competir (i, i) → compitiendo / *competing*
      conseguir (i, i) → consiguiendo / *obtaining*
      decir (i, i) → diciendo / *saying, telling*
      medir (i, i) → midiendo / *measuring*
      pedir (i, i) → pidiendo / *requesting, asking for*
      reír (i, i) → riendo / *laughing*
      repetir (i, i) → repitiendo / *repeating*
      seguir (i, i) → siguiendo / *following*
      servir (i, i) → sirviendo / *serving*

GRAMMAR NOTE

Many dictionaries include a convention in their notation to alert the reader to the fact that -ir stem-changing verbs undergo a vowel change in the present participle (gerund). There are two parenthetical vowels in the dictionary entry, the first indicates a change in the present tense, and the second indicates a change in the present participle (gerund) and in certain forms of the preterite tense (see Chapter 7), the present subjunctive (see Chapter 15), and the past subjunctive (see Chapter 16) as illustrated below.

      dormir (ue, u) / *to sleep*
      mentir (ie, i) / *to lie*
      pedir (i, i) / *to request, to order, to ask for*

It should be noted that decir (i, i) / *to say, to tell* is irregular in the preterite and does not have this change in that tense. From now on, we will use this convention in this book.

NOTE

Verb with the change u → ue. Jugar (ue) / *to play (a game)* is the only verb that does not have this change in the gerund.

      jugar (ue) / *to play (a game)* → jugando / *playing (a game)*

EXERCISE Set 6-3

A. Supply the missing present progressive forms of the verb escribir, giving the English equivalent.

EXAMPLE: *él* _____   = _____

                él está escribiendo =   *he is writing*

1. (yo) _____   = _____

2. (tú) _____   = _____

3. (nosotros) _____   =   _____

4. (ellos) _____   =   _____

5. (vosotros) _____   =   _____

6. (Ud.) _____   =   _____

Now, supply the missing present progressive forms of the verb **leer**, giving the English equivalent.

1. (yo) _____   =   _____

2. (Isabel y yo) _____   =   _____

3. (Uds.) _____   =   _____

4. (ellos) _____   =   _____

5. (nosotros) _____   =   _____

6. (tú) _____   =   _____

Now, supply the missing present progressive forms of the verb **servir** (**i, i**), giving the English equivalent.

1. (yo) _____   =   _____

2. (tú) _____   =   _____

3. (nosotros) _____   =   _____

4. (ellos) _____   =   _____

5. (vosotros) _____   =   _____

6. (Uds.) _____   =   _____

Now, supply the missing present progressive forms of the verb **morir** (**ue, u**), giving the English equivalent.

1. (yo) _____   =   _____

2. (tú) _____   =   _____

3. (nosotros) _____   =   _____

4. (ellos) _____   =   _____

5. (vosotros) _____   =   _____

6. (Uds.) _____   =   _____

Now, supply the missing present progressive forms of the verb **bañarse**, giving the English equivalent. In this case, place the reflexive pronouns before the verb **estar** / *to be*.

1. (yo) _____ = _____

2. (tú) _____ = _____

3. (nosotros) _____ = _____

4. (ellos) _____ = _____

5. (vosotros) _____ = _____

6. (Uds.) _____ = _____

Now, supply the missing present progressive forms of the verb **bañarse**, giving the English equivalent. In this case, place the reflexive pronoun following the present participle (gerund) and attached to it. Remember to include the written accent mark on the last vowel of the present participle ending.

1. (yo) _____ = _____

2. (tú) _____ = _____

3. (nosotros) _____ = _____

4. (ellos) _____ = _____

5. (vosotros) _____ = _____

6. (Uds.) _____ = _____

B. How do you say the following sentences in Spanish?

1. She's studying for her exam right now.

_____

2. They are practicing Spanish at this moment.

_____

3. We are serving the dinner to our friends.

_____

4. I am playing soccer at this moment.

_____

5. You (fam. sg.) are sleeping right now.

_____

6. I am telling the truth.

_____

7. He is eating the Chilean food now.

_____

GRAMMAR NOTE

There are two categories of verbs: (1) transitive verbs, and (2) intransitive verbs. Transitive verbs take a direct object. Intransitive verbs do not.

The following examples illustrate this property of verbs. The first example shows a transitive verb—one that takes a direct object (= a noun, a person, place, object, or concept). We have underlined the direct object in the first sentence.

The second sentence shows an intransitive verb—one that does not require a direct object.

   1. **Juan compra** el libro. / *John buys the book.*
   2. **María sale.** / *Mary leaves.*

Direct Object Pronouns

In Chapter 4, you learned about reflexive pronouns. Remember that a pronoun stands in the place of a noun, i.e., it substitutes for a noun. Now you will learn about direct object pronouns. Just like reflexive pronouns, direct object pronouns come immediately before a conjugated verb. Direct objects answer the question *whom?* or *what?* as shown below (the direct object pronouns are underlined).

> **Whom** do you see?
> I see **Mary**. **Mary** is the direct object.

> **What** do you wear?
> I wear **new shoes**. **New shoes** is the direct object.

Here are the Spanish direct object pronouns:

Singular		Plural	
1st person	me / *me*	1st person	nos / *us*
2nd person	te / *you* (fam. sg.)	2nd person	os / *you* (fam. sg.)
3rd person	lo / *him, you* (m. pol. sg.)	3rd person	los / *them, you* (m. pol. pl.)
	la / *her, you* (f. pol. sg.)		las / *them, you* (f. pol. pl.)

The English direct object pronoun *it* (or plural *them*) is expressed by the third person direct object pronoun forms above. Be careful! Choose the pronoun according to the gender and number of the noun that has been replaced. The following examples illustrate the process of changing direct objects to direct object pronouns (the direct objects and direct object pronouns are underlined).

> Eva compra <u>el libro.</u> / *Eva is buying the book.*
>
> Eva <u>lo</u> compra. / *Eva is buying it.*

> Jorge compra <u>los boletos.</u> / *Jorge is buying the tickets.*
>
> Jorge <u>los</u> compra. / *Jorge is buying them.*

> Berta compra la <u>revista.</u> / *Berta is buying the magazine.*
>
> Berta <u>la</u> compra. / *Berta is buying it.*

> Jorge compra <u>las revistas.</u> / *Jorge is buying the magazines.*
>
> Jorge <u>las</u> compra. / *Jorge is buying them.*

The placement of object pronouns relative to the verb (reflexive pronouns, direct object pronouns, indirect object pronouns) follows set patterns. As we have already noted, object pronouns must appear immediately before a conjugated verb. The situation is different, however, when there is an infinitive or a present participle (gerund) as shown below. In these two cases, the object pronoun may follow and be attached to the infinitive/present participle (gerund), or it may also go immediately before the conjugated verb.

It is precisely because of their close association with verbs that we pay so much attention to object pronouns. You will use them frequently in conversation and in writing, so you need to know how to use them. We have underlined the direct objects.

A. INFINITIVES
Eva necesita comprar <u>el libro</u>. / *Eva needs to buy the book.*
Eva necesita comprar<u>lo</u>. / *Eva needs to buy it.*
Eva <u>lo</u> necesita comprar. / *Eva needs to buy it.*

B. PRESENT PARTICIPLES
Eva está comprando <u>el libro</u>. / *Eva is buying the book.*
Eva está comprándo<u>lo</u>. / *Eva is buying it.*
Eva <u>lo</u> está comprando. / *Eva is buying it.*

EXERCISE Set 6-4

A. Replace the direct objects with direct object pronouns. Remember that there are two options with infinitives and present participles (gerunds). In these cases, write both possibilities.

EXAMPLE: Rosa hace <u>el trabajo</u>.
            Rosa <u>lo</u> hace.

            Rosa no quiere hacer <u>el trabajo</u>.
            Rosa no quiere hacer<u>lo</u>.
            Rosa no <u>lo</u> quiere hacer.

            Rosa está haciendo <u>el trabajo</u>.
            Rosa está haciéndo<u>lo</u>.
            Rosa <u>lo</u> está haciendo.

1. Pablo lee <u>las revistas</u>.

   _____

2. Pilar está bebiendo <u>el café</u>.

   _____

   _____

3. Quiero cantar <u>la canción</u>.

   _____

   _____

4. Excribimos <u>las cartas</u>.

   _____

5. Ella come <u>los frijoles</u>.

   _____

B. Provide the Spanish for the following sentences. Use a direct object pronoun in your answer. If there are two ways of writing the answer, please do so.

1. I see her in the car.

   _____

2. You (fam. sg.) want to watch it (soap opera).

_____

3. She is reading it (the book) right now.

_____

4. They need it (money) now.

_____

C. Answer the following questions in Spanish. Use a direct object pronoun in your answer. If there are two ways of writing the answer, please do so.

1. ¿Lees los poemas de _Gabriela Mistral_[1]?

_____

2. ¿Necesitas hacer el trabajo ahora?

_____

3. ¿Están Uds. estudiando el libro de texto?

_____

[1]Chilean poet, 1889–1957; winner of the Nobel Prize, 1945.

Indirect Object Pronouns

By now, you are probably telling yourself that you have had enough of Spanish pronouns! What you need to remember is that once you learn the pronouns and the rules for their use, you will be able to use them throughout the rest of this book and in your daily communication in Spanish. They are always used in association with verbs, so you need to know how to use them. Because the third person singular (**le**) and third person plural (**les**) forms are ambiguous, it is necessary to use clarifying prepositional pronouns (with the preposition **a** / _to_) to specify the reference for these two pronominal forms. We have already seen their use with **gustar**-type constructions previously. We reproduce the indirect object pronouns here for your reference.

Singular		Plural	
1st person	me / _to me_	1st person	nos / _to us_
2nd person	te / _to you_ (fam. sg.)	2nd person	os / _to you_ (fam. pl.)
3rd person	le / _to him, to her, to you_ (pol. sg.)	3rd person	les / _to them, to you_ (pol. pl.)

Indirect object pronouns normally occur with verbs of communication and verbs of giving and transmitting. Again, just like other object pronouns (direct and reflexive), indirect object pronouns come immediately before a conjugated verb. Indirect object pronouns answer the question *to whom?* or *for whom?* (the indirect objects are underlined).

To whom are you speaking?
I am speaking **to Mary**. **To Mary** is the indirect object.

For whom are you buying the book?
I am buying the book **for Mary**. **For Mary** is the indirect object.

Indirect object pronouns appear in the same positions as reflexive pronouns and direct object pronouns, i.e., immediately before a conjugated verb but optionally following and attached to an infinitive or present participle (gerund). The following examples illustrate this. But first, the third person singular (**le**) and plural (**les**) indirect object pronoun must always be used even though it seems unnecessary to English speakers. For this reason, it is called the "redundant indirect object pronoun." You will also note that the examples include prepositional pronouns (those that are used after a preposition).

1. Conjugated verb.
   Le doy el libro <u>a él</u>. / *I give the book to him.*

2. Infinitive.
   Quiero decir**le** la verdad <u>a ella</u>. / *I want to tell the truth to her.*
   Le quiero decir la verdad <u>a ella</u>. / *I want to tell the truth to her.*

3. Present participle (gerund).
   Estoy escribiéndo**les** la carta <u>a ellos</u>. / *I am writing the letter to them.*
   Les estoy escribiendo la carta <u>a ellos</u>. / *I am writing the letter to them.*

Common Verbs of Communication

contar (ue)	*to tell (a story)*	gritar	*to shout*
decir (i)	*to say, to tell*	hablar	*to speak*
escribir	*to write*		

Common Verbs of Giving or Transmitting

dar	*to give*	mostrar (ue)	*to show*
entregar	*to hand over*	vender	*to sell*
mandar	*to send*		

GRAMMAR NOTE

If you add two pronouns to an infinitive, you must write a graphic accent mark on the place where the stress originally fell to indicate that it is maintained there as illustrated below.

Voy a mostrár**telo**. / *I am going to show it to you.*

If you add one or two pronouns to a present participle, you must write a graphic accent mark on the place where the stress originally fell to indicate that it is maintained there as we illustrate below.

Estoy haciéndo**lo**. / *I am doing it.*
Estoy dándo**telo**. / *I am giving it to you.*

EXERCISE Set 6-5

A. Provide the Spanish for the following sentences. Use an indirect object pronoun in your answer. Remember to use the redundant indirect object pronoun in the third person singular and plural. If there are two ways of writing the answer, please do so.

1. I tell the truth to her.

   _____

2. They have to write the letter to them (our friends).

   _____

   _____

3. They are speaking in Spanish to us.

   _____

   _____

B. Answer the following questions in Spanish. Use an indirect object pronoun in your answer. If there are two ways of writing the answer, please do so.

1. ¿Le das los libros a Magdalena?

   _____

2. ¿Prefieres darle los regalos a tu novia?

   _____

   _____

3. ¿Estás entregándole el paquete a Manolo?

   _____

   _____

Double Object Pronouns

It is possible to make pronouns of both indirect and direct objects in Spanish as exemplified here. When there are two object pronouns, the order is always: INDIRECT + DIRECT.

>Alba *me* da <u>el libro</u>. / *Alba gives me the book.* →
>Alba *me* <u>lo</u> da. / *Alba gives it to me.*
>
>Alberto *te* manda <u>la carta</u>. / *Alberto sends you the letter.* →
>Alberto *te* <u>la</u> manda. / *Albert sends it to you.*

When you use two object pronouns and one of them is either le or les, you must change the indirect object pronoun to se as shown below.

>le + direct object → se + direct object
>les + direct object → se + direct object

The following examples illustrate this change.

>Alicia *le* habla <u>español</u> a Félix. / *Alicia speaks Spanish to Félix.* →
>Alicia *se* <u>lo</u> habla a él. / *Alicia speaks it to him.*
>
>Guillermo *les* canta <u>las canciones chilenas</u> a Teresa y a Tomás. / *Guillermo sings the Chilean songs to Teresa and Tomás.* →
>Guillermo *se* <u>las</u> canta a ellos. / *Guillermo sings them (songs) to them.*

When you use two object pronouns with an infinitive, you may place them before the conjugated verb or after it, as illustrated below.

>Gustavo no quiere decir*le* <u>la verdad</u> a Julia. / *Gustavo doesn't want to tell the truth to Julia.*
>Gustavo no quiere decír*se*<u>la</u> a ella. / *Gustavo doesn't want to tell it to her.*
>Gustavo no *se* <u>la</u> quiere decir a ella. / *Gustavo doesn't want to tell it to her.*

When you use two object pronouns with a present participle (gerund), you may place them before the conjugated verb or after it, as illustrated below.

>Gustavo está diciéndo*le* <u>la verdad</u> a Julia. / *Gustavo is telling the truth to Julia.*
>Gustavo está diciéndo*se*<u>la</u> a ella. / *Gustavo is telling it to her.*
>Gustavo *se* <u>la</u> está diciendo a ella. / *Gustavo is telling it to her.*

EXERCISE Set 6-6

A. Replace the indirect and direct objects with indirect and direct object pronouns. Remember that there are two options with infinitives and present participles (gerunds). In these cases, write both possibilities. Remember that the order of these pronouns is always INDIRECT + DIRECT. If there are two ways of writing the answer, please do so.

EXAMPLES: Gustavo *le* dice <u>la verdad</u> *a Julia.*
Gustavo *se* <u>la</u> dice *a ella.*

Gustavo no quiere decir*le* <u>la verdad</u> *a Julia.*
Gustavo no quiere decír*se*<u>la</u> *a ella.*
Gustavo no *se* <u>la</u> quiere decir *a ella.*

Gustavo está diciéndo*le* <u>la verdad</u> *a Julia.*
Gustavo está diciéndo*se*<u>la</u> *a ella.*
Gustavo *se* <u>la</u> está diciendo *a ella.*

1. Aristófanes les escribe muchas cartas a sus padres.

   _____

2. Irene está contándole el cuento a Luisa.

   _____

   _____

3. Francisco necesita venderle la casa a Marina.

   _____

   _____

4. Ellas están dándoles el dinero a sus amigos.

   _____

   _____

5. Carlos me muestra la casa.

   _____

B. Provide the Spanish for the following sentences. Use an indirect object pronoun and a direct object in your answer. If there are two ways of writing the answer, please do so.

1. They sell them (books) to us.

   _____

2. We want to show them (photos) to them (our friends).

   _____

   _____

3. He is giving it (gift) to her.

   _____

   _____

C. Answer the following questions in Spanish. Use an indirect object and a direct object pronoun in your answer.

1. ¿Le muestras las joyas a tu novia?

   _____

2. ¿Vas a escribirles una carta a tus padres?

   _____

   _____

3. ¿Estás dándole el coche a tu hermano?

   _____

   _____

Crossword Puzzle 6

Fill in the blanks. The clues indicate the verb tenses.

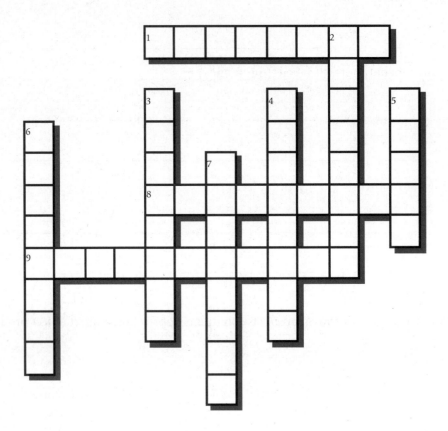

Horizontales
  1. ¿Qué estás . . . (drinking)?
  8. Está . . . (raining) ahora.
  9. Uds. están . . . (learning) español ahora.

Verticales
  2. ¿Qué estás . . . (saying) ahora?
  3. En este momento, están . . . (dancing).
  4. ¿Qué estás . . . (doing) ahora?
  5. Yo . . . (am) trabajando ahora.
  6. Él está . . . (singing) ahora.
  7. Ella está . . . (eating).

Part Two
The Past Indicative Tenses

The Past Indicative Tenses: An Overview

What Is a Past Tense?

A past tense is any tense indicating time gone by or some former action or state. There are four main indicative past tenses in Spanish:

1. The preterit, called the **pretérito**:

> **Gloria comió pescado ayer.** / *Gloria ate fish yesterday.*
> **Bebimos mucho café ayer.** / *We drank a lot of coffee yesterday.*

This tense shows that an event was completed at the time of speaking. It is equivalent to *I spoke* or *I did speak*.

2. The imperfect tense, called the **imperfecto de indicativo**:

> **Reinaldo comía pescado muchas veces.** / *Reinaldo used to eat fish often.*
> **Viajábamos a España muchas veces.** / *We used to travel to Spain often.*

This tense is used to indicate incomplete, continued, or customary past actions. English has no "true" imperfect tense, but some constructions, such as *she was studying* and *he used to study* render the meaning of imperfect verbs in Spanish in a fairly accurate way.

3. The present perfect, or the **perfecto de indicativo**:

> **Teresa ha ido a Venezuela.** / *Teresa has gone to Venezuela.*
> **Ellos han estudiado mucho en casa.** / *They have studied a lot at home.*

The present perfect is used to indicate an action that was completed prior to the present time and that has some bearing on the present time. It is equivalent to *I have gone, I have returned*.

4. The pluperfect, also known as the past perfect, or the **pluscuamperfecto de indicativo**:

> **Salvador había perdido las llaves.** / *Salvador had lost the keys.*
> **Habías encontrado a tu amigo en el centro cuando estabas en el parque.** / *You had found your friend downtown when you were in the park.*

The pluperfect (past perfect) is used to indicate that an action was completed prior to some other action that may be implied or expressed in a sentence. It is equivalent to *I had talked, I had eaten*.

Compound Tenses

The present perfect and the pluperfect (past perfect) are compound tenses. This means that they are verbs constructed of two parts, an auxiliary verb and a past participle, in that order:

1. Present Perfect Tense

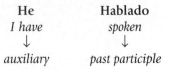

2. Past Perfect or Pluperfect Tense

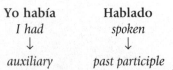

In Spanish, the tense of the auxiliary verb, present or imperfect, determines the tense of the compound verb, either present perfect, or pluperfect (past perfect).

7
The Preterit
(*el pretérito*)

Uses and Features of the Preterit

The preterit describes the past as a completed action. The preterit may report on past events as complete units of time. It may focus on the beginning, the end, or the entire event.

1. The preterit may focus on the beginning of an action:
   > Pablo empezó la nueva lección a las ocho. / *John began the new lesson at 8 o'clock.*

2. The preterit may focus on the end of an action:
   > Teresa terminó la novela ayer. / *Teresa finished the novel yesterday.*

3. The preterit may view a period of time as a completed unit of time:
   > En España la guerra civil duró tres años. / *In Spain, the Civil War lasted three years.*

Regular Verbs

First Conjugation Verbs

As you learned in the preceding unit, the infinitives of regular Spanish verbs end in -ar, -er, or -ir. Those ending in -ar are first-conjugation verbs. To form the preterit, called the pretérito, of such verbs in Spanish, do the following:

1. Drop the infinitive ending, -ar. This produces the verb stem.
   > <u>habl</u>ar / *to speak* → habl-

2. Add the following endings to the stem:

(yo)	-é
(tú)	-aste
(él, ella, Ud.)	-ó
(nosotros/-as)	-amos
(vosotros/-as)	-asteis
(ellos/-as, Uds.)	-aron

3. Here's the result:

hablar / to speak

Subject Pronoun	Verb Form	Meaning
(yo)	habl+é	*I spoke, I did speak*
(tú)	habl+aste	*you (fam. sg.) spoke, you did speak*
(él, ella, Ud.)	habl+ó	*he, she, you (pol. sg.) spoke, he, she, you did speak*
(nosotros/-as)	habl+amos	*we spoke, we did speak*
(vosotros/-as)	habl+asteis	*you (fam. pl.) spoke, you did speak*
(ellos/-as, Uds.)	habl+aron	*they, you (pol. pl.) spoke, they, you did speak*

Second Conjugation Verbs

Those verbs ending in -er are second conjugation verbs. To form the preterit, called the **pretérito**, of such verbs in Spanish, do the following:

1. Drop the infinitive ending, -er. This produces the verb stem.

com<u>er</u> / to eat → com-

2. Add the following endings to the stem:

(yo)	-í
(tú)	-iste
(él, ella, Ud.)	-ió
(nosotros/-as)	-imos
(vosotros/-as)	-isteis
(ellos/-as, Uds.)	-ieron

3. Here's the result:

comer / to eat

Subject Pronoun	Verb Form	Meaning
(yo)	com+í	*I ate, I did eat*
(tú)	com+iste	*you (fam. sg.) ate, you did eat*
(él, ella, Ud.)	com+ió	*he, she, you (pol. sg.) ate, he, she, you did eat*
(nosotros/-as)	com+imos	*we ate, we did eat*
(vosotros/-as)	com+isteis	*you (fam. pl.) ate, you did eat*
(ellos/-as, Uds.)	com+ieron	*they, you (pol. pl.) ate, they, you did eat*

Third Conjugation Verbs

Those verbs ending in -ir are third conjugation verbs. To form the preterit, called the **pretérito**, of such verbs in Spanish, do the following:

1. Drop the infinitive ending, -ir. This produces the verb stem.
   <u>escrib</u>ir / *to write* → escrib-

2. Add the following endings to the stem:

(yo)	-í
(tú)	-iste
(él, ella, Ud.)	-ió
(nosotros/-as)	-imos
(vosotros/-as)	-isteis
(ellos/-as, Uds.)	-ieron

3. Here's the result:

escribir / *to write*

Subject Pronoun	Verb Form	Meaning
(yo)	<u>escrib</u>+í	*I wrote, I did write*
(tú)	<u>escrib</u>+iste	*you (fam. sg.) wrote, you did write*
(él, ella, Ud.)	<u>escrib</u>+ió	*he, she, you (pol. sg.) wrote, he, she, you did write*
(nosotros/-as)	<u>escrib</u>+imos	*we wrote, we did write*
(vosotros/-as)	<u>escrib</u>+isteis	*you (fam. pl.) wrote, you did write*
(ellos/-as, Uds.)	<u>escrib</u>+ieron	*they, you (pol. pl.) wrote, they, you did write*

You have, by now, noted that the endings for second and third conjugation verbs in the preterit are <u>identical</u>. When you learn a new tense, however, it is useful to see how the endings for each conjugation work.

TIP

You will note that the **nosotros, nosotras** / *we* form of the first conjugation and the third conjugation are identical in the present indicative and the preterit tenses, as shown below. You can often distinguish the tense by the context and by the presence of adverbs of time.

Hablamos español ahora. / *We speak Spanish now.*
Hablamos español ayer. / *We spoke Spanish yesterday.*

Vivimos en Lima hoy. / *We live in Lima today.*
Vivimos en Lima hace diez años. / *We lived in Lima ten years ago.*

The Preterit Tense of Reflexive Verbs

Reflexive verbs always use reflexive pronouns in the preterit, as shown below. They always appear immediately before the conjugated verb, as they do in the present tense and all other tenses.

lavarse / *to wash oneself*

Subject Pronoun	Reflexive Pronoun	Conjugated Verb	Meaning
(yo)	me	lav+é	*I washed myself, I did wash myself*
(tú)	te	lav+aste	*you (fam. sg.) washed yourself, you did wash yourself*
(él, ella, Ud.)	se	lav+ó	*he, she, you (pol. sg.) washed himself/herself/yourself, he, she, you did wash himself/herself/yourself*
(nosotros/-as)	nos	lav+amos	*we washed ourselves, we did wash ourselves*
(vosotros/-as)	os	lav+asteis	*you (fam. pl.) washed yourselves, you did wash yourselves*
(ellos/-as, Uds.)	se ·	lav+aron	*they, you (pol. pl.) washed themselves/yourselves, they, you did wash themselves/yourselves*

GRAMMAR NOTE

Hace (from the verb hacer / *to do, to make* may be used with the preterit tense to mean *ago*, as shown in the following examples.

Construí la casa hace dos años. / *I built the house two years ago.*
Estudié esa lección hace dos semanas. / *I studied that lesson two weeks ago.*

TIP

Certain adverbial expressions of time are often used with the preterit tense. The following is a list of some of the more common ones.

anoche / *last night*
ayer / *yesterday*
anteayer / *day before yesterday*
la semana pasada / *last week*
el mes pasado / *last month*
el año pasado / *last year*

EXERCISE Set 7-1

A. Supply the missing preterit forms of the verb **cantar**, giving the English equivalent.

EXAMPLE: él _____   =   _____

él cantó   =   *he sang, he did sing*

1. (yo) _____   =   _____

2. (tú) _____   =   _____

3. (nosotros) _____   =   _____

4. (ellos) _____   =   _____

5. (vosotros) _____   =   _____

6. (Ud.) _____   =   _____

Now, supply the missing preterit forms of the verb **vender**, giving the English equivalent.

1. (yo) _____   =   _____

2. (Raquel y yo) _____   =   _____

3. (Uds.) _____   =   _____

4. (ellos) _____   =   _____

5. (vosotros) _____   =   _____

6. (tú) _____   =   _____

Now, supply the missing preterit forms of the verb **vivir**, giving the English equivalent.

1. (yo) _____   =   _____

2. (tú) _____   =   _____

3. (nosotros) _____   =   _____

4. (ellos) _____   =   _____

5. (vosotros) _____   =   _____

6. (Ud.) _____   =   _____

Now, supply the missing preterit forms of the verb **bañarse**, giving the English equivalent. Be sure to place the reflexive pronoun immediately before the conjugated verb.

1. (yo) _____   =   _____

2. (tú) _____   =   _____

3. (nosotros) _____ =   _____

4. (ellos) _____   =   _____

5. (vosotros) _____ =   _____

6. (Ud.) _____   =   _____

B. How do you say the following sentences in Spanish?

1. I traveled from *Lima* to *Cuzco*[1].

_____

2. They ate and drank at *Antaño*[2].

_____

3. We visited *Arequipa*[3] in the south of Peru.

_____

4. I lived in that neighborhood two years ago.

_____

5. She sang the same song last night.

_____

6. I bought a new car yesterday morning.

_____

7. You (fam. sg.) wrote an e-mail last night.

_____

8. You (pol. sg.) opened the door.

_____

9. I drank a lot of coffee this morning.

_____

10. Did you (fam. sg.) receive the gift from Elena yesterday?

_____

11. I liked the trip to *Huancayo*[4].

_____

12. His head ached last night.

_____

[1]Capital city of the Incan empire in southern Peru.
[2]Restaurant with typical Peruvian food in Central Lima.
[3]Tourist center located near Lake Titicaca.
[4]Central Andean city known for its natural beauty and local handicrafts.

Stem-Changing Verbs

First conjugation (-ar) and second conjugation (-er) stem-changing verbs (see Chapter 2) do not have stem changes in the preterit tense. Third conjugation stem-changing verbs, however, do have stem changes that occur in the <u>third person singular and plural</u>. There are two patterns: o → u, and e → i. We will illustrate these patterns below. We will indicate where the stem changes with underlined italic type. The endings for stem-changing verbs are regular.

When you look up these verbs in a dictionary, you will find in parentheses the following standard notations.

> **dormir (ue, u)** / *to sleep*
> **mentir (ie, i)** / *to lie*
> **servir (i, i)** / *to serve*

Remember that the first vowel(s) mean(s) that there is a stem change in present tense in the form of a shoe (see Chapter 2). The second vowel means that there is also a stem change in the preterit tense in the third person singular and plural, as well as the present participle (gerund; see Chapter 6). We will see examples of all three of these verbs.

dormir (ue, u) / *to sleep*

Subject Pronoun	Verb Form	Meaning
(yo)	<u>dorm</u>+í	*I slept, I did sleep*
(tú)	<u>dorm</u>+iste	*you (fam. sg.) slept, you did sleep*
(él, ella, Ud.)	<u>durm</u>+ió	*he, she, you (pol. sg.) slept, he, she, you did sleep*
(nosotros/-as)	<u>dorm</u>+imos	*we slept, we did sleep*
(vosotros/-as)	<u>dorm</u>+isteis	*you (fam. pl.) slept, you did sleep*
(ellos/-as, Uds.)	<u>durm</u>+ieron	*they, you (pol. pl.) slept, they, you did sleep*

The following verbs follow this pattern:

dormir (ue, u)   *to sleep*   **morir (ue, u)**   *to die*

mentir (ie, i) / *to lie*

Subject Pronoun	Verb Form	Meaning
(yo)	ment+í	*I lied, I did lie*
(tú)	ment+iste	*you (fam. sg.) lied, you did lie*
(él, ella, Ud.)	mint+ió	*he, she, you (pol. sg.) lied, he, she, you did lie*
(nosotros/-as)	ment+imos	*we lied, we did lie*
(vosotros/-as)	ment+isteis	*you (fam. pl.) lied, you did lie*
(ellos/-as, Uds.)	mint+ieron	*they, you (pol. pl.) lied, they, you did lie*

The following verbs follow this pattern:

advertir (ie, i)   *to notice*   **sentir(se) (ie, i)**   *to feel sorry, to regret*
mentir (ie, i)   *to lie*   **sugerir (ie, i)**   *to suggest*
preferir (ie, i)   *to prefer*

servir (i, i) / *to serve*

Subject Pronoun	Verb Form	Meaning
(yo)	serv+í	*I served, I did serve*
(tú)	serv+iste	*you (fam. sg.) served, you did serve*
(él, ella, Ud.)	sirv+ió	*he, she, you (pol. sg.) served, he, she, you did serve*
(nosotros/-as)	serv+imos	*we served, we did serve*
(vosotros/-as)	serv+isteis	*you (fam. pl.) served, you did serve*
(ellos/-as, Uds.)	sirv+ieron	*they, you (pol. pl.) served, they, you did serve*

The following verbs have this pattern:

despedir (i, i)   *to fire*   **pedir (i, i)**   *to request, to ask for, to order*
elegir (i, i)   *to elect*   **reír (i, i)**   *to laugh*
freír (i, i)   *to fry*   **repetir (i, i)**   *to repeat*
impedir (i, i)   *to impede, to hinder* **seguir (i, i)**   *to follow*
medir (i, i)   *to measure*   **servir (i, i)**   *to serve*

EXERCISE Set 7-2

A. Supply the missing preterit forms of the verb **morir (ue, u)**, giving the English equivalent.

EXAMPLE: *él* _____   =   _____

   él murió   =   *he died, he did die*

1. (yo) _____   =   _____

2. (tú) _____   =   _____

3. (Marta y yo) _____   =   _____

4. (ellas) _____   =   _____

5. (vosotros) _____   =   _____

6. (Ud.) _____   =   _____

Now, supply the missing preterit forms of the verb **preferir (ie, i)**, giving the English equivalent.

1. (yo) _____   =   _____

2. (nosotros) _____   =   _____

3. (Uds.) _____   =   _____

4. (ellos) _____   =   _____

5. (vosotros) _____   =   _____

6. (tú) _____   =   _____

Now, supply the missing preterit forms of the verb **repetir (i, i)**, giving the English equivalent.

1. (yo) _____   =   _____

2. (nosotras) _____   =   _____

3. (Uds.) _____   =   _____

4. (ellos) _____   =   _____

5. (vosotros) _____   =   _____

6. (tú) _____   =   _____

B. How do you say the following sentences in Spanish?

1. They served a good meal in *Pisco*[1].

   _____

2. Inés slept very late today.

   _____

3. My friends preferred to go to the *Museo de la Nación*[2] in Lima.

   _____

4. I repeated the conjugation of the preterit.

   _____

5. I measured the room last night.

   _____

6. He followed the teacher (m.) to the classroom.

   _____

7. His grandfather died last night.

   _____

8. They fried the meat in olive oil.

   _____

9. He fired the employee two days ago.

   _____

10. My parents never lied.

    _____

[1]Town on the Southern coast of Peru.
[2]Museum of Aboriginal art in Lima.

Irregular Preterits

The preterit tense has some irregular forms characterized by an irregular stem and irregular endings. There are two basic patterns that we will now illustrate. It should be noted that irregular preterit verbs do not have written accents.

Irregular Preterit: Pattern 1

1. Learn the irregular preterit stem to which you add the Pattern-1 irregular preterit endings. We list them below.

   andar / *to walk* → anduv-
   caber / *to fit* → cup-
   estar / *to be* → estuv-
   haber / *to have* (auxiliary) → hub-
   hacer / *to do, to make* → hic- (hiz- in third person singular)
   poder / *can, to be able* → pud-
   poner / *to put, to place* → pus-
   querer / *to want* → quis-
   saber / *to know* → sup-
   tener / *to have* → tuv-
   venir / *to come* → vin-

2. Add the following irregular preterit tense endings to the irregular stems listed above. You will note that there are no written accents on these endings.

(yo)	-e
(tú)	-iste
(él, ella, Ud.)	-o
(nosotros/-as)	-imos
(vosotros/-as)	-isteis
(ellos/-as, Uds.)	-ieron

3. Here's the result:

venir / *to come*

Subject Pronoun	Verb Form	Meaning
(yo)	vin+e	*I came, I did come*
(tú)	vin+iste	*you (fam. sg.) came, you did come*
(él, ella, Ud.)	vin+o	*he, she, you (pol. sg.) came, he, she, you did come*
(nosotros/-as)	vin+imos	*we came, we did come*
(vosotros/-as)	vin+isteis	*you (fam. pl.) came, you did come*
(ellos/-as, Uds.)	vin+ieron	*they, you (pol. pl.) came, they, you did come*

Irregular Preterit: Pattern 2

The second pattern of irregular preterits is slightly different. All of the stems of these irregular preterits end in j-, and the third person plural form is -eron.

1. Learn the irregular preterit stem to which you add the Pattern-2 irregular preterit endings. We list them below. All of these verbs have an irregular stem that ends in a j-.

    > atraer / *to attract* → atraj-
    > conducir / *to drive* → conduj-
    > decir / *to say, to tell* → dij-
    > deducir / *to deduce, to infer* → deduj-
    > distraer / *to distract* → distraj-
    > introducir / *to introduce* → introduj-
    > producir / *to produce* → produj-
    > retraer / *to bring back, to dissuade* → retraj-
    > sustraer / *to subtract, to take away* → sustraj-
    > traducir / *to translate* → traduj-
    > traer / *to bring* → traj-

2. Add the following irregular preterit tense endings to the irregular stems listed above. You will note that there are no written accents on these endings. The only difference between irregular preterit Pattern-1 and Pattern-2 endings is in the third person plural form. Pattern-2 endings have no -i- in this ending (-eron).

(yo)	-e
(tú)	-iste
(él, ella, Ud.)	-o
(nosotros/-as)	-imos
(vosotros/-as)	-isteis
(ellos/-as, Uds.)	-eron

3. Here's the result:

decir / *to say, to tell*

Subject Pronoun	Verb Form	Meaning
(yo)	dij+e	*I said, told, I did say, tell*
(tú)	dij+iste	*you (fam. sg.) said, told, you did say, tell*
(él, ella, Ud.)	dij+o	*he, she, you (pol. sg.) said, told, he, she, you did say, tell*
(nosotros/-as)	dij+imos	*we said, told, we did say, tell*
(vosotros/-as)	dij+isteis	*you (fam. pl.) said, told, you did say, tell*
(ellos/-as, Uds.)	dij+eron	*they, you (pol. pl.) said, told, they, you did say, tell*

TIP

You will note that the <u>third person singular</u> of the preterit tense ends in a stressed -ó for regular verbs and an unstressed -o for irregular verbs. Do not confuse this verb form with the unstressed -o of the present indicative tense that stands for the first person singular (**yo**).

Consider the following examples:

habl<u>o</u> / *I speak, I am speaking, I do speak*
habl<u>ó</u> / *he, she, you spoke, he, she, you did speak*

tuv<u>e</u> / *I had, I did have*
tuv<u>o</u> / *he, she, you had, he, she, you did have*

The Preterit of Ir / *to go* and Ser / *to be*

The preterit of the verbs ir / *to go* and ser / *to be* are identical. You will also note that the first and third persons singular are different from the irregular preterit patterns noted above. We will provide conjugations of both verbs here. You will need context to distinguish the meaning.

ir / *to go*

Subject Pronoun	Verb Form	Meaning
(yo)	<u>fu</u>+i	*I went, I did go*
(tú)	<u>fu</u>+iste	*you (fam. sg.) went, you did go*
(él, ella, Ud.)	<u>fu</u>+e	*he, she, you (pol. sg.) went, he, she, you did go*
(nosotros/-as)	<u>fu</u>+imos	*we went, we did go*
(vosotros/-as)	<u>fu</u>+isteis	*you (fam. pl.) went, you did go*
(ellos/-as, Uds.)	<u>fu</u>+eron	*they, you (pol. pl.) went, they, you did go*

ser / *to be*

Subject Pronoun	Verb Form	Meaning
(yo)	<u>fu</u>+i	*I was*
(tú)	<u>fu</u>+iste	*you (fam. sg.) were*
(él, ella, Ud.)	<u>fu</u>+e	*he, she, you (pol. sg.) was, were*
(nosotros/-as)	<u>fu</u>+imos	*we were*
(vosotros/-as)	<u>fu</u>+isteis	*you (fam. pl.) were*
(ellos/-as, Uds.)	<u>fu</u>+eron	*they, you (pol. pl.) were*

The Preterit of Dar / *to give and* Ver / *to see*

There are two more verbs that have a slightly different pattern from preceding ones. They are the verbs dar / *to give* and ver / *to see*. The endings for the first and third person singular are distinct.

dar / *to give*

Subject Pronoun	Verb Form	Meaning
(yo)	d+i	*I gave, I did give*
(tú)	d+iste	*you (fam. sg.) gave, you did give*
(él, ella, Ud.)	d+io	*he, she, you (pol. sg.) gave, he, she, you did give*
(nosotros/-as)	d+imos	*we gave, we did give*
(vosotros/-as)	d+isteis	*you (fam. pl.) gave, you did give*
(ellos/-as, Uds.)	d+ieron	*they, you (pol. pl.) gave, they, you did give*

ver / *to see*

Subject Pronoun	Verb Form	Meaning
(yo)	v+i	*I saw, I did see*
(tú)	v+iste	*you (fam. sg.) saw, you did see*
(él, ella, Ud.)	v+io	*he, she, you (pol. sg.) saw, he, she, you did see*
(nosotros/-as)	v+imos	*we saw, we did see*
(vosotros/-as)	v+isteis	*you (fam. pl.) saw, you did see*
(ellos/-as, Uds.)	v+ieron	*they, you (pol. pl.) saw, they, you did see*

The Preterit of Hay / *there is, there are*

The preterit of the verb hay / *there is, there are* is hubo / *there was, there were*. It is used to refer to a situation as it existed in the past, but which no longer exists. The following sentences illustrate its use.

> Hubo una plaga en el pasado. / *There was a plague in the past.*
> Hubo guerras terribles en el pasado. / *There were terrible wars in the past.*

Remember also that the idiomatic form hay que / *it is necessary, one must* may also appear in the preterit as hubo que / *it was necessary*. The following sentence illustrates this usage.

> Hubo que ir a clase. / *It was necessary to go to class.*

EXERCISE Set 7-3

A. Supply the missing preterit forms of the verb **tener**, giving the English equivalent.

EXAMPLE: *él* _____   =   _____

   él tuvo   =   *he had, he did have*

1. (yo) _____   =   _____

2. (tú) _____   =   _____

3. (Marta y yo) _____   =   _____

4. (ellas) _____   =   _____

5. (vosotros) _____   =   _____

6. (Ud.) _____   =   _____

Now, supply the missing preterit forms of the verb **querer (ie)**, giving the English equivalent.

1. (yo) _____   =   _____

2. (nosotros) _____   =   _____

3. (Uds.) _____   =   _____

4. (ellos) _____   =   _____

5. (vosotros) _____   =   _____

6. (tú) _____   =   _____

Now, supply the missing preterit forms of the verb **hacer**, giving the English equivalent.

1. (yo) _____   =   _____

2. (tú) _____   =   _____

3. (nosotras) _____   =   _____

4. (Uds.) _____   =   _____

5. (vosotros) _____   =   _____

6. (Ud.) _____   =   _____

Now, supply the missing preterit forms of the verb **estar**, giving the English equivalent.

1. (yo) _____   =   _____

2. (tú) _____   =   _____

3. (nosotras) _____   =   _____

4. (Uds.) _____   =   _____

5. (vosotros) _____   =   _____

6. (Ud.) _____   =   _____

Now, supply the missing preterit forms of the verb **poder (ue)**, giving the English equivalent.

1. (yo) _____   =   _____

2. (tú) _____   =   _____

3. (nosotras) _____   =   _____

4. (Uds.) _____   =   _____

5. (vosotros) _____   =   _____

6. (Ud.) _____   =   _____

Now, supply the missing preterit forms of the verb **venir**, giving the English equivalent.

1. (yo) _____   =   _____

2. (tú) _____   =   _____

3. (nosotras) _____   =   _____

4. (Uds.) _____   =   _____

5. (vosotros) _____   =   _____

6. (Ud.) _____   =   _____

Now, supply the missing preterit forms of the verb **ser**, giving the English equivalent.

1. (yo) _____   =   _____

2. (tú) _____   =   _____

3. (nosotros) _____   =   _____

4. (Uds.) _____ = _____

5. (vosotros) _____ = _____

6. (Ud.) _____ = _____

Now, supply the missing preterit forms of the verb **traducir**, giving the English equivalent.

1. (yo) _____ = _____

2. (tú) _____ = _____

3. (nosotros) _____ = _____

4. (Uds.) _____ = _____

5. (vosotros) _____ = _____

6. (Ud.) _____ = _____

Now, supply the missing preterit forms of the verb **ir**, giving the English equivalent.

1. (yo) _____ = _____

2. (tú) _____ = _____

3. (nosotros) _____ = _____

4. (Uds.) _____ = _____

5. (vosotros) _____ = _____

6. (Ud.) _____ = _____

Now, supply the missing preterit forms of the verb **conducir**, giving the English equivalent.

1. (yo) _____ = _____

2. (tú) _____ = _____

3. (nosotros) _____ = _____

4. (Uds.) _____ = _____

5. (vosotros) _____ = _____

6. (Ud.) _____ = _____

B. How do you say the following sentences in Spanish?

1. We drove from *Lima* to *Tacna*[1].

   _____

2. I gave the money to my friend.

   _____

3. Raquel and I went downtown to eat dinner.

   _____

4. They took a walk in *Parque Kennedy*[2].

   _____

5. I came to class late.

   _____

6. I fell in the street.

   _____

7. I told the truth to Marco.

   _____

8. I translated the verbs from English to Spanish.

   _____

9. We were at home when I saw her.

   _____

10. I was president of the organization last year.

    _____

11. Yesterday it was bad weather because it rained a lot.

    _____

12. It was very cold in February because it snowed a lot.

    _____

[1]City in Southern Peru near the Chilean border.
[2]Beautiful park in the suburban Miraflores section of Lima.

13. I know that María told the truth.

_____

14. She said that she read the book last night.

_____

15. They said that we lied.

_____

Spelling Changes in the Preterit

Certain verbs have spelling changes in some forms of the preterit tense. There are three types of spelling changes as shown here. It must be remembered that the endings for each verb are completely regular and that they all follow the pattern for regular -ar preterit verbs.

1. Verbs that end in -gar, the first person singular (yo) form is -gué.
2. Verbs that end in -car, the first person singular (yo) form is -qué.
3. Verbs that end in -zar, the first person singular (yo) form is -cé.

We will now look at a conjugation in the preterit for each verb category. We will also provide a list of common verbs for each of these verb types.

llegar / *to arrive*

Subject Pronoun	Verb Form	Meaning
(yo)	<u>llegu</u>+é	*I arrived, I did arrive*
(tú)	<u>lleg</u>+aste	*you (fam. sg.) arrived, you did arrive*
(él, ella, Ud.)	<u>lleg</u>+ó	*he, she, you (pol. sg.) arrived, he, she, you did arrive*
(nosotros/-as)	<u>lleg</u>+amos	*we arrived, we did arrive*
(vosotros/-as)	<u>lleg</u>+asteis	*you (fam. pl.) arrived, you did arrive*
(ellos/-as, Uds.)	<u>lleg</u>+aron	*they, you (pol. pl.) arrived, they, you did arrive*

The following verbs have this pattern.

conjugar	*to conjugate*	regar (ie)	*to water (a plant)*
llegar	*to arrive*	tragar	*to swallow*
jugar (ue)	*to play (a game)*	vagar	*to wander*
pagar	*to pay for*		

buscar / *to look for*

Subject Pronoun	Verb Form	Meaning
(yo)	bus*qu*+é	*I looked for, I did look for*
(tú)	busc+aste	*you (fam. sg.) looked for, you did look for*
(él, ella, Ud.)	busc+ó	*he, she, you (pol. sg.) looked for, he, she, you did look for*
(nosotros/-as)	busc+amos	*we looked for, we did look for*
(vosotros/-as)	busc+asteis	*you (fam. pl.) looked for, you did look for*
(ellos/-as, Uds.)	busc+aron	*they, you (pol. pl.) looked for, they, you did look for*

The following verbs have this pattern.

buscar	*to look for*	practicar	*to practice*
clasificar	*to classify*	sacar	*to take, to take a photo*
destacar	*to stand out*	tocar	*to touch, to play (an instrument)*
justificar	*to justify*		

organizar / *to organize*

Subject Pronoun	Verb Form	Meaning
(yo)	organic+é	*I organized, I did organize*
(tú)	organiz+aste	*you (fam. sg.) organized, you did organize*
(él, ella, Ud.)	organiz+ó	*he, she, you (pol. sg.) organized, he, she, you did organize*
(nosotros/-as)	organiz+amos	*we organized, we did organize*
(vosotros/-as)	organiz+asteis	*you (fam. pl.) organized, you did organize*
(ellos/-as, Uds.)	organiz+aron	*they, you (pol. pl.) organized, they, you did organize*

The following verbs have this pattern.

autorizar	*to authorize*	rezar	*to pray*
comenzar (ie)	*to begin*	trazar	*to trace*
empezar (ie)	*to begin*	tropezarse (ie) (con)	*to stumble (into)*

Verbs with i → y *Change in the Preterit*

There is another group of verbs that have the change i → y in the preterit in the third person singular and plural. This change occurs because the unstressed i appears between two vowels. The following conjugation illustrates this spelling change. Note that in all of the other forms of the verb, there is a written accent over the í.

leer / *to read*

Subject Pronoun	Verb Form	Meaning
(yo)	le+í	*I read, I did read*
(tú)	le+íste	*you (fam. sg.) read, you did read*
(él, ella, Ud.)	le+yó	*he, she, you (pol. sg.) read, he, she, you did read*
(nosotros/-as)	le+ímos	*we read, we did read*
(vosotros/-as)	le+ísteis	*you (fam. pl.) read, you did read*
(ellos/-as, Uds.)	le+yeron	*they, you (pol. pl.) read, they, you did read*

The following verbs have this pattern.

caer	to fall	oír	to hear
caerse	to fall down	poseer	to possess
creer	to believe	proveer	to provide

There is another slightly different verbal pattern in the preterit in which i → y. This group of verbs ends in -uir. This group is different from the previous one because the written accent occurs only over the **yo** form of the verb (**í**). The vowel -i- in the remaining verbal endings (second person singular, first and second person plural) does not receive a written accent. The following conjugation illustrates this spelling change.

huir / *to flee*

Subject Pronoun	Verb Form	Meaning
(yo)	hu+í	*I fled, I did flee*
(tú)	hu+iste	*you (fam. sg.) fled, you did flee*
(él, ella, Ud.)	hu+yó	*he, she, you (pol. sg.) fled, he, she, you did flee*
(nosotros/-as)	hu+imos	*we fled, we did flee*
(vosotros/-as)	hu+isteis	*you (fam. pl.) fled, you did flee*
(ellos/-as, Uds.)	hu+yeron	*they, you (pol. pl.) fled, they, you did flee*

The following verbs have this pattern.

construir	to build	fluir	to flow
contribuir	to contribute	incluir	to include
destruir	to destroy	influir	to influence

EXERCISE Set 7-4

A. Supply the missing preterit forms of the verb **jugar** (**ue**), giving the English equivalent.

EXAMPLE: *él* _____   =   _____

   él jugó   =   *he played, he did play*

1. (yo) _____   =   _____

2. (tú) _____   =   _____

3. (nosotras) _____   =   _____

4. (Uds.) _____   =   _____

5. (vosotros) _____   =   _____

6. (Ud.) _____   =   _____

Now, supply the missing preterit forms of the verb tocar, giving the English equivalent.

1. (yo) _____   =   _____

2. (tú) _____   =   _____

3. (nosotras) _____   =   _____

4. (Uds.) _____   =   _____

5. (vosotros) _____   =   _____

6. (Ud.) _____   =   _____

Now, supply the missing preterit forms of the verb empezar (ie), giving the English equivalent.

1. (yo) _____   =   _____

2. (tú) _____   =   _____

3. (nosotras) _____   =   _____

4. (Uds.) _____   =   _____

5. (vosotros) _____   =   _____

6. (Ud.) _____   =   _____

Now, supply the missing preterit forms of the verb oír, giving the English equivalent.

1. (yo) _____   =   _____

2. (tú) _____   =   _____

3. (nosotras) _____   =   _____

4. (Uds.) _____   =   _____

5. (vosotros) _____   =   _____

6. (Ud.) _____   =   _____

Now, supply the missing preterit forms of the verb construir, giving the English equivalent.

1. (yo) _____   =   _____

2. (tú) _____   =   _____

3. (nosotras) _____   =   _____

4. (Uds.) _____   =   _____

5. (vosotros) _____ =   _____

6. (Ud.) _____ =   _____

B. How do you say the following sentences in Spanish?

1. I ate lunch with my friend (m.) in a good Peruvian restaurant.

   _____

2. I read *La República*[1] early this morning.

   _____

3. I contributed 100 *soles* yesterday.

   _____

4. We heard the woman in the street.

   _____

5. They built an expensive home.

   _____

6. The guilty man fled from the police.

   _____

7. It began to rain yesterday.

   _____

8. He stumbled into the chair.

   _____

9. I played the guitar for my sister.

   _____

10. The storm destroyed my home.

    _____

[1]Peruvian newspaper.

C. Provide the corresponding preterit forms for the following verbs in the present indicative tense.

1. hablamos _____

2. tienen _____

3. van _____

4. somos _____

5. estás _____

6. dice _____

7. comemos _____

8. vivimos _____

9. me acuesto _____

10. soy _____

11. duermen _____

12. pide _____

13. hace _____

14. tienes _____

15. entiendo _____

16. puedo _____

17. quieren _____

18. empiezo _____

Meaning Change in Preterit Verbs

There is a small group of verbs that has a change of meaning when they are used in the preterit. The following is a list of these verbs.

Verb	Meaning in Present Tense	Meaning in Preterit Tense
conocer	to know (a person)	Conocí a Luis ayer. / I <u>met</u> Louis yesterday.
poder	to be able	Pude ir a Trujillo. I <u>managed</u> to go to Trujillo.
no poder	not to be able	No pude estudiar español anoche. / I <u>failed</u> to study Spanish last night.
querer	to want	Quise visitar Iquitos. / I <u>tried</u> to visit Iquitos.
no querer	not to want	No quise leer el libro. / I <u>refused</u> to read the book.
saber	to know (a fact)	Supe la verdad. / I <u>found out</u> the truth.
tener	to have	Tuve una carta de mi familia. / I <u>received</u> a letter from my family.

EXERCISE Set 7-5

A. How do you say the following sentences in Spanish?

1. I received a gift from my mother last night.

_____

2. I failed to conjugate all of the Spanish verbs.

_____

3. He met his wife in an elevator.

_____

4. We discovered the truth last year.

_____

5. I managed to find my book at home.

_____

6. They tried to study but they failed.

_____

Crossword Puzzle 7

Fill in the blanks. Use the following verbs in the preterit tense in your answers: andar, beber, conocer, decir, estar, gustar, hacer, ir, leer, perder.

Horizontales
2. . . . mucho calor ayer.
5. Félix y Juana . . . el libro anoche.
6. (Tú) . . . la bolsa.
9. Me . . . los libros.
10. Ellos . . . a Marta en la fiesta.

Verticales
1. ¿ . . . (tú) la verdad?
3. Marisol . . . en el parque ayer.
4. (Nosotros) . . . mucho café ayer.
7. . . . nublado ayer.
8. Laura y yo . . . al centro.

8

The Imperfect Indicative (*el imperfecto de indicativo*) and the Imperfect Progressive (*el imperfecto progresivo*)

Uses and Features

"Imperfect indicative" means incomplete. The imperfect indicative is, thus, a tense used to express or describe an action, event, or state of being that was incomplete, continuous, or habitual in the past. Specifically, it is used:

1. To express an action in the past that went on simultaneously with another action:

> **Mientras que mi madre leía, mi padre miraba la televisión.** / *While my mother was reading, my father was watching TV.*
> **Mientras que mi madre estaba leyendo, mi padre estaba mirando la televisión.** / *While my mother was reading, my father was watching TV.*

2. To express an action that was ongoing while another action occurred in the past:

> **Mi hermana escuchaba un disco cuando llamé por teléfono.** / *My sister was listening to a CD when I telephoned.*
> **Mi hermana estaba escuchando un disco cuando llamé por teléfono.** / *My sister was listening to a CD when I telephoned.*

3. To indicate a past action, desire, condition, etc., that took place habitually:

> **Cuando estábamos en Ecuador, íbamos con frecuencia al mar.** / *When we were in Ecuador, we frequently went to the sea.*
> **De niño, yo siempre quería comer las alcachofas.** / *As a child, I always wanted to eat artichokes.*

4. To describe a former, earlier, or bygone mental, emotional, or physical condition or situation. The most common verbs used in this way are:

> creer / *to think*, estar / *to be*, pensar / *to think*, poder / *to be able*, preferir / *to prefer*, querer / *to want*, saber / *to know*, sentir / *to feel*, ser / *to be*, tener / *to have*.
>
> De niña, ella tenía el pelo rubio. / *As a child, she had blonde hair.*
> De niño, yo sabía hablar dos idiomas. / *As a child, I knew how to speak two languages.*

5. To refer to routine time of the day in the past:

> ¿A qué hora tenías la clase de español? / *At what time did you used to have Spanish class?*

6. To quote someone directly in the past:

> Carlos dijo que él iba a la fiesta. / *Carlos said that he was going to the party.*

7. To express time and age:

> Eran las cinco de la tarde cuando regresé a casa. / *It was 5 P.M. when I returned home.*
> Yo tenía treinta años el año pasado. / *I was thirty last year.*

Regular -ar Verbs

To form the imperfect indicative, called the **imperfecto de indicativo**, of regular -ar verbs, do the following:

1. Drop the -ar from the infinitive:
   hablar / *to speak* → habl-

2. Add the following endings to the stem according to person and number (note that the **nosotros/-as** / *we* form has a graphic accent):

(yo)	-aba
(tú)	-abas
(él, ella, Ud.)	-aba
(nosotros/-as)	-ábamos
(vosotros/-as)	-abais
(ellos/-as, Uds.)	-aban

3. Here's the result:

hablar / *to speak*

Subject Pronoun	Verb Form	Meaning
(yo)	habl+aba	*I was speaking, I used to speak*
(tú)	habl+abas	*you (fam. sg.) were speaking, you used to speak*
(él, ella, Ud.)	habl+aba	*he, she, you (pol. sg.) was/were speaking, he, she, you used to speak*
(nosotros/-as)	habl+ábamos	*we were speaking, we used to speak*
(vosotros/-as)	habl+abais	*you (fam. pl.) were speaking, you used to speak*
(ellos/-as, Uds.)	habl+aban	*they, you (pol. pl.) were speaking, they, you used to speak*

Regular -er and -ir Verbs

To form the imperfect indicative of regular -er and -ir verbs, called the **imperfecto de indicativo**, do the following:

1. Drop the -er and -ir from the infinitive (the endings are the same for second and third conjugation verbs in the imperfect tense):

   <u>com</u>er / *to eat* → com-
   <u>abr</u>ir / *to open* → abr-

2. Add the following endings to the stem according to person and number:

(yo)	-ía
(tú)	-ías
(él, ella, Ud.)	-ía
(nosotros/-as)	-íamos
(vosotros/-as)	-íais
(ellos/-as, Uds.)	-ían

3. Here's the result:

comer / *to eat*

Subject Pronoun	Verb Form	Meaning
(yo)	<u>com</u>+ía	*I was eating, I used to eat*
(tú)	<u>com</u>+ías	*you (fam. sg.) were eating, you used to eat*
(él, ella, Ud.)	<u>com</u>+ía	*he, she, you (pol. sg.) was/were eating, he, she, you used to eat*
(nosotros/-as)	<u>com</u>+íamos	*we were eating, we used to eat*
(vosotros/-as)	<u>com</u>+íais	*you (fam. pl.) were eating, you used to eat*
(ellos/-as, Uds.)	<u>com</u>+ían	*they, you (pol. pl.) were eating, they, you used to eat*

abrir / *to open*

Subject Pronoun	Verb Form	Meaning
(yo)	<u>abr</u>+ía	*I was opening, I used to open*
(tú)	<u>abr</u>+ías	*you (fam. sg.) were opening, you used to open*
(él, ella, Ud.)	<u>abr</u>+ía	*he, she, you (pol. sg.) was/were opening, he, she, you used to open.*
(nosotros/-as)	<u>abr</u>+íamos	*we were opening, we used to open*
(vosotros/-as)	<u>abr</u>+íais	*you (fam. pl.) were opening, you used to open*
(ellos/-as, Uds.)	<u>abr</u>+ían	*they, you (pol. pl.) were opening, they, you used to open*

The Imperfect Indicative of Reflexive Verbs

Reflexive verbs always use reflexive pronouns in the imperfect indicative as shown below. They always appear immediately before the conjugated verb as they do in all tenses.

lavarse / *to wash oneself*

Subject Pronoun	Reflexive Pronoun	Conjugated Verb	Meaning
(yo)	me	<u>lav</u>+aba	*I was washing myself, I used to wash myself*
(tú)	te	<u>lav</u>+abas	*you (fam. sg.) were washing yourself, you used to wash yourself*
(él, ella, Ud.)	se	<u>lav</u>+aba	*he, she, you (pol. sg.) was/were washing himself/herself/yourself, he, she, you used to wash himself/herself/yourself*
(nosotros/-as)	nos	<u>lav</u>+ábamos	*we were washing ourselves, we used to wash ourselves*
(vosotros/-as)	os	<u>lav</u>+abais	*you (fam. pl.) were washing yourselves, you used to wash yourselves*
(ellos/-as, Uds.)	se	<u>lav</u>+aban	*they, you (pol. pl.) were washing themselves/yourselves, they, you used to wash themselves/yourselves*

Irregular Imperfect Indicative Verbs

You will be delighted to learn that there are only three irregular imperfect indicative verbs: ir / *to go*, ser / *to be*, and ver / *to see*. Their conjugations in the imperfect indicative follow.

ir / *to go*

Subject Pronoun	Verb Form	Meaning
(yo)	<u>ib</u>+a	*I was going, I used to go*
(tú)	<u>ib</u>+as	*you (fam. sg.) were going, you used to go*
(él, ella, Ud.)	<u>ib</u>+a	*he, she, you (pol. sg.) was/were going, he, she, you used to go*
(nosotros/-as)	<u>íb</u>+amos	*we were going, we used to go*
(vosotros/-as)	<u>ib</u>+ais	*you (fam. pl.) were going, you used to go*
(ellos/-as, Uds.)	<u>ib</u>+an	*they, you (pol. pl.) were going, they, you used to go*

ser / *to be*

Subject Pronoun	Verb Form	Meaning
(yo)	<u>er</u>+a	*I was, I used to be*
(tú)	<u>er</u>+as	*you (fam. sg.) were, you used to be*
(él, ella, Ud.)	<u>er</u>+a	*he, she, you (pol. sg.) was/were, he, she, you used to be*
(nosotros/-as)	<u>ér</u>+amos	*we were, we used to be*
(vosotros/-as)	<u>er</u>+ais	*you (fam. pl.) were, you used to be*
(ellos/-as, Uds.)	er+an	*they, you (pol. pl.) were, they, you used to be*

ver / *to see*

Subject Pronoun	Verb Form	Meaning
(yo)	<u>ve</u>+ía	*I was seeing, I used to see*
(tú)	<u>ve</u>+ías	*you (fam. sg.) were seeing, you used to see*
(él, ella, Ud.)	<u>ve</u>+ía	*he, she, you (pol. sg.) was/were seeing, he, she, you used to see*
(nosotros/-as)	<u>ve</u>+íamos	*we were seeing, we used to see*
(vosotros/-as)	<u>ve</u>+íais	*you (fam. pl.) were seeing, you used to see*
(ellos/-as, Uds.)	<u>ve</u>+ían	*they, you (pol. pl.) were seeing, they, you used to see*

TIP

There are no stem changes in the imperfect indicative tense. So you don't have to worry about remembering!

NOTE

You have probably noticed that the first person singular (yo) and third person singular (él, ella, Ud.) forms of the imperfect tense are identical in form. For this reason, you must normally use the subject pronoun yo / *I* to distinguish these forms.

GRAMMAR NOTE

The verb hacer / *to do, to make* may appear in a special idiomatic construction with the imperfect indicative tense as illustrated below. This construction indicates that a specified activity began in the past and continued in the past.

¿Cuánto tiempo hacía que estudiabas español? / *How long had you been studying Spanish?*
Hacía un año que yo estudiaba español. / *I had been studying Spanish for a year.*

The above question and answer may be expressed in a different way as seen below.

¿Desde cuándo estudiabas español? / *How long had you been studying Spanish?*
Yo estudiaba español desde hacía un año. / *I had been studying Spanish for a year.*

EXERCISE Set 8-1

A. Supply the missing imperfect indicative forms of the verb **cantar**, giving the English equivalent.

EXAMPLE: *él* _____   =   _____

            él cantaba   =   *he was singing, he used to sing*

1. (yo) _____   =   _____

2. (tú) _____   =   _____

3. (nosotros) _____   =   _____

4. (ellos) _____   =   _____

5. (vosotros) _____   =   _____

6. (Ud.) _____   =   _____

Now, supply the missing imperfect indicative forms of the verb tener, giving the English equivalent.

1. (yo) _____   =   _____

2. (Rachel y yo) _____   =   _____

3. (Uds.) _____   =   _____

4. (ellos) _____   =   _____

5. (vosotros) _____   =   _____

6. (tú) _____   =   _____

Now, supply the missing imperfect indicative forms of the verb decir (i, i), giving the English equivalent.

1. (yo) _____   =   _____

2. (tú) _____   =   _____

3. (nosotros) _____   =   _____

4. (ellos) _____   =   _____

5. (vosotros) _____   =   _____

6. (Ud.) _____   =   _____

Now, supply the missing imperfect indicative forms of the verb ser, giving the English equivalent.

1. (yo) _____   =   _____

2. (tú) _____   =   _____

3. (nosotros) _____   =   _____

4. (ellos) _____   =   _____

5. (vosotros) _____   =   _____

6. (Ud.) _____   =   _____

Now, supply the missing imperfect indicative forms of the verb ir, giving the English equivalent.

1. (yo) _____   =   _____

2. (tú) _____   =   _____

3. (nosotros) _____   =   _____

4. (ellos) _____   =   _____

5. (vosotros) _____   =   _____

6. (Ud.) _____   =   _____

Now, supply the missing imperfect indicative forms of the verb ver, giving the English equivalent.

1. (yo) _____   =   _____

2. (tú) _____   =   _____

3. (nosotros) _____   =   _____

4. (ellos) _____   =   _____

5. (vosotros) _____   =   _____

6. (Ud.) _____   =   _____

Now, supply the missing imperfect indicative forms of the verb levantarse, giving the English equivalent.

1. (yo) _____   =   _____

2. (tú) _____   =   _____

3. (nosotros) _____   =   _____

4. (ellos) _____   =   _____

5. (vosotros) _____   =   _____

6. (Ud.) _____   =   _____

B. How do you say the following sentences in Spanish?

1. I used to live in Quito.

    _____

2. I was very nice as a child.

    _____

3. It was 9 P.M.

    _____

4. We used to go to school every day.

    _____

5. As a child, Isabel had blond hair.

    _____

6. It was raining and it was cloudy.

    _____

7. They wanted to see the latest movie.

    _____

8. I liked to read the books of *Jorge Icaza*[1].

    _____

9. Were you (fam. sg.) playing soccer?

    _____

10. I used to work in that store.

    _____

[1]Ecuadorean novelist, 1906–1978; author of *Huasipungo*, 1934.

11. They were studying in the library.

_____

12. I used to think that Jorge studied frequently.

_____

13. Elena was working, and I was writing.

_____

14. We believed that he was driving to San Antonio.

_____

Imperfect Indicative of Hay

The imperfect indicative of **hay** / *there is, there are* is **había** / *there was, there were*. It is used in the same way that **hay** is used, except that it is in the imperfect indicative tense. The following sentences illustrate this point.

> **Había mucho papel en la calle.** / *There was a lot of paper in the street.*
> **Había muchas personas en la fiesta.** / *There were a lot of people at the party.*

The imperfect indicative of the idiomatic expression **hay que** / *one must, it is necessary to* is **había que** / *it was necessary to*. The following sentence illustrates this usage.

> **Había que ir a Quito para estudiar la literatura ecuatoriana.** / *It was necessary to go to Quito to study Ecuadorean literature.*

Imperfect Progressive

The imperfect progressive, called the **imperfecto progresivo** in Spanish, is an alternative to the imperfect indicative. It corresponds, basically, to the present progressive (Chapter 6), allowing you to zero in on an action in the past that was ongoing at the time (usually relative to another action):

> **Ayer, mientras mi hermana estaba comiendo, yo estaba mirando la televisión.** / *Yesterday, while my sister was eating, I was watching TV.*

The imperfect progressive is formed with the imperfect indicative tense of **estar** / *to be* and the present participle of the verb. Review Chapter 6 for the formation of the present participle (gerund) and for its irregular forms.

Here are three verbs conjugated in the imperfect progressive:

hablar / *to speak*

Subject Pronoun	Estar	Present Participle	Meaning
(yo)	<u>est</u>+aba	<u>habl</u>+ando	*I was speaking*
(tú)	<u>est</u>+abas	<u>habl</u>+ando	*you (fam. sg.) were speaking*
(él, ella, Ud.)	<u>est</u>+aba	<u>habl</u>+ando	*he, she, you (pol. sg.) was/were speaking*
(nosotros/-as)	<u>est</u>+ábamos	<u>habl</u>+ando	*we were speaking*
(vosotros/-as)	<u>est</u>+abais	<u>habl</u>+ando	*you (fam. pl.) were speaking*
(ellos/-as, Uds.)	<u>est</u>+aban	<u>habl</u>+ando	*they, you (pol. pl.) were speaking*

comer / *to eat*

Subject Pronoun	Estar	Present Participle	Meaning
(yo)	<u>est</u>+aba	<u>com</u>+iendo	*I was eating*
(tú)	<u>est</u>+abas	<u>com</u>+iendo	*you (fam. sg.) were eating*
(él, ella, Ud.)	<u>est</u>+aba	<u>com</u>+iendo	*he, she, you (pol. sg.) was/were eating*
(nosotros/-as)	<u>est</u>+ábamos	<u>com</u>+iendo	*we were eating*
(vosotros/-as)	<u>est</u>+abais	<u>com</u>+iendo	*you (fam. pl.) were eating*
(ellos/-as, Uds.)	<u>est</u>+aban	<u>com</u>+iendo	*they, you (pol. pl.) were eating*

vivir / *to live*

Subject Pronoun	Estar	Present Participle	Meaning
(yo)	<u>est</u>+aba	<u>viv</u>+iendo	*I was living*
(tú)	<u>est</u>+abas	<u>viv</u>+iendo	*you (fam. sg.) were living*
(él, ella, Ud.)	<u>est</u>+aba	<u>viv</u>+iendo	*he, she, you (pol. sg.) was/were living*
(nosotros/-as)	<u>est</u>+ábamos	<u>viv</u>+iendo	*we were living*
(vosotros/-as)	<u>est</u>+abais	<u>viv</u>+iendo	*you (fam. pl.) were living*
(ellos/-as, Uds.)	<u>est</u>+aban	<u>viv</u>+iendo	*they, you (pol. pl.) were living*

The Imperfect Progressive of Reflexive Verbs

Reflexive verbs always also use reflexive pronouns in the imperfect progressive tense. As we noted in our discussion of the present progressive of reflexive verbs (see Chapter 6), there are, in fact, two ways of placing the reflexive pronoun. We illustrate both possibilities here. The first example shows the placement of the reflexive pronoun before the verb estar / *to be*. The second example shows the placement of the reflexive pronoun following and attached to the present participle. In the latter case, you will note that there is a written accent over the first vowel of the present participle ending to indicate that the accent is retained in its original position. We have highlighted the graphic accent with italics in the second example.

Reflexive Pronoun Before Estar

lavarse / *to wash oneself*

Subject Pronoun	Reflexive Pronoun	Estar	Past Participle	Meaning
(yo)	me	est+aba	lav+ando	*I was washing myself*
(tú)	te	est+abas	lav+ando	*you (fam. sg.) were washing yourself*
(él, ella, Ud.)	se	est+aba	lav+ando	*he, she, you (pol. sg.) was/were washing himself/ herself/ yourself*
(nosotros/-as)	nos	est+ábamos	lav+ando	*we were washing ourselves*
(vosotros/-as)	os	est+abais	lav+ando	*you (fam. pl.) were washing yourselves*
(ellos/-as, Uds.)	se	est+aban	lav+ando	*they, you (pol. pl.) were washing themselves/yourselves*

Reflexive Pronoun Following and Attached to Present Participle (Gerund)

lavarse / *to wash oneself*

Subject Pronoun	Estar	Present Participle	Meaning
(yo)	est+aba	lav+ándo+me	*I was washing myself*
(tú)	est+abas	lav+ándo+te	*you (fam. sg.) were washing yourself*
(él, ella, Ud.)	est+aba	lav+ándo+se	*he, she, you (pol. sg.) was/were washing himself/herself/yourself*
(nosotros/-as)	est+ábamos	lav+ándo+nos	*we were washing ourselves*
(vosotros/-as)	est+abais	lav+ándo+os	*you (fam. pl.) were washing yourselves*
(ellos/-as, Uds.)	est+aban	lav+ándo+se	*they, you (pol. pl.) were washing themselves/yourselves*

EXERCISE Set 8-2

A. Replace the imperfect indicative forms of the given verbs with the corresponding imperfect progressive forms.

EXAMPLE: *él comía*   =   _____

            él estaba comiendo =   *he was eating*

1. yo pagaba   =   _____

2. empezabas   =   _____

3. comíamos   =   _____

4. ellos preferían   = _____

5. jugabais   = _____

6. Ud. estudiaba   = _____

7. ellas cantaban   = _____

8. dábamos   = _____

9. yo creía   = _____

10. Uds. hacían   = _____

11. escribíamos   = _____

12. yo salía   = _____

13. te levantabas (2 ways) = _____

                          = _____

B. How do you say the following sentences in Spanish? Use the imperfect progressive in your answers.

1. You (fam. sg.) were reading *Hoy*[1].

    _____

2. Sofía was studying Spanish verbs.

    _____

3. Roberto and I were watching television.

    _____

4. My friends were playing soccer.

    _____

5. He was preparing the meal.

    _____

[1]Daily newspaper in Quito.

C. Describe what the people in the pictures were doing when Pablo rang the doorbell. Use the appropriate verbs in the imperfect tense.

1. Pablo _____

2. Claudio _____

3. Carolina _____

4. Carlos _____

5. Soledad _____

6. Laura _____

7. Ignacio _____

8. Jorge _____

9. Marina y Alejandro _____

10. Marta _____

VOCABULARY TIP

Certain adverbs of time are commonly used with the imperfect indicative because they express repeated or habitual action.

a menudo / *often*	siempre / *always*
con frecuencia / *frequently*	todas las noches / *every night*
de niño/-a / *as a child*	todas las semanas / *every week*
frecuentemente / *frequently*	todos los años / *every year*
generalmente / *generally*	todos los días / *every day*
muchas veces / *often*	todos los meses / *every month*

A Comparison of the Meaning of Selected Verbs in the Imperfect Indicative and the Preterit

There is a small group of verbs that has a change of meaning when they are used in the preterit (see Chapter 7). The following is a list of the meanings of these verbs in the imperfect indicative and the preterite tenses.

Verb	Meaning in Imperfect Tense	Meaning in Preterite Tense
conocer / *to know a person*	Yo conocía a Luis. / *I used to know Luis.*	Conocí a Luis. / *I met Luis.*
poder / *to be able, can*	Yo podía ir a Cuenca. / *I was able to go to Cuenca.*	Pude ir a Cuenca. / *I managed to go to Cuenca.*
no poder / *not to be able, can*	Yo no podía estudiar español anoche. / *I could not study Spanish last night.*	No pude estudiar español anoche. / *I failed to study Spanish last night.*
querer / *to want*	Yo quería visitar Otavalo. / *I wanted to visit Otavalo.*	Quise visitar Otavalo. / *I tried to visit Otavalo.*
no querer / *not to want*	Yo no quería leer el libro. / *I did not want to read the book.*	No quise leer el libro. / *I refused to read the book.*
saber / *to know (a fact)*	Yo sabía la verdad. / *I knew the truth.*	Supe la verdad. / *I found out the truth.*
tener / *to have*	Yo tenía una carta de mi familia. / *I had a letter from my family.*	Tuve una carta de mi familia. / *I received a letter from my family.*

A Comparison of the Uses of the Imperfect Indicative and the Preterit Tenses

The imperfect indicative and the preterit tenses may be described in general terms in the following way.

Imperfect Indicative Uses

Imperfect Indicative Uses	Examples
1. Repeated or habitual past action	**Vicente estudiaba todos los días.** / *Vincent studied every day.*
2. To tell time	**Eran las dos de la tarde.** / *It was 2 P.M.*
3. To express the English phrase "used to," i.e., a repeated activity in the past	**Clara iba a la universidad por la mañana.** / *Clara used to go to the university in the morning.*
4. To express the English past progressive "was … -ing"	**Cuando Ricardo llegó, Teresa salía.** / *When Richard arrived, Teresa was leaving.*
5. To express (1) mental, (2) physical, or (3) emotional activity	**Pilar pensaba que llovía.** / *Pilar thought that it was raining.* **Fernando estaba cansado.** / *Fernando was tired.* **Bernardo quería mucho a Gloria.** / *Bernard loved Gloria a lot.*
6. To refer to two actions that occur simultaneously in the past	**Mientras Carla bailaba, Ignacio hablaba con Antonio.** / *While Carla was dancing, Ignacio was speaking with Antonio.*
7. To refer to an activity in progress in the past while something else took place	**Mientras Inés preparaba la comida, Jorge terminó su tarea.** / *While Inés was preparing the meal, George completed his homework.*

Preterit Uses

Uses	Examples
1. To express a completed past action	**Rosa leyó toda la novela.** / *Rosa read the entire novel.*
2. To describe a series of completed past actions	**Beatriz se despertó, se levantó, se duchó y se vistió.** / *Beatriz woke up, got up, took a shower, and got dressed.*
3. To indicate the beginning of an activity	**Alvaro empezó a mirar televisión.** / *Alvaro began to watch television.*
4. To indicate the end of an actvity	**Margarita cesó de fumar.** / *Margarita stopped smoking.*
5. To describe a change of state	**Laura se puso enferma cuando vio el examen.** / *Laura became ill when she saw the test.*

EXERCISE Set 8-3

A. Provide the corresponding preterit and imperfect indicative forms for the following verbs in the present indicative tense.

1. hablamos _____   _____

2. tengo _____   _____

3. vamos _____   _____

4. somos _____   _____

5. estoy _____   _____

6. digo _____   _____

7. comemos _____   _____

8. vivimos _____   _____

9. se acuesta _____   _____

10. son _____   _____

11. dormimos _____   _____

12. pides _____   _____

13. hace _____   _____

14. tienen _____   _____

15. entiende _____   _____

16. puede _____   _____

17. queremos _____   _____

18. empiezo _____   _____

B. How do you say the following sentences in Spanish? Use the imperfect indicative or preterit according to the meaning of the sentence.

1. I used to study when you (fam. sg.) went to school.

   _____

2. Gloria was taking a shower when the telephone rang.

   _____

3. I went to the store while it was raining.

   _____

4. Francisco was reading a magazine when María entered the house.

   _____

5. My father used to drink coffee when it was snowing.

   _____

C. Fill in the blanks with the appropriate form of the verb in the preterit or imperfect indicative according to the context.

1. De niña, yo (estudiar) _____ mucho.

2. Nicolás (afeitarse) _____ esta mañana.

3. Pilar y yo (llegar) _____ a las ocho en punto.

4. (Ser) _____ las nueve de la mañana cuando yo (levantarse) _____ .

5. Ella siempre (tocar) _____ la guitarra.

6. Mi hermano (leer) _____ toda la novela anoche.

Crossword Puzzle 8

Supply the correct form of the imperfect indicative tense according to the meaning. Use the following verbs in your answers: **beber, cantar, comer, estar, llover, hablar, ir, saber, ser**.

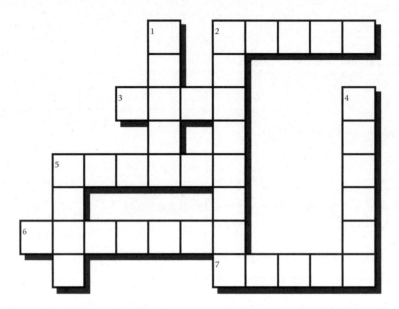

Horizontales
  2. Él . . . la pizza.
  3. De niños, ellos . . . al mar.
  5. Ud. . . . muy cansado.
  6. Mi amigo siempre . . . .
  7. Yo . . . tocar el piano.

Verticales
  1. Yo . . . mucho café.
  2. Tú siempre . . . mi canción favorita.
  4. . . . mucho.
  5. . . . las ocho de la mañana.

9

The Present Perfect Indicative (*el perfecto de indicativo*)

Past Participles

A regular past participle, called participio, is formed in the following way:

1. Drop the infinitive ending:

   <u>habl</u>ar / *to speak* → habl-
   <u>com</u>er / *to eat* → com-
   <u>viv</u>ir / *to live* → viv-

2. Add the appropriate past participle ending to the stem: -ado for -ar verbs and -ido for -er and -ir verbs:

   habl + ado → hablado / *spoken*
   com + ido → comido / *eaten*
   viv + ido → vivido / *lived*

Irregular Past Participles

There are a number of irregular past participles in Spanish. The following is a list of the most common ones. Most of these end in -to. Two (decir / *to tell*, hacer / *to do*) end in -cho, and one (pudrir / *to rot*) has a change in the stem, podrido / *rotten*.

abrir / *to open*	abierto	morir (ue, u) / *to die*	muerto
cubrir / *to cover*	cubierto	oponer / *to oppose*	opuesto
describir / *to describe*	descrito	poner / *to put, to place*	puesto
descubrir / *to discover*	descubierto	proveer / *to provide*	provisto
devolver (ue) / *to return*	devuelto	pudrir / *to rot*	podrido
envolver (ue) / *to wrap*	envuelto	resolver / *to resolve*	resuelto
escribir / *to write*	escrito	romper / *to break*	roto
freír (i, i) / *to fry*	frito	ver / *to see*	visto
hacer / *to do, to make*	hecho	volver (ue) / *to return*	vuelto

Additional Irregular Past Participles

Regular -er and -ir verbs with a vowel immediately preceding the past participle ending -ido have a graphic accent. The following is a list of the common verbs.

atraer / *to attract*	atraído	oír / *to hear*	oído
caer / *to fall*	caído	poseer / *to possess*	poseído
creer / *to believe*	creído	reír / *to laugh*	reído
leer / *to read*	leído	traer / *to bring*	traído

GRAMMAR NOTE

The past participle of derived verbs will have the same past participle of the basic verb. The following examples illustrate this.

<u>volver</u> / *to return* → <u>vuelto</u> / *returned*
de<u>volver</u> / *to return (something)* → de<u>vuelto</u> / *returned*
en<u>volver</u> / *to wrap* → en<u>vuelto</u> / *wrapped*

EXERCISE Set 9-1

A. Give the past participle of the following verbs.

1. llegar = _____

2. comer = _____

3. recibir = _____

4. ser = _____

5. estar = _____

6. tener = _____

7. hacer = _____

8. saber = _____

9. conocer = _____

10. mentir = _____

11. perder = _____

12. poder = _____

13. ofrecer = _____

14. seguir = _____

15. corregir = _____

16. empezar = _____

17. querer = _____

18. almorzar = _____

B. Now give the infinitive of the following past participles.

1. roto = _____

2. escrito = _____

3. visto = _____

4. abierto = _____

5. puesto = _____

6. frito = _____

7. dicho = _____

8. podrido = _____

9. muerto = _____

10. caído = _____

11. hecho = _____

12. vuelto = _____

13. envuelto = _____

14. resuelto = _____

15. descubierto = _____

16. creído = _____

17. devuelto = _____

18. provisto = _____

The Present Perfect Indicative Tense

The present perfect indicative, called el perfecto de indicativo in Spanish, is a tense that talks about the past and continues into the present. The present perfect indicative may refer to an action that started in the past and that may be ongoing in the present. The sentence "Siempre he comido a las seis / *I have always eaten at six*" means that you did this in the past and you still do it today. At the same time, the present perfect indicative may refer to a recently completed action, as "He estudiado todo el capítulo / *I have studied the entire chapter*" illustrates.

Uses and Features

The present perfect indicative is a compound tense that uses the present tense of the auxiliary verb haber / *to have* and the past participle in that order. You use the present perfect indicative in the following situations.

1. To refer to a situation that was true in the past and remains true in the present.
      He comido la comida colombiana toda mi vida. / *I have eaten Colombian cuisine my entire life.*

2. To indicate a recently completed action.
      He conjugado los verbos en el perfecto de indicativo. / *I have conjugated the verbs in the present perfect.*

   To form the present perfect indicative of regular verbs, this is what you have to do:

1. Use the present tense of the auxiliary verb haber / *to have*, which we provide here. Remember that haber is an auxiliary verb. It does not mean *to have* in the sense of *to possess*. To indicate that you have or possess something, you must use the verb tener / *to have*.

haber / *to have*

Subject Pronoun	Verb Form	Meaning
(yo)	he	*I have*
(tú)	has	*you (fam. sg.) have*
(él, ella, Ud.)	ha	*he, she, you (pol. sg.) has/have*
(nosotros/-as)	hemos	*we have*
(vosotros/-as)	habéis	*you (fam. pl.) have*
(ellos/-as, Uds.)	han	*they, you (pol. pl.) have*

2. Place the past participle after the present tense of the auxiliary verb haber / *to have*. The following conjugations of -ar, -er, and -ir verbs illustrate the format of the present perfect indicative tense.

hablar / *to talk*

Subject Pronoun	Haber	Past Participle	Meaning
(yo)	he	habl+ado	*I have spoken*
(tú)	has	habl+ado	*you (fam. sg.) have spoken*
(él, ella, Ud.)	ha	habl+ado	*he, she, you (pol. sg.) has/have spoken*
(nosotros/-as)	hemos	habl+ado	*we have spoken*
(vosotros/-as)	habéis	habl+ado	*you (fam. pl.) have spoken*
(ellos/-as, Uds.)	han	habl+ado	*they, you (pol. pl.) have spoken*

comer / *to eat*

Subject Pronoun	Haber	Past Participle	Meaning
(yo)	he	<u>cóm</u>+ido	*I have eaten*
(tú)	has	<u>com</u>+ido	*you (fam. sg.) have eaten*
(él, ella, Ud.)	ha	<u>com</u>+ido	*he, she, you (pol. sg.) has/have eaten*
(nosotros/-as)	hemos	<u>com</u>+ido	*we have eaten*
(vosotros/-as)	habéis	<u>com</u>+ido	*you (fam. pl.) have eaten*
(ellos/-as, Uds.)	han	<u>com</u>+ido	*they, you (pol. pl.) have eaten*

vivir / *to live*

Subject Pronoun	Haber	Past Participle	Meaning
(yo)	he	<u>viv</u>+ido	*I have lived*
(tú)	has	<u>viv</u>+ido	*you (fam. sg.) have lived*
(él, ella, Ud.)	ha	<u>viv</u>+ido	*he, she, you (pol. sg.) has/have lived*
(nosotros/-as)	hemos	<u>viv</u>+ido	*we have lived*
(vosotros/-as)	habéis	<u>viv</u>+ido	*you (fam. pl.) have lived*
(ellos/-as, Uds.)	han	<u>viv</u>+ido	*they, you (pol. pl.) have lived*

The Present Perfect Indicative of Reflexive Verbs

Reflexive verbs always use reflexive pronouns in the present perfect indicative as shown below. Remember that you must place the reflexive pronoun immediately before the conjugated auxiliary verb haber / *to have*.

lavarse / *to wash oneself*

Subject Pronoun	Reflexive Pronoun	Haber	Past Participle	Meaning
(yo)	me	he	<u>lav</u>+ado	*I have washed myself*
(tú)	te	has	<u>lav</u>+ado	*you (fam. sg.) have washed yourself*
(él, ella, Ud.)	se	ha	<u>lav</u>+ado	*he, she, you (pol. sg.) has/have washed himself/herself/yourself*
(nosotros/-as)	nos	hemos	<u>lav</u>+ado	*we have washed ourselves*
(vosotros/-as)	os	habéis	<u>lav</u>+ado	*you (fam. pl.) have washed yourselves*
(ellos/-as, Uds.)	se	han	<u>lav</u>+ado	*they, you (pol. pl.) have washed themselves/yourselves*

The Present Perfect Indicative of Hay

The present perfect indicative form of **hay** / *there is, there are* is **ha habido** / *there has been, there have been.* The following examples illustrate this usage.

> **Ha habido mucha lluvia.** / *There has been a lot of rain.*
> **Ha habido muchos exámenes.** / *There have been a lot of tests.*

The present perfect of the idiomatic expression **hay que** / *one must, it is necessary to* is **ha habido que** / *it has been necessary to.* The following sentence illustrates this usage.

> **Ha habido que ir a Colombia para estudiar la cultura colombiana.** / *It has been necessary to go to Colombia to study Colombian culture.*

EXERCISE Set 9-2

A. Supply the missing present perfect indicative forms of the verb **cantar**, giving the English equivalent.

EXAMPLE: *él* _____   =   _____

él ha cantado   =   *he has sung*

1. (yo) _____   =   _____

2. (tú) _____   =   _____

3. (nosotros) _____   =   _____

4. (ellos) _____   =   _____

5. (vosotros) _____   =   _____

6. (Ud.) _____   =   _____

Now, supply the missing present perfect indicative forms of the verb **vender**, giving the English equivalent.

1. (yo) _____   =   _____

2. (Raquel y yo) _____   =   _____

3. (Uds.) _____   =   _____

4. (ellos) _____   =   _____

5. (vosotros) _____   =   _____

6. (tú) _____   =   _____

Now, supply the missing present perfect indicative forms of the verb recibir, giving the English equivalent.

1. (yo) _____ = _____

2. (tú) _____ = _____

3. (nosotros) _____ = _____

4. (ellos) _____ = _____

5. (vosotros) _____ = _____

6. (Ud.) _____ = _____

Now, supply the missing present perfect indicative forms of the verb bañarse, giving the English equivalent.

1. (yo) _____ = _____

2. (tú) _____ = _____

3. (nosotros) _____ = _____

4. (ellos) _____ = _____

5. (vosotros) _____ = _____

6. (Ud.) _____ = _____

Now, supply the missing present perfect indicative forms of the verb volver (ue), giving the English equivalent.

1. (yo) _____ = _____

2. (tú) _____ = _____

3. (nosotros) _____ = _____

4. (ellos) _____ = _____

5. (vosotros) _____ = _____

6. (Ud.) _____ = _____

Now, supply the missing present perfect indicative forms of the verb estar, giving the English equivalent.

1. (yo) _____ = _____

2. (tú) _____ = _____

3. (nosotros) _____ = _____

4. (ellos) _____ = _____

5. (vosotros) _____ = _____

6. (Ud.) _____ = _____

Now, supply the missing present perfect indicative forms of the verb **ser**, giving the English equivalent.

1. (yo) _____ = _____

2. (tú) _____ = _____

3. (nosotros) _____ = _____

4. (ellos) _____ = _____

5. (vosotros) _____ = _____

6. (Ud.) _____ = _____

B. How do you say the following sentences in Spanish?

1. I have visited Bogotá often.

   _____

2. We have been in *Cartagena*[1].

   _____

3. Have you (fam. sg.) taken a shower?

   _____

4. Have you (pol. sg.) seen my wife?

   _____

5. It has rained a lot.

   _____

6. Have they resolved their problems?

   _____

7. You (pol. pl.) have been thirsty all day.

   _____

[1]Colonial resort city on Colombia's Northern Caribbean coast.

8. We have seen *Leticia*[2].

_____

8. She has told the truth.

_____

10. I have always liked this beach.

_____

11. You (fam. sg.) have had to work hard.

_____

12. He has been very nice.

_____

13. You (pol. pl.) have opened all the doors.

_____

14. I have provided the food.

_____

15. They have gotten dressed.

_____

16. We have always believed our son.

_____

17. You (fam. sg.) have taken a trip to *Cali*[3].

_____

18. We have read the writings of *José Eustacio Rivera*[4].

_____

19. Why hasn't she returned?

_____

[2]Located in the Amazon region on the border with Peru and Brazil.
[3]Second city located in Southwestern Colombia; founded in 1536.
[4]Colombian writer, 1889–1928, author of *La vorágine*, 1924.

20. The telephone has rung all night and I have not been able to sleep.

_____

21. There have been many tests in this book.

_____

The Present Perfect Indicative with Object Pronouns

We have already seen that reflexive pronouns appear in the same place as in other tenses, namely, immediately before the conjugated verb, in this case the auxiliary verb haber / *to have.* You must remember that all object pronouns (direct, indirect, and reflexive) follow the same rules. They are placed immediately before the conjugated auxiliary verb haber / *to have.* Likewise, the order of the object pronouns (indirect and direct) is the same: INDIRECT OBJECT + DIRECT OBJECT. The following selected sentences show these patterns.

He leído <u>la novela</u>. / *I have read the novel.*

<u>La</u> he leído. / *I have read it.*

Le he dado <u>los libros</u> *a Pablo.* / *I have given the books to Pablo.*

Se <u>los</u> he dado *a él.* / *I have given them to him.*

When you use the infinitive form of the auxiliary verb, the object pronouns (reflexive, indirect, direct) may follow and be attached to the infinitive or they may appear immediately before the conjugated verb, as illustrated below.

1. Reflexive Verbs
   Debo haber<u>me</u> despertado temprano. / *I should have woken up early.*
   <u>Me</u> debo haber despertado temprano. / *I should have woken up early.*

2. Direct Object Pronouns
   Debo haber comprado <u>el libro</u>. / *I should have bought the book.*
   Debo haber<u>lo</u> comprado. / *I should have bought it.*
   <u>Lo</u> debo haber comprado. / *I should have bought it.*

3. Indirect Object Pronouns
   Debo haber<u>le</u> dado el coche *a Marta.* / *I should have given the car to Marta.*
   Le debo haber dado el coche *a Marta.* / *I should have given the car to Marta.*
   Debo haber<u>le</u> dado el coche *a ella.* / *I should have given the car to her.*
   Le debo haber dado el coche *a ella.* / *I should have given the car to her.*

4. Double Object Constructions
   Debo haber<u>le</u> dado <u>el coche</u> *a Marta.* / *I should have given the car to Marta.*
   Debo habér<u>selo</u> dado *a ella.* / *I should have given it to her.*
   Se <u>lo</u> debo haber dado *a ella.* / *I should have given it to her.*

EXERCISE Set 9-3

A. Replace the direct objects with direct object pronouns. Remember that there are two options for pronoun placement with infinitives. In these cases, write both possibilities.

1. He leído <u>los libros</u>.

   _____

2. Pilar ha bebido <u>el café</u>.

   _____

3. Debo haber cantado <u>la canción</u>.

   _____

4. Ella ha escrito <u>la carta</u>.

   _____

B. Replace both indirect and direct objects with indirect and direct object pronouns. You will need to use prepositional pronouns to "clarify" the reference (see Chapter 6). Remember that there are two options with infinitives and present participles. In such cases, write both possibilities. Remember also that you need the "redundant indirect object pronoun" with the indirect object in the third person singular and plural. And finally, remember that the order of these pronouns is always INDIRECT + DIRECT.

1. Ramón le ha hablado español a Rosalba.

   _____

2. Marina debe haber escrito la carta a su hijo.

   _____

3. Uds. les han dicho la verdad a sus amigos.

   _____

C. Provide the Spanish for the following sentences. Use an indirect object pronoun in your answer. Remember to use the redundant indirect object pronoun in the third person singular and plural. If there are two ways of writing the answer, please do so.

1. I have sold the car to my brother.

_____

2. They should have spoken to us.

_____

D. Replace the indirect and direct objects with indirect and direct object pronouns. Remember the order of these pronouns is always INDIRECT + DIRECT.

1. Vicente le ha mandado el paquete a Raquel.

_____

2. Le he leído el cuento a mi hija.

_____

3. Le hemos dicho la verdad a Antonio.

_____

4. Berta le ha enseñado toda la lección a su amigo.

_____

E. Provide the Spanish for the following sentences. Use an indirect object pronoun and a direct object in your answer. Remember to use the redundant indirect object pronoun.

1. You (fam. sg.) have sent it to him (the letter).

_____

2. We have given them (books) to them (our cousins).

_____

3. They have sold it (the car) to her.

_____

F. Answer the following questions in Spanish. Use an indirect object and a direct object pronoun in your answer. Remember to use the redundant indirect object pronoun.

1. ¿Le has dado los regalos a Marta?

   _____

2. ¿Les has hablado español a tus amigos?

   _____

3. ¿Le has servido el té a tu amiga?

   _____

EXERCISE Set 9-4

A. Provide the corresponding preterit, imperfect, and present perfect indicative forms for the following verbs in the present indicative tense.

1. comemos

2. tiene

3. voy

4. soy

5. estoy

6. decimos

7. vivimos

8. hacemos

9. se baña

10. hay

11. muere

12. piden

13. hace

14. tienen

15. entiendes

16. pueden _____ _____ _____

17. quiero _____ _____ _____

18. empieza _____ _____ _____

Crossword Puzzle 9

Fill in the blanks. All of the clues both vertical and horizontal require that you use the appropriate past participle form.

Horizontales
  5. Ud. ha . . . (escuchar) la música.
  6. Ellos han . . . (abrir) las ventanas.
  8. Uds. han . . . (decir) la verdad.
  9. Él ha . . . (ser) generoso.

Verticales
  1. ¿Qué tiempo ha . . . (hacer)?
  2. Ella ha . . . (estar) enferma.
  3. He . . . (escribir) un libro.
  4. ¿A qué hora te has . . . (levantarse)?
  7. ¿Quién ha . . . (romper) el plato?

10

The Pluperfect (Past Perfect) Indicative (*el pluscuamperfecto de indicativo*)

The Conjugation of the Pluperfect (Past Perfect) Indicative Tense

The pluperfect tense, sometimes called the past perfect tense, and known as the **pluscuamperfecto de indicativo** in Spanish, is a compound tense. Therefore, it is conjugated with the auxiliary verb **haber** / *to have*. See Chapter 9 for the relevant details regarding past participles. In the pluperfect, the auxiliary verbs are in the imperfect tense.

The pluperfect indicative (past perfect indicative) refers to an action that took place before another action or event. You use the pluperfect indicative (past perfect indicative) to refer to an event prior in time to another event in the past. The following sentences illustrate this point.

> **Yo ya había bebido el café cuando Dolores entró.** / *I had already drunk the coffee when Dolores entered.*
> **Después de que ella había llegado, me llamó por teléfono.** / *After she had arrived, she phoned me.*

To form the pluperfect indicative (past perfect indicative) tense of regular verbs, this is what you have to do:

1. Use the imperfect tense of the auxiliary verb **haber** / *to have* that we provide here. Remember that **haber** is an auxiliary verb. It does not mean *to have* in the sense of *to possess*. To indicate that you have or possess something, you must use the verb **tener** / *to have, to possess.*

haber / *to have*

Subject Pronoun	Verb Form	Meaning
(yo)	<u>hab</u>+ía	*I had*
(tú)	<u>hab</u>+ías	*you (fam. sg.) had*
(él, ella, Ud.)	<u>hab</u>+ía	*he, she, you (pol. sg.) had*
(nosotros/-as)	<u>hab</u>+íamos	*we had*
(vosotros/-as)	<u>hab</u>+íais	*you (fam. pl.) had*
(ellos/-as, Uds.)	<u>hab</u>+ían	*they, you (pol. pl.) had*

2. Place the past participle after the imperfect form of the auxiliary verb **haber** / *to have*. The following are examples of -ar, -er, and -ir verbs.

hablar / *to talk*

Subject Pronoun	Haber	Past Participle	Meaning
(yo)	hab+ía	habl+ado	*I had spoken*
(tú)	hab+ías	habl+ado	*you (fam. sg.) had spoken*
(él, ella, Ud.)	hab+ía	habl+ado	*he, she, you (pol. sg.) had spoken*
(nosotros/-as)	hab+íamos	habl+ado	*we had spoken*
(vosotros/-as)	hab+íais	habl+ado	*you (fam. pl.) had spoken*
(ellos/-as, Uds.)	hab+ían	habl+ado	*they, you (pol. pl.) had spoken*

comer / *to eat*

Subject Pronoun	Haber	Past Participle	Meaning
(yo)	hab+ía	com+ido	*I had eaten*
(tú)	hab+ías	com+ido	*you (fam. sg.) had eaten*
(él, ella, Ud.)	hab+ía	com+ido	*he, she, you (pol. sg.) had eaten*
(nosotros/-as)	hab+íamos	com+ido	*we had eaten*
(vosotros/-as)	hab+íais	com+ido	*you (fam. pl.) had eaten*
(ellos/-as, Uds.)	hab+ían	com+ido	*they, you (pol. pl.) had eaten*

vivir / *to live*

Subject Pronoun	Haber	Past Participle	Meaning
(yo)	hab+ía	viv+ido	*I had lived*
(tú)	hab+ías	viv+ido	*you (fam. sg.) had lived*
(él, ella, Ud.)	hab+ía	viv+ido	*he, she, you (pol. sg.) had lived*
(nosotros/-as)	hab+íamos	viv+ido	*we had lived*
(vosotros/-as)	hab+íais	viv+ido	*you (fam. pl.) had lived*
(ellos/-as, Uds.)	hab+ían	viv+ido	*they, you (pol. pl.) had lived*

The Pluperfect Indicative (Past Perfect Indicative) of Reflexive Verbs

Reflexive verbs always use reflexive pronouns in the pluperfect indicative (past perfect indicative) tense as shown below. Remember that you must place the reflexive pronoun immediately before the conjugated auxiliary verb haber / *to have*.

lavarse / *to wash oneself*

Subject Pronoun	Reflexive Pronoun	Haber	Past Participle	Meaning
(yo)	me	<u>hab</u>+ía	<u>lav</u>+ado	*I had washed myself*
(tú)	te	<u>hab</u>+ías	<u>lav</u>+ado	*you (fam. sg.) had washed yourself*
(él, ella, Ud.)	se	<u>hab</u>+ía	<u>lav</u>+ado	*he, she, you (pol. sg.) had washed himself/herself/yourself*
(nosotros/-as)	nos	<u>hab</u>+íamos	<u>lav</u>+ado	*we had washed ourselves*
(vosotros/-as)	os	<u>hab</u>+íais	<u>lav</u>+ado	*you (fam. pl.) had washed yourselves*
(ellos/-as, Uds.)	se	<u>hab</u>+ían	<u>lav</u>+ado	*they, you (pol. pl.) had washed themselves/yourselves*

NOTE

You have probably noticed that the first person singular (yo) and third person singular (él, ella, Ud.) are identical in form. For this reason, you must normally use the subject pronoun yo / *I* to distinguish these forms. You will recall that this was necessary in the imperfect tense, and since the pluperfect indicative (past perfect indicative) uses the imperfect of the auxiliary verb haber / *to have*, this is simply a continuation of that usage.

The Pluperfect Indicative (Past Perfect Indicative) of Hay

The pluperfect indicative (past perfect indicative) form of hay / *there is, there are* is había habido / *there had been*. The following examples illustrate this usage.

> Había habido mucha nieve. / *There had been a lot of snow.*
> Había habido muchas tormentas. / *There had been many storms.*

The pluperfect (past perfect) of the idiomatic expression hay que / *one must, it is necessary to* is había habido que / *it had been necessary to*. The following sentence illustrates this usage.

> Había habido que conjugar los verbos en el pluscuamperfecto. / *It had been necessary to conjugate the verbs in the pluperfect.*

EXERCISE Set 10-1

A. Supply the missing pluperfect indicative (past perfect indicative) forms of the verb **dar**, giving the English equivalent.

EXAMPLE: *él* _____   =   _____

          él había dado   =   *he had given*

1. (yo) _____   =   _____

2. (tú) _____   =   _____

3. (nosotros) _____   =   _____

4. (ellos) _____   =   _____

5. (vosotros) _____   =   _____

6. (Ud.) _____   =   _____

     Now, supply the missing pluperfect indicative (past perfect indicative) forms of the verb **aprender**, giving the English equivalent.

1. (yo) _____   =   _____

2. (Raquel y yo) _____ =   _____

3. (Uds.) _____   =   _____

4. (ellos) _____   =   _____

5. (vosotros) _____   =   _____

6. (tú) _____   =   _____

     Now, supply the missing pluperfect indicative (past perfect indicative) forms of the verb **sufrir**, giving the English equivalent.

1. (yo) _____   =   _____

2. (tú) _____   =   _____

3. (nosotros) _____   =   _____

4. (ellos) _____   =   _____

5. (vosotros) _____ = _____

6. (Ud.) _____ = _____

Now, supply the missing pluperfect indicative (past perfect indicative) forms of the verb **vestirse (i, i)**, giving the English equivalent.

1. (yo) _____ = _____

2. (tú) _____ = _____

3. (nosotros) _____ = _____

4. (ellos) _____ = _____

5. (vosotros) _____ = _____

6. (Ud.) _____ = _____

Now, supply the missing pluperfect indicative (past perfect indicative) forms of the verb **cubrir**, giving the English equivalent.

1. (yo) _____ = _____

2. (tú) _____ = _____

3. (nosotros) _____ = _____

4. (ellos) _____ = _____

5. (vosotros) _____ = _____

6. (Ud.) _____ = _____

Now, supply the missing pluperfect indicative (past perfect indicative) forms of the verb **estar**, giving the English equivalent.

1. (yo) _____ = _____

2. (tú) _____ = _____

3. (nosotros) _____ = _____

4. (ellos) _____ = _____

5. (vosotros) _____ = _____

6. (Ud.) _____ = _____

Now, supply the missing pluperfect indicative (past perfect indicative) forms of the verb **ser**, giving the English equivalent.

1. (yo) _____   =   _____

2. (tú) _____   =   _____

3. (nosotros) _____ =   _____

4. (ellos) _____   =   _____

5. (vosotros) _____ =   _____

6. (Ud.) _____   =   _____

B. How do you say the following sentences in Spanish?

1. I had seen the *Museo Bolivariano*[1] in Caracas.

   _____

2. I had heard the folkloric music of Venezuela.

   _____

3. I had purchased *El Diario de Caracas*[2].

   _____

4. There had been many houses there.

   _____

5. It had rained last night.

   _____

6. Pablo had lived in Madrid before coming to Venezuela.

   _____

7. I had seen the latest Venezuelan movie.

   _____

8. I had played the guitar.

   _____

[1]Museum for Simón Bolivar, 1783–1830, Venezuelan soldier and South American liberator.
[2]Daily newspaper in Caracas.

9. I had traveled to *Mérida*[3].

_____

10. I had gotten up very late.

_____

11. You (fam. sg.) had studied Spanish verbs a lot.

_____

12. We had entered the capital of Venezuela.

_____

13. It had begun to rain.

_____

14. They had driven to Maracaibo[4].

_____

15. Where had he found the money?

_____

16. I had done the puzzle.

_____

17. You (pol. sg.) had had the book before.

_____

18. Had you (pol. pl.) discovered the secret?

_____

19. The flowers had died in the fall.

_____

20. She had laughed a lot.

_____

[3]Colonial city founded in 1558 in Western Venezuela.
[4]Oil producing center in Northwestern Venezuela; second largest city.

EXERCISE Set 10-2

A. Provide the corresponding present perfect indicative and pluperfect indicative (past perfect indicative) forms for the following verbs in the present indicative tense.

1. vivimos   _____   _____

2. llueve   _____   _____

3. va   _____   _____

4. eres   _____   _____

5. estamos   _____   _____

6. dicen   _____   _____

7. bebemos   _____   _____

8. hago   _____   _____

9. se ducha   _____   _____

10. hay   _____   _____

11. muere   _____   _____

12. pide   _____   _____

13. hace   _____   _____

14. tengo   _____   _____

15. entiendes   _____   _____

16. puede   _____   _____

17. quieres   _____   _____

18. comienza   _____   _____

Crossword Puzzle 10

Fill in the blanks. All of the clues both vertical and horizontal require that you use the appropriate past participle form.

Horizontales
4. Habías . . . (poner) la mesa.
5. Mi amigo y yo habíamos . . .
   (resolver) el problema.
9. Habíamos . . . (entrar) en casa.
10. Ud. había . . . (oír) la música.
11. Había . . . (hacer) buen tiempo.

Verticales
1. Yo había . . . (ver) la película.
2. Habías . . . (ir) a casa.
3. Ella se había . . . (despertarse) tarde.
6. Jorge había . . . (estar) cansado.
7. Ellos habían . . . (traer) los libros.
8. Elena había . . . (comer) la comida.

Part Three

The Future and Conditional Tenses

The Future and the Conditional: An Overview

What Is the Future Tense?

In English, the *future* tense is expressed by the "modal" form *will* to indicate something that will take place in the time to come. In Spanish, the same tense is constructed with endings added on to the stem base of the infinitive:

> Mañana llamaré a Marta por teléfono. / *Tomorrow I will phone Marta.*
> Estudiaremos la lección mañana. / *We will study the lesson tomorrow.*

There is also a *future perfect* tense in English and Spanish that is used to express or indicate past time with respect to some point in future time, as in:

> La semana próxima ya habrás partido. / *Next week you will have left already.*
> Habré leído todo el libro para mañana. / *I shall have read the entire book by tomorrow.*

As you can see, it is a compound tense made up of an auxiliary verb in the future tense and the past participle of the verb.

What Is the Conditional Tense?

In English, the *conditional* tense is expressed by the modal form *would* to indicate or make reference to conditions. In Spanish the same tense is constructed with endings added on to the base of the infinitive:

> Yo iría a la casa de Laura, pero ella no está allí. / *I would go to Laura's home, but she isn't there.*
> Iríamos a España, pero no tenemos el dinero. / *We would go to Spain, but we don't have the money.*

There is also a *conditional perfect* tense in English and Spanish that is used to express or indicate an action or event that would have taken place under certain conditions:

> Yo habría hecho el trabajo, pero yo no tenía el tiempo. / *I would have done the work, but I did not have the time.*
> Marco habría pagado la cuenta, pero él no tenía su cartera. / *Marco would have paid the bill, but he didn't have his wallet.*

As you can see, it is also a compound tense made up of an auxiliary verb in the conditional tense and the past participle of the verb.

11
The Future
(*el futuro*)

Uses and Features

The simple future is used most of the time as follows:

1. To express an action or state of being that will take place at some time in the future:
   Mañana iré al cine. / *Tomorrow I will go the movies.*
   Lo haré si tengo el tiempo. / *I will do it if I have the time.*

2. To express probability:
   ¿Qué hora será? / *I wonder what time it is?*
   Serán las ocho. / *It is probably eight o'clock.*

3. To express conjecture (wondering, guessing):
   ¿Quién llamará a esta hora? / *I wonder who is calling at this hour?*

Regular Verbs

To form the future tense, called the futuro in Spanish, do the following:

1. Use the entire infinitive as the stem: <u>hablar</u> / *to speak*, <u>comer</u> / *to eat*, and <u>vivir</u> / *to live*.

2. Add the following endings to the stem. Note that there is a single set of endings for the future tense:

(yo)	-é
(tú)	-ás
(él, ella, Ud.)	-á
(nosotros/-as)	-emos
(vosotros/-as)	-éis
(ellos/-as, Uds.)	-án

3. Here's the result:

hablar / *to speak*

Subject Pronoun	Verb Form	Meaning
(yo)	hablar+é	*I will speak*
(tú)	hablar+ás	*you (fam. sg.) will speak*
(él, ella, Ud.)	hablar+á	*he, she, you (pol. sg.) will speak*
(nosotros/-as)	hablar+emos	*we will speak*
(vosotros/-as)	hablar+éis	*you (fam. pl.) will speak*
(ellos/-as, Uds.)	hablar+án	*they, you (pol. pl.) will speak*

comer / *to eat*

Subject Pronoun	Verb Form	Meaning
(yo)	comer+é	*I will eat*
(tú)	comer+ás	*you (fam. sg.) will eat*
(él, ella, Ud.)	comer+á	*he, she, you (pol. sg.) will eat*
(nosotros/-as)	comer+emos	*we will eat*
(vosotros/-as)	comer+éis	*you (fam. pl.) will eat*
(ellos/-as, Uds.)	comer+án	*they, you (pol. pl.) will eat*

vivir / *to live*

Subject Pronoun	Verb Form	Meaning
(yo)	vivir+é	*I will live*
(tú)	vivir+ás	*you (fam. sg.) will live*
(él, ella, Ud.)	vivir+á	*he, she, you (pol. sg.) will live*
(nosotros/-as)	vivir+emos	*we will live*
(vosotros/-as)	vivir+éis	*you (fam. pl.) will live*
(ellos/-as, Uds.)	vivir+án	*they, you (pol. pl.) will live*

The Future Tense of Reflexive Verbs

Reflexive verbs always use reflexive pronouns in the future, as shown below. They always appear immediately before the conjugated verb, as they do in the present and all other tenses.

lavarse / *to wash oneself*

Subject Pronoun	Reflexive Pronoun	Conjugated Verb	Meaning
(yo)	me	lavar+é	*I will wash myself*
(tú)	te	lavar+ás	*you (fam. sg.) will wash yourself*
(él, ella, Ud.)	se	lavar+á	*he, she, you (pol. sg.) will wash himself/herself/yourself*
(nosotros/-as)	nos	lavar+emos	*we will wash ourselves*
(vosotros/-as)	os	lavar+éis	*you (fam. pl.) will wash yourselves*
(ellos/-as, Uds.)	se	lavar+án	*they, you (pol. pl.) will wash themselves/yourselves*

NOTE

Notice that the future generally is rendered in English by the following two translations:

Ella llegará mañana. = *She will arrive tomorrow.*
= *She will be arriving tomorrow.*

You will be pleased to know that there are no stem changes in the future tense.

TIP

There are no stem changes in the future tense. There are, however, twelve verbs that have an irregular stem to which the regular future tense endings are added. These verbs appear right after the following exercises.

EXERCISE Set 11-1

A. Supply the missing future forms of the verb **estudiar**, giving the English equivalent.

EXAMPLE: *él* _____ = _____

él estudiará = he will study

1. (yo) _____ = _____

2. (tú) _____ = _____

3. (nosotros) _____ = _____

4. (ellos) _____ = _____

5. (vosotros) _____ = _____

6. (Ud.) _____ = _____

Now, supply the missing future forms of the verb **aprender**, giving the English equivalent.

1. (yo) _____ = _____

2. (Raquel y yo) _____ = _____

3. (Uds.) _____ = _____

4. (ellos) _____ = _____

5. (vosotros) _____ = _____

6. (tú) _____ = _____

Now, supply the missing future forms of the verb **escribir**, giving the English equivalent.

1. (yo) _____ = _____

2. (tú) _____ = _____

3. (nosotros) _____ = _____

4. (ellos) _____ = _____

5. (vosotros) _____ = _____

6. (Ud.) _____ = _____

Now, supply the missing future forms of the verb **sentarse (ie)**, giving the English equivalent.

1. (yo) _____ = _____

2. (tú) _____ = _____

3. (nosotros) _____ = _____

4. (ellos) _____ = _____

5. (vosotros) _____ = _____

6. (Ud.) _____ = _____

B. How do you say the following sentences in Spanish?

1. I will travel to *David*[1].

_____

2. That program will begin at 8 P.M.

_____

3. She will take a shower tomorrow.

_____

[1]Panama's southwestern province on the border of Costa Rica, noted for its natural beauty.

4. Rosalba and I will buy our books tomorrow.

_____

5. I will get up late tomorrow.

_____

6. I will see the *Museo afro-antillano*[2] on Friday.

_____

7. She will not like that movie.

_____

8. He will sleep until noon.

_____

9. I will attend the university next year.

_____

10. They will arrive at 1 P.M.

_____

[2]Museum dedicated to Panama's West Indian community, located in Panama City.

Irregular Future Tense Verbs

There are twelve irregular verbs in the future tense. What makes these verbs irregular is the fact that they have an irregular stem. As we noted earlier, there is a single set of regular endings for the future tense.

Irregular Future Stems: Pattern 1

Learn the irregular future stem to which you add the future tense endings. In this group, you take the infinitive and you delete the vowel in the infinitive ending: -er → -r-. We list them below.

> **caber** / *to fit, to be contained* → **cabr-**
> **haber** / *to have (auxiliary verb)* → **habr-**
> **poder** / *can, to be able* → **podr-**
> **querer** / *to want* → **querr-**
> **saber** / *to know, to know how* → **sabr-**

Irregular Future Stems: Pattern 2

Learn the irregular future stem, to which you add the future tense endings. In this group, you take the infinitive and you delete the vowel in the infinitive ending. Then you insert the consonant -d-: -er → -dr-. We list them below.

poner / *to put, to place* → pondr-
salir / *to leave* → saldr-
tener / *to have* → tendr-
valer / *to be worth* → valdr-
venir / *to come* → vendr-

Irregular Future Stems: Pattern 3

Learn the irregular future stem, to which you add the future tense endings. In this group, a completely different stem is used. We list them below:

decir (i, i) / *to say, to tell* → dir-
hacer / *to do, to make* → har-

To each of these irregular stems, you add the regular future tense endings that we reproduce here:

(yo)	-é
(tú)	-ás
(él, ella, Ud.)	-á
(nosotros/-as)	-emos
(vosotros/-as)	-éis
(ellos/-as, Uds.)	-án

We now provide one conjugation from each of the three categories we just saw.

querer / *to want*

Subject Pronoun	Verb Form	Meaning
(yo)	querr+é	*I will want*
(tú)	querr+ás	*you (fam. sg.) will want*
(él, ella, Ud.)	querr+á	*he, she, you (pol. sg.) will want*
(nosotros/-as)	querr+emos	*we will want*
(vosotros/-as)	querr+éis	*you (fam. pl.) will want*
(ellos/-as, Uds.)	querr+án	*they, you (pol. pl.) will want*

tener / *to have*

Subject Pronoun	Verb Form	Meaning
(yo)	tendr+é	*I will have*
(tú)	tendr+ás	*you (fam. sg.) will have*
(él, ella, Ud.)	tendr+á	*he, she, you (pol. sg.) will have*
(nosotros/-as)	tendr+emos	*we will have*
(vosotros/-as)	tendr+éis	*you (fam. pl.) will have*
(ellos/-as, Uds.)	tendr+án	*they, you (pol. pl.) will have*

hacer / *to do, to make*

Subject Pronoun	Verb Form	Meaning
(yo)	<u>har</u>+é	*I will do/make*
(tú)	<u>har</u>+ás	*you (fam. sg.) will do/make*
(él, ella, Ud.)	<u>har</u>+á	*he, she, you (pol. sg.) will do/make*
(nosotros/-as)	<u>har</u>+emos	*we will do/make*
(vosotros/-as)	<u>har</u>+éis	*you (fam. pl.) will do/make*
(ellos/-as, Uds.)	<u>har</u>+án	*they, you (pol. pl.) will do/make*

GRAMMAR NOTE

There are several verbs derived from these twelve verbs that also have an irregular future stem. The following are some common ones.

1. <u>hacer</u> / *to do, to make* → <u>har</u>-
   des<u>hacer</u> / *to undo, to untie (a knot)* → des<u>har</u>-

2. <u>poner</u> / *to put, to place* → <u>pondr</u>-
   com<u>poner</u> / *to compose* → com<u>pondr</u>-
   o<u>ponerse</u> / *to oppose* → o<u>pondr</u>-
   su<u>poner</u> / *to suppose* → su<u>pondr</u>-

3. <u>tener</u> / *to have* → <u>tendr</u>-
   con<u>tener</u> / *to contain, to hold* → con<u>tendr</u>-
   de<u>tener</u> / *to detain, to arrest* → de<u>tendr</u>-
   man<u>tener</u> / *to maintain* → man<u>tendr</u>-
   ob<u>tener</u> / *to obtain* → ob<u>tendr</u>-
   sos<u>tener</u> / *to sustain, to support* → sos<u>tendr</u>-

Future Tense of Hay

The future of hay / *there is, there are* is habrá / *there will be*. It is used in the same way that hay is used, except that it is in the future tense. The following sentences illustrate this point.

> Habrá un examen mañana. / *There will be an exam tomorrow.*
> Habrá muchas tareas mañana. / *There will be many chores tomorrow.*

The future of the idiomatic expression hay que / *one must, it is necessary to* is habrá que / *it will be necessary to*. The following sentence illustrates this usage.

> Habrá que ir a la Ciudad de Panamá mañana. / *It will be necessary to go to Panama City tomorrow.*

EXERCISE Set 11-2

A. Supply the missing future forms of the verb caber, giving the English equivalent.

EXAMPLE: él _____   =   _____

él cabrá   =   he will fit

1. (yo) _____   =   _____

2. (tú) _____   =   _____

3. (nosotros) _____   =   _____

4. (ellos) _____   =   _____

5. (vosotros) _____   =   _____

6. (Ud.) _____   =   _____

Now, supply the missing future forms of the verb salir, giving the English equivalent.

1. (yo) _____   =   _____

2. (Raquel y yo) _____   =   _____

3. (Uds.) _____   =   _____

4. (ellos) _____   =   _____

5. (vosotros) _____   =   _____

6. (tú) _____   =   _____

Now, supply the missing future forms of the verb decir (i, i), giving the English equivalent.

1. (yo) _____   =   _____

2. (tú) _____   =   _____

3. (nosotros) _____   =   _____

4. (ellos) _____   =   _____

5. (vosotros) _____   =   _____

6. (Ud.) _____   =   _____

Now, supply the missing future forms of the auxiliary verb **haber**, giving the English equivalent.

1. (yo) _____ = _____

2. (tú) _____ = _____

3. (nosotros) _____ = _____

4. (ellos) _____ = _____

5. (vosotros) _____ = _____

6. (Ud.) _____ = _____

Now, supply the missing future forms of the verb **poder**, giving the English equivalent.

1. (yo) _____ = _____

2. (tú) _____ = _____

3. (nosotros) _____ = _____

4. (ellos) _____ = _____

5. (vosotros) _____ = _____

6. (Ud.) _____ = _____

Now, supply the missing future forms of the verb **venir**, giving the English equivalent.

1. (yo) _____ = _____

2. (tú) _____ = _____

3. (nosotros) _____ = _____

4. (ellos) _____ = _____

5. (vosotros) _____ = _____

6. (Ud.) _____ = _____

Now, supply the missing future forms of the verb **saber**, giving the English equivalent.

1. (yo) _____ = _____

2. (tú) _____ = _____

3. (nosotros) _____ = _____

4. (ellos) _____ = _____

5. (vosotros) _____ = _____

6. (Ud.) _____ = _____

Now, supply the missing future forms of the verb **poner**, giving the English equivalent.

1. (yo) _____ = _____

2. (tú) _____ = _____

3. (nosotros) _____ = _____

4. (ellos) _____ = _____

5. (vosotros) _____ = _____

6. (Ud.) _____ = _____

B. How do you say the following sentences in Spanish?

1. When will Elena arrive?

_____

2. It will be six o'clock soon.

_____

3. There will be many people there.

_____

4. They will have to be here.

_____

5. You (fam. sg.) will leave tomorrow.

_____

6. We will come at 11 A.M.

_____

7. Cristina will know the answer.

_____

8. My parents will want to see the photos of Panama.

_____

9. The *balboa*[1] will be worth more in the future.

_____

10. You (pol. pl.) will place the books on the table.

_____

11. It will be cold in December.

_____

12. They will go to *Isla Contadora*[2].

_____

13. It will be cloudy tomorrow.

_____

14. I will tell the truth.

_____

[1]Unit of money in Panama, though the U.S. dollar is commonly used. *Balboa* = Vasco Núñez de Balboa, Spanish explorer, 1475–1517.
[2]Best known of the Pearl Islands, about fifty miles off Panama's coast.

EXERCISE Set 11-3

A. Match the two columns logically.

1. ¿Qué tiempo …?	a. haré
2. (Yo) … un viaje a Panamá.	b. conjugarás
3. ¿Qué hora …?	c. diremos
4. ¿… los verbos mañana?	d. cantará
5. (Tú) … a casa más tarde.	e. será
6. (Nosotros) … la verdad.	f. hará
7. Ud. … esa canción.	g. vendrán
8. Ellos … tarde.	h. irás

B. How do you say the following sentences in Spanish?

1. I wonder where he will be?

_____

2. It will be necessary to conjugate more verbs.

_____

3. They will leave tomorrow.

_____

4. I will have to work in the evening.

_____

5. You (fam. sg.) will want to see the latest film.

_____

6. There will be many students in this class.

_____

7. We will tell her the truth.

_____

8. You (pol. pl.) will have to buy more food.

_____

9. I wonder what day it is.

_____

10. I will go to Pablo's house.

_____

C. Provide the corresponding future forms for the following verbs in the present indicative tense.

1. llegan _____

2. rompo _____

3. cubres _____

4. es _____

5. están _____

6. va _____

7. tengo _____

8. hay _____

9. sé _____

10. conozco _____

11. podemos _____

12. quiere _____

13. hace _____

14. digo _____

15. vale _____

16. salgo _____

17. venimos _____

18. te vistes _____

Crossword Puzzle 11

Fill in the blanks. All of the clues both vertical and horizontal require that you use the appropriate future form.

Horizontales
 3. Juanita y yo . . . (venir) mañana.
 6. . . . (haber) muchas personas en casa.
 7. . . . (hacer) calor mañana.
 9. . . . (ser) las ocho.
10. Elena . . . (ir) a la fiesta.

Verticales
 1. Ellos . . . (beber) café.
 2. Ud. . . . (poder) hacer la tarea.
 4. Ellos . . . (estar) aquí.
 5. Él . . . (saber) la verdad.
 8. (Yo) te lo . . . (decir) mañana.

12

The Future Perfect
(*el futuro perfecto*)

Uses and Features

The future perfect is used to refer to an action that occurred before another simple future action (Chapter 11):

> **Cuando habré comido la cena, iré al cine.** / *When I will have eaten, I will go to the movies.*

And, like the simple future, it can be used to convey probability.

> **Habrá habido un accidente.** / *There must have been an accident.*
> **Él habrá mentido en la corte.** / *He must have lied in court.*

The Conjugation of the Future Perfect Tense

The future perfect, called the **futuro perfecto** in Spanish, is a compound tense. Therefore, it is conjugated with the auxiliary verb **haber** / *to have*, and the past participle of the verb, in that order. See Chapter 9 for the relevant details regarding past participles.

To form the future perfect tense of regular verbs, this is what you have to do:

1. Use the future tense of the auxiliary verb **haber** / *to have* which we provide here. Remember that **haber** is an auxiliary verb. It does not mean *to have* in the sense of *to possess*. To indicate that you have or possess something, you must use the verb **tener** / *to have, to possess*.

haber / *to have*

Subject Pronoun	Verb Form	Meaning
(yo)	habr+é	*I will have*
(tú)	habr+ás	*you (fam. sg.) will have*
(él, ella, Ud.)	habr+á	*he, she, you (pol. sg.) will have*
(nosotros/-as)	habr+emos	*we will have*
(vosotros/-as)	habr+éis	*you (fam. pl.) will have*
(ellos/-as, Uds.)	habr+án	*they, you (pol. pl.) will have*

2. The combination of the future tense of the auxiliary verb **haber** / *to have* and the past participle of a verb produces the following results:

hablar / to talk

Subject Pronoun	Haber	Past Participle	Meaning
(yo)	habr+é	habl+ado	*I will have spoken*
(tú)	habr+ás	habl+ado	*you (fam. sg.) will have spoken*
(él, ella, Ud.)	habr+á	habl+ado	*he, she, you (pol. sg.) will have spoken*
(nosotros/-as)	habr+emos	habl+ado	*we will have spoken*
(vosotros/-as)	habr+éis	habl+ado	*you (fam. pl.) will have spoken*
(ellos/-as, Uds.)	habr+án	habl+ado	*they, you (pol. pl.) will have spoken*

comer / to eat

Subject Pronoun	Haber	Past Participle	Meaning
(yo)	habr+é	com+ido	*I will have eaten*
(tú)	habr+ás	com+ido	*you (fam. sg.) will have eaten*
(él, ella, Ud.)	habr+á	com+ido	*he, she, you (pol. sg.) will have eaten*
(nosotros/-as)	habr+emos	com+ido	*we will have eaten*
(vosotros/-as)	habr+éis	com+ido	*you (fam. pl.) will have eaten*
(ellos/-as, Uds.)	habr+án	com+ido	*they, you (pol. pl.) will have eaten*

vivir / to live

Subject Pronoun	Haber	Past Participle	Meaning
(yo)	habr+é	viv+ido	*I will have lived*
(tú)	habr+ás	viv+ido	*you (fam. sg.) will have lived*
(él, ella, Ud.)	habr+á	viv+ido	*he, she, you (pol. sg.) will have lived*
(nosotros/-as)	habr+emos	viv+ido	*we will have lived*
(vosotros/-as)	habr+éis	viv+ido	*you (fam. pl.) will have lived*
(ellos/-as, Uds.)	habr+án	viv+ido	*they, you (pol. pl.) will have lived*

The Future Perfect of Reflexive Verbs

Reflexive verbs always use reflexive pronouns in the future perfect tense, as shown below. They always appear immediately before the conjugated verb, as they do in the present and all other tenses.

lavarse / *to wash oneself*

Subject Pronoun	Reflexive Pronoun	Haber	Past Participle	Meaning
(yo)	me	habr+é	lav+ado	*I will have washed myself*
(tú)	te	habr+ás	lav+ado	*you (fam. sg.) will have washed yourself*
(él, ella, Ud.)	se	habr+á	lav+ado	*he, she, you (pol. sg.) will have washed himself/herself/yourself*
(nosotros/-as)	nos	habr+emos	lav+ado	*we will have washed ourselves*
(vosotros/-as)	os	habr+éis	lav+ado	*you (fam. pl.) will have washed yourselves*
(ellos/-as, Uds.)	se	habr+án	lav+ado	*they, you (pol. pl.) will have washed themselves/yourselves*

The Future Perfect of Hay

The future perfect form of hay / *there is, there are* is habrá habido / *there will have been*. The following examples illustrate this usage.

> Habrá habido una tormenta para mañana. / *There will have been a storm by tomorrow.*
> Habrá habido muchas tormentas. / *There will have been many storms.*

The future perfect of the idiomatic expression hay que / *one must, it is necessary to* is habrá habido que / *it will have been necessary to*. The following sentence illustrates this usage.

> Habrá habido que ir a San José. / *It will have been necessary to go to San Jose.*

VOCABULARY TIP

The future perfect is often used with words and expressions such as:

> cuando / *when*
> ya / *already*

EXERCISE Set 12-1

A. Supply the missing future forms of the verb **trabajar**, giving the English equivalent.

EXAMPLE: *él* _____   =   _____

             él habrá trabajado =   *he will have worked*

1. (yo) _____   =   _____

2. (tú) _____   =   _____

3. (nosotros) _____ =   _____

4. (ellos) _____   =   _____

5. (vosotros) _____ =   _____

6. (Ud.) _____   =   _____

Now, supply the missing future perfect forms of the verb **creer**, giving the English equivalent.

1. (yo) _____   =   _____

2. (Raquel y yo) _____ =   _____

3. (Uds.) _____   =   _____

4. (ellos) _____   =   _____

5. (vosotros) _____   =   _____

6. (tú) _____   =   _____

Now, supply the missing future perfect forms of the verb **decidir**, giving the English equivalent.

1. (yo) _____   =   _____

2. (tú) _____   =   _____

3. (nosotros) _____ =   _____

4. (ellos) _____   =   _____

5. (vosotros) _____ =   _____

6. (Ud.) _____   =   _____

Now, supply the missing future perfect forms of the verb **afeitarse**, giving the English equivalent.

1. (yo) _____   =   _____

2. (tú) _____   =   _____

3. (nosotros) _____ =   _____

4. (ellos) _____   =   _____

5. (vosotros) _____ =   _____

6. (Ud.) _____   =   _____

Now, supply the missing future perfect forms of the verb **ser**, giving the English equivalent.

1. (yo) _____   =   _____

2. (tú) _____   =   _____

3. (nosotros) _____ =   _____

4. (ellos) _____   =   _____

5. (vosotros) _____ =   _____

6. (Ud.) _____   =   _____

Now, supply the missing future perfect forms of the verb **estar**, giving the English equivalent.

1. (yo) _____   =   _____

2. (tú) _____   =   _____

3. (nosotros) _____ =   _____

4. (ellos) _____   =   _____

5. (vosotros) _____ =   _____

6. (Ud.) _____   =   _____

Now, supply the missing future perfect forms of the verb **hacer**, giving the English equivalent.

1. (yo) _____   =   _____

2. (tú) _____   =   _____

3. (nosotros) _____ =   _____

4. (ellos) _____   =   _____

5. (vosotros) _____   =   _____

6. (Ud.) _____   =   _____

B. How do you say the following sentences in Spanish?

1. When they will have married, they will live in San José.

   _____

2. When you (pol. pl.) will have graduated, where will you work?

   _____

3. When I will have learned many Spanish verbs, I will be able to speak Spanish.

   _____

4. They will have arrived tomorrow morning.

   _____

5. He will have read the book by tomorrow.

   _____

C. Provide the corresponding future and future perfect forms for the following verbs in the present indicative tense.

1. veo   _____   _____

2. cubres   _____   _____

3. abren   _____   _____

4. son   _____   _____

5. estoy   _____   _____

6. digo   _____   _____

7. vendemos   _____   _____

8. escribimos   _____   _____

9. te bañas   _____   _____

10. tenéis _____   _____

11. piden _____   _____

12. volvemos _____   _____

13. hace _____   _____

14. tienen _____   _____

15. cierras _____   _____

16. muere _____   _____

17. pongo _____   _____

18. hay _____   _____

Crossword Puzzle 12

Fill in the blanks. All of the clues both vertical and horizontal require that you use the appropriate past participle form. Supply the appropriate auxiliary verb in the future tense.

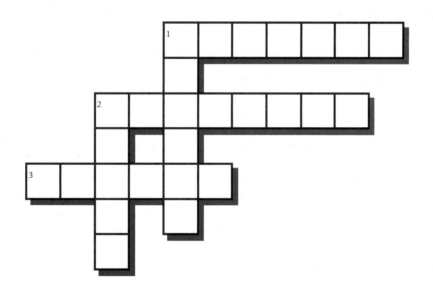

Horizontales
1. (Vosotros) . . . vuelto.
2. (Nosotros) . . . estudiado mucho.
3. (Tú) . . . dicho la verdad.

Verticales
1. Ellos . . . sido buenos.
2. (Yo) . . . estado en casa.

13
The Conditional
(*el potencial simple*)

Uses and Features

The conditional is used most of the time as follows:

1. To express a conditional, potential, or hypothetical action:
   Yo iría al teatro pero no tengo el tiempo. / *I would go to the theater but I don't have the time.*

2. To convey courtesy or politeness:
   ¿Me podría Ud. ayudar? / *Could you help me?*
   ¿Qué querría Ud.? / *What would you like?*

3. To express an indirect quotation:
   María dijo que vendría mañana. / *María said that she would be coming tomorrow.*

4. To express probability:
   Serían las diez de la noche. / *It was probably 10 P.M.*

Regular Verbs

The conditional of regular verbs, called the **potencial simple** in Spanish, is formed in a similar manner to the future tense (Chapter 11).

1. Use the entire infinitive as the stem: <u>hablar</u> / *to speak*, <u>comer</u> / *to eat*, and <u>vivir</u> / *to live*.

2. Add the following endings to the stem. Note that there is a single set of endings for the conditional tense:

(yo)	-ía
(tú)	-ías
(él, ella, Ud.)	-ía
(nosotros/-as)	-íamos
(vosotros/-as)	-íais
(ellos/-as, Uds.)	-ían

3. Here's the result:

hablar / *to speak*

Subject Pronoun	Verb Form	Meaning
(yo)	hablar+ía	*I would speak*
(tú)	hablar+ías	*you (fam. sg.) would speak*
(él, ella, Ud.)	hablar+ía	*he, she, you (pol. sg.) would speak*
(nosotros/-as)	hablar+íamos	*we would speak*
(vosotros/-as)	hablar+íais	*you (fam. pl.) would speak*
(ellos/-as, Uds.)	hablar+ían	*they, you (pol. pl.) would speak*

comer / *to eat*

Subject Pronoun	Verb Form	Meaning
(yo)	comer+ía	*I would eat*
(tú)	comer+ías	*you (fam. sg.) would eat*
(él, ella, Ud.)	comer+ía	*he, she, you (pol. sg.) would eat*
(nosotros/-as)	comer+íamos	*we would eat*
(vosotros/-as)	comer+íais	*you (fam. pl.) would eat*
(ellos/-as, Uds.)	comer+ían	*they, you (pol. pl.) would eat*

vivir / *to live*

Subject Pronoun	Verb Form	Meaning
(yo)	vivir+ía	*I would live*
(tú)	vivir+ías	*you (fam. sg.) would live*
(él, ella, Ud.)	vivir+ía	*he, she, you (pol. sg.) would live*
(nosotros/-as)	vivir+íamos	*we would live*
(vosotros/-as)	vivir+íais	*you (fam. pl.) would live*
(ellos/-as, Uds.)	vivir+ían	*they, you (pol. pl.) would live*

The Conditional Tense of Reflexive Verbs

Reflexive verbs always use reflexive pronouns in the conditional, as shown below. They always appear immediately before the conjugated verb, as they do in the present and all other tenses.

lavarse / *to wash oneself*

Subject Pronoun	Reflexive Pronoun	Conjugated Verb	Meaning
(yo)	me	lavar+ía	*I would wash myself*
(tú)	te	lavar+ías	*you (fam. sg.) would wash yourself*
(él, ella, Ud.)	se	lavar+ía	*he, she, you (pol. sg.) would wash herself/yourself*
(nosotros/-as)	nos	lavar+íamos	*we would wash ourselves*
(vosotros/-as)	os	lavar+íais	*you (fam. pl.) would wash yourselves*
(ellos/-as, Uds.)	se	lavar+ían	*they/you (pol. pl.) would wash themselves/yourselves*

> **TIP**
>
> While there are no stem changes in the conditional tense, there are, however, twelve verbs that have irregular stems. You will learn these forms in the next section. These irregular stems are exactly the same as those for the future tense (Chapter 11).

> **NOTE**
>
> You have probably noticed that the first person singular (yo) and third person singular (él, ella, Ud.) are identical in form in the conditional tense. For this reason, you must normally use the subject pronoun yo / I to distinguish these forms in the conditional.

> **TIP**
>
> Notice that the conditional is rendered in English generally by the following two translations:
>
> Alfonso llegaría ... = *Alfonso would arrive ...*
> = *Alfonso would be arriving ...*

EXERCISE Set 13-1

A. Supply the missing conditional forms of the verb **entrar**, giving the English equivalent.

EXAMPLE: *él* _____ = _____

él entraría = *he would enter*

1. (yo) _____ = _____

2. (tú) _____ = _____

3. (nosotros) _____ = _____

4. (ellos) _____ = _____

5. (vosotros) _____ = _____

6. (Ud.) _____ = _____

Now, supply the missing conditional forms of the verb **temer**, giving the English equivalent.

1. (yo) _____ = _____

2. (Raquel y yo) _____ = _____

3. (Uds.) _____ = _____

4. (ellos) _____ = _____

5. (vosotros) _____ = _____

6. (tú) _____ = _____

Now, supply the missing conditional forms of the verb **descubrir**, giving the English equivalent.

1. (yo) _____ = _____

2. (tú) _____ = _____

3. (nosotros) _____ = _____

4. (ellos) _____ = _____

5. (vosotros) _____ = _____

6. (Ud.) _____ = _____

Now, supply the missing conditional forms of the verb **casarse (con)**, giving the English equivalent.

1. (yo) _____ = _____

2. (tú) _____ = _____

3. (nosotros) _____ = _____

4. (ellos) _____ = _____

5. (vosotros) _____ = _____

6. (Ud.) _____ = _____

VOCABULARY TIP

The conditional is often followed by the conjunction **pero** / *but*.

Concepción estudiaría, pero no tiene su libro. / *Concepción would study but she doesn't have her book.*

B. How do you say the following sentences in Spanish?

1. I would speak Spanish more, but I must study the verbs.

_____

2. Would you (fam. sg.) go, please?

_____

3. They would pay for the coffee, but they have no money.

_____

4. Where would you (fam. sg.) find an open store at this hour?

_____

5. Who would see it?

_____

6. They would go to the _Reserva Natural Volcán Mombacho_[1].

_____

7. I would go shopping, but I don't have money.

_____

8. Would you (fam. sg.) give me that newspaper?

_____

9. Would he marry Carmen?

_____

10. I would like to learn more Spanish verbs.

_____

[1]Government-protected natural reserve with a volcano that was last active in 1570; biodiversity area.

Irregular Verbs

There are twelve irregular verbs in the conditional tense. What makes these verbs irregular is the fact that they have an irregular stem. As we said before, there is a single set of endings for the conditional tense. Also, you will be pleased to know that the verbs with irregular stems in the conditional tense are the same as for those in the future tense (see Chapter 11), so you will not have to learn new forms. You will simply add the single set of conditional endings to these forms. We repeat the three groups of irregular conditional stems for your convenience.

Irregular Conditional Stems: Pattern 1

Learn the irregular conditional stem to which you add the conditional tense endings. In this group, you take the infinitive and you delete the vowel in the infinitive ending: -er → -r-. We list them below.

> **caber** / _to fit, to be contained_ → **cabr-**
> **haber** / _to have (auxiliary verb)_ → **habr-**
> **poder** / _can, to be able_ → **podr-**
> **querer** / _to want_ → **querr-**
> **saber** / _to know, to know how_ → **sabr-**

Irregular Conditional Stems: Pattern 2

Learn the irregular conditional stem to which you add the conditional tense endings. In this group, you take the infinitive and you delete the vowel in the infinitive ending. Then you insert the consonant -d-: -er → -dr-. We list them below.

> **poner** / *to put, to place* → **pondr-**
> **salir** / *to leave* → **saldr-**
> **tener** / *to have* → **tendr-**
> **valer** / *to be worth* → **valdr-**
> **venir** / *to come* → **vendr-**

Irregular Conditional Stems: Pattern 3

Learn the irregular conditional stem to which you add the conditional tense endings. In this group, a completely different stem is used. We list them below:

> **decir** / *to say, to tell* → **dir-**
> **hacer** / *to do, to make* → **har-**

To each of these irregular stems, you add the conditional tense endings that we reproduce here:

(yo)	-ía
(tú)	-ías
(él, ella, Ud.)	-ía
(nosotros/-as)	-íamos
(vosotros/-as)	-íais
(ellos/-as, Uds.)	-ían

We now provide one conjugation from each of the three categories we just saw.

saber/ *to know*

Subject Pronoun	Verb Form	Meaning
(yo)	sabr+ía	*I would know*
(tú)	sabr+ías	*you (fam. sg.) would know*
(él, ella, Ud.)	sabr+ía	*he, she, you (pol. sg.) would know*
(nosotros/-as)	sabr+íamos	*we would know*
(vosotros/-as)	sabr+íais	*you (fam. pl.) would know*
(ellos/-as, Uds.)	sabr+ían	*they, you (pol. pl.) would know*

salir / *to leave*

Subject Pronoun	Verb Form	Meaning
(yo)	saldr+ía	*I would leave*
(tú)	saldr+ías	*you (fam. sg.) would leave*
(él, ella, Ud.)	saldr+ía	*he, she, you (pol. sg.) would leave*
(nosotros/-as)	saldr+íamos	*we would leave*
(vosotros/-as)	saldr+íais	*you (fam. pl.) would leave*
(ellos/-as, Uds.)	saldr+ían	*they, you (pol. pl.) would leave*

decir / *to say, to tell*

Subject Pronoun	Verb Form	Meaning
(yo)	<u>dir</u>+ía	*I would say/tell*
(tú)	<u>dir</u>+ías	*you (fam. sg.) would say/tell*
(él, ella, Ud.)	<u>dir</u>+ía	*he, she, you (pol. sg.) would say/tell*
(nosotros/-as)	<u>dir</u>+íamos	*we would say/tell*
(vosotros/-as)	<u>dir</u>+íais	*you (fam. pl.) would say/tell*
(ellos/-as, Uds.)	<u>dir</u>+ían	*they, you (pol. pl.) would say/tell*

Conditional of Hay

The conditional of **hay** / *there is, there are* is **habría** / *there would be*. It is used in the same way that **hay** is used, except that it is in the conditional tense. The following sentences illustrate this point.

> **Habría más dinero pero no tuve empleo entonces.** / *There would be more money but I had no job then.*
> **Habría más muebles pero no tuvimos el dinero.** / *There would be more furniture but we didn't have the money.*

The conditional of the idiomatic expression **hay que** / *one must, it is necessary to* is **habría que** / *it would be necessary to*. The following sentence illustrates this usage.

> **Habría que ir a Managua.** / *It would be necessary to go to Managua.*

EXERCISE Set 13-2

A. Supply the missing conditional forms of the verb **querer (ie)**, giving the English equivalent.

EXAMPLE: *él* _____   =   _____

               él querría   =   *he would want*

1. (yo) _____   =   _____

2. (tú) _____   =   _____

3. (nosotros) _____   =   _____

4. (ellos) _____   =   _____

5. (vosotros) _____   =   _____

6. (Ud.) _____   =   _____

Now, supply the missing conditional forms of the verb **caber**, giving the English equivalent.

1. (yo) _____ = _____

2. (Raquel y yo) _____ = _____

3. (Uds.) _____ = _____

4. (ellos) _____ = _____

5. (vosotros) _____ = _____

6. (tú) _____ = _____

Now, supply the missing conditional forms of the verb **hacer**, giving the English equivalent.

1. (yo) _____ = _____

2. (tú) _____ = _____

3. (nosotros) _____ = _____

4. (ellos) _____ = _____

5. (vosotros) _____ = _____

6. (Ud.) _____ = _____

Now, supply the missing conditional forms of the verb **haber**, giving the English equivalent.

1. (yo) _____ = _____

2. (tú) _____ = _____

3. (nosotros) _____ = _____

4. (ellos) _____ = _____

5. (vosotros) _____ = _____

6. (Ud.) _____ = _____

Now, supply the missing conditional forms of the verb **poder (ue)**, giving the English equivalent.

1. (yo) _____ = _____

2. (tú) _____ = _____

3. (nosotros) _____ = _____

4. (ellos) _____   =   _____

5. (vosotros) _____   =   _____

6. (Ud.) _____   =   _____

Now, supply the missing conditional forms of the verb **venir**, giving the English equivalent.

1. (yo) _____   =   _____

2. (tú) _____   =   _____

3. (nosotros) _____   =   _____

4. (ellos) _____   =   _____

5. (vosotros) _____   =   _____

6. (Ud.) _____   =   _____

Now, supply the missing conditional forms of the verb **tener**, giving the English equivalent.

1. (yo) _____   =   _____

2. (tú) _____   =   _____

3. (nosotros) _____   =   _____

4. (ellos) _____   =   _____

5. (vosotros) _____   =   _____

6. (Ud.) _____   =   _____

B. How do you say the following sentences in Spanish?

1. I would do the exercises, but I am very tired.

_____

2. She would be able to do that job.

_____

3. We would put the plates on the table.

_____

4. I would leave in the evening.

_____

5. You (pol. sg.) would know the answer.

_____

6. He would say that it is late.

_____

7. You (pol. pl.) would have to be here on time.

_____

8. The car would be worth 10.000 *córdobas*[1].

_____

9. Would you (fam. sg.) want to go to the theater?

_____

10. It would rain in the evening.

_____

11. You (fam. sg.) would tell the truth.

_____

12. The books would fit on the shelf.

_____

13. We would know how to conjugate the conditional tense.

_____

14. It would be necessary to get up early.

_____

[1]Unit of money in Nicaragua.

EXERCISE Set 13-3

A. How do you say the following sentences in Spanish?

1. It was probably five P.M. when Lidia arrived.

_____

2. It would be necessary to work all night.

_____

3. What would you (fam. sg.) do during a storm?

_____

4. It probably would cost a lot of money.

_____

5. I would buy another car, but I don't have the money.

_____

B. Provide the corresponding conditional forms for the following verbs in the present indicative tense.

1. van   _____

2. hago   _____

3. dices   _____

4. son   _____

5. estoy   _____

6. canta   _____

7. tienes   _____

8. hay   _____

9. sé   _____

10. encuentro _____

11. puede   _____

12. queremos _____

13. hace _____

14. cierro _____

15. vale _____

16. salen _____

17. vengo _____

18. te afeitas _____

Crossword Puzzle 13

Fill in the blanks. Supply the corresponding conditional tense form for the present tense indicative form given in the clue.

Horizontales
2. Beben
5. Cabe
7. Valen
8. Dice
9. Puede
10. Quieres

Verticales
1. Hay
3. Salimos
4. Hacéis
6. Cantas
7. Vive

14
The Conditional Perfect
(*el potencial compuesto*)

Uses and Features

The conditional perfect is used most of the time as follows:

1. To express an action that would have occurred if something else had been possible.

> **Ella habría cantado, pero tenía un dolor de garganta.** / *She would have sung, but she had a sore throat.*
> **Ellos habrían ido, pero no tenían el tiempo.** / *They would have gone, but they didn't have the time.*

2. To express what would have happened.

> **Él me dijo que él habría venido.** / *He said that he would have come.*
> **Él sabía que yo habría comprendido.** / *He knew that I would have understood.*

3. To convey probability.

> **Habría habido un accidente.** / *There had to have been an accident.*
> **Él habría mentido en la corte.** / *He had to have lied in court.*

The Conjugation of the Conditional Perfect Tense

The conditional perfect, called the **potencial compuesto** in Spanish, is a compound tense. Therefore, it is conjugated with the auxiliary verb **haber** / *to have*, and the past participle of the verb, in that order. See Chapter 9 for the relevant details regarding past participles.

To form the conditional perfect tense of regular verbs, this is what you have to do:

1. Use the conditional tense of the auxiliary verb **haber** / *to have*, which we provide here. Remember that **haber** is an auxiliary verb. It does not mean *to have* in the sense of *to possess*. To indicate that you have or possess something, you must use the verb **tener** / *to have, to possess*.

haber / *to have*

Subject Pronoun	Verb Form	Meaning
(yo)	habr+ía	*I would have*
(tú)	habr+ías	*you (fam. sg.) would have*
(él, ella, Ud.)	habr+ía	*he, she, you (pol. sg.) would have*
(nosotros/-as)	habr+íamos	*we would have*
(vosotros/-as)	habr+íais	*you (fam. pl.) would have*
(ellos/-as, Uds.)	habr+ían	*they, you (pol. pl.) would have*

The combination of the conditional tense of the auxiliary verb haber / *to have* produces the following results:

hablar / *to talk*

Subject Pronoun	Haber	Past Participle	Meaning
(yo)	habr+ía	habl+ado	*I would have spoken*
(tú)	habr+ías	habl+ado	*you (fam. sg.) would have spoken*
(él, ella, Ud.)	habr+ía	habl+ado	*he, she, you (pol. sg.) would have spoken*
(nosotros/-as)	habr+íamos	habl+ado	*we would have spoken*
(vosotros/-as)	habr+íais	habl+ado	*you (fam. pl.) would have spoken*
(ellos/-as, Uds.)	habr+ían	habl+ado	*they, you (pol. pl.) would have spoken*

comer / *to eat*

Subject Pronoun	Haber	Past Participle	Meaning
(yo)	habr+ía	com+ido	*I would have eaten*
(tú)	habr+ías	com+ido	*you (fam. sg.) would have eaten*
(él, ella, Ud.)	habr+ía	com+ido	*he, she, you (pol. sg.) would have eaten*
(nosotros/-as)	habr+íamos	com+ido	*we would have eaten*
(vosotros/-as)	habr+íais	com+ido	*you (fam. pl.) would have eaten*
(ellos/-as, Uds.)	habr+ían	com+ido	*they, you (pol. pl.) would have eaten*

vivir / *to live*

Subject Pronoun	Haber	Past Participle	Meaning
(yo)	habr+ía	viv+ido	*I would have lived*
(tú)	habr+ías	viv+ido	*you (fam. sg.) would have lived*
(él, ella, Ud.)	habr+ía	viv+ido	*he, she, you (pol. sg.) would have lived*
(nosotros/-as)	habr+íamos	viv+ido	*we would have lived*
(vosotros/-as)	habr+íais	viv+ido	*you (fam. pl.) would have lived*
(ellos/-as, Uds.)	habr+ían	viv+ido	*they, you (pol. pl.) would have lived*

The Conditional Perfect of Reflexive Verbs·

Reflexive verbs always use reflexive pronouns in the conditional perfect tense, as shown below. They always appear immediately before the conjugated verb, as they do in the present and all other tenses.

lavarse / *to wash oneself*

Subject Pronoun	Reflexive Pronoun	Haber	Past Participle	Meaning
(yo)	me	habr+ía	lav+ado	*I would have washed myself*
(tú)	te	habr+ías	lav+ado	*you (fam. sg.) would have washed yourself*
(él, ella, Ud.)	se	habr+ía	lav+ado	*he, she, you (pol. sg.) would have washed himself/herself/yourself*
(nosotros/-as)	nos	habr+íamos	lav+ado	*we would have washed ourselves*
(vosotros/-as)	os	habr+íais	lav+ado	*you (fam. pl.) would have washed yourselves*
(ellos/-as, Uds.)	se	habr+ían	lav+ado	*they, you (pol. pl.) would have washed themselves/yourselves*

NOTE

You have probably noticed that the first person singular (yo) and third person singular (él, ella, Ud.) are identical in form in the conditional perfect tense. For this reason, you must normally use the subject pronoun yo / *I* to distinguish these forms in the conditional.

TIP

Notice that the conditional perfect is rendered in English generally by the following translation:

Alfonso habría dicho …   = *Alfonso would have said …*

The Conditional Perfect of Hay

The conditional perfect form of hay / *there is, there are* is habría habido / *there would have been*. The following examples illustrate this usage.

Habría habido un problema, pero no pasó nada. / *There would have been a problem, but nothing happened.*
Habría habido muchos estudiantes allí, pero llovió. / *There would have been many students there, but it rained.*

The conditional perfect of the idiomatic expression hay que / *one must, it is necessary to* is habría habido que / *it would have been necessary to*. The following sentence illustrates this usage.

Habría habido que ir a Tegucigalpa. / *It would have been necessary to go to Tegucigalpa.*

VOCABULARY TIP

As is the case with the conditional tense (Chapter 13), the conditional perfect tense is often followed by the conjunction pero / *but*:

Julio se habría levantado temprano, pero estaba muy cansado. / *Julio would have gotten up early, but he was very tired.*

EXERCISE Set 14-1

A. Supply the missing conditional perfect forms of the verb llegar, giving the English equivalent.

EXAMPLE: *él* _____ = _____

él habría llegado = *he would have arrived*

1. (yo) _____ = _____

2. (tú) _____ = _____

3. (nosotros) _____ = _____

4. (ellos) _____ = _____

5. (vosotros) _____ = _____

6. (Ud.) _____ = _____

Now, supply the missing conditional perfect forms of the verb comprender, giving the English equivalent.

1. (yo) _____ = _____

2. (Raquel y yo) _____ = _____

3. (Uds.) _____ = _____

4. (ellos) _____ = _____

5. (vosotros) _____ = _____

6. (tú) _____ = _____

Now, supply the missing conditional perfect forms of the verb **discutir**, giving the English equivalent.

1. (yo) _____   =   _____

2. (tú) _____   =   _____

3. (nosotros) _____   =   _____

4. (ellos) _____   =   _____

5. (vosotros) _____   =   _____

6. (Ud.) _____   =   _____

Now, supply the missing conditional perfect forms of the verb **quitarse**, giving the English equivalent.

1. (yo) _____   =   _____

2. (tú) _____   =   _____

3. (nosotros) _____   =   _____

4. (ellos) _____   =   _____

5. (vosotros) _____   =   _____

6. (Ud.) _____   =   _____

Now, supply the missing conditional perfect forms of the verb **ser**, giving the English equivalent.

1. (yo) _____   =   _____

2. (tú) _____   =   _____

3. (nosotros) _____   =   _____

4. (ellos) _____   =   _____

5. (vosotros) _____   =   _____

6. (Ud.) _____   =   _____

Now, supply the missing conditional perfect forms of the verb **estar**, giving the English equivalent.

1. (yo) _____   = _____

2. (tú) _____   = _____

3. (nosotros) _____   = _____

4. (ellos) _____   = _____

5. (vosotros) _____   = _____

6. (Ud.) _____   = _____

Now, supply the missing conditional perfect forms of the verb **hacer**, giving the English equivalent.

1. (yo) _____   = _____

2. (tú) _____   = _____

3. (nosotros) _____   = _____

4. (ellos) _____   = _____

5. (vosotros) _____   = _____

6. (Ud.) _____   = _____

B. How do you say the following sentences in Spanish?

1. I would have gone to the party, but I didn't have the time.

_____

2. My parents would have gone to Honduras, but they didn't have the money.

_____

3. I would have gone with them, but I had to study.

_____

4. They would have gotten up early, but they slept late.

_____

5. He would have bought the car, but it cost too much.

_____

C. Provide the corresponding conditional and conditional perfect forms for the following verbs in the present indicative tense.

1. voy _____ _____

2. escribes _____ _____

3. dicen _____ _____

4. sois _____ _____

5. están _____ _____

6. dice _____ _____

7. comemos _____ _____

8. vivimos _____ _____

9. te lavas _____ _____

10. tengo _____ _____

11. mueren _____ _____

12. vuelvo _____ _____

13. vienes _____ _____

14. sé _____ _____

15. conozco _____ _____

16. resuelvo _____ _____

17. ponemos _____ _____

18. hay _____ _____

Crossword Puzzle 14

Fill in the blanks. All of the clues both vertical and horizontal require that you use the appropriate past participle form.

Horizontales
1. Ud. habría . . . (ser) bueno.
6. Ella lo habría . . . (hacer).
7. Mis amigos habrían . . . (ir).
8. Yo habría . . . (estar) allí.

Verticáles
2. (Vosotros) habríais . . . (decir) la verdad.
3. (Nosotros) habríamos . . . (escribir) la tarea.
4. Habría . . . (llover).
5. (Tú) habrías . . . (abrir) la puerta.

Part Four
The Subjunctive Tenses

The Subjunctive Tenses: An Overview

What Is the Subjunctive?

The subjunctive is a mood that allows you to express a point of view—fear, doubt, hope, possibility—in sum, anything that is not a fact. In a way, the subjunctive is a counterpart to the indicative, the mood that allows you to convey facts and information.

The main thing to note about the subjunctive is that it is used, primarily, in a subordinate clause. What is a subordinate clause, you might ask?

A complex sentence has at least one subordinate clause—a clause, by the way, is a group of related words that contains a subject and predicate and is part of the main sentence. The subjunctive is used, as mentioned, mainly in a subordinate clause, generally introduced by que / *that, which, who*. So, when expressing something that is a doubt, etc., with a verb in the main clause (the verb to the left of que), put the verb in the subordinate clause (the verb to the right of que) in the subjunctive:

<u>Espero</u> <u>que</u> ellos <u>hablen</u> español. / *I hope that they speak Spanish.*
   ↓   ↓
indicative   subjunctive

Subjunctive vs. Indicative

Not all verbs in subordinate clauses (those after **que**) are necessarily to be put in the subjunctive—only those connected with a main clause verb that expresses a "nonfact" (fear, supposition, anticipation, wish, hope, doubt, etc.).

Indicative	Subjunctive
<u>Sé</u> que <u>es</u> la verdad. / *I know that it is the truth.*	<u>Quiero</u> que <u>sea</u> la verdad. / *I want it to be the truth.*
<u>Es cierto</u> que él <u>paga</u>. / *It's certain that he is paying.*	<u>Es probable</u> que él <u>pague</u>. / *It's probable that he is paying.*

15

The Present Subjunctive (*el presente de subjuntivo*)

Uses and Features

The subjunctive allows you to convey a point of view, emotion, doubt, hope, possibility—anything that is not a fact or certainty.

There is a useful memory tool to help you to remember when to use the subjunctive. It is the acronym WEDDING. This acronym stands for the various situations in which the subjunctive is used.

Will
Emotion
Desire
Doubt
Impersonal expression
Negative
Generalized Characteristics

The WEDDING acronym thus covers noun clauses introduced by verbs of volition, emotion, desire, doubt, and impersonal expressions. Likewise, it covers the use of the subjunctive with negative or indefinite antecedents.

Will (verbs of volition such as **preferir (ie, i)** / *to prefer*, and so forth).

<u>Prefiero</u> que Jorge <u>llegue</u> a tiempo./ *I prefer that Jorge arrive on time.*

Emotion (verbs and verbal expressions of emotion such as **sentir (ie, i)** / *to regret*, and so forth).

<u>Siento</u> que María <u>esté</u> enferma. / *I regret that María is sick.*

Desire (verbs such as **querer (ie)** / *to want*, and so forth).

<u>Quiero</u> que Juan <u>escriba</u> la carta. / *I want John to write the letter.*

Doubt (verbs such as **dudar** / *to doubt*, and so forth).

<u>Dudo</u> que <u>llueva</u> hoy. / *I doubt that it will rain today.*

Impersonal expression (verbal expressions such as **es posible** / *it is possible*, and so forth).

<u>Es posible</u> que <u>haya</u> mucha gente allí. / *It is possible that there will be a lot of people there.*

Negative (clauses with negative antecedents such as **nadie** / *no one*, and so forth).

> No hay <u>nadie</u> que <u>pueda</u> trabajar el domingo. / *There is no one that can work on Sunday.*

Generalized characteristics (clauses with unspecified antecedents).

> ¿Hay <u>alguien</u> que <u>tenga</u> la tarea de hoy? / *Is there someone who has today's homework?*

Formation of the Present Subjunctive

To form the present subjunctive of regular verbs, called the **presente de subjuntivo** in Spanish, do the following:

1. Take the first person singular of the present indicative. You need to note that this includes all regular and irregular verbs, with the exception of six irregular verbs (see further in this chapter) and stem-changing -ir verbs. We include selective examples of each type of verb here.

> hablo / *I speak*
> como / *I eat*
> vivo / *I live*
> tengo / *I have*
> hago / *I do/make*
> salgo / *I leave*
> concluyo / *I conclude*
> caigo / *I fall*

2. Remove the -o ending:
> habl+o → habl-
> com+o → com-
> viv+o → viv-
> teng+o → teng-
> hag+o → hag-
> salg+o → salg-
> concluy+o → concluy-
> caig+o → caig-

3. Add the following endings for -ar verbs (we use suspension points […] to indicate that verbs in the subjunctive appear in subordinate clauses, and we will use this convention in the remaining chapters of this section):

. . . (yo)	-e
. . . (tú)	-es
. . . (él, ella, Ud.)	-e
. . . (nosotros/-as)	-emos
. . . (vosotros/-as)	-éis
. . . (ellos/-as, Uds.)	-en

4. Add the following endings for -er and -ir verbs:

. . . (yo)	-a
. . . (tú)	-as
. . . (él, ella, Ud.)	-a
. . . (nosotros/-as)	-amos
. . . (vosotros/-as)	-áis
. . . (ellos/-as, Uds.)	-an

5. Here's the result for the examples given above:

habl+e
com+a
viv+a
teng+a
hag+a
salg+a
concluy+a
caig+a

We now provide exemplary and complete conjugations of the verb types used above. Again, we remind you that we use suspension points (…) in all examples to indicate that the subjunctive appears in subordinate clauses.

hablar / *to speak*

Subject Pronoun	Verb Form	Meaning
…(yo)	habl+e	…*I speak, I am speaking, I may speak*
…(tú)	habl+es	…*you (fam. sg.) speak, you are speaking, you may speak*
…(él, ella, Ud.)	habl+e	…*he, she, you (pol. sg.) speak(s), he, she, you is/are speaking, he, she, you may speak*
…(nosotros/-as)	habl+emos	…*we speak, we are speaking, we may speak*
…(vosotros/-as)	habl+éis	…*you (fam. pl.) speak, you are speaking, you may speak*
…(ellos/-as, Uds.)	habl+en	…*they, you (pol. pl.) speak, they, you are speaking, they, you may speak*

comer / *to eat*

Subject Pronoun	Verb Form	Meaning
…(yo)	com+a	…*I eat, I am eating, I may eat*
…(tú)	com+as	…*you (fam. sg.) eat, you are eating, you may eat*
…(él, ella, Ud.)	com+a	…*he, she, you (pol. sg.) eat(s), he, she, you is/are eating, he, she, you may eat*
…(nosotros/-as)	com+amos	…*we eat, we are eating, we may eat*
…(vosotros/-as)	com+áis	…*you (fam. pl.) eat, you are eating, you may eat*
…(ellos/-as, Uds.)	com+an	…*they, you (pol. pl.) eat, they, you are eating, they, you may eat*

vivir / *to live*

Subject Pronoun	Verb Form	Meaning
...(yo)	<u>viv</u>+a	...I live, I am living, I may live
...(tú)	<u>viv</u>+as	...you (fam. sg.) live, you are living, you may live
...(él, ella, Ud.)	<u>viv</u>+a	...he, she, you (pol. sg.) live(s), he, she, you is/are living, he, she, you may live
...(nosotros/-as)	<u>viv</u>+amos	...we live, we are living, we may live
...(vosotros/-as)	<u>viv</u>+áis	...you (fam. pl.) live, you are living, you may live
...(ellos/-as, Uds.)	<u>viv</u>+an	...they, you (pol. pl.) live, they, you are living, they, you may live

tener / *to have*

Subject Pronoun	Verb Form	Meaning
...(yo)	<u>teng</u>+a	...I have, I am having, I may have
...(tú)	<u>teng</u>+as	...you (fam. sg.) have, you are having, you may have
...(él, ella, Ud.)	<u>teng</u>+a	... he, she, you (pol. sg.) has/have, he, she, you is/are having, he, she, you may have
...(nosotros/-as)	<u>teng</u>+amos	...we have, we are having, we may have
...(vosotros/-as)	<u>teng</u>+áis	...you (fam. pl.) have, you are having, you may have
...(ellos/-as, Uds.)	<u>teng</u>+an	...they, you (pol. pl.) have, they, you are having, they, you may have

hacer / *to do, to make*

Subject Pronoun	Verb Form	Meaning
...(yo)	<u>hag</u>+a	...I do/make, I am doing/making, I may do/make
...(tú)	<u>hag</u>+as	...you (fam. sg.) do/make, you are doing/making, you may do/make
...(él, ella, Ud.)	<u>hag</u>+a	...he, she, you (pol. sg.) does/do, makes/make, he, she, you is/are doing/making, he, she, you may do/make
...(nosotros/-as)	<u>hag</u>+amos	...we do/make, we are doing/making, we may do/make
...(vosotros/-as)	<u>hag</u>+áis	...you (fam. pl.) do/make, you are doing/making, you may do/make
...(ellos/-as, Uds.)	<u>hag</u>+an	...they, you (pol. pl.) do/make, they, you are doing/making, they, you may do/make

salir / *to leave*

Subject Pronoun	Verb Form	Meaning
...(yo)	<u>salg</u>+a	...*I leave, I am leaving, I may leave*
...(tú)	<u>salg</u>+as	...*you (fam. sg.) leave, you are leaving, you may leave*
...(él, ella, Ud.)	<u>salg</u>+a	...*he, she, you (pol. sg.) leave(s), he, she, you is/are leaving, he, she, you may leave*
...(nosotros/-as)	<u>salg</u>+amos	...*we leave, we are leaving, we may leave*
...(vosotros/-as)	<u>salg</u>+áis	...*you (fam. pl.) leave, you are leaving, you may leave*
...(ellos/-as, Uds.)	<u>salg</u>+an	... *they, you (pol. pl.) leave, they, you are leaving, they, you may leave*

concluir / *to conclude*

Subject Pronoun	Verb Form	Meaning
...(yo)	<u>concluy</u>+a	...*I conclude, I am concluding, I may conclude*
...(tú)	<u>concluy</u>+as	...*you (fam. sg.) conclude, you are concluding, you may conclude*
...(él, ella, Ud.)	<u>concluy</u>+a	...*he, she, you (pol. sg.) conclude(s), he, she, you is/are concluding, he, she, you may conclude*
...(nosotros/-as)	<u>concluy</u>+amos	...*we conclude, we are concluding, we may conclude*
...(vosotros/-as)	<u>concluy</u>+áis	...*you (fam. pl.) conclude, you are concluding, you may conclude*
...(ellos/-as, Uds.)	<u>concluy</u>+an	...*they, you (pol. pl.) conclude, they, you are concluding, they, you may conclude*

caer / *to fall*

Subject Pronoun	Verb Form	Meaning
...(yo)	<u>caig</u>+a	...*I fall, I am falling, I may fall*
...(tú)	<u>caig</u>+as	...*you (fam. sg.) fall, you are falling, you may fall*
...(él, ella, Ud.)	<u>caig</u>+a	...*he, she, you (pol. sg.) fall(s), he, she, you is/are fallling, he, she, you may fall*
...(nosotros/-as)	<u>caig</u>+amos	...*we fall, we are falling, we may fall*
...(vosotros/-as)	<u>caig</u>+áis	...*you (fam. pl.) fall, you are falling, you may fall*
...(ellos/-as, Uds.)	<u>caig</u>+an	...*they, you (pol. pl.) fall, they, you are falling, they, you may fall*

NOTE

The English translation of the present subjunctive is often the same as the English translation of the present indicative. In English, the subjunctive has virtually disappeared from everyday usage. It is used rarely in such expressions as "*If he be*" and "*I prefer that he be here.*" Nevertheless, it remains a viable form in Spanish even though its English translation does not reflect this grammatical fact.

The Present Subjunctive of Reflexive Verbs

Reflexive verbs always use reflexive pronouns in the present subjunctive, as shown below. They always appear immediately before the conjugated verb, as they do in all other tenses.

lavarse / to wash oneself

Subject Pronoun	Reflexive Pronoun	Conjugated Verb	Meaning
...(yo)	me	lav+e	...I wash myself, I am washing myself, I may wash myself
...(tú)	te	lav+es	...you (fam. sg.) wash yourself, you are washing yourself, you may wash yourself
...(él, ella, Ud.)	se	lav+e	...he, she, you (pol. sg.) wash(es) himself, herself, yourself, he, she, you does/do wash himself/herself/yourself, he, she, you may wash himself/herself/yourself
...(nosotros/-as)	nos	lav+emos	...we wash ourselves, we are washing ourselves, we may wash ourselves
...(vosotros/-as)	os	lav+éis	...you (fam. pl.) wash yourselves, you are washing yourselves, you may wash yourselves
...(ellos/-as, Uds.)	se	lav+en	...they, you (pol. pl.) wash themselves/yourselves, they, you are washing themselves/yourselves, they, you may wash themselves/yourselves

Stem-Changing Verbs

Stem-changing verbs have the same changes in the stem as they do in the present indicative (see Chapter 2 to review this pattern). We provide two selected examples (cerrar (ie) / to close and volver (ue) / to return) of this type of verb in the present subjunctive. You will note that the subjunctive endings are the same as for regularly formed subjunctive verbs.

cerrar (ie) / to close

Subject Pronoun	Verb Form	Meaning
...(yo)	cierr+e	...I close, I am closing, I may close
...(tú)	cierr+es	...you (fam. sg.) close, you are closing, you may close
...(él, ella, Ud.)	cierr+e	...he, she, you (pol. sg.) close(s), he, she, you is/are closing, he, she, you may close
...(nosotros/-as)	cerr+emos	...we close, we are closing, we may close
...(vosotros/-as)	cerr+éis	...you (fam. pl.) close, you are closing, you may close
...(ellos/-as, Uds.)	cierr+en	... they, you (pol. pl.) close, they, you are closing, they, you may close

volver (ue) (a) / *to return*

Subject Pronoun	Verb Form	Meaning
...(yo)	<u>vuelv</u>+a	...*I return, I am returning, I may return*
...(tú)	<u>vuelv</u>+as	...*you (fam. sg.) return, you are returning, you may return*
...(él, ella, Ud.)	<u>vuelv</u>+a	...*he, she, you (pol. sg.) return(s), he, she, you is/are returning, he, she, you may return*
...(nosotros/-as)	<u>volv</u>+amos	...*we return, we are returning, we may return*
...(vosotros/-as)	<u>volv</u>+áis	...*you (fam. pl.) return, you are returning, you may return*
...(ellos/-as, Uds.)	<u>vuelv</u>+an	... *they, you (pol. pl.) return, they, you are returning, they, you may return*

Stem-Changing *-ir* Verbs

Third conjugation stem-changing verbs (-ir) also have a stem change in the **nosotros/-as** / *we* and **vosotros/-as** / *you* (fam. pl.) forms. Verbs such as **medir (i, i)** / *to measure* have an -i- in these forms, and verbs such as **dormir (ue, u)** / *to sleep* have a -u- in these forms. We provide conjugations of each one below.

medir (i, i) / *to measure*

Subject Pronoun	Verb Form	Meaning
...(yo)	<u>mid</u>+a	...*I measure, I am measuring, I may measure*
...(tú)	<u>mid</u>+as	...*you (fam. sg.) measure, you are measuring, you may measure*
...(él, ella, Ud.)	<u>mid</u>+a	...*he, she, you (pol. sg.) measure(s), he, she, you is/are measuring, he, she, you may measure*
...(nosotros/-as)	<u>mid</u>+amos	...*we measure, we are measuring, we may measure*
...(vosotros/-as)	<u>mid</u>+áis	...*you (fam. pl.) measure, you are measuring, you may measure*
...(ellos/-as, Uds.)	<u>mid</u>+an	...*they, you (pol. pl.) measure, they, you are measuring, they, you may measure*

dormir (ue, u) / *to sleep*

Subject Pronoun	Verb Form	Meaning
...(yo)	<u>duerm</u>+a	...*I sleep, I am sleeping, I may sleep*
...(tú)	<u>duerm</u>+as	...*you (fam. sg.) sleep, you are sleeping, you may sleep*
...(él, ella, Ud.)	<u>duerm</u>+a	...*he, she, you (pol. sg.) sleep(s), he, she, you is/are sleeping, he, she, you may sleep*
...(nosotros/-as)	<u>durm</u>+amos	...*we sleep, we are sleeping, we may sleep*
...(vosotros/-as)	<u>durm</u>+áis	... *you (fam. pl.) sleep, you are sleeping, you may sleep*
...(ellos/-as, Uds.)	<u>duerm</u>+an	...*they, you (pol. pl.) sleep, they, you are sleeping, they, you may sleep*

> **TIP**
>
> Remember that third conjugation verbs have a parenthetical -i- or a -u- in their dictionary entry to indicate this additional change. In the case of e → i verbs, it is the second i that indicates the change in the present subjunctive.
>
>   servir (i, i) / *to serve*
>   dormir (ue, u) / *to sleep*
>
> Recall also that the second vowel in these stem-changing -ir verbs means that there is a change in the present participle (gerund; see Chapter 6) and the preterit tense (see Chapter 7).

Irregular Verbs

As noted previously, there are six verbs that are irregular in the present subjunctive. There is a useful memory aid to help you remember them. The acronym DISHES spells out the first letter of each of these irregular verbs as illustrated below:

   Dar / *to give*
   Ir / *to go*
   Ser / *to be*
   Haber / *to have*
   Estar / *to be*
   Saber / *to know*

We provide a complete conjugation of each of these verbs here:

dar / *to give*

Subject Pronoun	Verb Form	Meaning
...(yo)	d+é	...*I give, I am giving, I may give*
...(tú)	d+es	...*you (fam. sg.) give, you are giving, you may give*
...(él, ella, Ud.)	d+é	...*he, she, you (pol. sg.) give(s), he, she, you is/are giving, he, she, you may give*
...(nosotros/-as)	d+emos	...*we give, we are giving, we may give*
...(vosotros/-as)	d+eis	...*you (fam. pl.) give, you are giving, you may give*
...(ellos/-as, Uds.)	d+en	...*they, you (pol. pl.) give, they, you are giving, they, you may give*

ir / *to go*

Subject Pronoun	Verb Form	Meaning
…(yo)	<u>vay</u>+a	…*I go, I am going, I may go*
…(tú)	<u>vay</u>+as	…*you (fam. sg.) go, you are going, you may go*
…(él, ella, Ud.)	<u>vay</u>+a	…*he, she, you (pol. sg.) go(es), he, she, you is/are going, he, she, you may go*
…(nosotros/-as)	<u>vay</u>+amos	…*we go, we are going, we may go*
…(vosotros/-as)	<u>vay</u>+áis	…*you (fam. pl.) go, you are going, you may go*
…(ellos/-as, Uds.)	<u>vay</u>+an	…*they, you (pol. pl.) go, they, you are going, they, you may go*

ser / *to be*

Subject Pronoun	Verb Form	Meaning
…(yo)	<u>se</u>+a	…*I am, I may be*
…(tú)	<u>se</u>+as	…*you (fam. sg.) are, you may be*
…(él, ella, Ud.)	<u>se</u>+a	…*he, she, you (pol. sg.) is/are, he, she, you may be*
…(nosotros/-as)	<u>se</u>+amos	…*we are, we may be*
…(vosotros/-as)	<u>se</u>+áis	…*you (fam. pl.) are, you may be*
…(ellos/-as, Uds.)	<u>se</u>+an	…*they, you (pol. pl.) are, they, you may be*

haber / *to have*

Subject Pronoun	Verb Form	Meaning
…(yo)	<u>hay</u>+a	…*I have, I may have*
…(tú)	<u>hay</u>+as	…*you (fam. sg.) have, you may have*
…(él, ella, Ud.)	<u>hay</u>+a	…*he, she, you (pol. sg.) has/have, he, she, you may have*
…(nosotros/-as)	<u>hay</u>+amos	…*we have, we may have*
…(vosotros/-as)	<u>hay</u>+áis	…*you (fam. pl.) have, you may have*
…(ellos/-as, Uds.)	<u>hay</u>+an	…*they, you (pol. pl.) have, they, you may have*

estar / *to be*

Subject Pronoun	Verb Form	Meaning
…(yo)	<u>est</u>+é	…*I am, I may be*
…(tú)	<u>est</u>+és	…*you (fam. sg.) are, you may be*
…(él, ella, Ud.)	<u>est</u>+é	…*he, she, you (pol. sg.) is/are, he, she, you may be*
…(nosotros/-as)	<u>est</u>+emos	… *we are, we may be*
…(vosotros/-as)	<u>est</u>+éis	… *you (fam. pl.) are, you may be*
…(ellos/-as, Uds.)	<u>est</u>+én	…*they, you (pol. pl.) are, they, you may be*

saber / *to know*

Subject Pronoun	Verb Form	Meaning
...(yo)	<u>sep</u>+a	...*I know, I am knowing, I may know*
...(tú)	<u>sep</u>+as	...*you (fam. sg.) know, you are knowing, you may know*
...(él, ella, Ud.)	<u>sep</u>+a	...*he, she, you (pol. sg.) know(s), he, she, you is/are knowing, he, she, you may know*
...(nosotros/-as)	<u>sep</u>+amos	...*we know, we are knowing, we may know*
...(vosotros/-as)	<u>sep</u>+áis	...*you (fam. pl.) know, you are knowing, you may know*
...(ellos/-as, Uds.)	<u>sep</u>+an	...*they, you (pol. pl.) know, they, you are knowing, they, you may know*

Spelling Change in the Present Subjunctive

Certain verbs have spelling changes in the present subjunctive (see Chapter 4 and Chapter 7 for spelling changes in the present indicative and preterit tenses, respectively). These spelling changes do not affect the pronunciation; they are simply spelling conventions. We provide examples of each type and lists of verbs that follow these spelling patterns. It should be remembered that the present subjunctive endings will follow one of the two patterns noted above, namely, one set of endings for -ar verbs and another for -er and -ir verbs.

There are five types of spelling changes shown here.

1. Verbs that end in -gar, the -g- changes to -gu-.
2. Verbs that end in -car, the -c- changes to -qu-.
3. Verbs that end in -zar, the -z- changes to -c-.
4. Verbs that end in -ger or -gir, the -g- changes to -j-.
5. Verbs that end in -cer or -cir preceded by a consonant, the -c- changes to a -z-.

We will now look at a conjugation in the present subjunctive for each one of these five verb types.

Verbs Ending in -gar

Verbs that end in -gar have a spelling change to -gu- in the present subjunctive, as illustrated below.

llegar / *to arrive*

Subject Pronoun	Verb Form	Meaning
...(yo)	<u>llegu</u>+e	...*I arrive, I am arriving, I may arrive*
...(tú)	<u>llegu</u>+es	...*you (fam. sg.) arrive, you are arriving, you may arrive*
...(él, ella, Ud.)	<u>llegu</u>+e	...*he, she, you (pol. sg.) arrive(s), he, she, you is/are arriving, he, she, you may arrive*
...(nosotros/-as)	<u>llegu</u>+emos	...*we arrive, we are arriving, we may arrive*
...(vosotros/-as)	<u>llegu</u>+éis	...*you (fam. pl.) arrive, you are arriving, you may arrive*
...(ellos/-as, Uds.)	<u>llegu</u>+en	...*they, you (pol. pl.) arrive, they, you are arriving, they, you may arrive*

The following verbs have this pattern.

conjugar	*to conjugate*	regar (ie)	*to water (a plant)*
llegar	*to arrive*	tragar	*to swallow*
jugar (ue)	*to play (a game)*	vagar	*to wander*
pagar	*to pay for*		

Verbs Ending in -car

Verbs that end in -car have a spelling change to -qu- in the present subjunctive, as illustrated below.

buscar / *to look for*

Subject Pronoun	Verb Form	Meaning
...(yo)	bus*qu*+e	...*I look for, I am looking for, I may look for*
...(tú)	bus*qu*+es	...*you (fam. sg.) look for, you are looking for, you may look for*
...(él, ella, Ud.)	bus*qu*+e	...*he, she, you (pol. sg.) look(s) for, he, she, you is/are looking for, he, she, you may look for*
...(nosotros/-as)	bus*qu*+emos	...*we look for, we are looking for, we may look for*
...(vosotros/-as)	bus*qu*+éis	...*you (fam. pl.) look for, you are looking for, you may look for*
...(ellos/-as, Uds.)	bus*qu*+en	...*they, you (pol. pl.) look for, they, you are looking for, they, you may look for*

The following verbs have this pattern.

buscar	*to look for*	practicar	*to practice*
clasificar	*to classify*	sacar	*to take, to take a photo*
destacar	*to stand out*	tocar	*to touch, to play (an instrument)*
justificar	*to justify*		

Verbs Ending in -zar

Verbs that end in -zar have a spelling change to -c- in the present subjunctive, as illustrated below.

organizar / *to organize*

Subject Pronoun	Verb Form	Meaning
...(yo)	organi*c*+e	...*I organize, I am organizing, I may organize*
...(tú)	organi*c*+es	...*you (fam. sg.) organize, you are organizing, you may organize*
...(él, ella, Ud.)	organi*c*+e	...*he, she, you (pol. sg.) organize(s), he, she, you is/are organizing, he, she, you may organize*
...(nosotros/-as)	organi*c*+emos	...*we organize, we are organizing, we may organize*
...(vosotros/-as)	organi*c*+éis	...*you (fam. pl.) organize, you are organizing, you may organize*
...(ellos/-as, Uds.)	organi*c*+en	...*they, you (pol. pl.) organize, they, you are organizing, they, you may organize*

The following verbs have this pattern.

autorizar	to authorize	rezar	to pray
comenzar (ie) (a)	to begin	trazar	to trace
empezar (ie) (a)	to begin	tropezar (ie) (con)	to stumble (into)

Verbs Ending in -ger and -gir

Verbs that end in -ger and -gir have a spelling change to -j- in the present subjunctive, as illustrated below.

proteger / to protect

Subject Pronoun	Verb Form	Meaning
...(yo)	protej+a	...I protect, I am protecting, I may protect
...(tú)	protej+as	...you (fam. sg.) protect, you are protecting, you may protect
...(él, ella, Ud.)	protej+a	...he, she, you (pol. sg.) protect(s), he, she, you is/are protecting, he, she, you may protect
...(nosotros/-as)	protej+amos	...we protect, we are protecting, we may protect
...(vosotros/-as)	protej+áis	...you (fam. pl.) protect, you are protecting, you may protect
...(ellos/-as, Uds.)	protej+an	...they, you (pol. pl.) protect, they, you are protecting, they, you may protect

corregir (i, i) / to correct

Subject Pronoun	Verb Form	Meaning
...(yo)	corrij+a	...I correct, I am correcting, I may correct
...(tú)	corrij+as	...you (fam. sg.) correct, you are correcting, you may correct
...(él, ella, Ud.)	corrij+a	...he, she, you (pol. sg.) correct(s), he, she, you is/are correcting, he, she, you may correct
...(nosotros/-as)	corrij+amos	...we correct, we are correcting, we may correct
...(vosotros/-as)	corrij+áis	...you (fam. pl.) correct, you are correcting, you may correct
...(ellos/-as, Uds.)	corrij+an	...they, you (pol. pl.) correct, they, you are correcting, they, you may correct

The following verbs have this pattern.

coger	to grasp, to seize	fingir	to pretend
corregir (i, i)	to correct	proteger	to protect
dirigir	to direct	regir (i, i)	to rule
elegir (i, i)	to elect, to choose	recoger	to pick up
escoger	to select	surgir	to surge, to spur
exigir (i, i)	to demand, to require		

Verbs Ending in -cer or -cir Preceded by a Consonant

Certain verbs that end in -cer or -cir that are preceded by a consonant have a spelling change to -z- in the present subjunctive, as illustrated below.

convencer / *to convince*

Subject Pronoun	Verb Form	Meaning
...(yo)	convenz+a	...I convince, I am convincing, I may convince
...(tú)	convenz+as	...you (fam. sg.) convince, you are convincing, you may convince
...(él, ella, Ud.)	convenz+a	...he, she, you (pol. sg.) convince(s), he, she, you is/are convincing, he, she, you may convince
...(nosotros/-as)	convenz+amos	...we convince, we are convincing, we may convince
...(vosotros/-as)	convenz+áis	...you (fam. pl.) convince, you are convincing, you may convince
...(ellos/-as, Uds.)	convenz+an	...they, you (pol. pl.) convince, they, you are convincing, they, you may convince

zurcir / *to mend, to darn*

Subject Pronoun	Verb Form	Meaning
...(yo)	zurz+a	...I mend/darn, I am mending/darning, I may mend/darn
...(tú)	zurz+as	...you (fam. sg.) mend/darn, you are mending/darning, you may mend/darn
...(él, ella, Ud.)	zurz+a	...he, she, you (pol. sg.) mend(s)/darn(s), he, she, you is/are mending/darning, he, she, you may mend/darn
...(nosotros/-as)	zurz+amos	...we mend/darn, we are mending/darning, we may mend/darn
...(vosotros/-as)	zurz+áis	...you (fam. pl.) mend/darn, you are mending/darning, you may mend/darn
...(ellos/-as, Uds.)	zurz+an	...they, you (pol. pl.) mend/darn, they, you are mending/darning, they, you may mend/darn

The following verbs have this same pattern.

convencer	*to convince*	vencer	*to defeat, to conquer*
ejercer	*to exercise*	zurcir	*to mend, to darn*
esparcir	*to scatter, to spread*		

NOTE

You have probably noticed that the first person singular (yo) and third person singular (él, ella, Ud.) are identical in form in the present subjunctive. For this reason, you must use the subject pronoun yo / *I* to distinguish these forms in the present subjunctive.

EXERCISE Set 15-1

A. Supply the missing present subjunctive forms of the verb **mirar**, giving the English equivalent.

EXAMPLE: ... *él* _____   =   _____

            ... *él mire*   =   *... he looks at, he is looking at, he may look at*

Es necesario que ...

1. (yo) _____   = _____

2. (tú) _____   = _____

3. (nosotros) _____   = _____

4. (ellos) _____   = _____

5. (vosotros) _____   = _____

6. (Ud.) _____   = _____

Now, supply the missing present subjunctive forms of the verb **creer**, giving the English equivalent.

1. (yo) _____   = _____

2. (Raquel y yo) _____   = _____

3. (Uds.) _____   = _____

4. (ellos) _____   = _____

5. (vosotros) _____   = _____

6. (tú) _____   = _____

Now, supply the missing present subjunctive forms of the verb **discutir**, giving the English equivalent.

1. (yo) _____   = _____

2. (tú) _____   = _____

3. (nosotros) _____   = _____

4. (ellos) _____   = _____

5. (vosotros) _____   = _____

6. (Ud.) _____   = _____

Now, supply the missing present subjunctive forms of the verb ducharse, giving the English equivalent.

1. (yo) _____   =   _____

2. (tú) _____   =   _____

3. (nosotros) _____ =   _____

4. (ellos) _____   =   _____

5. (vosotros) _____ =   _____

6. (Ud.) _____   =   _____

Now, supply the missing present subjunctive forms of the verb contar (ue), giving the English equivalent.

1. (yo) _____   =   _____

2. (tú) _____   =   _____

3. (nosotros) _____ =   _____

4. (ellos) _____   =   _____

5. (vosotros) _____ =   _____

6. (Ud.) _____   =   _____

Now, supply the missing present subjunctive forms of the verb negar (ie), giving the English equivalent.

1. (yo) _____   =   _____

2. (tú) _____   =   _____

3. (nosotros) _____ =   _____

4. (ellos) _____   =   _____

5. (vosotros) _____ =   _____

6. (Ud.) _____   =   _____

Now, supply the missing present subjunctive forms of the verb morir (ue, u), giving the English equivalent.

1. (yo) _____   =   _____

2. (tú) _____   =   _____

3. (nosotros) _____ =   _____

4. (ellos) _____   =   _____

5. (vosotros) _____   =   _____

6. (Ud.) _____   =   _____

Now, supply the missing present subjunctive forms of the verb **conseguir** (i, i), giving the English equivalent.

1. (yo) _____   =   _____

2. (tú) _____   =   _____

3. (nosotros) _____   =   _____

4. (ellos) _____   =   _____

5. (vosotros) _____   =   _____

6. (Ud.) _____   =   _____

Now, supply the missing present subjunctive forms of the verb **regir** (i, i), giving the English equivalent.

1. (yo) _____   =   _____

2. (tú) _____   =   _____

3. (nosotros) _____   =   _____

4. (ellos) _____   =   _____

5. (vosotros) _____   =   _____

6. (Ud.) _____   =   _____

Now, supply the missing present subjunctive forms of the verb **obtener**, giving the English equivalent.

1. (yo) _____   =   _____

2. (tú) _____   =   _____

3. (nosotros) _____   =   _____

4. (ellos) _____   =   _____

5. (vosotros) _____   =   _____

6. (Ud.) _____   =   _____

Now, supply the missing present subjunctive forms of the verb **componer**, giving the English equivalent.

1. (yo) _____ = _____

2. (tú) _____ = _____

3. (nosotros) _____ = _____

4. (ellos) _____ = _____

5. (vosotros) _____ = _____

6. (Ud.) _____ = _____

Now, supply the missing present subjunctive forms of the verb **ser**, giving the English equivalent.

1. (yo) _____ = _____

2. (tú) _____ = _____

3. (nosotros) _____ = _____

4. (ellos) _____ = _____

5. (vosotros) _____ = _____

6. (Ud.) _____ = _____

Now, supply the missing present subjunctive forms of the verb **estar**, giving the English equivalent.

1. (yo) _____ = _____

2. (tú) _____ = _____

3. (nosotros) _____ = _____

4. (ellos) _____ = _____

5. (vosotros) _____ = _____

6. (Ud.) _____ = _____

Now, supply the missing present subjunctive forms of the verb **vencer**, giving the English equivalent.

1. (yo) _____ = _____

2. (tú) _____ = _____

3. (nosotros) _____ = _____

4. (ellos) _____ = _____

5. (vosotros) _____   =   _____

6. (Ud.) _____   =   _____

Use of the Subjunctive

As mentioned in the previous overview unit, the subjunctive is used in subordinate clauses, and it is generally introduced by **que** / *that*. So, when expressing something that is in doubt, hope, fear, and so forth with a verb in the main clause (the verb to the left of **que**), put the verb in the subordinate clause (the verb to the right of **que**) in the subjunctive.

The best way to learn which main clause verbs require the subjunctive is to memorize the most commonly used ones. These verbs form "meaning classes," or verbs that share a common meaning. The following are the common meaning classes: verbs of desire (**preferir (ie, i)** / *to prefer*, **querer (ie)** / *to want*, **desear** / *to wish*), verbs of command (**mandar** / *to order*), verbs of emotion (**temer** / *to fear*), verbs of doubt and denial (**dudar** / *to doubt*, **negar (ie)** / *to deny*), and many impersonal expressions (**es importante** / *it is important*). We shall discuss each group now. We will also provide selected lists of verbs for each category.

Verbs of Desire

The following sentences exemplify this group of verbs. These verbs indicate that you exert your will over someone else.

> **Prefiero** que Inés me **devuelva** el dinero. / *I prefer that Inés return the money to me.*
> Jorge **quiere** que Emilia **haga** la tarea. / *Jorge wants Emilia to do the homework.*
> Matilde **desea** que Gaspar **mire** la televisión menos. / *Matilde wants Gaspar to look at the TV less.*

The following is a list of verbs that belong to this class.

desear	*to desire*	**querer (ie)**	*to want*
preferir (ie, i)	*to prefer*		

Verbs of Command

Notice that in these sentences, you use an indirect object to specify the subject of the subordinate clause. Recall also the use of the redundant indirect object pronoun.

> Le **mando** *a Carlos* que **regrese** a casa. / *I order Carlos to return home.*
> Les **mando** *a mis amigos* que **canten** una canción. / *I order my friends to sing a song.*

aconsejar	*to advise*	**preferir (ie, i)**	*to prefer*
exigir	*to demand*	**recomendar (ie)**	*to recommend*
mandar	*to order*	**rogar (ue)**	*to pray, to beg*
pedir (i, i)	*to request*	**sugerir (ie, i)**	*to suggest*

Verbs of Emotion

Verbs of emotion constitute another meaning class.

> <u>Temo</u> que Roberto no <u>llegue</u> a tiempo. / *I fear that Roberto may not arrive on time.*
> Teresa <u>siente</u> que Ricardo no <u>esté</u> aquí. / *Teresa regrets that Ricardo isn't here.*

The following are some common verbs in this category.

alegrarse (de)	*to be glad*	sentir (ie, i)	*to regret*
esperar	*to hope*	temer	*to fear*
lamentar	*to regret*		

Verbs of Doubt and Denial

The following examples belong to the meaning class of doubt and denial.

> <u>Dudo</u> que Tomás <u>venga</u>. / *I doubt that Tomás is coming.*
> Esmeralda <u>niega</u> que él <u>sea</u> generoso. / *Esmeralda denies that he is generous.*

The following verbs belong to this category.

no creer	*not to believe*	no estar seguro/a de que	*not to be sure*
dudar	*to doubt*		
no estar convencido de que	*not to be convinced*	negar (ie)	*to deny*
		no pensar (ie)	*not to think*

GRAMMAR NOTE

With the affirmative version of verbs of doubt, you use the indicative because you are asserting a fact, as illustrated below.

> <u>Creo</u> que mis amigos <u>son</u> simpáticos. / *I believe that my friends are nice.*
> <u>Estoy seguro/a de</u> que <u>hace</u> viento. / *I am sure that it is windy.*
> <u>Pienso</u> que Amparo <u>está</u> cansada. / *I think that Amparo is tired.*
> <u>Estoy convencido/a</u> de que <u>tienes</u> razón. / *I am convinced that you are right.*

Impersonal Expressions

The following impersonal expressions are followed by the subjunctive.

> <u>Es importante</u> que Silvia <u>trabaje</u> más. / *It is important that Silvia work more.*
> <u>Es fácil</u> que Raúl <u>sepa</u> la verdad. / *It is likely that Raúl knows the truth.*

The following are some common impersonal expressions.

conviene	*it is advisable*	es increíble	*it is incredible*
es (una) lástima	*it is a pity*	es mejor	*it is better*
es difícil	*it is unlikely*	es necesario	*it is necessary*
es fácil	*it is likely*	es posible	*it is possible*
es fantástico	*it is fantastic*	es probable	*it is probable*
es importante	*it is important*	es ridículo	*it is ridiculous*
es imposible	*it is impossible*	puede ser	*it may be*

GRAMMAR NOTE

There are a few impersonal expressions listed below that are followed by the indicative. The indicative is used because these expressions introduce information that is factual. You use the indicative when these sentences are in the affirmative.

Es verdad que Claudia habla español. / *It is true that Claudia speaks Spanish.*
Es obvio que José está aquí. / *It is obvious that José is here.*
Es cierto que Pilar sabe mucho. / *It is certain that Pilar knows a lot.*
Es evidente que hay un problema. / *It is evident that there is a problem.*

When these impersonal expressions are negative, you use the subjunctive, as illustrated below.

No es verdad que Claudia hable español. / *It is not true that Claudia speaks Spanish.*
No es obvio que José esté aquí. / *It is not obvious that José is here.*
No es cierto que Pilar sepa mucho. / *It is not certain that Pilar knows a lot.*
No es evidente que haya un problema. / *It is not evident that there is a problem.*

TIP

When you use the verbs from the different "meaning classes" or groups discussed above, you must always use a word that connects the main clause with the subordinate clause. This word is que / *that*. The following sentences illustrate this usage.

Dudo que vaya a llover. / *I doubt that it is going to rain.*
Es posible que Blanca lea el libro. / *It is possible that Blanca is reading the book.*

In English, it is possible to omit the word "that" as shown below.

I don't think (that) he's coming.

The word que / *that* can never be deleted in Spanish, as shown below.

No creo que él venga. / *I don't think (that) he's coming.*

> **GRAMMAR NOTE**
>
> When there is a change of subject with various meaning classes of verbs, you always use the subjunctive. However, when there is <u>no change of subject</u>, you use the <u>infinitive</u> (-r) form of the verb, as shown below.
>
> Quiero <u>ver</u> esa película. / *I want to see that film.*
> Prefieres <u>dar</u> un paseo en el parque. / *You prefer to take a stroll in the park.*

More Information About the Use of the Subjunctive

In this section, we shall discuss additional cases when you use the subjunctive. The first involves indefinite and negative references. This means that the person or thing referred to is vague or uncertain, or does not exist. The second involves what are called conjunctions. As the name implies, these are words that connect, or conjoin, two clauses. The third involves some miscellaneous expressions that require the subjunctive.

Indefinite or Negative Reference

The subjunctive is used when there is an indefinite or negative antecedent in a sentence. The following sentences illustrate this usage. We have indicated the antecedent noun in the main clause and the verb in the subjunctive in the subordinate clause with an underline. The first case is an example of an indefinite antecedent. We do not know if such a person exists. The second sentence illustrates a negative antecedent. The person does not exist.

Busco <u>un empleado</u> que <u>trabaje</u> mucho. / *I am looking for an employee who works hard.*

No hay <u>nadie</u> que <u>toque</u> la guitarra. / *There is no one who plays the guitar.*

Adverbial Conjunctions

The subjunctive is used after certain adverbial conjunctions, or connectors, in Spanish. These are words that you use to connect two sentences. Some of them indicate the time when an action is occurring. Others indicate purpose. Still others, by their very meaning, involve uncertainty. We shall look at each group now.

Conjunctions of Time

The following adverbs of time take the subjunctive when the time referred to has not yet taken place. We have indicated the adverb of time and the verb in the subjunctive with an underline.

Él vendrá <u>cuando</u> <u>pueda</u>. / *He will come when he can.*
<u>En cuanto</u> <u>haga</u> buen tiempo, iré a la playa. / *As soon as the weather is nice, I will go to the beach.*

The following are some common adverbs of time.

cuando	*when*	hasta que	*until*
en cuanto	*as soon as*	tan pronto como	*as soon as*

GRAMMAR NOTE

Cuando / *when* takes the subjunctive if the action has not yet occurred, as shown below.

> **Voy a hablar con Amparo cuando ella llegue.** / *I am going to speak with Amparo when she arrives.*

If you are speaking about a regularly occurring activity, you use the indicative as illustrated below. In this usage, cuando / *when* often has the meaning of "whenever."

> **Cuando Mauricio enseña, él habla en voz alta.** / *When Mauricio teaches, he speaks in a loud voice.*

Another conjunction, aunque / *even if/although/even though*, uses the subjunctive when the action of the verb has not yet occurred, as illustrated below.

> **Aunque Sofía llegue tarde, iremos al cine.** / *Even though Sofía may arrive late, we will go to the movies.*

Other Conjunctions

Certain conjunctions always take the subjunctive. The following sentences show how these work. We have indicated the conjunction and the verb in the subjunctive with an underline.

> A menos que vayas a clase, no puedes aprender. / *Unless you go to class, you can't learn.*
> Para que ganes más, debes buscar otro empleo. / *In order for you to earn more, you ought to look for another job.*

The following are some common conjunctions that always take the subjunctive.

a menos que	*unless*	en caso de que	*in case that*
antes de que	*before*	para que	*in order that*
con tal de que	*provided that*	sin que	*without*

There is a useful memory aid to help you remember these words. It is the acronym ESCAPA, which is the first letter of each conjunction, as illustrated below.

En caso de que / *in case that*
Sin que / *without*
Con tal de que / *provided that*
Antes de que / *before*
Para que / *in order that*
A menos que / *unless*

Miscellaneous Expressions

There are a few other expressions that require the subjunctive because they express uncertainty. These are the words for "perhaps," namely, **acaso** (usually reserved for writing), **quizá(s)**, and **tal vez**. The following sentences illustrate this usage. Note that **quizá** is more commonly used now.

> <u>Quizá(s)</u> él <u>esté</u> aquí. / *Perhaps he is here.*
> <u>Tal vez</u> ellos <u>sean</u> simpáticos. / *Perhaps they are nice.*

There is another expression, **ojalá** / *I hope that*, that derives from the Arabic word meaning "may Allah grant that" that takes the subjunctive, as shown below.

> <u>Ojalá</u> que no <u>llueva</u>. / *I hope that it doesn't rain.*

Present Subjunctive of Hay

The present subjunctive of **hay** / *there is, there are* is ...**haya** / *...there is, there are, there may be*. It is used in the same way that **hay** is used, except that it is in the present subjunctive. The following sentences illustrate this point. This form of **hay** always appears in a subordinate clause, i.e., it is to the right of the word **que**.

> <u>Temo</u> que <u>haya</u> un examen. / *I fear that there is an exam.*
> <u>Espero</u> que no <u>haya</u> muchas tareas. / *I hope that there aren't many chores.*

The present subjunctive of the idiomatic expression **hay que** / *one must, it is necessary to* is ...**haya que** / *...it is necessary to, it may be necessary to*. The following sentence illustrates this usage.

> <u>Dudo</u> que <u>haya que</u> ir a San Salvador. / *I doubt that it is necessary to go to San Salvador.*

EXERCISE Set 15-2

A. How do you say the following sentences in Spanish?

1. Concepción doubts that it is going to snow.

_____

2. I want Oscar to be here at 9 P.M.

_____

3. You (fam. sg.) regret that the test is tomorrow.

_____

4. Unless we work hard, we will never finish.

_____

5. It is likely that Rosa has the book.

   _____

6. He doesn't believe that there are many students there today.

   _____

7. I hope that Julio reads the novel.

   _____

8. There is no one that knows how to use this computer.

   _____

9. She will write the composition before she watches television.

   _____

10. It is possible that he pays the bill.

    _____

11. As soon as I arrive in San Salvador, I will go to the *Museo Nacional de Antropología David J. Guzmán*[1].

    _____

12. They are not sure that their parents are in El Salvador.

    _____

13. It is unlikely that Laura knows Enrique.

    _____

14. I want Salvador to see this program.

    _____

15. My parents insist that my brother attend class.

    _____

[1]Excellent museum that houses El Salvador's major archaeological finds.

EXERCISE Set 15-3

A. Change the verbs into the subjunctive by adding the indicated expression to the given sentence.

1. Ellos van a San Salvador este año (Es probable que ...)

   _____

2. Tengo sueño (Mi esposa niega que ...)

   _____

3. Mis amigos beben mucha cerveza (Temo que ...)

   _____

4. Este libro es muy bueno (Espero que ...)

   _____

5. Pablo estudia demasiado (No creo que ...)

   _____

6. Mis niños están enfermos (Es una lástima que ...)

   _____

7. Ellos juegan al fútbol (Prefiero que ...)

   _____

8. Aurora viene mañana (Tal vez ...)

   _____

9. Voy a El Salvador (Es fácil que ...)

   _____

10. Hace calor (No pienso que ...)

   _____

| EXERCISE Set 15-4 |

A. How do you say the following sentences in Spanish?

1. Provided it is cool, we will swim in *La Libertad*[1].

_____

2. Perhaps they are going to Central America. Do you (fam. sg.) know?

_____

3. It's possible that it is cloudy.

_____

4. It may be that she is tired.

_____

5. I will go to the library when Mario arrives.

_____

6. I want him to write a letter.

_____

7. He doesn't believe that there is a storm.

_____

8. I fear that Esperanza may not know the answer.

_____

[1]Beach closest to the capital of El Salvador.

EXERCISE Set 15-5

A. Provide the corresponding present subjunctive forms for the following verbs in the present indicative tense.

1. tiene _____

2. ponemos _____

3. pedís _____

4. son _____

5. estás _____

6. van _____

7. sé _____

8. conocemos _____

9. dormimos _____

10. corrigen _____

11. hay _____

12. decimos _____

13. traes _____

14. te bañas _____

15. busco _____

16. salen _____

17. viene _____

18. hace _____

Crossword Puzzle 15

Change the following verbs in the present indicative to their corresponding present subjunctive forms.

Horizontales
4. Practico
5. Conoces
7. Vas
8. Hay

Verticales
1. Dormimos
2. Decimos
3. Somos
4. Proteges
6. Hace

16

The Imperfect Subjunctive (*el imperfecto de subjuntivo*)

Uses and Features

The imperfect subjunctive is used in subordinate clauses for the same reasons as for the present subjunctive (see Chapter 15). The main difference between the use of the present subjunctive and the imperfect subjunctive is the time of the action.

1. If the main clause is in the present tense, and if the subordinate clause refers to the past, then the imperfect subjunctive in the dependent clause is normally called for.

   <u>Es posible</u> que mis amigos <u>fueran</u> al espectáculo. / *It's possible that my friends went to the show.*
   <u>Niego</u> que Matilde <u>estuviera</u> aquí ayer. / *I deny that Matilde was here yesterday.*

2. If the main clause is in the past tense, then the past subjunctive in the subordinate clause is normally called for.

   Yo <u>quería</u> que mis amigos <u>fueran</u> al espectáculo. / *I wanted my friends to go to the show.*
   <u>Era necesario</u> que Juanita <u>dijera</u> la verdad. / *It was necessary that Juanita tell the truth.*

3. In contrary-to-fact clauses (si clauses), use the imperfect subjunctive if the main clause is in the conditional tense.

   Si yo <u>fuera</u> rico, yo <u>compraría</u> un palacio. / *If I were rich, I would buy a palace.*
   Si ella <u>tuviera</u> mucho tiempo, <u>iría</u> a Guatemala por un año. / *If she had a lot of time, she would go to Guatemala for a year.*

4. You use the imperfect subjunctive in main clauses if you want to make a polite request. This usage is normally restricted to the imperfect subjunctive of two verbs: **querer** / *to want* and **poder** / *can, be able.*

   ¿<u>Pudiera</u> Ud. ayudarme? / *Could you help me?*
   Yo <u>quisiera</u> ir al teatro. / *I would like to go to the theater.*

5. In *as if* clauses (como si), use the imperfect subjunctive.

   Él <u>estudia</u> como si <u>tuviera</u> un examen. / *He is studying as if he had a test.*
   Ella <u>vivió</u> como si <u>estuviera</u> muy contenta. / *She lived as if she were very happy.*

Regular Verbs

To form the imperfect subjunctive, or the **imperfecto de subjuntivo** in Spanish, do the following:

1. Take the third person plural of the preterit tense of <u>all</u> verbs.

> hablaron
> comieron
> · vivieron
> midieron
> durmieron
> quisieron
> dijeron
> fueron

2. Remove the **-ron** to get the stem for the imperfect subjunctive tense.

> <u>habla</u>ron → habla-
> <u>comie</u>ron → comie-
> <u>vivie</u>ron → vivie-
> <u>midie</u>ron → midie-
> <u>durmie</u>ron → durmie-
> <u>quisie</u>ron → quisie-
> <u>dije</u>ron → dije-
> <u>fue</u>ron → fue-

3. Add the following endings to form the imperfect subjunctive endings. You should note that the **nosotros/-as** / *we* form of the verb has an accent (´) on the vowel that precedes the ending for the imperfect subjunctive (-´ramos): <u>hablá</u>**ramos**, <u>comié</u>**ramos**, <u>vivié</u>**ramos**.

(yo)	-ra
(tú)	-ras
(él, ella, Ud.)	-ra
(nosotros/-as)	-´ramos
(vosotros/-as)	-rais
(ellos/-as, Uds.)	-ran

4. There is an alternative set of endings for the imperfect subjunctive. These endings are added to the same stem as noted in 2 above. These endings tend to be found in literary works. Nevertheless, you may hear them in use in some parts of the Spanish-speaking world. Both are interchangeable and there is no meaningful difference between the two. We will provide the endings here, but we will only use the following endings for the exercises in this book: **-ra, -ras, -ra, ´ramos, -rais, -ran**. We provide the alternative set of endings for your reference. You should also note that the **nosotros/-as** / *we* form of the verb of this set of endings has an accent (´) on the vowel that precedes the ending for the imperfect subjunctive (-´semos): <u>hablá</u>**semos**, <u>comié</u>**semos**, <u>vivié</u>**semos**.

(yo)	-se
(tú)	-ses
(él, ella, Ud.)	-se
(nosotros/-as)	-´semos
(vosotros/-as)	-seis
(ellos/-as, Uds.)	-sen

5. Here's the result. We will provide the -se forms (in parentheses) in the first three verb conjugations so that you may become familiar with these forms. Both have the same translations.

hablar / *to speak*

Subject Pronoun	Verb Form	Meaning
…(yo)	habla+ra (habla+se)	…*I spoke, I was speaking, I might speak*
…(tú)	habla+ras (habla+ses)	…*you (fam. sg.) spoke, you were speaking, you might speak*
…(él, ella, Ud.)	habla+ra (habla+se)	…*he, she, you (pol. sg.) spoke, he, she, you was/were speaking, he, she, you might speak*
…(nosotros/-as)	hablá+ramos (hablá+semos)	…*we spoke, we were speaking, we might speak*
…(vosotros/-as)	habla+rais (habla+seis)	…*you (fam. pl.) spoke, you were speaking, you might speak*
…(ellos/-as, Uds.)	habla+ran (habla+sen)	…*they, you (pol. pl.) spoke, they, you were speaking, they, you might speak*

comer / *to eat*

Subject Pronoun	Verb Form	Meaning
…(yo)	comie+ra (comie+se)	…*I ate, I was eating, I might eat*
…(tú)	comie+ras (comie+ses)	…*you (fam. sg.) ate, you were eating, you might eat*
…(él, ella, Ud.)	comie+ra (comie+se)	…*he, she, you (pol. sg.) ate, he, she, you was/were eating, he, she you might eat*
…(nosotros/-as)	comié+ramos (comié+semos)	…*we ate, we were eating, we might eat*
…(vosotros/-as)	comie+rais (comie+seis)	…*you (fam. pl.) ate, you were eating, you might eat*
…(ellos/-as, Uds.)	comie+ran (comie+sen)	…*they, you (pol. pl.) ate, they, you were eating, they, you might eat*

vivir / *to live*

Subject Pronoun	Verb Form	Meaning
...(yo)	vivie+ra (vivie+se)	...I lived, I was living, I might live
...(tú)	vivie+ras (vivie+ses)	...you (fam. sg.) lived, you were living, you might live
...(él, ella, Ud.)	vivie+ra (vivie+se)	...he, she, you (pol. sg.) lived, he, she, you was/were living, he, she, you might live
...(nosotros/-as)	vivié+ramos (vivié+semos)	...we lived, we were living, we might live
...(vosotros/-as)	vivie+rais (vivie+seis)	...you (fam. pl.) lived, you were living, you might live
...(ellos/-as, Uds.)	vivie+ran (vivie+sen)	...they, you (pol. pl.) lived, they, you were living, they, you might live

The Imperfect Subjunctive of Reflexive Verbs

Reflexive verbs always use reflexive pronouns in the imperfect subjunctive, as shown below. They always appear immediately before the conjugated verb, as they do in the present subjunctive and all other tenses.

lavarse / *to wash oneself*

Subject Pronoun	Reflexive Pronoun	Conjugated Verb	Meaning
...(yo)	me	lava+ra	...I washed myself, I was washing myself, I might wash myself
...(tú)	te	lava+ras	...you (fam. sg.) washed yourself, you were washing yourself, you might wash yourself
...(él, ella, Ud.)	se	lava+ra	...he, she, you (pol. sg.) washed himself/herself/yourself, he, she, you was/were washing himself/herself/yourself, he, she, you might wash himself/herself/yourself
...(nosotros/-as)	nos	lavá+ramos	...we washed ourselves, we were washing ourselves, we might wash ourselves
...(vosotros/-as)	os	lava+rais	...you (fam. pl.) washed yourselves, you were washing yourselves, you might wash yourselves
...(ellos/-as, Uds.)	se	lava+ran	...they, you (pol. pl.) washed themselves/yourselves, they, you were washing themselves/yourselves, they, you might wash themselves/yourselves

> **GRAMMAR NOTE**
>
> Remember to write the graphic accent on the nosotros/-as / *we* form of the verb in the past subjunctive.
>
> habláramos   comiéramos   viviéramos

> **GRAMMAR REMINDER**
>
> Remember to determine the stem to which you add the imperfect subjunctive endings by removing the -ron (third person plural) form of the preterit tense. Then add the imperfect subjunctive endings (see 1 and 2 under "Regular Verbs" in this chapter). See Chapter 7 for a list of the preterit tense forms with an irregular stem.

> **NOTE**
>
> You have probably noticed that the first person singular (yo) and third person singular (él, ella, Ud.) are identical in form in the imperfect subjunctive. For this reason, you must use the subject pronoun yo / *I* to distinguish these forms in the imperfect subjunctive.

EXERCISE Set 16-1

A. Supply the missing imperfect subjunctive forms of the verb **pagar**, giving the English equivalent.

EXAMPLE: ... *él* _____ = _____

         ... *él pagara* = *... he paid, he was paying, he might pay*

Era difícil que ...

1. (yo) _____ = _____

2. (tú) _____ = _____

3. (nosotros) _____ = _____

4. (ellos) _____ = _____

5. (vosotros) _____ = _____

6. (Ud.) _____ = _____

Now, supply the missing imperfect subjunctive forms of the verb **cometer**, giving the English equivalent.

1. (yo) _____ = _____

2. (Raquel y yo) _____ = _____

3. (Uds.) _____ = _____

4. (ellos) _____ = _____

5. (vosotros) _____ = _____

6. (tú) _____ = _____

Now, supply the missing imperfect subjunctive forms of the verb **permitir**, giving the English equivalent.

1. (yo) _____ = _____

2. (tú) _____ = _____

3. (nosotros) _____ = _____

4. (ellos) _____ = _____

5. (vosotros) _____ = _____

6. (Ud.) _____ = _____

Now, supply the missing imperfect subjunctive forms of the verb **quitarse**, giving the English equivalent.

1. (yo) _____ = _____

2. (tú) _____ = _____

3. (nosotros) _____ = _____

4. (ellos) _____ = _____

5. (vosotros) _____ = _____

6. (Ud.) _____ = _____

Now, supply the missing imperfect subjunctive forms of the verb **confesar (ie)**, giving the English equivalent.

1. (yo) _____ = _____

2. (tú) _____ = _____

3. (nosotros) _____ = _____

4. (ellos) _____ = _____

5. (vosotros) _____ = _____

6. (Ud.) _____ = _____

Now, supply the missing imperfect subjunctive forms of the verb **volar (ue)**, giving the English equivalent.

1. (yo) _____   =   _____

2. (tú) _____   =   _____

3. (nosotros) _____   =   _____

4. (ellos) _____   =   _____

5. (vosotros) _____   =   _____

6. (Ud.) _____   =   _____

Now, supply the missing imperfect subjunctive forms of the verb **medir (i, i)**, giving the English equivalent.

1. (yo) _____   =   _____

2. (tú) _____   =   _____

3. (nosotros) _____   =   _____

4. (ellos) _____   =   _____

5. (vosotros) _____   =   _____

6. (Ud.) _____   =   _____

Now, supply the missing imperfect subjunctive forms of the verb **morir (ue, u)**, giving the English equivalent.

1. (yo) _____   =   _____

2. (tú) _____   =   _____

3. (nosotros) _____   =   _____

4. (ellos) _____   =   _____

5. (vosotros) _____   =   _____

6. (Ud.) _____   =   _____

Now, supply the missing imperfect subjunctive forms of the verb **ser**, giving the English equivalent.

1. (yo) _____   =   _____

2. (tú) _____   =   _____

3. (nosotros) _____ = _____

4. (ellos) _____ = _____

5. (vosotros) _____ = _____

6. (Ud.) _____ = _____

Now, supply the missing imperfect subjunctive forms of the verb **tener**, giving the English equivalent.

1. (yo) _____ = _____

2. (tú) _____ = _____

3. (nosotros) _____ = _____

4. (ellos) _____ = _____

5. (vosotros) _____ = _____

6. (Ud.) _____ = _____

Now, supply the missing imperfect subjunctive forms of the verb **hacer**, giving the English equivalent.

1. (yo) _____ = _____

2. (tú) _____ = _____

3. (nosotros) _____ = _____

4. (ellos) _____ = _____

5. (vosotros) _____ = _____

6. (Ud.) _____ = _____

Now, supply the missing imperfect subjunctive forms of the verb **ir**, giving the English equivalent.

1. (yo) _____ = _____

2. (tú) _____ = _____

3. (nosotros) _____ = _____

4. (ellos) _____ = _____

5. (vosotros) _____ = _____

6. (Ud.) _____ = _____

Now, supply the missing imperfect subjunctive forms of the verb estar, giving the English equivalent.

1. (yo) _____ = _____

2. (tú) _____ = _____

3. (nosotros) _____ = _____

4. (ellos) _____ = _____

5. (vosotros) _____ = _____

6. (Ud.) _____ = _____

Now, supply the missing imperfect subjunctive forms of the verb conducir, giving the English equivalent.

1. (yo) _____ = _____

2. (tú) _____ = _____

3. (nosotros) _____ = _____

4. (ellos) _____ = _____

5. (vosotros) _____ = _____

6. (Ud.) _____ = _____

Tense and the Imperfect Subjunctive

We will discuss the cases in which the imperfect subjunctive is used and we will provide illustrations for each instance.

Main Verb in the Present Tense and Subordinate Verb in the Past

The imperfect subjunctive is used when the main clause is in the present and there is a past tense in the subordinate clause (see Chapter 15 for when to use the subjunctive). You will notice that in the indicative mood, there are two simple past tenses: the preterit (see Chapter 7) and the imperfect (see Chapter 8). With the imperfect subjunctive, there is only one simple past tense. Even though there are two different forms, these forms have the same meaning. For this reason, the imperfect subjunctive may correspond, depending on the context of the sentence, to the preterit or imperfect indicative. The following are selected examples.

> **Es posible** que lloviera. / *It's possible that it was raining.*
> **Dudo** que Ramón se **levantara** temprano. / *I doubt that Ramón got up early.*

Main Clause in the Past Tense

If there is a past tense in the main clause, then the verb in the subordinate clause will be in the past (imperfect subjunctive). The following are selected examples.

> Pilar <u>quería</u> que Camilo <u>fuera</u> a la tienda. / *Pilar wanted Camilo to go to the store.*
> <u>Era probable</u> que Mónica <u>diera</u> un paseo en el parque. / *It was probable that Mónica took a walk in the park.*

Imperfect Subjunctive of Hay

The imperfect subjunctive of hay / *there is, there are* is …hubiera / *there was/there were, there might be*. It is used in the same way that hay is used, except that it is in the past subjunctive. The following sentences illustrate this point. This form of hay (…hubiera) always appears in a subordinate clause, that is, it is to the right of the word que.

> <u>Dudábamos</u> que <u>hubiera</u> un examen. / *We feared that there was an exam.*
> Ella <u>temía</u> que no <u>hubiera</u> bebidas en la fiesta. / *She feared that there were no drinks at the party.*

The imperfect subjunctive of the idiomatic expression hay que / *one must, it is necessary to* is …hubiera que / *…it was necessary to, it might be necessary to*. The following sentence illustrates this usage.

> Yo <u>no creía</u> que <u>hubiera que</u> conjugar los verbos españoles. / *I didn't think that it was necessary to conjugate Spanish verbs.*

If Clauses

Clauses that begin with si / *if* are sometimes called contrary-to-fact clauses, counterfactuals, or hypothetical statements, because they refer to a situation that has not yet occurred. We will look at two examples of "if clauses." The first group is in the present and does not use the subjunctive, as illustrated below. In these examples, the si clause verb is in the present indicative tense and the main clause verb is in the future tense.

> Si <u>tengo</u> el dinero, <u>iré</u> a Guatemala. / *If I have the money, I will go to Guatemala.*
> Si <u>veo</u> a Roberto, le <u>daré</u> el dinero a él. / *If I see Roberto, I will give him the money.*

In the second type of "if clause," commonly called contrary-to-fact sentences, the "if clause" is in the imperfect subjunctive and the main clause is in the conditional tense. A typical example in English is *"If I were rich, I would travel more."* It is clear that the verb in the "if clause" is in the subjunctive because of the subjunctive form of the verb *to be*. The meaning of this sentence is hypothetical because the conditions for it to be true have not been met. Therefore, the past subjunctive is used. The following sentences illustrate this usage.

> Si yo <u>tuviera</u> mucho dinero, yo <u>iría</u> a la Ciudad de Guatemala. / *If I had a lot of money, I would go to Guatemala City.*
> Si <u>hiciera</u> calor, yo <u>nadaría</u> en el Mar Caribe. / *If it were hot, I would swim in the Caribbean.*
> Eva <u>compraría</u> un coche nuevo, si ella <u>tuviera</u> un empleo. / *Eva would buy a new car, if she had a job.*

EXERCISE Set 16-2

A. How do you say the following sentences in Spanish?

1. If I had the money, I would buy a lottery ticket.

   _____

2. I would read *El señor presidente*[1] by (de) *Miguel Ángel Asturias,*[2] if I had the time.

   _____

3. If it weren't so hot, I would run in the park.

   _____

4. If I weren't so tired, I would clean the house.

   _____

5. She would come, if she could.

   _____

6. We would buy the house if it weren't so expensive.

   _____

7. We would go to *Quetzaltenango,*[3] if we didn't work.

   _____

8. If she were here, she would be happy.

   _____

9. If you (pol. pl.) saw *Chichecastenango,*[4] you wouldn't leave.

   _____

10. If there were more time, I would go to Guatemala more often.

    _____

[1]Novel written in 1946 by Miguel Ángel Asturias, 1899–1974.
[2]Nobel Prize winner in 1967.
[3]Mayan city located in the Western highlands of Guatemala. also known as Xela.
[4]Important Cakchiquel commercial center before the arrival of the Spaniards, still a center of trade for Mayan Indians.

B. Change the verb into the subjunctive by adding the indicated expression.

EXAMPLE: María leía una novela (Era posible que...)

Era posible que María leyera una novela.

1. Yo empezaba a estudiar (Ellos dudaban que...)

_____

2. Querías ir a Guatemala (Él temía que...)

_____

3. No hacía mucho frío (Esperábamos que ...)

_____

4. Ud. tenía razón (Yo no estaba seguro/a de que...)

_____

5. Ellos no miraban la televisión (Era increíble que...)

_____

6. Yo sabía hablar español (Ella no creía que...)

_____

7. Íbamos a la capital de Guatemala (Era fácil que...)

_____

8. Llovía mucho (Yo no pensaba que...)

_____

Querer / *to want* and Poder/ *can, be able*

The verbs **querer** / *to want* and **poder** / *can, be able* may be used in the imperfect subjunctive tense. They may be used alone and they don't have to be in a subordinate clause. When they are used this way, they are "polite" ways of making a request. In English, for example, it is possible to make requests in a very direct fashion that some people may perceive to be impolite or even ill-mannered. We have all heard people say "I want a hamburger," or "Give me a hamburger." These same requests can be phrased in English by saying "Could you please give me a hamburger," or "I would like to have a hamburger." In Spanish, you can also use the verbs **querer** / *want* and **poder** / *can, be able* in the imperfect to make a polite request, as shown below.

> ¿<u>Pudiera</u> traerme la sopa del día? / *Could you bring me the soup of the day?*
> Yo <u>quisiera</u> una cerveza. / *I would like a beer.*

A. How do you say the following sentences in Spanish?

1. Where would you (fam. sg.) like to go?

_____

2. Would you (pol. sg.) show me the novel by (de) the new Guatemalan writer?

_____

3. Could you (pol. sg.) drive me to the university?

_____

4. My wife would like to see the Mayan ruins.

_____

5. Could (pol. sg.) you repeat the question?

_____

Como si / *as if*

The imperfect subjunctive is used after the phrase **como si** / *as if*. The main clause may be in the present, the conditional, or the past tense, as illustrated below.

Ellos <u>corrieron</u> como si <u>fueran</u> culpables. / *They ran as if they were guilty.*
Carlos <u>habló</u> como si él lo <u>supiera</u> todo. / *Carlos spoke as if he knew everything.*
<u>Canté</u> como si yo <u>fuera</u> Julio Iglesias. / *I sang as if I were Julio Iglesias.*

A. How do you say the following sentences in Spanish?

1. I felt as if I were sick.

_____

2. I played the guitar as if I were *Andrés Segovia*[1].

_____

[1]Classical Spanish guitarist, 1893–1987.

3. He paints as if he were *Pablo Picasso*[2].

_____

4. I used to write as if I were *Miguel Angel Asturias*[3].

_____

5. You (fam. sg.) speak as if you were from Guatemala.

_____

6. He drove as if he were drunk.

_____

[2]Spanish painter, 1881–1973.
[3]Guatemalan writer and Nobel Prize winner (1967); 1899–1974.

EXERCISE Set 16-5

A. Provide the corresponding present subjunctive and imperfect subjunctive forms for the following verbs in the present indicative tense.

1. compra

_____   _____

2. creen

_____   _____

3. vivimos

_____   _____

4. somos

_____   _____

5. estoy

_____   _____

6. va

_____   _____

7. conozco

_____   _____

8. sé

_____   _____

9. morís

_____   _____

10. dicen

_____   _____

11. hay

_____   _____

12. corriges

_____   _____

13. cae

_____   _____

14. se ducha

_____   _____

15. pongo

       _____   _____

16. salimos

       _____   _____

17. vienes

       _____   _____

18. hace

       _____   _____

Crossword Puzzle 16

Change the verb in the following sentences to the appropriate imperfect subjunctive form.

Era fácil que…

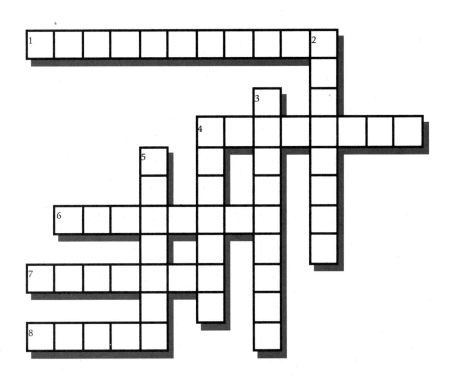

Horizontales
1. Es probable que tú . . . (entender).
4. No creo que mi amigo . . . (dormir).
6. Ella esperaba que no . . . (llover).
7. Yo temía que . . . (hacer) mal tiempo.
8. Era posible que él . . . (ser) mexicano.

Verticales
2. Yo quería que (tú) . . . (saber) hablar español.
3. Era mejor que Enrique . . . (trabajar).
4. Era fácil que mis amigos . . . (decir) la verdad.
5. Yo negaba que ella . . . (tener) frío.

17
The Present Perfect Subjunctive (*el perfecto de subjuntivo*)

Uses and Features

The present perfect subjunctive corresponds to the present perfect in temporal usage. The difference is that it comes after a verb, a conjunction, or an expression that requires the subjunctive mood (see Chapter 15 for a discussion of the various uses of the subjunctive). The following examples illustrate these uses.

> Espero que Mauricio haya llegado. / *I hope that Mauricio has arrived.*
> Busco un estudiante que haya leído la lección. / *I'm looking for a student who has read the lesson.*
> Voy a esperar hasta que Berta haya llegado. / *I am going to wait until Berta has arrived.*

Conjugation of the Present Perfect Subjunctive

The present perfect subjunctive, called the perfecto de subjuntivo in Spanish, is a compound tense. Therefore, it is conjugated with the auxiliary verb haber / *to have*, and the past participle. See Chapter 9 for the relevant details regarding past participles and the use of the auxiliary verb.

In the case of the present perfect subjunctive, the auxiliary verb haber / *to have* is conjugated in the present subjunctive as shown here.

haber / *to have*

Subject Pronoun	Verb Form	Meaning
...(yo)	hay+a	...*I have, I may have*
...(tú)	hay+as	...*you (fam. sg.) have, you may have*
...(él, ella, Ud.)	hay+a	...*he, she, you (pol. sg.) has/have, he, she, you may have*
...(nosotros/-as)	hay+amos	...*we have, we may have*
...(vosotros/-as)	hay+áis	...*you (fam. pl.) have, you may have*
...(ellos/-as, Uds.)	hay+an	...*they, you (pol. pl.) have, they, you may have*

hablar / *to talk*

Subject Pronoun	Haber	Past Participle	Meaning
...(yo)	<u>hay</u>+a	<u>habl</u>+ado	...I have spoken, I may have spoken
...(tú)	<u>hay</u>+as	<u>habl</u>+ado	...you (fam. sg.) have spoken, you may have spoken
...(él, ella, Ud.)	<u>hay</u>+a	<u>habl</u>+ado	...he, she, you (pol. sg.) has/have spoken, he, she, you may have spoken
...(nosotros/-as)	<u>hay</u>+amos	<u>habl</u>+ado	...we have spoken, we may have spoken
...(vosotros/-as)	<u>hay</u>+áis	<u>habl</u>+ado	...you (fam. pl.) have spoken, you may have spoken
...(ellos/-as, Uds.)	<u>hay</u>+an	<u>habl</u>+ado	...they, you (pol. pl.) have spoken, they, you may have spoken

comer / *to eat*

Subject Pronoun	Haber	Past Participle	Meaning
...(yo)	<u>hay</u>+a	<u>com</u>+ido	...I have eaten, I may have eaten
...(tú)	<u>hay</u>+as	<u>com</u>+ido	...you (fam. sg.) have eaten, you may have eaten
...(él, ella, Ud.)	<u>hay</u>+a	<u>com</u>+ido	...he, she, you (pol. sg.) has/have eaten, he, she, you may have eaten
...(nosotros/-as)	<u>hay</u>+amos	<u>com</u>+ido	...we have eaten, we may have eaten
...(vosotros/-as)	<u>hay</u>+áis	<u>com</u>+ido	...you (fam. pl.) have eaten, you may have eaten
...(ellos/-as, Uds.)	<u>hay</u>+an	<u>com</u>+ido	...they, you (pol. pl.) have eaten, they, you may have eaten

vivir / *to live*

Subject Pronoun	Haber	Past Participle	Meaning
...(yo)	<u>hay</u>+a	<u>viv</u>+ido	...I have lived, I may have lived
...(tú)	<u>hay</u>+as	<u>viv</u>+ido	...you (fam. sg.) have lived, you may have lived
...(él, ella, Ud.)	<u>hay</u>+a	<u>viv</u>+ido	...he, she, you (pol. sg.) has/have lived, he, she, you may have lived
...(nosotros/-as)	<u>hay</u>+amos	<u>viv</u>+ido	...we have lived, we may have lived
...(vosotros/-as)	<u>hay</u>+áis	<u>viv</u>+ido	...you (fam. pl.) have lived, you may have lived
...(ellos/-as, Uds.)	<u>hay</u>+an	<u>viv</u>+ido	... they, you (pol. pl.) have lived, they, you may have lived

The Present Perfect Subjunctive of Reflexive Verbs

Reflexive verbs always use reflexive pronouns in the present perfect subjunctive, as shown below. They always appear immediately before the conjugated verb, as they do in the present subjunctive and all other tenses.

lavarse / *to wash oneself*

Subject Pronoun	Reflexive Pronoun	Haber	Past Participle	Meaning
...(yo)	me	hay+a	lav+ado	...*I have washed myself, I may have washed myself*
...(tú)	te	hay+as	lav+ado	...*you (fam. sg.) have washed yourself, you may have washed yourself*
...(él, ella, Ud.)	se	hay+a	lav+ado	...*he, she, you (pol. sg.) has/have washed himself/herself/yourself, he she, you may have washed himself/herself/yourself*
...(nosotros/-as)	nos	hay+amos	lav+ado	...*we have washed ourselves, we may have washed ourselves*
...(vosotros/-as)	os	hay+áis	lav+ado	...*you (fam. pl.) have washed yourselves, you may have washed yourselves*
...(ellos/-as, Uds.)	se	hay+an	lav+ado	...*they, you (pol. pl.) have washed themselves/yourselves, they, you may have washed themselves/yourselves*

NOTE

You have probably noticed that the first person singular (yo) and third person singular (él, ella, Ud.) are identical in form. For this reason, you must normally use the subject pronoun yo / *I* to distinguish these forms.

TIP

The present perfect subjunctive corresponds to the present perfect in temporal usage and overall features (see Chapter 9). For a review of the formation of past participles, see Chapter 9. For a review of the uses of the subjunctive, see Chapter 15. Essentially, it expresses a completed action, usually a recently completed one.

The Present Perfect Subjunctive of **Hay**

The present perfect subjunctive form of hay / *there is, there are* is ...haya habido / ...*there has been, there have been*. The following examples illustrate this usage.

Es increíble que haya habido tanta lluvia. / *It is unbelievable that there has been so much rain.*
Dudo que no haya habido exámenes. / *I doubt that there have been no tests.*

The present perfect subjunctive of the idiomatic expression **hay que** / *one must, it is necessary to* is ...**haya habido que** / ...*it has been necessary to, it may have been necessary to*. The following sentence illustrates this usage.

Él <u>teme</u> que <u>haya habido que</u> estudiar más. / *He fears that it may have been necessary to study more.*

EXERCISE Set 17-1

A. Supply the missing present perfect subjunctive forms of the verb **estudiar**, giving the English equivalent.

EXAMPLE: ... *él* _____ = _____

... *él haya estudiado* = ... *he has studied, he may have studied*

Es posible que ...

1. (yo) _____   = _____

2. (tú) _____   = _____

3. (nosotros) _____ = _____

4. (ellos) _____   = _____

5. (vosotros) _____ = _____

6. (Ud.) _____   = _____

Now, supply the missing present perfect subjunctive forms of the verb **correr**, giving the English equivalent.

1. (yo) _____   = _____

2. (Raquel y yo) _____ = _____

3. (Uds.) _____   = _____

4. (ellos) _____   = _____

5. (vosotros) _____   = _____

6. (tú) _____   = _____

Now, supply the missing present perfect subjunctive forms of the verb **sufrir**, giving the English equivalent.

1. (yo) _____   = _____

2. (tú) _____   = _____

3. (nosotros) _____   =   _____

4. (ellos) _____   =   _____

5. (vosotros) _____   =   _____

6. (Ud.) _____   =   _____

Now, supply the missing present perfect subjunctive forms of the verb *afeitarse*, giving the English equivalent.

1. (yo) _____   =   _____

2. (tú) _____   =   _____

3. (nosotros) _____   =   _____

4. (ellos) _____   =   _____

5. (vosotros) _____   =   _____

6. (Ud.) _____   =   _____

B. How do you say the following sentences in Spanish?

1. It is unlikely that she has read *El laberinto de la soledad*[1] by (de) *Octavio Paz*[2].

_____

2. I doubt that Eulalia has arrived.

_____

3. Antonio doesn't know anyone who has seen that movie.

_____

4. In case that Clara has arrived, I will have to go to the airport.

_____

5. You (fam. sg.) fear that she has already returned home.

_____

6. It is possible that they have eaten all of the sweets.

_____

[1]Essays published in 1950.
[2]Winner of the Nobel Prize, 1990; 1914–1998.

7. I don't think that Benito has done his homework.

_____

8. They deny that Blas has gone to México.

_____

9. I hope that Gloria has not been sick.

_____

10. César doesn't believe that Amalia has done the work.

_____

C. Choose **a** (present subjunctive) or **b** (present perfect subjunctive) according to the meaning.

1. Es probable que ella … Jorge mañana.
   a. se case con
   b. se haya casado con

2. Niego que Juana ya …
   a. parta
   b. haya partido

3. Quiero que Marina … la verdad.
   a. diga
   b. haya dicho

4. Es probable que Ramón ya se …
   a. despierte
   b. haya despertado

5. Temo que Teresa no … todavía.
   a. llegue
   b. haya llegado

EXERCISE Set 17-2

A. Change the verb to the present perfect subjunctive by adding the indicated expression.

1. He comenzado a estudiar (Es fantástico que…)

_____

2. Mi hermana ha llegado (Dudo que…)

_____

3. Ha hecho mal tiempo (Temo que...)

_____

4. He leído esos poemas (Mi esposo niega que...)

_____

5. Mi amiga ha visto esa película (Espero que...)

_____

6. Ha estado nublado (Es posible que...)

_____

7. Me he divertido mucho (Ella no cree que...)

_____

8. Mi hermano ha pagado la cuenta (Es increíble que...)

_____

9. Te has levantado muy tarde (Es improbable que...)

_____

10. Ellos han estado aquí por dos semanas (Puede ser que...)

_____

EXERCISE Set 17-3

A. Provide the corresponding present perfect subjunctive forms for the following verbs in the present indicative tense.

1. tenemos   _____

2. podéis   _____

3. pide   _____

4. soy   _____

5. estamos   _____

6. voy   _____

7. saben _____

8. conozco _____

9. duermes _____

10. rompe _____

11. hay _____

12. digo _____

13. traen _____

14. se ducha _____

15. cree _____

16. abro _____

17. cubres _____

18. hace _____

Crossword Puzzle 17

The auxiliary form of the verb haber / *to have* for the present perfect subjunctive is missing in each sentence.

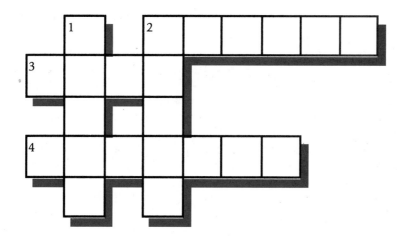

Horizontales
2. No creo que (vosotros) . . . visto a Juan.
3. Es probable que . . . nevado.
4. Ella teme que Enrique y yo no . . .
   estudiado poco.

Verticales
1. Dudo que ellos . . . hecho la tarea.
2. Espero que (tú) . . . escrito la carta.

18

The Pluperfect (Past Perfect) Subjunctive (*el pluscuamperfecto de subjuntivo*)

Uses and Features

The pluperfect (past perfect) subjunctive corresponds to the pluperfect (past perfect) indicative. The difference is that it comes after a verb, conjunction, or expression that requires the subjunctive mood in the subordinate clause.

> Era posible que ellos hubieran venido. / *It was possible that they had come.*
> Si yo no hubiera visto a Matilde, yo la habría llamado. / *If I hadn't seen Matilde, I would have called her.*

Conjugation of the Pluperfect (Past Perfect) Subjunctive

The pluperfect or past perfect subjunctive, called the **pluscuamperfecto de subjuntivo** in Spanish, is a compound tense. It is conjugated with the auxiliary verb **haber** / *to have* and the past participle of the verb, in that order. See Chapter 9 for the relevant details regarding past participles and the use of the auxiliary verb.

In the case of the pluperfect, or past perfect subjunctive, the auxiliary verb **haber** / *to have* is conjugated in the imperfect subjunctive. Again, there are two forms of **haber** / *to have* in the imperfect subjunctive. The first set has endings in -ra, -ras, -ra, -´ramos, -rais, -ran shown below. Remember that the **nosotros/-as** / *we* form of this verb has an accent (´) on the vowel that precedes the ending for the imperfect subjunctive (-´ramos): hubiéramos.

haber / *to have* (-ra endings)

Subject Pronoun	Verb Form	Meaning
...(yo)	hubie+ra	...*I had, I might have*
...(tú)	hubie+ras	...*you (fam. sg.) had, you might have*
...(él, ella, Ud.)	hubie+ra	...*he, she, you (pol. sg.) had, he, she, you might have*
...(nosotros/-as)	hubié+ramos	...*we had, we might have*
...(vosotros/-as)	hubie+rais	...*you (fam. pl.) had, you might have*
...(ellos/-as, Uds.)	hubie+ran	...*they, you (pol. pl.) had, they, you might have*

The second set's endings are -se, -ses, -se, -´semos, -seis, -sen. Remember that the nosotros/-as / *we* form of this verb has an accent (´) on the vowel that precedes the ending for the imperfect subjunctive (-´semos): hubié*semos*. In this book, we will only use the first set of endings for the exercises.

haber / to have (-se endings)

Subject Pronoun	Verb Form	Meaning
...(yo)	hubie+se	...I had, I might have
...(tú)	hubie+ses	...you (fam. sg.)had, you might have
...(él, ella, Ud.)	hubie+se	...he, she, you (pol. sg.) had, he, she, you might have
...(nosotros/-as)	hubié+semos	...we had, we might have
...(vosotros/-as)	hubie+seis	...you (fam. pl.) had, you might have
...(ellos/-as, Uds.)	hubie+sen	...they, you (pol. pl.) had, they, you might have

hablar / to talk

Subject Pronoun	Haber	Past Participle	Meaning
...(yo)	hubie+ra	habl+ado	...I had spoken, I might have spoken
...(tú)	hubie+ras	habl+ado	...you (fam. sg.) had spoken, you might have spoken
...(él, ella, Ud.)	hubie+ra	habl+ado	...he, she, you (pol. sg.) had spoken, he, she, you might have spoken
...(nosotros/-as)	hubié+ramos	habl+ado	...we had spoken, we might have spoken
...(vosotros/-as)	hubie+rais	habl+ado	...you (fam. pl.) had spoken, you might have spoken
...(ellos/-as, Uds.)	hubie+ran	habl+ado	...they, you (pol. pl.) had spoken, they, you might have spoken

comer / to eat

Subject Pronoun	Haber	Past Participle	Meaning
...(yo)	hubie+ra	com+ido	...I had eaten, I might have eaten
...(tú)	hubie+ras	com+ido	...you (fam. sg.) had eaten, you might have eaten
...(él, ella, Ud.)	hubie+ra	com+ido	...he, she, you (pol. sg.) had eaten, he, she, you might have eaten
...(nosotros/-as)	hubié+ramos	com+ido	...we had eaten, we might have eaten
...(vosotros/-as)	hubie+rais	com+ido	...you (fam. pl.) had eaten, you might have eaten
...(ellos/-as, Uds.)	hubie+ran	com+ido	...they, you (pol. pl.) had eaten, they, you might have eaten

vivir / *to live*

Subject Pronoun	Haber	Past Participle	Meaning
...(yo)	<u>hubie</u>+ra	<u>viv</u>+ido	...I had lived, I might have lived
...(tú)	<u>hubie</u>+ras	<u>viv</u>+ido	...you (fam. sg.) had lived, you might have lived
...(él, ella, Ud.)	<u>hubie</u>+ra	<u>viv</u>+ido	...he, she, you (pol. sg.) had lived, he, she, you might have lived
...(nosotros/-as)	<u>hubié</u>+ramos	<u>viv</u>+ido	...we had lived, we might have lived
...(vosotros/-as)	<u>hubie</u>+rais	<u>viv</u>+ido	...you (fam. pl.) had lived, you might have lived
...(ellos/-as, Uds.)	<u>hubie</u>+ran	<u>viv</u>+ido	... they, you (pol. pl.) had lived, they, you might have lived

The Pluperfect (Past Perfect) Subjunctive of Reflexive Verbs

Reflexive verbs always use reflexive pronouns in the pluperfect (past perfect) subjunctive, as shown below. They always appear immediately before the conjugated verb, as they do in the present subjunctive and all other tenses.

lavarse / *to wash oneself*

Subject Pronoun	Reflexive Pronoun	Haber	Past Participle	Meaning
...(yo)	me	<u>hubie</u>+ra	<u>lav</u>+ado	...I had washed myself, I might have washed myself
...(tú)	te	<u>hubie</u>+ras	<u>lav</u>+ado	...you (fam. sg.) had washed yourself, you might have washed yourself
...(él, ella, Ud.)	se	<u>hubie</u>+ra	<u>lav</u>+ado	...he, she, you (pol. sg.) had washed himself/herself/yourself, he, she, you might have washed himself/herself/yourself
...(nosotros/-as)	nos	<u>hubié</u>+ramos	<u>lav</u>+ado	...we had washed ourselves, we might have washed ourselves
...(vosotros/-as)	os	<u>hubie</u>+rais	<u>lav</u>+ado	...you (fam. pl.) had washed yourselves, you might have washed yourselves
...(ellos/-as, Uds.)	se	<u>hubie</u>+ran	<u>lav</u>+ado	...they, you (pol. pl.) had washed themselves/yourselves, they, you might have washed themselves/yourselves

---

NOTE

You have probably noticed that the first person singular (yo) and third person singular (él, ella, Ud.) are identical in form. For this reason, you must normally use the subject pronoun yo / *I* to distinguish these forms.

The Pluperfect (Past Perfect) Subjunctive

The pluperfect (past perfect) subjunctive corresponds to the pluperfect (past perfect) indicative (Chapter 10) in usage and overall features. It allows you to express a past action that occurred before another past action. We will discuss the cases in which the pluperfect (past perfect) subjunctive is used and we will provide illustrations for each instance.

<u>Era fácil</u> que él <u>hubiera dicho</u> la verdad. / *It was likely that he had told the truth.*
<u>Temíamos</u> que Víctor <u>hubiera entrado</u> en la cueva. / *We feared that Víctor had entered the cave.*
<u>Esperando que</u> <u>hubiera llovido</u> mucho, <u>llevamos</u> botas. / *Assuming that it had rained a lot, we wore boots.*

If Clauses

As was the case with the imperfect subjunctive (see Chapter 16), the pluperfect (past perfect) subjunctive is also used after si / *if* contrary-to-fact clauses (sometimes known as counterfactual or hypothetical statements). In this case, it is used when the main clause verb is in the conditional perfect.

Si Miguel <u>se hubiera levantado</u> a tiempo, él no <u>habría llegado</u> a la universidad tarde. / *If Miguel had gotten up on time, he wouldn't have arrived at the university late.*
Si yo <u>hubiera tenido</u> el dinero, yo <u>habría comprado</u> la casa. / *If I had had the money, I would have bought the house.*

The Pluperfect (Past Perfect) Subjunctive of Hay

The pluperfect (past perfect) subjunctive form of hay / *there is, there are* is ...hubiera habido / *...there had been*. The following examples illustrate this usage.

Era difícil que hubiera habido un problema. / *It was unlikely that there had been a problem.*
Yo dudaba que no hubiera habido muchos problemas. / *I doubted that there had been many problems.*

The present perfect subjunctive of the idiomatic expression hay que / *one must, it is necessary to* is ...hubiera habido que / *...it had been necessary to, it might have been necessary to*. The following sentence illustrates this usage.

Él <u>temía</u> que <u>hubiera habido que</u> estudiar más. / *He feared that it might have been necessary to study more.*

EXERCISE Set 18-1

A. Supply the missing pluperfect (past perfect) subjunctive forms of the verb **dudar**, giving the English equivalent.

EXAMPLE: ... *él* _____ = _____

         ... él hubiera dudado = ... he had doubted, he might have doubted

Era posible que...

1. (yo) _____ = _____

2. (tú) _____ = _____

3. (nosotros) _____ = _____

4. (ellos) _____ = _____

5. (vosotros) _____ = _____

6. (Ud.) _____ = _____

Now, supply the missing pluperfect (past perfect) subjunctive forms of the verb **beber**, giving the English equivalent.

1. (yo) _____ = _____

2. (Raquel y yo) _____ = _____

3. (Uds.) _____ = _____

4. (ellos) _____ = _____

5. (vosotros) _____ = _____

6. (tú) _____ = _____

Now, supply the missing pluperfect (past perfect) subjunctive forms of the verb **escribir**, giving the English equivalent.

1. (yo) _____ = _____

2. (Raquel y yo) _____ = _____

3. (Uds.) _____ = _____

4. (ellos) _____ = _____

5. (vosotros) _____ = _____

6. (Ud.) _____ = _____

Now, supply the missing pluperfect (past perfect) subjunctive forms of the verb ducharse, giving the English equivalent.

1. (yo) _____ = _____

2. (tú) _____ = _____

3. (nosotros) _____ = _____

4. (ellos) _____ = _____

5. (vosotros) _____ = _____

6. (Ud.) _____ = _____

B. How do you say the following sentences in Spanish?

1. I doubted that you (fam. sg.) had read *Tres tristes tigres*[1] by (de) *Guillermo Cabrera Infante*[2].

_____

2. Was it likely that they had seen my sister?

_____

3. I did not believe that Beatriz had visited Havana.

_____

4. The teacher hoped that his students had conjugated the verbs in the pluperfect subjunctive.

_____

5. You (fam. sg.) denied that I had been in Cuba.

_____

6. There was no one who had seen the news on TV.

_____

7. It was unlikely that Julio had been very busy.

_____

[1]Novel published in 1967.
[2]Famous Cuban novelist, 1929–2005.

8. It was possible that my parents had arrived late.

_____

9. Inés didn't believe that my brother had broken the dishes.

_____

10. It was probable that there had been an accident there.

_____

C. How do you say the following sentences in Spanish?

1. If I had had the time, I would have gone to Cuba.

_____

2. Bárbara would have driven to the university if she had known how to drive.

_____

3. If I had known of the test, I would have read the book.

_____

4. If Oscar had bought a ticket, he would have won the lottery.

_____

5. If Rosa hadn't been tired, she would not have had an accident.

_____

6. If it hadn't rained so much, we would have gone to the party.

_____

7. If Raúl hadn't lied, he wouldn't have gone to jail.

_____

8. If you (fam. sg.) had told me the truth, I wouldn't have been so angry.

_____

9. If there hadn't been so many problems, we would have arrived on time.

_____

10. If I had remembered my wallet, I would have been able to pay the bill.

_____

EXERCISE Set 18-2

A. Provide the corresponding present perfect and pluperfect (past perfect) subjunctive forms for the following verbs in the present indicative tense.

1. tenéis _____   _____

2. canto _____   _____

3. hace _____   _____

4. están _____   _____

5. somos _____   _____

6. van _____   _____

7. sé _____   _____

8. conoce _____   _____

9. mueres _____   _____

10. abrimos _____   _____

11. hay _____   _____

12. dices _____   _____

13. cae _____   _____

14. se baña _____   _____

15. cree _____   _____

16. abro _____   _____

17. cubren _____   _____

18. mido _____   _____

Crossword Puzzle 18

The auxiliary form of the verb haber / *to have* for the pluperfect (past perfect) subjunctive is missing from each verb.

Horizontales

2. Él temía que (nosotros) . . . escuchado.
3. Yo no creía que ella ya . . . llegado.
4. Si (tú) . . . tenido el dinero, habrías comprado el coche.

Verticales

1. Yo esperaba que (vosotros) . . . ganado.
2. Era difícil que ellos . . . llegado.

Part Five

Other Verb Forms

Other Verb Forms: An Overview

What Is the Imperative?

The imperative is a verbal mood that allows you to express a command, request, or warning. The request may be affirmative or negative and it may be familiar or polite. It may also include yourself (*let's* command).

¡Abre la boca! / *Open your mouth!* (fam. sg.)
¡No abras la boca! / *Don't open your mouth!* (fam. sg.)

¡Comed la fruta! / *Eat the fruit!* (fam. pl.)
¡No comáis la fruta! / *Don't eat the fruit!* (fam. pl.)

¡Diga la verdad! / *Tell the truth!* (pol. sg.)
¡No diga la verdad! / *Don't tell the truth!* (pol. sg.)

¡Trabajen más! / *Work more!* (pol. pl.)
¡No trabajen tanto! / *Don't work so much!* (pol. pl.)

¡Estudiemos los verbos españoles! / *Let's study Spanish verbs!* (*Let's* command)
¡No estudiemos los verbos españoles! / *Let's not study Spanish verbs!* (*Let's* command).

Notice that there is no first person singular form in the imperative, for it would make no sense.

What Is the Passive?

All the sentences and exercises that have preceded this unit have been *active* in their form. The verb in such sentences expresses the action performed by the subject. But for many active sentences there are corresponding *passive* ones in which the action is performed on the subject.

Active Sentence	Passive Sentence
<u>María</u> compra <u>el coche</u>. / *María buys the car.*	<u>El coche</u> es comprado por <u>María</u>. / *The car is bought by María.*

An alternative to the passive voice is the use of the pronoun se + verb in the third person singular or third person plural, as illustrated below.

<u>Se vende</u> tobaco aquí. / *Tobacco is sold here (one sells tobacco here).*
<u>Se venden</u> coches aquí. / *Cars are sold here (one sells cars here).*

What Is a Non-Finite Verb Form?

A verb in a *non-finite* form such as an infinitive, gerund, or past participle allows you to express an action that does not specify the subject. The following are examples of expressions with an infinitive (= a verbal noun), a present participle (= a verbal adverb), and a past participle (= a verbal adjective).

1. Infinitive

   El <u>comer</u> es necesario para <u>vivir</u>. / *Eating is necessary to live.*

2. Present Participle

   Marina llegó <u>cantando</u> canciones populares. / *Marina arrived singing popular songs.*

3. Past Participle

   <u>Hecha</u> la tarea, el estudiante cerró el libro. / *With the homework completed, the student closed the book.*

19
The Imperative
(*el imperativo*)

Imperative Forms of Regular Verbs

The imperative of regular verbs is called the **imperativo** in Spanish. This form is also called the command form of the verb, known as **mandato** in Spanish. The imperative is a mood and not a tense.

The imperative, or command form, of the verb has two forms. The first is the familiar imperative (**tú** / *you* [fam. sg.], and **vosotros-as** / *you* [fam. pl.]). The second is the polite imperative (**Ud.** / *you* [pol. sg.], and **Uds.** / *you* [pol. pl.]). We shall discuss all of these imperative forms in this chapter. Finally, we shall discuss the *let's* imperative in Spanish.

It will be helpful to review Chapter 15 (Present Subjunctive) since many of the imperative forms are the same as certain present subjunctive forms. Review, also, the section on spelling changes in verbs in that same chapter.

The imperative forms follow specific rules for their formation. Likewise, the placement of object pronouns (reflexive, indirect, direct) also follow a certain order depending on whether or not the imperatives are affirmative or negative. At first, the rules for formation of the two imperative forms (familiar, polite) and the placement of object pronouns with relation to these imperative forms may seem complex. If you follow the step-by-step discussion below, you will have no problems. Remember that the imperative forms in Spanish use an upside down exclamation point (¡) at the beginning of the sentence.

We shall examine imperative forms in the following step-by-step order:

Familiar Imperative

1. Affirmative familiar singular imperative
2. Affirmative familiar plural imperative
3. Negative familiar singular imperative
4. Negative familiar plural imperative
5. Irregular affirmative familiar singular imperative
6. Irregular negative familiar singular imperative
7. Affirmative familiar singular imperative with object pronouns
8. Negative familiar singular imperative with object pronouns
9. Affirmative familiar plural imperative with object pronouns
10. Negative familiar plural imperative with object pronouns

Polite Imperative

1. Affirmative polite singular imperative
2. Affirmative polite plural imperative
3. Negative polite singular imperative
4. Negative polite plural imperative
5. Irregular affirmative polite singular and plural imperative
6. Irregular negative polite singular and plural imperative
7. Affirmative polite singular imperative with object pronouns
8. Negative polite singular imperative with object pronouns
9. Affirmative polite plural imperative with object pronouns
10. Negative polite plural imperative with object pronouns

Let's Imperative

1. Affirmative *let's* imperative
2. Negative *let's* imperative
3. Affirmative *let's* imperative with object pronouns
4. Negative *let's* imperative with object pronouns

Familiar Imperative Forms

Affirmative Familiar Singular Imperative

The affirmative familiar singular imperative form (tú / *you*) of regular verbs is formed as follows:

The tú / *you* imperative form is the same as the third person singular present indicative as illustrated below.

> ¡Entra! / *Enter!*
> ¡Come! / *Eat!*
> ¡Escribe! / *Write!*
> ¡Cierra! / *Close!*
> ¡Vuelve! / *Return!*
> ¡Pide! / *Order!*

Affirmative Familiar Plural Imperative

The plural of the affirmative familiar imperative (vosotros/as / *you*) is very simple to form.

1. With the exception of the reflexive verbs (see below), the stem for the familiar plural imperative form is achieved by dropping the -r from the infinitive, as illustrated.

> entrar / *to enter* → entra-
> comer / *to eat* → come-
> escribir / *to write* → escribi-
> cerrar (ie) / *to close* → cerra-
> volver (ue) / *to return* → volve-
> pedir (i, i) / *to order* → pedi-

2. Add -d to the stem indicated in 1 above.

      entra- → ¡Entrad! / *Enter!*
      come- → ¡Comed! / *Eat!*
      escribi- → ¡Escribid! / *Write!*
      cerra- → ¡Cerrad! / *Close!*
      volve- → ¡Volved! / *Return!*
      pedi- → ¡Pedid! / *Order!*

Negative Familiar Singular Imperative

The negative form of the familiar singular imperative (tú / *you*) is formed by using the second person singular form of the present subjunctive (see Chapter 15) plus the negative word no before the verb, as illustrated below.

      ¡No entres! / *Don't enter!*
      ¡No comas! / *Don't eat!*
      ¡No escribas! / *Don't write!*
      ¡No cierres! / *Don't close!*
      ¡No vuelvas! / *Don't return!*
      ¡No pidas! / *Don't order!*

Negative Familiar Plural Imperative

The negative form of the familiar plural imperative (vosotros/-as / *you*) is formed by using the second person plural form of the present subjunctive (see Chapter 15) plus the negative word no before the verb, as illustrated below.

      ¡No entréis! / *Don't enter!*
      ¡No comáis! / *Don't eat!*
      ¡No escribáis! / *Don't write!*
      ¡No cerréis! / *Don't close!*
      ¡No volváis! / *Don't return!*
      ¡No pidáis! / *Don't order!*

Irregular Affirmative Familiar Singular Imperative

The affirmative familiar singular imperative has a few irregular forms. These irregularities are limited to the tú / *you* form only. In all other respects, these forms follow the rules outlined above. The following are the most common irregular (tú / *you*) imperative forms.

      decir (i, i) / *to say/to tell* → ¡Di!
      hacer / *to do/to make* → ¡Haz!
      ir / *to go* → ¡Ve!
      poner / *to put/to place* → ¡Pon!
      salir / *to leave* → ¡Sal!
      ser / *to be* → ¡Sé!
      tener / *to have* → ¡Ten!
      venir / *to come* → ¡Ven!

Irregular Negative Familiar Singular Imperative

The negative familiar singular imperatives (**tú** / *you*) for the previous verbs are completely regular, i.e., you use the second person singular present subjunctive of the verb preceded by the word **no**. Nevertheless, we illustrate them below to help you become familiar with them.

> **decir (i, i)** / *to say/to tell* → **¡No digas!**
> **hacer** / *to do/to make* → **¡No hagas!**
> **ir** / *to go* → **¡No vayas!**
> **poner** / *to put/to place* → **¡No pongas!**
> **salir** / *to leave* → **¡No salgas!**
> **ser** / *to be* → **¡No seas!**
> **tener** / *to have* → **¡No tengas!**
> **venir** / *to come* → **¡No vengas!**

EXERCISE Set 19-1

A. Supply the missing affirmative familiar singular imperative (**tú**) forms of **comprar, beber, abrir, tener, salir**, giving the English equivalents.

1. _____ = _____

2. _____ = _____

3. _____ = _____

4. _____ = _____

5. _____ = _____

B. Supply the missing negative familiar singular imperative (**tú**) forms of **preparar, correr, cubrir, hacer, venir**, giving the English equivalents.

1. _____ = _____

2. _____ = _____

3. _____ = _____

4. _____ = _____

5. _____ = _____

C. Supply the missing affirmative familiar plural imperative (**vosotros/-as**) forms of **comprar, beber, abrir, tener, salir**, giving the English equivalents.

1. _____ = _____

2. _____ = _____

3. _____ = _____

4. _____ = _____

5. _____ = _____

D. Supply the missing negative familiar plural imperative (**vosotros/-as**) forms of **preparar, correr, cubrir, hacer, venir**, giving the English equivalents.

1. _____ = _____

2. _____ = _____

3. _____ = _____

4. _____ = _____

5. _____ = _____

Affirmative Familiar Singular Imperative with Object Pronouns

As with other verb forms, the familiar singular imperative (**tú** / *you*) may be used with object pronouns (reflexive, indirect, direct). In this section, we shall consider first the affirmative familiar imperatives.

With affirmative familiar imperatives, the object pronouns follow and are attached to the familiar imperative form (see Chapter 6 for the section on object pronouns). We provide examples with direct object pronouns, indirect object pronouns, combinations of indirect and direct object pronouns (in that order), and reflexive pronouns below.

You will note that when you add one or two pronouns to a multi-syllable affirmative familiar singular imperative verb form (**tú**), you must write an accent mark over <u>the next to the last syllable</u> of the base imperative form (the verb before you add object pronoun(s)).

If the affirmative familiar singular imperative (**tú**) has only one syllable, and you add only one object pronoun, it is not necessary to write a graphic accent. We have examples of these cases below. The written accent means that you retain the stress in its original position. We have indicated the base imperative form of the verb, minus the object pronoun(s), with an underline. We have also used italic type to indicate the syllable that receives a written stress mark.

1. *Direct object pronoun*
   ¡<u>Cié*rra*</u>la! / *Close it!*
   ¡<u>*Có*me</u>la! / *Eat it!*
   ¡<u>*Á*bre</u>la! / *Open it!*
   ¡<u>Haz</u>lo! / *Do it!* (Single syllable; no written accent)
   ¡<u>Pon</u>lo aquí! / *Put it here!* (Single syllable; no written accent)

2. *Indirect object pronoun*
   ¡<u>*Há*bla</u>me! / *Speak to me!*
   ¡<u>Mué*stra*</u>me! / *Show me!*

3. *Indirect and direct object pronouns*
   ¡<u>*Dí*</u>melo! / *Tell it to me!* (Single syllable; two object pronouns added)
   ¡<u>*Cán*ta</u>mela! / *Sing it to me!*

4. *Reflexive pronoun.*
   ¡<u>Le*ván*</u>tate! / *Get up!*
   ¡<u>*Vís*te</u>te! / *Get dressed!*

> **TIP**
>
> 1. If a word ends in a vowel, n or s, the stress falls on the next to the last syllable as shown below. No written accent is necessary.
>
>   h<u>a</u>blo / *I speak*
>   h<u>a</u>blas / *you (fam. sg.) speak*
>   h<u>a</u>bla / *he, she, you (pol. sg.) speak(s)*
>
> 2. If a word ends in a consonant other than n or s, the stress falls on the last syllable as shown below. No written accent is necessary.
>
>   habl<u>a</u>r / *to speak*
>   ¡Habl<u>a</u>d! / *Speak!*
>
> If you add extra syllables (object pronouns), you will need to indicate that the stress is retained in its original place with a written accent.

Negative Familiar Singular Imperative with Object Pronouns

To form the negative familiar singular imperative (tú / *you*) of the above verb examples, you use the second person singular present subjunctive (fam. sg.). First you place the negative word no before the verb. Next, you place the object pronoun(s) immediately before the imperative form. The order would thus be: No + object pronoun(s) + verb.

The order of the words in a negative familiar singular imperative is the following: No + object pronoun(s) + second person singular present subjunctive. We reproduce the examples from the previous section, but in a negative format. We use an underline to indicate the imperative form.

1. *Direct object pronoun*
    ¡No la <u>cierres</u>! / *Don't close it!*
    ¡No la <u>comas</u>! / *Don't eat it!*
    ¡No la <u>abras</u>! / *Don't open it!*
    ¡No lo <u>hagas</u>! / *Don't do it!*
    ¡No lo <u>pongas</u> aquí! / *Don't put it here!*

2. *Indirect object pronoun*
    ¡No me <u>hables</u>! / *Don't speak to me!*
    ¡No me <u>muestres</u>! *Don't show me!*

3. *Indirect and direct object pronouns.*
    ¡No me lo <u>digas</u>! / *Don't tell it to me!*
    ¡No me la <u>cantes</u>! / *Don't sing it to me!*

4. *Reflexive pronoun*
    ¡No te <u>levantes</u>! / *Don't get up!*
    ¡No te <u>vistas</u>! / *Don't get dressed!*

Affirmative Familiar Plural Imperative with Object Pronouns

As with other verbs, the affirmative familiar plural imperative (**vosotros-as** / *you*) may be used with object pronouns (reflexive, indirect, direct). In this section, we shall consider first the affirmative familiar plural imperatives. With affirmative familiar plural imperatives, the object pronouns follow and are attached to the familiar imperative form (see Chapter 6 for the section on object pronouns). We provide examples with direct object pronouns, indirect object pronouns, combinations of indirect and direct object pronouns (in that order), as well as reflexive pronouns below.

You will note that with the affirmative familiar plural imperative (**vosotros-as** / *you*), you drop the -d from the stem before you add the reflexive pronoun. We have indicated the base imperative form with an underline.

We use the same verbs from the previous section, but this time they are in the **vosotros-as** / *you* form. We have indicated the base imperative form with an underline.

1. *Direct object pronoun*
    ¡<u>Cerrad</u>la! / *Close it!*
    ¡<u>Comed</u>la! / *Eat it!*
    ¡<u>Abrid</u>la! / *Open it!*
    ¡<u>Haced</u>lo! / *Do it!*
    ¡<u>Poned</u>lo aquí! / *Put it here!*

2. *Indirect object pronoun*
    ¡<u>Hablad</u>me! / *Speak to me!*
    ¡<u>Mostrad</u>me! / *Show me!*

3. *Indirect and direct object pronouns*
    ¡<u>Decíd</u>melo! / *Tell it to me!* (Written accent because you have added two syllables)
    ¡<u>Cantád</u>mela! / *Sing it to me!* (Written accent because you have added two syllables)

4. *Reflexive pronoun*
    ¡<u>Levanta</u>os! / *Get up!*
    ¡<u>Vestí</u>os! / *Get dressed!* (Written accent to indicate two separate syllables)

Negative Familiar Plural Imperative with Object Pronouns

Finally, to form the negative familiar plural imperative (**vosotros/as** / *you*) of the verb examples just seen, you use the second person plural present subjunctive (fam. pl.). First you place the negative word **no** before the verb. Next, you place the object pronouns immediately before the imperative form. The order of the words in a negative familiar plural imperative is the following: **No** + object pronoun(s) + Verb. We reproduce the examples from the previous section, but in a negative format. We have indicated the imperative form with an underline.

1. *Direct object pronoun*
    ¡No la <u>cerréis</u> ! / *Don't close it!*
    ¡No la <u>comáis</u>! / *Don't eat it!*
    ¡No la <u>abráis</u>! / *Don't open it!*
    ¡No lo <u>hagáis</u>! / *Don't do it!*
    ¡No lo <u>pongáis</u> aquí! / *Don't put it here!*

2. *Indirect object pronoun*
    ¡No me <u>habléis</u>! / *Don't speak to me!*
    ¡No me <u>mostréis</u>! / *Don't show me!*

3. *Indirect and direct object pronouns*
   ¡No me lo <u>digáis</u>! / *Don't tell it to me!*
   ¡No me la <u>cantéis</u>! / *Don't sing it to me!*

4. *Reflexive pronoun*
   ¡No os <u>levantéis</u>! / *Don't get up!*
   ¡No os <u>vistáis</u>! / *Don't get dressed!*

EXERCISE Set 19-2

A. How do you say the following sentences in Spanish? Use the tú imperatives. Pay attention to the placement of the object pronouns (reflexive, indirect, direct).

1. Shave!

   _____

2. Don't give it (book) to me!

   _____

3. Study it (lesson)!

   _____

4. Read it (book) to me!

   _____

5. Don't go to bed!

   _____

6. Don't tell it (truth) to me!

   _____

7. Don't read it (novel)!

   _____

8. Buy it (car)!

   _____

Polite Imperative Forms of Regular Verbs

In this section, we deal with the polite imperative (Ud. / *you* [pol. sg.], and Uds. / *you* [pol. pl.]). The polite imperative forms follow certain rules of formation. Likewise, the placement of object pronouns (reflexive, indirect, direct) also follow a certain order depending on whether or not the imperatives are affirmative or negative. Again, we remind you that the rules for formation of the polite imperatives and the placement of object pronouns with relation to these imperative forms may seem complex. However, if you follow the step-by-step discussion below, you will have no problems.

Affirmative Polite Singular Imperative

First, we shall discuss the formation of the affirmative polite singular imperative (Ud. / *you*).

The Ud. / *you* imperative form is the same as the third person singular present subjunctive, as illustrated below.

¡Entre! / *Enter!*
¡Coma! / *Eat!*
¡Escriba! / *Write!*
¡Cierre! / *Close!*
¡Vuelva! / *Return!*
¡Pida! / *Order!*

Affirmative Polite Plural Imperative

The plural of the affirmative polite imperative (Uds. / *you*) is very simple to form.

To form an affirmative polite plural imperative form, use the third person plural present subjunctive form.

¡Entren! / *Enter!*
¡Coman! / *Eat!*
¡Escriban! / *Write!*
¡Cierren! / *Close!*
¡Vuelvan! / *Return!*
¡Pidan! / *Order!*

Negative Polite Singular Imperative

The negative form of the polite singular imperative (Ud. / *you*) is formed by using the third person singular form of the present subjunctive (see Chapter 15) plus the negative word no before the verb, as illustrated below.

¡No entre! / *Don't enter!*
¡No coma! / *Don't eat!*
¡No escriba! / *Don't write!*
¡No cierre! / *Don't close!*
¡No vuelva! / *Don't return!*
¡No pida! / *Don't order!*

Negative Polite Plural Imperative

The negative form of the polite plural imperative (**Uds.** / *you*) is formed by using the third person plural form of the present subjunctive (see Chapter 15) plus the negative word **no** before the verb, as illustrated below.

¡No entren! / *Don't enter!*
¡No coman! / *Don't eat!*
¡No escriban! / *Don't write!*
¡No cierren! / *Don't close!*
¡No vuelvan! / *Don't return!*
¡No pidan! / *Don't order!*

Irregular Affirmative Polite Singular and Plural Imperative

The polite imperative has a few irregular forms. In Chapter 15, we introduced the memory aid of the acronym DISHES, which we reproduce here for your convenience. The plural (**Uds.** / *you*) form is the same as the third person plural of the present subjunctive.

<u>D</u>ar / *to give* → ¡Dé(n)! (Plural has no written accent)
<u>I</u>r / *to go* → ¡Vaya(n)!
<u>S</u>er / *to be* → ¡Sea(n)!
<u>H</u>aber / *to have* → ¡Haya(n)!
<u>E</u>star / *to be* → ¡Esté(n)!
<u>S</u>aber / *to know* → ¡Sepa(n)!

Irregular Negative Polite Singular and Plural Imperative

The negative polite singular imperatives (**Ud.** / *you*) for the above verbs use the third person singular present subjunctive. The plural (**Uds.** / *you*) form is the same as the third person plural of the present subjunctive. Nevertheless, we illustrate them below to help you become familiar with them.

<u>D</u>ar / *to give* → ¡No dé(n)! (Plural has no written accent)
<u>I</u>r / *to go* → ¡No vaya(n)!
<u>S</u>er / *to be* → ¡No sea(n)!
<u>H</u>aber / *to have* → ¡No haya(n)!
<u>E</u>star / *to be* → ¡No esté(n)!
<u>S</u>aber / *to know* → ¡No sepa(n)!

EXERCISE Set 19-3

A. Supply the missing affirmative polite singular imperative (**Ud.**) forms of **cantar, comer, asistir, ser, dar**, giving the English equivalents.

1. _____ = _____

2. _____ = _____

3. _____ = _____

4. _____ = _____

5. _____ = _____

B. Supply the missing negative polite singular imperative (**Ud.**) forms of **comprar, beber, vivir, saber, ir,** giving the English equivalents.

1. _____ = _____

2. _____ = _____

3. _____ = _____

4. _____ = _____

5. _____ = _____

C. Supply the missing affirmative polite plural imperative (**Uds.**) forms of **buscar, leer, abrir, estar, volver,** giving the English equivalents.

1. _____ = _____

2. _____ = _____

3. _____ = _____

4. _____ = _____

5. _____ = _____

D. Supply the missing negative polite plural imperative (**Uds.**) forms of **preparar, creer, admitir, comenzar, proteger,** giving the English equivalents.

1. _____ = _____

2. _____ = _____

3. _____ = _____

4. _____ = _____

5. _____ = _____

Affirmative Polite Singular Imperative with Object Pronouns

As with other verbs, the polite singular imperative (Ud. / *you*) may be used with object pronouns (reflexive, indirect, direct). In this section, we shall consider first the affirmative polite imperatives. With polite imperatives, the object pronouns follow and are attached to the imperative form (see Chapter 6 for the section on object pronouns). We provide examples with direct object pronouns, indirect object pronouns, combinations of indirect and direct object pronouns (in that order), and reflexive pronouns below.

You will note that when you add one or two pronouns to an affirmative polite singular imperative (Ud. / *you*) form, you must write an accent mark over the next to the last syllable of the base imperative form (the verb before you add object pronoun(s)). We have examples of both below. The written accent means that you retain the stress in its original position. We have indicated the base imperative form of the verb (minus the object pronouns) with an underline. We have also used italic type to indicate the syllable that receives a written stress mark.

1. *Direct object pronoun*
   ¡Ciérrela! / *Close it!*
   ¡Cómala! / *Eat it!*
   ¡Ábrala! / *Open it!*
   ¡Hágalo! / *Do it!*
   ¡Póngalo aquí! / *Put it here!*

2. *Indirect object pronoun*
   ¡Hábleme! / *Speak to me!*
   ¡Muéstreme! / *Show me!*

3. *Indirect and direct object pronouns*
   ¡Dígamelo! / *Tell it to me!*
   ¡Cántemela! / *Sing it to me!*

4. *Reflexive pronoun*
   ¡Levántese! / *Get up!*
   ¡Vístase! / *Get dressed!*

Negative Polite Singular Imperative with Object Pronouns

To form the negative polite singular imperative (Ud. / *you*) of the above verb examples, you use the third person singular present subjunctive (pol. sg.). First you place the negative word no before the verb. Next, you place the object pronouns immediately before the imperative form. The order of the words in a negative polite singular imperative is the following: No + object pronoun(s) + third person singular present subjunctive. We reproduce the examples from the previous section, but in a negative format. We have used an underline to indicate the imperative form.

1. *Direct object pronoun*
   ¡No la cierre! / *Don't close it!*
   ¡No la coma! / *Don't eat it!*
   ¡No la abra! / *Don't open it!*
   ¡No lo haga! / *Don't do it!*
   ¡No lo ponga aquí! / *Don't put it here!*

2. *Indirect object pronoun*
   ¡No me hable! / *Don't speak to me!*
   ¡No me muestre! / *Don't show me!*

3. *Indirect and direct object pronouns*
     ¡No me lo <u>diga</u>! / *Don't tell it to me!*
     ¡No me la <u>cante</u>! / *Don't sing it to me!*

4. *Reflexive pronoun*
     ¡No se <u>levante</u>! / *Don't get up!*
     ¡No se <u>vista</u>! / *Don't get dressed!*

Affirmative Polite Plural Imperative with Object Pronouns

As with other verbs, the polite plural imperative (**Uds.** / *you*) may be used with object pronouns (reflexive, indirect, direct). In this section, we shall consider first the affirmative polite plural imperatives. With polite imperatives, the object pronouns follow and are attached to the imperative form (see Chapter 6 for the section on object pronouns). We provide examples with direct object pronouns, indirect object pronouns, combinations of indirect and direct object pronouns (in that order), and reflexive pronouns below.

You will note that when you add one or two pronouns to a multi-syllable imperative form, you must write an accent mark over the next to the last syllable of the basic imperative form. We have examples of both below. The written accent means that you retain the stress in its original position. We have indicated the base imperative form (minus the object pronouns) with an underline. We have also used italic type to indicate the syllable that receives a written stress mark.

You will note that the affirmative polite plural imperative (**Uds.** / *you*) is the same as the third person plural present subjunctive plus the object pronoun.

We use the same verbs from the previous section, but this time they are in the **Uds.** / *you* form. We have used an underline to indicate the imperative form.

1. *Direct object pronoun*
     !<u>Ci*é*rren</u>la! / *Close it!*
     ¡<u>C*ó*man</u>la! / *Eat it!*
     ¡<u>*Á*bran</u>la! / *Open it!*
     ¡<u>H*á*gan</u>lo! / *Do it!*
     ¡<u>P*ó*nganlo</u> aquí! / *Put it here!*

2. *Indirect object pronoun*
     ¡<u>H*á*blen</u>me! / *Speak to me!*
     ¡<u>Mu*é*stren</u>me! / *Show me!*

3. *Indirect and direct object pronouns*
     ¡<u>D*í*gan</u>melo! / *Tell it to me!*
     ¡<u>C*á*nten</u>mela! / *Sing it to me!*

4. *Reflexive pronoun*
     ¡<u>Lev*á*nten</u>se! / *Get up!*
     ¡<u>V*í*stan</u>se! / *Get dressed!*

Negative Polite Plural Imperative with Object Pronouns

Finally, to form the negative polite plural imperative (**Uds.** / *you*) of the verb examples we have seen, you use the third person plural present subjunctive (pol. pl.). First you place the negative word **no** before the verb. Next, you place the object pronouns immediately before the imperative form. The order of the words in a negative familiar plural imperative is the following: **No** + object pronoun(s) + third person plural present subjunctive. We reproduce the examples from the previous section, but in a negative format. We have used an underline to indicate the imperative form.

1. *Direct object pronoun*
   ¡No la <u>cierren</u>! / *Don't close it!*
   ¡No la <u>coman</u>! / *Don't eat it!*
   ¡No la <u>abran</u>! / *Don't open it!*
   ¡No lo <u>hagan</u>! / *Don't do it!*
   ¡No lo <u>pongan</u> aquí! / *Don't put it here!*

2. *Indirect object pronoun*
   ¡No me <u>hablen</u>! / *Don't speak to me!*
   ¡No me <u>muestren</u>! / *Don't show me!*

3. *Indirect and direct object pronouns*
   ¡No me lo <u>digan</u>! / *Don't tell it to me!*
   ¡No me la <u>canten</u>! / *Don't sing it to me!*

4. *Reflexive pronoun*
   ¡No se <u>levanten</u>! / *Don't get up!*
   ¡No se <u>vistan</u>! / *Don't get dressed!*

EXERCISE Set 19-4

A. How do you say the following sentences in Spanish? All are polite forms (Ud., Uds.). Pay attention to the placement of the object pronouns (reflexive, indirect, direct). Remember to use the redundant indirect object pronoun where necessary (see Chapter 6).

1. Go to bed! (pol. pl.)

   _____

2. Buy it (novel) for me! (pol. sg.)

   _____

3. Don't show it (book) to her! (pol. sg.)

   _____

4. Sing it (song) to her! (pol. pl.)

   _____

5. Get up! (pol. sg.)

   _____

6. Don't look at me! (pol. pl.)

   _____

7. Write it (letter) to them! (pol. sg.)

_____

8. Show them (books) to her! (pol. sg.)

_____

Let's Imperative

Imperatives may appear in the nosotros/-as / *we* form of the verb. The *let's* imperative form is identical to the first person plural of the present subjunctive (see Chapter 15).

Affirmative Let's Imperative

The following are selected examples of the affirmative form of this imperative.

¡Entremos! / *Let's enter!*
¡Comamos! / *Let's eat!*
¡Escribamos! / *Let's write!*
¡Cerremos! / *Let's close!*
¡Volvamos! / *Let's return!*
¡Pidamos! / *Let's order!*

Negative Let's Imperative

The following are selected examples of the negative form of this imperative. We use the same verbs as those above to illustrate this form of the verb.

¡No entremos! / *Let's not enter!*
¡No comamos! / *Let's not eat!*
¡No escribamos! / *Let's not write!*
¡No cerremos! / *Let's not close!*
¡No volvamos! / *Let's not return!*
¡No pidamos! / *Let's not order!*

GRAMMAR NOTE

The verb ir / *to go* may be used with an infinitive to express the meaning *let's*, as illustrated below in the affirmative and negative versions.

Vamos a cantar. / *Let's sing.*
No vamos a cantar. / *Let's not sing.*

A. How do you say the following sentences in Spanish?

1. Let's begin!

_____

2. Let's not go!

_____

3. Let's play the guitar!

_____

4. Let's be nice!

_____

5. Let's not conjugate verbs in Spanish!

_____

Affirmative Let's Imperative with Object Pronouns

As with other verbs, the *let's* imperative may be used with object pronouns (reflexive, indirect, direct). In this section, we shall consider first the affirmative *let's* imperatives. With affirmative *let's* imperatives, the object pronouns follow and are attached to the *let's* imperative form (see Chapter 6 for the section on object pronouns).

You will note that when you add one or two pronouns to a *let's* imperative form, you must write an accent mark over the next to the last syllable of the basic imperative form. We have examples of both cases below. We have indicated the stressed syllable that must bear a written accent with italic type. The written accent means that you retain the stress in its original position. We have also underlined the verbal portion of the *let's* command form. You will note that with reflexive verbs, you remove the final -s of the verb and then add the reflexive pronoun -**nos**.

1. *Direct object pronoun*
   ¡<u>Cerrémos</u>la! / *Let's close it!*
   ¡<u>Comámos</u>la! / *Let's eat it!*
   ¡<u>Abrámos</u>la! / *Let's open it!*
   ¡<u>Hagámos</u>lo! / *Let's do it!*
   ¡<u>Pongámos</u>lo aquí! / *Let's put it here!*

2. *Indirect object pronoun*
   ¡<u>Hablémos</u>le a ella! / *Let's speak to her!*
   ¡<u>Mostrémos</u>le a ella! / *Let's show her!*

3. *Indirect and direct object pronouns*
   ¡<u>Digámo</u>selo a ellos! / *Let's tell it to them!* (Note: you only have one -s-)
   ¡<u>Cantémo</u>selo a él! / *Let's sing it to him!* (Note: you only have one -s-)

4. *Reflexive pronoun*
   ¡<u>Levantémo</u>nos! / *Let's get up!* (Note: you delete the -s- of the verb stem)
   ¡<u>Vistámo</u>nos! / *Let's get dressed!* (Note: you delete the -s- of the verb stem)

Negative Let's Imperative with Object Pronouns

To form the negative *let's* imperative of the above verb examples, you use the first person plural present subjunctive. First you place the negative word **no** before the verb. Next, you place the object pronouns immediately before the imperative form. The order of the words in a negative familiar singular imperative is the following: **No** + object pronoun(s) + first person plural present subjunctive. We reproduce the examples from the previous section, but in a negative format. We have also underlined the verbal portion of the *let's* command form.

1. *Direct object pronoun*
   ¡No la <u>cerremos</u>! / *Let's not close it!*
   ¡No la <u>comamos</u>! / *Let's not eat it!*
   ¡No la <u>abramos</u>! / *Let's not open it!*
   ¡No lo <u>hagamos</u>! / *Let's not do it!*
   ¡No lo <u>pongamos</u> aquí! / *Let's not put it here!*

2. *Indirect object pronoun*
   ¡No le <u>hablemos</u> a ella! / *Let's not speak to her!*
   ¡No le <u>mostremos</u> a ella! *Let's not show her!*

3. *Indirect and direct object pronouns*
   ¡No se lo <u>digamos</u> a ellos! / *Let's not tell it to them!*
   ¡No se lo <u>cantemos</u> a él! / *Let's not sing it to him!*

4. *Reflexive pronoun*
   ¡No nos <u>levantemos</u>! / *Let's not get up!*
   ¡No nos <u>vistamos</u>! / *Let's not get dressed!*

EXERCISE Set 19-6

A. How do you say the following sentences in Spanish? Pay attention to the position of the object pronouns. Remember to use the redundant indirect object pronoun where necessary (see Chapter 6).

1. Let's sing it (song) to her!

---

2. Let's not say anything to him!

---

3. Let's get up late!

_____

4. Let's do it (work)!

_____

5. Let's not give it (gift) to him!

_____

6. Let's show it (home) to them!

_____

7. Let's not go to bed!

_____

8. Let's not drink it (coffee)!

_____

EXERCISE Set 19-7

A. Provide the affirmative and negative familiar singular imperatives (tú) for the following Spanish infinitives.

1. comprar   _____   _____

2. beber   _____   _____

3. vivir   _____   _____

4. ser   _____   _____

5. estar   _____   _____

6. hacer   _____   _____

7. tener   _____   _____

8. ducharse   _____   _____

9. buscar   _____   _____

10. encontrar   _____   _____

B. Provide the affirmative and negative polite singular imperatives (**Ud.**) for the following Spanish infinitives.

1. comprar

2. beber

3. vivir

4. ser

5. estar

6. hacer

7. tener

8. ducharse

9. buscar

10. encontrar

C. Provide the affirmative and negative *let's* command for the following Spanish infinitives.

1. hablar

2. comer

3. escribir

4. divertirse (ie, i)

Crossword Puzzle 19

Use imperative forms based on the sense of each sentence.

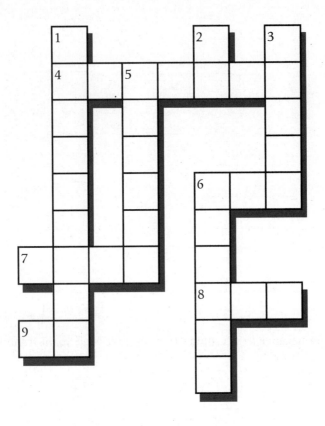

Horizontales
  4. Señorita Pérez, ¡(escribir) . . . en la pizarra!
  6. Alejandro, ¡(venir) . . . aquí!
  7. Señora Martínez, ¡(hacer) . . . esta tarea!
  8. Señora Rodríguez, ¡(leer) . . . este libro!
  9. Claudia, ¡(ir) . . . a la tienda!

Verticales
  1. Jorge, ¡(levantarse) . . . ahora!
  2. Ana, ¡(decir) . . . la verdad!
  3. Señores, ¡(ir) . . . !
  5. Carlos, ¡(comprar) . . . los libros!
  6. Señor González, ¡(volver) . . . !

20

The Passive Voice (*la voz pasiva*) and Non-Finite Verb Forms (*las formas no finitas del verbo*)

The True Passive Voice

Verbs can be in the active or passive voice. The active voice is used to indicate that the subject of the verb performs the action, whereas the passive voice, called la voz pasiva in Spanish, is used to indicate that the subject is the receiver of the action. It is sometimes called the "true passive."

> *Active*:   Mario compra los libros. / *Mario buys the books.*
> *Passive*: Los libros son comprados por Mario. / *The books are bought by Mario.*

Passive sentences can be formed from corresponding active ones as follows:

1. Change the order of the subject and the object.

> Mario compra los libros. / *Mario buys the books.*
>
> Los libros (compra) Mario.

2. Change the verb into the passive form by introducing the verb ser / *to be* in the same tense. Next, change the verb into its past participle form (see Chapter 9). Recall that when you use the verb ser / *to be*, there is agreement (gender and number) of the adjective with the subject of the sentence (the past participle is the adjectival form of the verb).

> Los libros son comprados.

3. Put **por** / *by* in front of the passive object.

        Los libros son comprados por Mario. / *The books are bought by Mario.*

Here are a few additional examples of "passivization."

Active	Passive
La mujer <u>lee</u> la revista. / *The woman reads the magazine.*	**La revista <u>es leída</u> por la mujer.** / *The magazine is read by the woman.*
Él <u>vendió</u> el coche. / *He sold the car.*	**El coche <u>fue vendido</u> por él.** / *The car was sold by him.*

EXERCISE Set 20-1

A. Rewrite the following sentences. Change them to the "true passive" voice. Remember that the verb may be in any tense. Remember also that the past participle agrees in number and gender with the subject of a "true passive" voice.

1. José construyó la casa.

---

2. Los hombres abren las puertas.

---

3. Ana leerá la novela.

---

4. Los estudiantes cantaron la canción.

---

5. *Cervantes*[1] escribió *Don Quijote*[2].

---

[1]Miguel de Cervantes Saavedra, 1547–1616.
[2]*Don Quijote*, novel in two parts, 1605, 1615.

B. How do you say the following sentences in Spanish? Remember that the past participle agrees in number and gender with the subject of a "true passive" voice.

1. The food was eaten by the children.

_____

2. The house was built by the workers.

_____

3. The window was broken by the men.

_____

4. The bill was paid by Carlos.

_____

5. The books were purchased by the students.

_____

The *Se* Passive

There is another, more common, way of formulating the passive voice, when you don't want to express the original subject of the sentence. In this version of the passive voice, there are two possible verb forms: Third person singular and third person plural. These two verb forms are always preceded by the object pronoun **se**, as illustrated below. You will also note that the order of the words is as follows: Se + verb (singular/plural) + subject (singular/plural).

se +	verb in third person + (singular or plural)	subject (singular or plural)

The following examples illustrate how the above formula works.

Singular	Plural
Se canta la canción. / *The song is sung.*	**Se cantan** las canciones. / *The songs are sung.*

It should be noted that the English translation of the **se** passive is not always equivalent to the traditional passive voice (*the man was seen by his son*). The following are some examples of other ways of translating the **se** passive forms into English and vice-versa. We provide the most common English glosses for this construction, namely, non-referential "you," non-referential "they," and impersonal "one."

    ¿Cómo se dice "book" en español? /*How do _you_ say book in Spanish?*
    Se habla italiano en Suiza. / *_They_ speak Italian in Switzerland.*
    Se debe estudiar mucho. / *_One_ must study a lot.*

Remember that the **se** passive may be used in any tense or mood just as with the "true passive" voice.

EXERCISE Set 20-2

A. How do you say the following sentences in Spanish? Use the se passive construction.

1. Spanish is spoken here.

_____

2. They say that it is raining.

_____

3. They sell newspapers here.

_____

4. The bills are paid on Fridays.

_____

5. You must eat three meals every day.

_____

Summary

The passive voice may be expressed in two ways, as illustrated below:

1. The "true passive" voice involves a step-by-step process:
    a. Change the order of the subject and object.
    b. Introduce the verb ser.
    c. Make the verb ser the same tense as the original verb.
    d. Change the original verb to the past participle.
    e. Remember to make the past participle agree in number and gender with the new subject of the sentence.

The following example shows the process in a nutshell.

Elena vende la casa. / *Elena sells the house.*
La casa <u>es vendida</u> por Elena. / *The house is sold by Elena.*

2. The se passive also has a formula for its use that we reproduce here. Remember that you do not express the agent (the person by whom the action of the verb is performed) in this construction.
    a. Use se and the third person (singular or plural) of the verb in any tense.
    b. Place the noun after the verb. The verb will be singular or plural depending on whether the noun is singular or plural.

The following examples illustrate this process.

Se vende tabaco aquí. / *Tobacco is sold here.*
Se venden casas aquí. / *Houses are sold here (houses for sale).*

Non-Finite Verb Forms

You will recall that conjugated verbs have endings to indicate the following pieces of information:

1. Person (first, second, third).
2. Number (singular, plural).
3. Tense (past, present, future).
4. Mood (indicative, subjunctive, imperative).

   Spanish also has three non-finite verb forms. This means that they have no subject expressed. You have already learned these three forms in previous chapters.

1. Infinitive (the form of the verb that ends in -r).
2. The present participle, or gerund (the form of the verb that ends in -ndo).
3. Past participle (the form of the verb that ends in -do, though there are irregular forms).

   We provide examples of how these three non-finite verb forms may be used in Spanish.

1. The infinitive after a preposition.

   Al <u>llegar</u> a casa, preparé la cena. / *Upon arriving home, I prepared dinner.*

2. The infinitive when there is no change of subject in a sentence.

   Quiero <u>leer</u> esa novela. / *I want to read that novel.*

3. It should be noted also that a perfect infinitive also exists, as illustrated below.

   Debo <u>haber conjugado</u> esos verbos. / *I should have conjugated those verbs.*

4. Remember that object pronouns (reflexive, indirect, direct) may follow and may be attached to infinitives.

   Voy a ver<u>lo</u>. / *I am going to see him.*

5. Alternatively, object pronouns (reflexive, indirect, direct) may appear immediately before the conjugated verb, as shown below.

   <u>Lo</u> voy a ver. / *I am going to see him.*

6. The present participle, or gerund, is used to create progressive verb forms (see Chapter 6) but it is also used to modify a sentence as illustrated below. Remember that object pronouns (reflexive, direct, indirect) follow and are attached to a present participle.

   <u>Corriendo</u>, pierdo peso. / *By running, I lose weight.*
   <u>Viéndolo</u>, lo saludé. / *Upon seeing him, I greeted him.*

7. The past participle may also be used to modify a sentence, as shown below.

   <u>Hecho</u> el trabajo, regresé a casa. / *With the work completed, I returned home.*

EXERCISE Set 20-3

A. How do you say the following sentences in Spanish? Use an infinitive, present participle, or past participle according to the meaning.

1. After reading the paper, Marisol started to work.

_____

2. While walking, I saw Pablo.

_____

3. With the game finished, we went to the restaurant.

_____

4. While reading the magazine, Lidia drank coffee.

_____

5. Before leaving, Juan bought a book.

_____

Crossword Puzzle 20

Provide an infinitive, present participle, or past participle according to the grammar and the meaning.

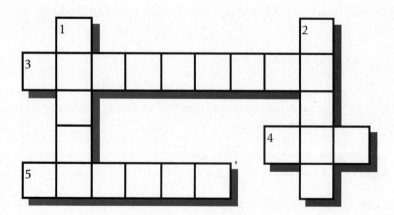

Horizontales
3. (Terminar) . . . la tarea, fui al cine.
4. Al (ver) . . . a Sara, la saludé.
5. Antes de (volver) . . . a casa, corrí
   en el parque.

Verticales
1. (Hacer) . . . el trabajo, él volvió a casa.
2. Después de (haber) . . . visto a María,
   él regresó a casa.

Answers

CHAPTER 1
Exercise Set 1-1

A.

1. toco	=	I play, I am playing, I do play
2. esperas	=	you (fam. sg.) hope/wait, you are hoping/waiting, you do hope/wait
3. preparamos	=	we prepare, we are preparing, we do prepare
4. llevan	=	they wear, they are wearing, they do wear
5. pagáis	=	you (fam. pl.) pay for, you are paying for, you do pay for
6. trabaja	=	you (pol. sg.) work, you are working, you do work
7. miran	=	they look at, they are looking at, they do look at
8. estudian	=	you (pol. pl.) study, you are studying, you do study
9. viajo	=	I travel, I am traveling, I do travel
10. bailas	=	you (fam. sg.) dance, you are dancing, you do dance
11. cantamos	=	we sing, we are singing, we do sing
12. compra	=	he buys, he is buying, he does buy
13. hablan	=	they speak, they are speaking, they do speak
14. entra	=	you (pol sg.) enter, you are entering, you do enter
15. buscan	=	you (pol. pl.) look for, you are looking for, you do look for

B.

1. Perdón, ¿habla Ud. inglés?
2. Sí, hablo inglés muy bien.
3. Ellos no hablan español muy bien.
4. Hablamos español un poco.
5. Rafael, hablas español también, ¿verdad?
6. No hablo español, pero mi hija habla español muy bien.
7. No, no es verdad. El autobús no llega ahora.
8. Gracias. Ud. es muy amable. No hablo español bien.
9. Alejandro toca el violoncelo como *Pablo Casals* y Claudia pinta como *Diego Velázquez*.
10. Ella escucha la radio demasiado.
11. Deseo mirar la corrida de toros en la televisión.
12. Ellos tocan el piano bien.
13. Siempre miras la televisión.
14. Ud. lleva una chaqueta nueva, ¿verdad?
15. Uds. esperan el autobús, ¿verdad?

Exercise Set 1-2

A.

1. aprendo	=	I learn, I am learning, I do learn
2. comprendes	=	you (fam. sg.) understand, you are understanding, you do understand
3. creemos	=	we believe, we are believing, we do believe
4. meten	=	they put (into), they are putting (into), they do put (into)
5. corréis	=	you (fam. pl.) run, you are running, you do run
6. lee	=	you (pol. sg.) read, you are reading, you do read
7. mi amiga teme	=	my friend (f.) fears, my friend is fearing, my friend does fear
8. rompen	=	they (f.) break, they are breaking, they do break
9. debo	=	I owe/ought/should, I am owing, I do owe

10. bebes	=	you (fam. sg.) drink, you are drinking, you do drink
11. vendemos	=	we sell, we are selling, we do sell
12. comen	=	you (pol. pl.) eat, you are eating, you do eat
13. aprende	=	he learns, he is learning, he does learn
14. comprenden	=	they understand, they are understanding, they do understand
15. cree	=	you (pol. sg.) believe, you are believing, you do believe

B.

1. ¿Lees *Don Quijote*?
2. No leo. Mando un correo electrónico.
3. Perdón, ¿manda Ud. un correo electrónico en español?
4. Sí, porque mi amiga habla, lee y escribe español muy bien.
5. Adiós. ¿Comprenden Uds.?
6. Debo mandar un correo electrónico en veinte minutos.
7. Mi amiga no vende el *Seat*.
8. Mi abuela bebe mucho café.
9. Temo los exámenes de español.
10. Mi hermano vende el coche.
11. Mi hermana siempre rompe algo.
12. Mi amiga mexicana lee *El País* con frecuencia.
13. Mi hijo debe leer más.
14. Mi hija aprende a hablar español en la Universidad de Salamanca.
15. ¿Comes mucho?

Exercise Set 1-3

A.

1. vivo	=	I live, I am living, I do live
2. asistes	=	you (fam. sg.) attend, you are attending, you do attend
3. describimos	=	we describe, we are describing, we do describe
4. cubren	=	they cover, they are covering, they do cover
5. sufrís	=	you (fam. pl.) suffer, you are suffering, you do suffer
6. admite	=	you (pol. sg.) admit, you are admitting, you do admit
7. mi amiga discute	=	my friend discusses, my friend is discussing, my friend does discuss
8. viven	=	they live, they are living, they do live
9. permito	=	I permit, I am permitting, I do permit
10. partes	=	you (fam. sg.) leave, you are leaving, you do leave
11. subimos	=	we go up, we are going up, we do go up
12. existen	=	you (pol. pl.) exist, you are existing, you do exist
13. escribe	=	he writes, he is writing, he does write
14. deciden	=	they decide, they are deciding, they do decide
15. recibe	=	you (pol. sg.) receive, you are receiving, you do receive

B.

1. ¿Recibes mucho correo electrónico?
2. Ellos discuten la película de *Luis Buñuel* ahora.
3. Asistimos a la clase ahora.
4. Ella parte para *Málaga* mañana.
5. Uds. viven cerca.
6. Escribo, leo y mando mucho correo electrónico.
7. Necesito asistir a la clase todos los días.

8. Ellos describen el cuadro de *Francisco Goya* ahora.
9. Mucha gente sufre hoy.
10. Decidís discutir el asunto.
11. Marta y yo abrimos las ventanas.
12. Descubro muchos secretos en clase.
13. Mi esposo escribe como *Calderón de la Barca*.
14. ¿Existen las hadas?
15. Cubres la mesa.

C.

1. a   2. a   3. a   4. a   5. b   6. a   7. b   8. a   9. b
10. a   11. b   12. a   13. b   14. a

Exercise Set 1-4

A.

1. toca   2. parten   3. vivimos   4. miran   5. llegan
6. limpiamos   7. comprendo   8. escucha   9. hablas

B.

1. b.   2. b   3. a   4. a   5. a   6. a   7. a   8. b   9. b

C.

1. ¿Baila Ud. el tango muy bien también?
2. ¿Qué leen Uds. en este momento?
3. ¿Qué estudia Ud.?
4. ¿Por qué mira Ud. la televisión tanto?
5. ¿Necesitan Uds. estudiar mucho?

D.

1. ¿Vivís en Madrid? (Spain)
2. Uds. viven en Barcelona. (Spain)
3. Uds. beben mucho café. (Latin America)
4. Uds. hablan español muy bien. (Latin America)
5. Uds. cantan muy bien. (Latin America)

Exercise Set 1-5

1. (Nosotros) compramos el balón de fútbol.
2. Juan y María compran el juguete.
3. Usted compra el helado.
4. (Yo) compro el teléfono.
5. (Tú) compras la sartén.
6. Ella compra el libro.

Crossword Puzzle 1

CHAPTER 2
Exercise Set 2-1

A.

1. empiezo	=	I begin, I am beginning, I do begin
2. empiezas	=	you (fam. sg.) begin, you are beginning, you do begin
3. empezamos	=	we begin, we are beginning, we do begin
4. empiezan	=	they begin, they are beginning, they do begin
5. empezáis	=	you (fam. pl.) begin, you are beginning, you do begin
6. empieza	=	you (pol. sg.) begin, you are beginning, you do begin

1. entiendo	=	I understand, I am understanding, I do understand
2. entendemos	=	Raquel and I understand, Raquel and I are understanding, Raquel and I do understand
3. entienden	=	you (pol. pl.) understand, you are understanding, you do understand
4. entienden	=	they understand, they are understanding, they do understand
5. entendéis	=	you (fam. pl.) understand, you are understanding, you do understand
6. entiendes	=	you (fam. sg.) understand, you are understanding, you do understand

1. miento	=	I lie, I am lying, I do lie
2. mientes	=	you (fam. sg.) lie, you are lying, you do lie
3. mentimos	=	we lie, we are lying, we do lie
4. mienten	=	they lie, they are lying, they do lie
5. mentís	=	you (fam. pl.) lie, you are lying, you do lie
6. miente	=	you (pol. sg.) lie, you are lying, you do lie

B.

1. Empiezo a leer la poesía de *Alfonsina Storni.*
2. ¿Quieres leer las novelas de *Eduardo Mallea*?
3. Encendemos la luz todas las noches.
4. ¿Entiende Ud. la pregunta?
5. ¿Sientes no leer *El túnel* de *Ernesto Sábato*?
6. Perdemos nuestras llaves mucho.
7. Ella confiesa que mira muchas telenovelas.

8. Queremos leer *Mafalda*.
9. Ellos prefieren ir a la *Calle Florida* para comprar la ropa.
10. Él sugiere el libro de *Ana María Shua*.
11. No mientes.

Exercise Set 2-2

A.

1. encuentro	=	I find, I am finding, I do find
2. encuentras	=	you (fam. sg.) find, you are finding, you do find
3. encontramos	=	we find, we are finding, we do find
4. encuentran	=	they find, they are finding, they do find
5. encuentran	=	you (pol. pl.) find, you are finding, you do find
6. encuentra	=	you (pol. sg.) find, you are finding, you do find

1. devuelvo	=	I return, I am returning, I do return
2. devolvemos	=	Javier and I return, Javier and I are returning, Javier and I do return
3. devuelven	=	they return, they are returning, they do return
4. devuelven	=	you (pol. pl.) return, you are returning, you do return
5. devolvéis	=	you (fam. pl.) return, you are returning, you do return
6. devuelves	=	you (fam. sg.) return, you are returning, you do return

1. muero	=	I die, I am dying, I do die
2. mueres	=	you (fam. sg.) die, you are dying, you do die
3. morimos	=	we die, we are dying, we do die
4. mueren	=	they die, they are dying, they do die
5. morís	=	you (fam. pl.) die, you are dying, you do die
6. muere	=	you (pol. sg.) die, you are dying, you do die

B.

1. Un bistec cuesta mucho en *La Cabaña*.
2. Uds. pueden leer *El puente* de *Carlos Gorostiza*.
3. Ella encuentra las llaves en el sofá.
4. Volamos a Ushuaia mañana.
5. Sueñas con ganar la lotería.
6. Ellos duermen tarde si pueden.
7. Cuelgo el teléfono si ellos venden algo.
8. Volvemos a *Mendoza* mañana en *Aerolíneas Argentinas*.
9. Él recuerda el ensayo de *Domingo Fausto Sarmiento*.
10. El teléfono suena constantemente.

Exercise Set 2-3

A.

1. compito	=	I compete, I am competing, I do compete
2. compites	=	you (fam. sg.) compete, you are competing, you do compete
3. competimos	=	we compete, we are competing, we do compette
4. compiten	=	they compete, they are competing, they do compete
5. compiten	=	you (pol. pl.) compete, you are competing, you do compete
6. compite	=	you (pol. sg.) compete, you are competing, you do compete

1. mido	=	I measure, I am measuring, I do measure
2. miden	=	they measure, they are measuring, they do measure
3. medimos	=	Lydia and I measure, Lydia and I are measuring, Lydia and I do measure

4. miden	=	you (pol. pl.) measure, you are measuring, you do measure
5. medimos	=	we measure, we are measuring, we do measure
6. mides	=	you (fam. sg.) measure, you are measuring, you do measure

1. sigo	=	I follow, I am following, I do follow
2. sigue	=	you (pol. sg.) follow, you are following, you do follow
3. seguimos	=	we follow, we are following, we do follow
4. siguen	=	they follow, they are following, they do follow
5. seguís	=	you (fam. pl.) follow, you are following, you do follow
6. seguimos	=	Joaquín and I follow, Joaquín and I are following, Joaquín and I do follow

B.

1. Ellos compiten por el premio.
2. Los profesores necesitan corregir los exámenes hoy.
3. Siempre sigo las reglas.
4. Pido el *churrasco* en *Dora*.
5. Cuando repites las palabras en voz alta, recuerdas.
6. Ella mide los ingredientes con cuidado.
7. Ellos sirven vino excelente en el restaurante.
8. Él despide a los empleados.
9. Uds. ríen mucho.
10. Ellos siempre fríen los huevos aquí.

Exercise Set 2-4

A.

1. prefiero   2. entienden   3. cerramos   4. friega   5. sueñas
6. vuelvo   7. competimos   8. vuela   9. sirven

B.

1. a   2. b   3. a   4. b   5. b   6. b   7. a   8. b   9. b

C.

1. Vuelvo a Buenos Aires.
2. Almuerzo en *Güerrín*.
3. Cierro las puertas
4. Sigo la misma ruta.
5. Empiezo a estudiar.

Exercise Set 2-5

A.

1. Pilar y Carlos juegan.
2. Juan escribe.
3. Jorge y Soledad duermen.
4. Juana usa la computadora.
5. Julián y Pedro leen.
6. Carlos come.
7. Pablo bebe.
8. Verónica escucha.
9. Carmen habla.

Crossword Puzzle 2

CHAPTER 3
Exercise Set 3-1

A.

1. soy	=	I am
2. eres	=	you (fam. sg.) are
3. somos	=	we are
4. son	=	they are
5. sois	=	you (fam. pl.) are
6. es	=	you (pol. sg.) are

B.

1. Son las ocho y veinte de la noche.
2. Son las siete y media (treinta) de la mañana.
3. Son las cinco menos cuarto (quince) de la tarde.
4. Son las diez y dieciocho de la mañana.
5. Son las doce menos veinticinco de la noche.
6. Son las nueve en punto de la mañana.
7. Son las dos y diez de la tarde.
8. Son las cuatro y media (treinta) de la mañana.

C.

1. ¿De dónde eres?
2. Mi esposa es de Uruguay, pero yo soy de España.
3. Ellos son uruguayos y son simpáticos.
4. La mujer española es rubia.
5. ¿De qué es el bolígrafo rojo? Es de plástico.
6. ¿De quién es el reloj? Es de Pilar.
7. Es importante estudiar español hoy.
8. Silvia es pelirroja y alta.
9. Mi casa es de madera.
10. La película es a las ocho de la noche.

Exercise Set 3-2

A.

1. estás	=	you (fam. sg.) are
2. estoy	=	I am
3. estamos	=	we are
4. están	=	they are
5. estáis	=	you (fam. pl.) are
6. están	=	you (pol. pl.) are

B.

1. Estoy en casa ahora porque estoy enfermo/-a.
2. Mi esposo está para salir para Montevideo.
3. Ella está cansada porque trabaja mucho.
4. Mi hermana está casada con un hombre simpático.
5. Estoy de acuerdo con Pablo.
6. Estamos de vacaciones en Uruguay ahora.
7. Blanca, estás cansada porque estás de pie tanto.
8. Cuando estudio mucho, estoy de buen humor porque aprendo.
9. Estoy aburrido/a porque no estoy de vacaciones.
10. Este color es muy vivo.

Exercise Set 3-3

A.

1. Hay seis libros aquí.
2. Hay una mujer uruguaya en la clase.
3. Hay que estar aquí a las ocho de la mañana.
4. Hay que ir a Montevideo.
5. Hay muchos estudiantes en la clase.

Exercise Set 3-4

A.

1. tiene	=	she has, she does have
2. tengo	=	I have, I do have
3. tienes	=	you (fam. sg.) have, you do have
4. tienen	=	they have, they do have
5. tiene	=	you (pol. sg.) have, you do have
6. tienen	=	you (pol. pl.) have, you do have

B.

1. Tengo ganas de ir al *Museo del Gaucho y de la Moneda*.
2. Cuando estoy en el casino, tengo mucha suerte.
3. Él tiene cincuenta años.
4. Ella tiene vergüenza de sus acciones.
5. Uds. tienen que comer en *La Silenciosa*.
6. Tengo mucha sed hoy y quiero beber agua.
7. Cuando tengo mucha hambre, como salchichas.
8. Tengo miedo de las arañas.
9. Siempre tengo mucha prisa cuando tengo que trabajar.
10. Ella tiene mucho sueño y necesita dormir.

Exercise Set 3-5

A.

1. haces = you (fam. sg.) do/make, you are doing/making, you do do/make
2. hago = I do/make, I am doing/making, I do do/make
3. hacemos = we do/make, we are doing/making, we do do/make
4. hacen = they do/make, they are doing/making, they do do/make
5. hacéis = you (fam. pl.) do/make, you are doing/making, you do do/make
6. hacen = you (pol. pl.) do/make, you are doing/making, you do do/make

B.

1. ¿Cuánto tiempo hace que estudias español?
2. Hace una hora que estudio español.
3. Hace frío en Montevideo en junio.
4. Cuando llueve, está nublado.
5. Hago caso a los verbos cuando estudio español.
6. Hace calor en Montevideo en diciembre.
7. Hago un viaje a *Punta del Este.*
8. Siempre nieva en invierno.
9. Siempre hace buen tiempo en junio.
10. Hace mucho viento en Chicago.
11. Es el treinta y uno de marzo, dos mil trece.

Exercise Set 3-6

A.

1. sabes = you (fam. sg.) know, you do know
2. sé = I know, I do know
3. sabemos = we know, we do know
4. saben = they know, they do know
5. sabéis = you (fam. pl.) know, you do know
6. saben = you (pol. pl.) know, you do know

B.

1. Sabes nadar bien.
2. Ella sabe que Raquel está aquí.
3. Sé que es necesario dormir ocho horas.
4. Sabemos que hace frío en enero.
5. Uds. saben que tengo que estar en Montevideo mañana.
6. Sabes la fecha de hoy.
7. Él sabe que estoy cansado/a.
8. Ud. sabe que el tango es muy popular en Montevideo.
9. Sabemos que *Piriápolis* está en Uruguay.
10. Ellos saben que estoy de buen humor.

Exercise Set 3-7

A.

1. conoces = you (fam.sg.) know, you do know
2. conozco = I know, I do know
3. conocemos = we know, we do know
4. conocen = they know, they do know

5. conocéis   =   you (fam. pl.) know, you do know
6. conocen   =   you (pol. pl.) know, you do know

B.

1. Conozco un buen restaurante en *Punta del Este.*
2. Conozco a Julio Rodríguez bien.
3. Conozco los cuentos de *Horacio Quiroga.*
4. Él conoce a los Hernández.
5. Conozco la ciudad de Montevideo muy bien.

Exercise Set 3-8

A.

1. Estoy seguro/-a de que tengo razón.
2. Sé que hace frío hoy.
3. Tengo que estar aquí a las seis en punto de la tarde.
4. Hay que ser simpático.
5. Ellos tienen sueño y están cansados.
6. Somos argentinos pero ellos son uruguayos.
7. Es la una y cuarto (quince) de la tarde.
8. Tengo veinte años de edad y soy estudiante.
9. Christina Aguilera es rubia y bonita.
10. Cuando hace calor, tengo mucha sed.

Exercise Set 3-9

A.

First, you are out during the day.

1. Son las nueve y media de la mañana. Son las nueve y treinta de la mañana.
2. Son las doce. Es el mediodía.
3. Son las cuatro y veinte de la tarde.
4. Son las seis menos un cuarto de la mañana. Son las seis menos quince de la mañana.

Now, you are out at night.

5. Son las ocho y cuarto de la noche. Son las ocho y quince de la noche.
6. Son las diez de la noche.
7. Son las once menos cuarto de la noche. Son las once menos quince de la noche.
8. Son las doce. Es la medianoche.

Exercise Set 3-10

Answers may vary. Examples are provided.

1. María y Juan juegan al tenis.
2. (Yo) como una hamburguesa.
3. Ustedes viajan por avión.
4. Ella llama por teléfono.
5. (Nosotros) leemos un libro.
6. (Tú) usas la computadora.
7. Usted maneja un coche.
8. Él duerme.
9. Ana y yo miramos la televisión.

Crossword Puzzle 3

CHAPTER 4
Exercise Set 4-1

A.

1. salgo	=	I leave, I am leaving, I do leave
2. sales	=	you (fam. sg.) leave, you are leaving, you do leave
3. salimos	=	she and I leave, she and I are leaving, she and I do leave
4. salen	=	they leave, they are leaving, they do leave
5. salís	=	you (fam. pl.) leave, you are leaving, you do leave
6. sale	=	you (pol. sg.) leave, you are leaving, you do leave

1. voy	=	I go, I am going, I do go
2. vamos	=	Isabel and I go, Isabel and I are going, Isabel and I do go
3. van	=	you (pol. pl.) go, you are going, you do go
4. van	=	they go, they are going, they do go
5. vamos	=	we go, we are going, we do go
6. vas	=	you (fam. sg.) go, you are going, you do go

1. vengo	=	I come, I am coming, I do come
2. vienes	=	you (fam. sg.) come, you are coming, you do come
3. venimos	=	Ignacio and I come, Ignacio and I are coming, Ignacio and I do come
4. vienen	=	they come, they are coming, they do come
5. venís	=	you (fam. pl.) come, you are coming, you do come
6. vienen	=	you (pol. pl.) come, you are coming, you do come

1. doy	=	I give, I am giving, I do give
2. das	=	you (fam. sg.) give, you are giving, you do give
3. damos	=	we give, we are giving, we do give
4. dan	=	they give, they are giving, they do give
5. dais	=	you (fam. pl.) give, you are giving, you do give
6. dan	=	you (pol. pl.) give, you are giving, you do give

1. oigo	=	I hear, I am hearing, I do hear
2. oyes	=	you (fam. sg.) hear, you are hearing, you do hear
3. oímos	=	we hear, we are hearing, we do hear
4. oyen	=	they hear, they are hearing, they do hear
5. oís	=	you (fam. pl.) hear, you are hearing, you do hear
6. oyen	=	you (pol. pl.) hear, you are hearing, you do hear

1. digo	=	I say/tell, I am saying/telling, I do say/tell
2. dices	=	you (fam. sg.) say/tell, you are saying/telling, you do say/tell
3. decimos	=	Isabel and I say/tell, Isabel and I are saying/telling, Isabel and I do say/tell
4. dicen	=	they say/tell, they are saying/telling, they do say/tell
5. decís	=	you (fam. pl.) say/tell, you are saying/telling, you do say/tell
6. dicen	=	you (pol. pl.) say/tell, you are saying/telling, you do say/tell

1. pongo	=	I put/place, I am putting/placing, I do put/place
2. pones	=	you (fam.sg.) put/place, you are putting/placing, you do put/place
3. ponemos	=	we put/place, we are putting/placing, we do put/place
4. ponen	=	they put/place, they are putting/placing, they do put/place
5. ponéis	=	you (fam. pl.) put/place, you are putting/placing, you do put/place
6. ponen	=	you (pol. pl.) put/place, you are putting/placing, you do put/place

1. veo	=	I see, I am seeing, I do see
2. ves	=	you (fam. sg.) see, you are seeing, you do see
3. vemos	=	we see, we are seeing, we do see
4. ven	=	they see, they are seeing, they do see
5. veis	=	you (fam. pl.) see, you are seeing, you do see
6. ven	=	you (pol. pl.) see, you are seeing, you do see

B.

1. Doy un paseo en el parque todos los días.
2. Salgo con mis amigos los viernes.
3. Vengo tarde a la universidad con frecuencia.
4. Veo el *Museo de Arte Indígena* ahora.
5. Pongo mi dinero en mi cartera.
6. Voy al *Chaco* mañana.
7. Oigo los sonidos de la selva.
8. No digo mentiras.

C.

1. c   2. a   3. b   4. c   5. b   6. c

Exercise Set 4-2

A.

1. ofrezco	=	I offer, I am offering, I do offer
2. ofreces	=	you (fam. sg.) offer, you are offering, you do offer
3. ofrecemos	=	she and I offer, she and I are offering, she and I do offer
4. ofrecen	=	they offer, they are offering, they do offer
5. ofrecéis	=	you (fam. pl.) offer, you are offering, you do offer
6. ofrece	=	you (pol. sg.) offer, you are offering, you do offer

1. produzco	=	I produce, I am producing, I do produce
2. producimos	=	we produce, we are producing, we do produce
3. producen	=	you (pol. pl.) produce, you are producing, you do produce
4. producen	=	they produce, they are producing, they do produce
5. producimos	=	we produce, we are producing, we do produce
6. produces	=	you (fam. sg.) produce, you are producing, you do produce

1. traigo	=	I bring, I am bringing, I do bring
2. traemos	=	Ignacio and I bring, Ignacio and I are bringing, Ignacio and I do bring
3. traen	=	you (pol. pl.) bring, you are bringing, you do bring
4. traen	=	they bring, they are bringing, they do bring
5. traemos	=	we bring, we are bringing, we do bring
6. traes	=	you (fam. sg.) bring, you are bringing, you do bring

1. incluyo	=	I include, I am including, I do include
2. incluimos	=	we include, we are including, we do include
3. incluyen	=	you (pol. pl.) include, you are including, you do include
4. incluyen	=	they include, they are including, they do include
5. incluye	=	she includes, she is including, she does include
6. incluyes	=	you (fam. sg.) include, you are including, you do include

1. venzo	=	I conquer/defeat, I am conquering/defeating, I do conquer/defeat
2. vencemos	=	Jorge and I conquer/defeat, Jorge and I are conquering/defeating, Jorge and I do conquer/defeat
3. vencen	=	you (pol. pl.) conquer/defeat, you are conquering/defeating, you do conquer/defeat
4. vencen	=	they conquer/defeat, they are conquering/defeating, they do conquer/defeat
5. vencemos	=	we conquer/defeat, we are conquering/defeating, we do conquer/defeat
6. vences	=	you (fam. sg.) conquer/defeat, you are conquering/defeating, you do conquer/defeat

1. protejo	=	I protect, I am protecting, I do protect
2. protegemos	=	we protect, we are protecting, we do protect
3. protegen	=	you (pol. pl.) protect, you are protecting, you do protect
4. protegen	=	they protect, they are protecting, they do protect
5. protege	=	he protects, he is protecting, he does protect
6. proteges	=	you (fam. sg.) protect, you are protecting, you do protect

B.

1. Conozco la ciudad de Asunción bien.
2. Este libro pertenece a Carmen.
3. Traduzco poesía del guaraní al español.
4. Voy a reducir mis horas de trabajo.
5. Traigo mis libros a la oficina hoy.
6. Incluyo un capítulo sobre la literatura paraguaya.
7. Ellos vencen a sus enemigos con alabanzas.
8. Protejo a mis niños.

C.

1. b   2. c   3. c   4. a   5. b   6. c

Crossword Puzzle 4

CHAPTER 5
Exercise Set 5-1

A.

1. me levanto	=	I get up, I am getting up, I do get up
2. te levantas	=	you (fam. sg.) get up, you are getting up, you do get up
3. nos levantamos	=	we get up, we are getting up, we do get up
4. se levantan	=	they get up, they are getting up, they do get up
5. os levantáis	=	you (fam. pl.) get up, you are getting up, you do get up
6. se levanta	=	you (pol. sg.) get up, you are getting up, you do get up

1. me despierto	=	I wake up, I am waking up, I do wake up
2. nos despertamos	=	Isabel and I wake up, Isabel and I are waking up, Isabel and I do wake up
3. se despiertan	=	you (pol. pl.) wake up, you are waking up, you do wake up
4. se despiertan	=	they wake up, they are waking up, they do wake up
5. nos despertamos	=	we wake up, we are waking up, we do wake up
6. te despiertas	=	you (fam. sg.) wake up, you are waking up, you do wake up

1. me visto	=	I get dressed, I am getting dressed, I do get dressed
2. te vistes	=	you (fam. sg.) get dressed, you are getting dressed, you do get dressed
3. nos vestimos	=	we get dressed, we are getting dressed, we do get dressed
4. se visten	=	they get dressed, they are getting dressed, they do get dressed
5. os vestís	=	you (fam. pl.) get dressed, you are getting dressed, you do get dressed
6. se visten	=	you (pol. pl.) get dressed, you are getting dressed, you do get dressed

B.

1. a   2. b   3. b   4. c   5. a   6. b   7. c

C.

1. Ana se acuesta muy temprano.
2. El autor de *Raza de bronce* se llama *Alcides Arguedas.*

3. Margarita quiere casarse en La Paz.
4. Por la mañana me despierto, me levanto, me ducho y me visto.
5. Cuando estudio los verbos españoles mucho, me canso.
6. Después de bañarme, me seco.
7. Estoy contento cuando aprendo los verbos españoles.
8. Me preocupo cuando tengo un examen.
9. Ellos se duermen a las once de la noche.
10. Guillermo se mira en el espejo por la mañana.

Exercise Set 5-2

1. Carlos se viste.
2. Juana se ducha.
3. Luis se despierta.
4. José se afeita.
5. Juan se cepilla los dientes.
6. Marta y Pedro se besan.
7. Raquel y Mónica se gritan.
8. María y Julia se ponen el maquillaje.

Crossword Puzzle 5

CHAPTER 6
Exercise Set 6-1

A.

1. Me gusta este libro.
2. A mis amigos les gusta aquel restaurante.
3. Te gusta mirar las telenovelas.
4. Nos gusta ese programa.
5. A ella le gusta esta película.
6. A ellos les gustan estas revistas.
7. A él le gusta visitar *Antofagasta*.
8. A Rosa le gusta *Concepción*.
9. ¿A Ud. le gusta la comida chilena?
10. A ellos les gusta viajar a *Punta Arenas*.

11. Me gustas.
12. Nos gusta ella.
13. Me caes bien.
14. Me gusta ir al *Museo de Santiago*.
15. A Uds. les gusta nadar en el mar.

Exercise Set 6-2

A.

1. A ella le duele el diente.
2. Me caes bien.
3. Me faltan veinte *pesos*.
4. Me interesan los libros viejos.
5. Me importa el arte chileno.
6. A él le molesta la gente tonta.
7. A los turistas les interesa Valdivia.
8. Te conviene trabajar mucho ahora.

B.

1. ¿A Ud. le gusta la literatura chilena?
2. ¿A Ud. le gustan los museos de Santiago?
3. ¿A Ud. le interesa ir al teatro chileno?
4. ¿A Ud. le bastan cien pesos?
5. ¿A Ud. le importa leer *La Nación*?
6. ¿A Ud. le conviene dormir tarde todos los días?

Exercise Set 6-3

A.

1. estoy escribiendo	=	I am writing
2. estás escribiendo	=	you (fam. sg.) are writing
3. estamos escribiendo	=	we are writing
4. ellos están escribiendo	=	they are writing
5. estáis escribiendo	=	you (fam. pl.) are writing
6. Ud. está escribiendo	=	you (pol. sg.) are writing

1. estoy leyendo	=	I am reading
2. estamos leyendo	=	Isabel and I are reading
3. Uds. están leyendo	=	you (pol. pl.) are reading
4. ellos están leyendo	=	they are reading
5. estamos leyendo	=	we are reading
6. estás leyendo	=	you (fam. sg.) are reading

1. estoy sirviendo	=	I am serving
2. estás sirviendo	=	you (fam. sg.) are serving
3. estamos sirviendo	=	we are serving
4. están sirviendo	=	they are serving
5. estáis sirviendo	=	you (fam. pl.) are serving
6. está sirviendo	=	you (pol. sg.) are serving

1. estoy muriendo	=	I am dying
2. estás muriendo	=	you (fam. sg.) are dying
3. estamos muriendo	=	we are dying
4. están muriendo	=	they are dying

5. estáis muriendo	=	you (fam.pl.) are dying
6. están muriendo	=	you (pol. pl.) are dying

1. me estoy bañando	=	I am bathing myself
2. te estás bañando	=	you (fam. sg.) are bathing yourself
3. nos estamos bañando	=	we are bathing ourselves
4. se están bañando	=	they are bathing themselves
5. os estáis bañando	=	you (fam. pl) are bathing yourselves
6. se están bañando	=	you (pol. pl.) are bathing yourselves

1. estoy bañándome	=	I am bathing myself
2. estás bañándote	=	you (fam. sg.) are bathing yourself
3. estamos bañándonos	=	we are bathing ourselves
4. están bañándose	=	they are bathing themselves
5. estáis bañándoos	=	you (fam. pl) are bathing yourselves
6. están bañándose	=	you (pol. pl.) are bathing yourselves

B.

1. Ella está estudiando para su examen ahora mismo.
2. Ellos están practicando español en este momento.
3. Estamos sirviéndoles la cena a nuestros amigos.
4. Estoy jugando al fútbol en este momento.
5. Estás durmiendo ahora mismo.
6. Estoy diciendo la verdad.
7. Él está comiendo la comida chilena ahora.

Exercise Set 6-4

A.

1. Pablo las lee.
2. Pilar está bebiéndolo. Pilar lo está bebiendo.
3. Quiero cantarla. La quiero cantar.
4. Las escribimos.
5. Ella los come.

B.

1. La veo en el coche.
2. Quieres mirarla. La quieres mirar.
3. Ella está leyéndolo. Ella lo está leyendo.
4. Ellos lo necesitan ahora.

C.

1. Los leo.
2. Necesito hacerlo ahora. Lo necesito hacer ahora.
3. Estamos estudiándolo. Lo estamos estudiando.

Exercise Set 6-5

A.

1. Le digo la verdad a ella.
2. Ellos tienen que escribirles la carta a ellos. Ellos les tienen que escribir la carta a ellos.
3. Ellos están hablándonos en español. Ellos nos están hablando en español.

B.

1. Le doy los libros a ella.
2. Prefiero darle los regalos a ella. Le prefiero dar los regalos a ella.
3. Estoy entregándole el paquete a él. Le estoy entregando el paquete a él.

Exercise Set 6-6

A.

1. Aristófanes se las escribe a ellos.
2. Irene está contándoselo a ella. Irene se lo está contando a ella.
3. Francisco necesita vendérsela a ella. Francisco se la necesita vender.
4. Ellas están dándoselo a ellos. Ellas se lo están dando a ellos.
5. Carlos me la muestra.

B.

1. Ellos nos los venden.
2. Queremos mostrárselas a ellos. Se las queremos mostrar a ellos.
3. Él está dándoselo a ella. Él se lo está dando a ella.

C.

1. Se las muestro a ella.
2. Voy a escribírsela a ellos. Se la voy a escribir a ellos.
3. Estoy dándoselo a él. Se lo estoy dando a él.

Crossword Puzzle 6

CHAPTER 7
Execise Set 7-1

A.

1. canté	=	I sang, I did sing
2. cantaste	=	you (fam. sg.) sang, you did sing
3. cantamos	=	we sang, we did sing

4. cantaron	=	they sang, they did sing
5. cantasteis	=	you (fam. pl.) sang, you did sing
6. cantó	=	you (pol. sg.) sang, you did sing

1. vendí	=	I sold, I did sell
2. vendimos	=	Raquel and I sold, Raquel and I did sell
3. vendieron	=	you (pol. pl.) sold, you did sell
4. vendieron	=	they sold, they did sell
5. vendisteis	=	you (fam. pl.) sold, you did sell
6. vendiste	=	you (fam. sg.) sold, you did sell

1. viví	=	I lived, I did live
2. viviste	=	you (fam. sg.) lived, you did live
3. vivimos	=	we lived, we did live
4. vivieron	=	they lived, they did live
5. vivisteis	=	you (fam. pl.) lived, you did live
6. vivió	=	you (pol. sg.) lived, you did live

1. me bañé	=	I bathed myself, I did bathe myself
2. te bañaste	=	you (fam. sg.) bathed yourself, you did bathe yourself
3. nos bañamos	=	we bathed ourselves, we did bathe ourselves
4. se bañaron	=	they bathed themselves, they did bathe themselves
5. os bañasteis	=	you (fam. pl.) bathed yourselves, you did bathe yourselves
6. se bañó	=	you (pol. sg.) bathed yourself, you did bathe yourself

B.

1. Viajé de *Lima* a *Cuzco*.
2. Ellos comieron y bebieron en *Antaño*.
3. Visitamos *Arequipa* en el sur de Perú.
4. Viví en aquel barrio hace dos años.
5. Ella cantó la misma canción anoche.
6. Compré un coche nuevo ayer por la mañana.
7. Escribiste un correo electrónico anoche.
8. Ud. abrió la puerta.
9. Bebí mucho café esta mañana.
10. ¿Recibiste el regalo de Elena ayer?
11. Me gustó el viaje a *Huancayo*.
12. A él le dolió la cabeza anoche.

Exercise Set 7-2

A.

1. morí	=	I died, I did die.
2. moriste	=	you (fam. sg.) died, you did die
3. morimos	=	Marta and I died, Marta and I did die
4. murieron	=	they died, they did die
5. moristeis	=	you (fam. pl.) died, you did die
6. murió	=	you (pol. sg.) died, you did die

1. preferí	=	I preferred, I did prefer
2. preferimos	=	we preferred, we did prefer
3. prefirieron	=	you (pol. pl.) preferred, you did prefer
4. prefirieron	=	they preferred, they did prefer

| 5. preferisteis | = | you (fam. pl.) preferred, you did prefer |
| 6. preferiste | = | you (fam. sg.) preferred, you did prefer |

1. repetí	=	I repeated, I did repeat
2. repetimos	=	we repeated, we did repeat
3. repitieron	=	you (pol. pl.) repeated, you did repeat
4. repitieron	=	they repeated, they did repeat
5. repetisteis	=	you (fam. pl.) repeated, you did repeat
6. repetiste	=	you (fam. sg.) repeated, you did repeat

B.

1. Ellos sirvieron una buena comida en *Pisco*.
2. Inés durmió muy tarde hoy.
3. Mis amigos prefirieron ir al *Museo de la Nación* en Lima.
4. Repetí la conjugación del pretérito.
5. Medí el cuarto anoche.
6. Él siguió al profesor a la clase.
7. Su abuelo murió anoche.
8. Ellos frieron la carne en aceite de oliva.
9. Él despidió al empleado hace dos días.
10. Mis padres no mintieron nunca.

Exercise Set 7-3

A.

1. tuve	=	I had, I did have
2. tuviste	=	you (fam. sg.) had, you did have
3. tuvimos	=	Marta and I had, Marta and I did have
4. tuvieron	=	they had, they did have
5. tuvisteis	=	you (fam. pl.) had, you did have
6. tuvo	=	you (pol. sg.) had, you did have

1. quise	=	I wanted, I did want
2. quisimos	=	we wanted, we did want
3. quisieron	=	you (pol. pl.) wanted, you did want
4. quisieron	=	they wanted, they did want
5. quisisteis	=	you (fam. pl.) wanted, you did want
6. quisiste	=	you (fam. sg.) wanted, you did want

1. hice	=	I did, I did do
2. hiciste	=	you (fam. sg.) did, you did do
3. hicimos	=	we did, we did do
4. hicieron	=	you (pol. pl.) did, you did do
5. hicisteis	=	you (fam. pl.) did, you did do
6. hizo	=	you (pol. sg.) did, you did do

1. estuve	=	I was
2. estuviste	=	you (fam. sg.) were
3. estuvimos	=	we were
4. estuvieron	=	you (pol. pl.) were
5. estuvisteis	=	you (fam. pl.) were
6. estuvo	=	you (pol. sg.) were

1. pude	=	I could/was able
2. pudiste	=	you (fam. sg.) could/were able
3. pudimos	=	we could/were able
4. pudieron	=	you (pol. pl.) could/were able
5. pudisteis	=	you (fam. pl.) could/were able
6. pudo	=	you (pol. sg.) could/were able

1. vine	=	I came, I did come
2. viniste	=	you (fam. sg.) came, you did come
3. vinimos	=	we came, we did come
4. vinieron	=	you (pol. pl.) came, you did come
5. vinisteis	=	you (fam. pl.) came, you did come
6. vino	=	you (pol. sg.) came, you did come

1. fui	=	I was
2. fuiste	=	you (fam. sg.) were
3. fuimos	=	we were
4. fueron	=	you (pol. pl.) were
5. fuisteis	=	you (fam. pl.) were
6. fue	=	you (pol. sg.) were

1. traduje	=	I translated, I did translate
2. tradujiste	=	you (fam. sg.) translated, you did translate
3. tradujimos	=	we translated, we did translate
4. tradujeron	=	you (pol. pl.) translated, you did translate
5. tradujisteis	=	you (fam. pl.) translated, you did translate
6. tradujo	=	you (pol. sg.) translated, you did translate

1. fui	=	I went, I did go
2. fuiste	=	you (fam. sg.) went, you did go
3. fuimos	=	we went, we did go
4. fueron	=	you (pol. pl.) went, you did go
5. fuisteis	=	you (fam. pl.) went, you did go
6. fue	=	you (pol. sg.) went, you did go

1. conduje	=	I drove, I did drive
2. condujiste	=	you (fam. sg.) drove, you did drive
3. condujimos	=	we drove, we did drive
4. condujeron	=	you (pol. pl.) drove, you did drive
5. condujisteis	=	you (fam. pl.) drove, you did drive
6. condujo	=	you (pol. sg.) drove, you did drive

B.

1. Condujimos de *Lima* a *Tacna*.
2. Le di el dinero a mi amigo.
3. Raquel y yo fuimos al centro a cenar.
4. Ellos dieron un paseo en el *Parque Kennedy*.
5. Vine a clase tarde.
6. Caí en la calle.
7. Le dije la verdad a Marco.
8. Traduje los verbos del inglés al español.
9. Estuvimos en casa cuando la vi.
10. Fui presidente/a de la organización el año pasado.
11. Ayer hizo mal tiempo porque llovió mucho.

12. Hizo mucho frío en febrero porque nevó mucho.
13. Sé que María dijo la verdad.
14. Ella dijo que leyó el libro anoche.
15. Ellos dijeron que mentimos.

Exercise Set 7-4

A.

1. jugué	=	I played, I did play
2. jugaste	=	you (fam. sg.) played, you did play
3. jugamos	=	we played, we did play
4. jugaron	=	you (pol. pl.) played, you did play
5. jugasteis	=	you (fam. pl.) played, you did play
6. jugó	=	you (pol. sg.) played, you did play

1. toqué	=	I played, I did play
2. tocaste	=	you (fam. sg.) played, you did play
3. tocamos	=	we played, we did play
4. tocaron	=	you (pol. pl.) played, you did play
5. tocasteis	=	you (fam. pl.) played, you did play
6. tocó	=	you (pol. sg.) played, you did play

1. empecé	=	I began, I did begin
2. empezaste	=	you (fam. sg.) began, you did begin
3. empezamos	=	we began, we did begin
4. empezaron	=	you (pol. pl.) began, you did begin
5. empezasteis	=	you (fam. pl.) began, you did begin
6. empezó	=	you (pol. sg.) began, you did begin

1. oí	=	I heard, I did hear
2. oíste	=	you (fam. sg.) heard, you did hear
3. oímos	=	we heard, we did hear
4. oyeron	=	you (pol. pl.) heard, you did hear
5. oísteis	=	you (fam. pl.) heard, you did hear
6. oyó	=	you (pol. sg.) heard, you did hear

1. construí	=	I built, I did build
2. constuiste	=	you (fam. sg.) built, you did build
3. construimos	=	we built, we did build
4. construyeron	=	you (pol. pl.) built, you did build
5. construisteis	=	you (fam. pl.) built, you did build
6. construyó	=	you (pol. sg.) built, you did build

B.

1. Almorcé con mi amigo en un buen restaurante peruano.
2. Leí *La República* temprano esta mañana.
3. Contribuí cien *soles* ayer.
4. Oímos a la mujer en la calle.
5. Ellos construyeron una casa cara.
6. El hombre culpable huyó de la policía.
7. Empezó a llover ayer.
8. Él se tropezó con la silla.
9. Toqué la guitarra para mi hermana.
10. La tormenta destruyó mi casa.

C.

1. hablamos	7. comimos	13. hizo
2. tuvieron	8. vivimos	14. tuviste
3. fueron	9. me acosté	15. entendí
4. fuimos	10. fui	16. pude
5. estuviste	11. durmieron	17. quisieron
6. dijo	12. pidió	18. empecé

Exercise Set 7-5

A.

1. Tuve un regalo de mi madre anoche.
2. No pude conjugar todos los verbos españoles.
3. Él conoció a su esposa en un ascensor.
4. Supimos la verdad el año pasado.
5. Pude encontrar mi libro en casa.
6. Ellos quisieron estudiar pero no pudieron.

Crossword Puzzle 7

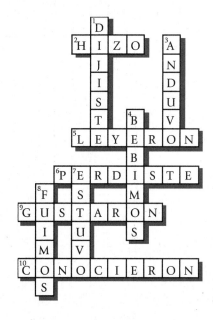

CHAPTER 8
Exercise Set 8-1

A.

1. cantaba	=	I was singing, I used to sing
2. cantabas	=	you (fam. sg.) were singing, you used to sing
3. cantábamos	=	we were singing, we used to sing
4. cantaban	=	they were singing, they used to sing
5. cantabais	=	you (fam. pl.) were singing, you used to sing
6. cantaba	=	you (pol. sg.) were singing, you used to sing

1. tenía	=	I was having, I used to have
2. teníamos	=	Raquel and I were having, Raquel and I used to have
3. tenían	=	you (pol. pl.) were having, you used to have
4. tenían	=	they were having, they used to have
5. teníais	=	you (fam. pl.) were having, you used to have
6. tenías	=	you (fam. sg.) were having, you used to have

1. decía	=	I was saying/telling, I used to say/tell
2. decías	=	you (fam. sg.) were saying/telling, you used to say/tell
3. decíamos	=	we were saying/telling, we used to say/tell
4. decían	=	they were saying/tellling, they used to say/tell
5. decíais	=	you (fam.pl.) were saying/telling, you used to say/tell
6. decía	=	you (pol. sg.) were saying/telling, you used to say/tell

1. era	=	I was, I used to be
2. eras	=	you (fam. sg.) were, you used to be
3. éramos	=	we were, we used to be
4. eran	=	they were, they used to be
5. erais	=	you (fam. pl.) were, you used to be
6. era	=	you (pol. sg.) were, you used to be

1. iba	=	I was going, I used to go
2. ibas	=	you (fam. sg.) were going, you used to go
3. íbamos	=	we were going, we used to go
4. iban	=	they were going, they used to go
5. ibais	=	you (fam. pl.) were going, you used to go
6. iba	=	you (pol. sg.) were going, you used to go

1. veía	=	I was seeing, I used to see
2. veías	=	you (fam. sg.) were seeing, you used to see
3. veíamos	=	we were seeing, we used to see
4. veían	=	they were seeing, they used to see
5. veíais	=	you (fam. pl.) were seeing, you used to see
6. veía	=	you (pol. sg.) were seeing, you used to see

1. me levantaba	=	I was getting up, I used to get up
2. te levantabas	=	you (fam. sg.) were getting up, you used to get up
3. nos levantábamos	=	we were getting up, we used to get up
4. se levantaban	=	they were getting up, they used to get up
5. os levantabais	=	you (fam. pl.) were getting up, you used to get up
6. se levantaba	=	you (pol. sg.) were getting up, you used to get up

B.

1. Yo vivía en Quito.
2. Yo era muy simpático/a de niño/a.
3. Eran las nueve de la noche.
4. Íbamos a la escuela todos los días.
5. De niña Isabel tenía el pelo rubio.
6. Llovía y estaba nublado.
7. Ellos querían ver la última película.
8. Me gustaba leer los libros de *Jorge Icaza*.
9. ¿Jugabas al fútbol?
10. Yo trabajaba en esa tienda.
11. Ellos estudiaban en la biblioteca.

12. Yo pensaba que Jorge estudiaba frecuentemente.
13. Elena trabajaba y yo escribía.
14. Creíamos que él conducía a San Antonio.

Exercise Set 8-2

A.

1. estaba pagando
2. estabas empezando
3. estábamos comiendo
4. estaban prefiriendo
5. estabais jugando
6. estaba estudiando
7. estaban cantando
8. estábamos dando
9. estaba creyendo
10. estaban haciendo
11. estábamos escribiendo
12. estaba saliendo
13. te estabas levantando, estabas levantándote

B.

1. Estabas leyendo *Hoy*.
2. Sofía estaba estudiando los verbos españoles.
3. Roberto y yo estábamos mirando la televisión.
4. Mis amigos estaban jugando al fútbol.
5. Él estaba preparando la comida.

C.

1. Pablo entraba.
2. Claudio dormía.
3. Carolina se cepillaba los dientes.
4. Carlos se bañaba.
5. Soledad leía.
6. Laura hablaba por teléfono.
7. Ignacio miraba la televisión.
8. Jorge comía.
9. Marina y Alejandro bebían.
10. Marta trabajaba en el jardín.

Exercise Set 8-3

A.

1. hablamos, hablábamos
2. tuve, tenía
3. fuimos, íbamos
4. fuimos, éramos
5. estuve, estaba
6. dije, decía
7. comimos, comíamos
8. vivimos, vivíamos
9. se acostó, se acostaba
10. fueron, eran

11. dormimos, dormíamos
12. pediste, pedías
13. hizo, hacía
14. tuvieron, tenían
15. entendió, entendía
16. pudo, podía
17. quisimos, queríamos
18. empecé, empezaba

B.

1. Yo estudiaba cuando fuiste a la escuela.
2. Gloria se duchaba cuando sonó el teléfono.
3. Fui a la tienda cuando llovía.
4. Francisco leía una revista cuando María entró en la casa.
5. Mi padre bebía café cuando nevaba.

C.

1. estudiaba
2. se afeitó
3. llegamos
4. eran me levanté
5. tocaba
6. leyó

Crossword Puzzle 8

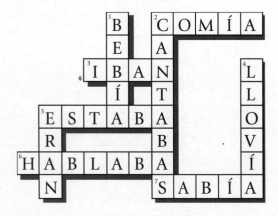

CHAPTER 9
Exercise Set 9-1

A.

1. llegado	7. hecho	13. ofrecido
2. comido	8. sabido	14. seguido
3. recibido	9. conocido	15. corregido
4. sido	10. mentido	16. empezado
5. estado	11. perdido	17. querido
6. tenido	12. podido	18. almorzado

B.

1. romper	7. decir	13. envolver
2. escribir	8. pudrir	14. resolver
3. ver	9. morir	15. descubrir
4. abrir	10. caer	16. creer
5. poner	11. hacer	17. devolver
6. freír	12. volver	18. proveer

Exercise Set 9-2

A.

1. he cantado	=	I have sung
2. has cantado	=	you (fam. sg.) have sung
3. hemos cantado	=	we have sung
4. han cantado	=	they have sung
5. habéis cantado	=	you (fam. pl.) have sung
6. ha cantado	=	you (pol. sg.) have sung

1. he vendido	=	I have sold
2. hemos vendido	=	Raquel and I have sold
3. han vendido	=	you (pol. pl.) have sold
4. han vendido	=	they have sold
5. habéis vendido	=	you (fam. pl.) have sold
6. has vendido	=	you (fam. sg.) have sold

1. he recibido	=	I have received
2. has recibido	=	you (fam. sg.) have received
3. hemos recibido	=	we have received
4. han recibido	=	they have received
5. habéis recibido	=	you (fam. pl.) have received
6. ha recibido	=	you (pol. sg.) have received

1. me he bañado	=	I have bathed myself
2. te has bañado	=	you (fam. sg.) have bathed yourself
3. nos hemos bañado	=	we have bathed ourselves
4. se han bañado	=	they have bathed themselves
5. os habéis bañado	=	you (fam. pl.) have bathed yourselves
6. se ha bañado	=	you (pol. sg.) have bathed yourself

1. he vuelto	=	I have returned
2. has vuelto	=	you (fam. sg.) have returned
3. hemos vuelto	=	we have returned
4. han vuelto	=	they have returned
5. habéis vuelto	=	you (fam. pl.) have returned
6. ha vuelto	=	you (pol. sg.) have returned

1. he estado	=	I have been
2. has estado	=	you (fam. sg.) have been
3. hemos estado	=	we have been
4. han estado	=	they have been
5. habéis estado	=	you (fam. pl.) have been
6. ha estado	=	you (pol. sg.) have been

1. he sido	=	I have been
2. has sido	=	you (fam. sg.) have been
3. hemos sido	=	we have been
4. han sido	=	they have been
5. habéis sido	=	you (fam. pl.) have been
6. ha sido	=	you (pol. sg.) have been

B.

1. He visitado Bogotá muchas veces.
2. Hemos estado en *Cartagena*.
3. ¿Te has duchado?
4. ¿Ha visto Ud. a mi esposa?
5. Ha llovido mucho.
6. ¿Han resuelto ellos sus problemas?
7. Uds. han tenido sed todo el día.
8. Hemos visto *Leticia*.
9. Ella ha dicho la verdad.
10. Siempre me ha gustado esta playa.
11. Has tenido que trabajar mucho.
12. Él ha sido muy simpático.
13. Uds. han abierto todas las puertas.
14. He provisto toda la comida.
15. Ellos se han vestido.
16. Hemos creído a nuestro hijo siempre.
17. Has hecho un viaje a *Cali*.
18. Hemos leído todos los escritos de *José Eustacio Rivera*.
19. ¿Por qué no ha vuelto ella?
20. El teléfono ha sonado toda la noche y no he podido dormir.
21. Ha habido muchos exámenes en este libro.

Exercise Set 9-3

A.

1. Los he leído.
2. Pilar lo ha bebido.
3. Debo haberla cantado. La debo haber cantado.
4. Ella la ha escrito.

B.

1. Ramón se lo ha hablado a ella.
2. Marina debe habérsela escrito a él. Marina se la debe haber escrito a él.
3. Uds. se la han dicho a ellos.

C.

1. Le he vendido el coche a mi hermano.
2. Ellos deben habernos hablado. Ellos nos deben haber hablado.

D.

1. Vicente se lo ha mandado a ella.
2. Se lo he leído a ella.
3. Se la hemos dicho a él.
4. Berta se la ha enseñado a él.

E.

1. Se la has enviado a él.
2. Se los hemos dado a ellos.
3. Ellos se lo han vendido a ella.

F.

1. Se los he dado a ella.
2. Se lo he hablado a ellos.
3. Se lo he servido a ella.

Exercise Set 9-4

A.

1. comimos, comíamos, hemos comido
2. tuvo, tenía, ha tenido
3. fui, iba, he ido
4. fui, era, he sido
5. estuve, estaba, he estado
6. dijimos, decíamos, hemos dicho
7. vivimos, vivíamos, hemos vivido
8. hicimos, hacíamos, hemos hecho
9. se bañó, se bañaba, se ha bañado
10. hubo, había, ha habido
11. murió, moría, ha muerto
12. pidieron, pedían, han pedido
13. hizo, hacía, ha hecho
14. tuvieron, tenían, han tenido
15. entendiste, entendías, has entendido
16. pudieron, podían, han podido
17. quise, quería, he querido
18. empezó, empezaba, ha empezado

Crossword Puzzle 9

CHAPTER 10
Exercise Set 10-1

A.

1. había dado	=	I had given
2. habías dado	=	you (fam. sg.) had given
3. habíamos dado	=	we had given
4. habían dado	=	they had given
5. habíais dado	=	you (fam. pl.) had given
6. había dado	=	you (pol. sg.) had given

1. había aprendido	=	I had understood
2. habíamos aprendido	=	Raquel and I had understood
3. habían aprendido	=	you (pol. pl.) had understood
4. habían aprendido	=	they had understood
5. habíais aprendido	=	you (fam. pl.) had understood
6. habías aprendido	=	you (fam. sg.) had understood

1. había sufrido	=	I had suffered
2. habías sufrido	=	you (fam. sg.) had suffered
3. habíamos sufrido	=	we had suffered
4. habían sufrido	=	they had suffered
5. habíais sufrido	=	you (fam. pl.) had suffered
6. había sufrido	=	you (pol. sg.) had suffered

1. me había vestido	=	I had gotten dressed
2. te habías vestido	=	you (fam. sg.) had gotten dressed
3. nos habíamos vestido	=	we had gotten dressed
4. se habían vestido	=	they had gotten dressed
5. os habíais vestido	=	you (fam. pl.) had gotten dressed
6. se había vestido	=	you (pol. sg.) had gotten dressed

1. había cubierto	=	I had covered
2. habías cubierto	=	you (fam. sg.) had covered
3. habíamos cubierto	=	we had covered
4. habían cubierto	=	they had covered
5. habíais cubierto	=	you (fam. pl.) had covered
6. había cubierto	=	you (pol. sg.) had covered

1. había estado	=	I had been
2. habías estado	=	you (fam. sg.) had been
3. habíamos estado	=	we had been
4. habían estado	=	they had been
5. habíais estado	=	you (fam. pl.) had been
6. había estado	=	you (pol. sg.) had been

1. había sido	=	I had been
2. habías sido	=	you (fam. sg.) had been
3. habíamos sido	=	we had been
4. habían sido	=	they had been
5. habíais sido	=	you (fam. pl.) had been
6. había sido	=	you (pol. sg.) had been

B.

1. Yo había visto el *Museo Boliviariano* en Caracas.
2. Yo había oído la música folklórica de Venezuela.
3. Yo había comprado *El Diario de Caracas*.
4. Había habido muchas casas allí.
5. Había llovido anoche.
6. Pablo había vivido en Madrid antes de venir a Venezuela.
7. Yo había visto la última película venezolana.
8. Yo había tocado la guitarra.
9. Yo había viajado a *Mérida*.
10. Me había levantado muy tarde.
11. Habías estudiado los verbos españoles mucho.
12. Habíamos entrado en la capital de Venezuela.
13. Había empezado a llover.
14. Ellos habían conducido a Maracaibo.
15. ¿Dónde había encontrado él el dinero?
16. Yo había hecho el rompecabezas.
17. Ud. había tenido el libro antes.
18. ¿Habían descubierto Uds. el secreto?
19. Las flores habían muerto en el otoño.
20. Ella había reído mucho.

Exercise Set 10-2

A.

1. hemos vivido, habíamos vivido
2. ha llovido, había llovido
3. ha ido, había ido
4. has sido, habías sido
5. hemos estado, habíamos estado
6. han dicho, habían dicho
7. hemos bebido, habíamos bebido
8. he hecho, había hecho
9. se ha duchado, se había duchado
10. ha habido, había habido
11. ha muerto, había muerto
12. ha pedido, había pedido
13. ha hecho, había hecho
14. he tenido, había tenido
15. has entendido, habías entendido
16. ha podido, había podido
17. has querido, habías querido
18. ha comenzado, había comenzado

Crossword Puzzle 10

CHAPTER 11
Exercise Set 11-1

A.

1. estudiaré	=	I will study
2. estudiarás	=	you (fam. sg.) will study
3. estudiaremos	=	we will study
4. estudiarán	=	they will study
5. estudiaréis	=	you (fam. pl.) will study
6. estudiará	=	you (pol. sg.) will study

1. aprenderé	=	I will learn
2. aprenderemos	=	Raquel and I will learn
3. aprenderán	=	you (pol. pl.) will learn
4. aprenderán	=	they will learn
5. aprenderéis	=	you (fam. pl.) will learn
6. aprenderás	=	you (fam. sg.) will learn

1. escribiré	=	I will write
2. escribirás	=	you (fam sg.) will write
3. escribiremos	=	we will write
4. escribirán	=	they will write
5. escribiréis	=	you (fam. pl.) will write
6. escribirá	=	you (pol. sg.) will write

1. me sentaré	=	I will sit down
2. te sentarás	=	you (fam. sg.) will sit down
3. nos sentaremos	=	we will sit down
4. se sentarán	=	they will sit down
5. os sentaréis	=	you (fam. pl.) will sit down
6. se sentará	=	you (pol. sg.) will sit down

B.

1. Viajaré a *David*.
2. Ese programa comenzará a las ocho de la noche.
3. Ella se duchará mañana.
4. Rosalba y yo compraremos nuestros libros mañana.
5. Me levantaré tarde mañana.
6. Veré el *Museo afro-antillano* el viernes.
7. A ella no le gustará esa película.
8. Él dormirá hasta el mediodía.
9. Asistiré a la universidad el año próximo.
10. Ellos llegarán a la una de la tarde.

Exercise Set 11-2

A.

1. cabré	=	I will fit
2. cabrás	=	you (fam. sg.) will fit
3. cabremos	=	we will fit
4. cabrán	=	they will fit
5. cabréis	=	you (fam. pl.) will fit
6. cabrá	=	you (pol. sg.) will fit

1. saldré	=	I will leave
2. saldremos	=	Raquel and I will leave
3. saldrán	=	you (pol. pl.) will leave
4. saldrán	=	they will leave
5. saldréis	=	you (fam. pl.) will leave
6. saldrás	=	you (fam. sg.) will leave

1. diré	=	I will say/tell
2. dirás	=	you (fam. sg.) will say/tell
3. diremos	=	we will say/tell
4. dirán	=	they will say/tell
5. diréis	=	you (fam. pl.) will say/tell
6. dirá	=	you (pol. sg.) will say/tell

1. habré	=	I will have
2. habrás	=	you (fam. sg.) will have
3. habremos	=	we will have
4. habrán	=	they will have
5. habréis	=	you (fam. pl.) will have
6. habrá	=	you (pol. sg.) will have

1. podré	=	I will be able
2. podrás	=	you (fam. sg.) will be able
3. podremos	=	we will be able
4. podrán	=	they will be able
5. podréis	=	you (fam. pl.) will be able
6. podrá	=	you (pol. sg.) will be able

1. vendré	=	I will come
2. vendrás	=	you (fam. sg.) will come
3. vendremos	=	we will come

4. vendrán	=	they will come
5. vendréis	=	you (fam. pl.) will come
6. vendrá	=	you (pol. sg.) will come
1. sabré	=	I will know
2. sabrás	=	you (fam. sg.) will know
3. sabremos	=	we will know
4. sabrán	=	they will know
5. sabréis	=	you (fam. pl.) will know
6. sabrá	=	you (pol. sg.) will know
1. pondré	=	I will put/place
2. pondrás	=	you (fam. sg.) will put/place
3. pondremos	=	we will put/place
4. pondrán	=	they will put/place
5. pondréis	=	you (fam. pl.) will put/place
6. pondrá	=	you (pol. sg.) will put/place

B.

1. ¿Cuándo llegará Elena?
2. Serán las seis pronto.
3. Habrá mucha gente allí.
4. Ellos tendrán que estar aquí.
5. Saldrás mañana.
6. Vendremos a las once de la mañana.
7. Cristina sabrá la respuesta.
8. Mis padres querrán ver las fotos de Panamá.
9. El *balboa* valdrá más en el futuro.
10. Uds. pondrán los libros en la mesa.
11. Hará frío en diciembre.
12. Ellos irán a *la Isla Contadora*.
13. Estará nublado mañana.
14. Diré la verdad.

Exercise Set 11-3

A.

1. f   2. a   3. e   4. b   5. h   6. c   7. d   8. g

B.

1. ¿Dónde estará él?
2. Habrá que conjugar más verbos.
3. Ellos saldrán mañana.
4. Tendré que trabajar por la tarde.
5. Querrás ver la última película.
6. Habrá muchos estudiantes en esta clase.
7. Le diremos la verdad a ella.
8. Uds. tendrán que comprar más comida.
9. ¿Qué día será?
10. Iré a la casa de Pablo.

C.

1. llegarán	7. tendré	13. hará
2. romperé	8. habrá	14. diré
3. cubrirás	9. sabré	15. valdrá
4. será	10. conoceré	16. saldré
5. estarán	11. podremos	17. vendremos
6. irá	12. querrá	18. te vestirás

Crossword Puzzle 11

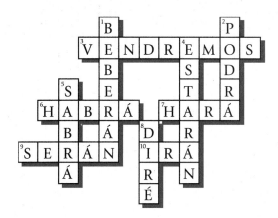

CHAPTER 12
Exercise Set 12-1

A.

1. habré trabajado	=	I will have worked
2. habrás trabajado	=	you (fam. sg.) will have worked
3. habremos trabajado	=	we will have worked
4. habrán trabajado	=	they will have worked
5. habréis trabajado	=	you (fam. pl.) will have worked
6. habrá trabajado	=	you (pol. sg.) will have worked

1. habré creído	=	I will have believed
2. habremos creído	=	Raquel and I will have believed
3. habrán creído	=	you (pol. pl.) will have believed
4. habrán creído	=	they will have believed
5. habréis creído	=	you (fam. pl.) will have believed
6. habrás creído	=	you (fam. sg.) will have believed

1. habré decidido	=	I will have decided
2. habrás decidido	=	you (fam. sg.) will have decided
3. habremos decidido	=	we will have decided
4. habrán decidido	=	they will have decided
5. habréis decidido	=	you (fam. pl.) will have decided
6. habrá decidido	=	you (pol. sg.) will have decided

1. me habré afeitado	=	I will have shaved
2. te habrás afeitado	=	you (fam. sg.) will have shaved
3. nos habremos afeitado	=	we will have shaved
4. se habrán afeitado	=	they will have shaved
5. os habréis afeitado	=	you (fam. pl.) will have shaved
6. se habrá afeitado	=	you (pol. sg.) will have shaved

1. habré sido	=	I will have been
2. habrás sido	=	you (fam. sg.) will have been
3. habremos sido	=	we will have been
4. habrán sido	=	they will have been
5. habréis sido	=	you (fam. pl.) will have been
6. habrá sido	=	you (pol. sg.) will have been

1. habré estado	=	I will have been
2. habrás estado	=	you (fam. sg.) will have been
3. habremos estado	=	we will have been
4. habrán estado	=	they will have been
5. habréis estado	=	you (fam. pl.) will have been
6. habrá estado	=	you (pol. sg.) will have been

1. habré hecho	=	I will have done/made
2. habrás hecho	=	you (fam. sg.) will have done/made
3. habremos hecho	=	we will have done/made
4. habrán hecho	=	they will have done/made
5. habréis hecho	=	you (fam. pl.) will have done/made
6. habrá hecho	=	you (pol. sg.) will have done/made

B.

1. Cuando ellos se habrán casado, vivirán en San José.
2. Cuando Uds. se habrán graduado, ¿dónde trabajarán Uds.?
3. Cuando habré aprendido muchos verbos españoles, podré hablar español.
4. Ellos habrán llegado mañana por la mañana.
5. Él habrá leído el libro para mañana.

C.

1. veré, habré visto
2. cubrirás, habrás cubierto
3. abrirán, habrán abierto
4. serán, habrán sido
5. estaré, habré estado
6. diré, habré dicho
7. venderemos, habremos vendido
8. escribiremos, habremos escrito
9. te bañarás, te habrás bañado
10. tendréis, habréis tenido
11. pedirán, habrán pedido
12. volveremos, habremos vuelto
13. hará, habrá hecho
14. tendrán, habrán tenido
15. cerrarás, habrás cerrado
16. morirá, habrá muerto
17. pondré, habré puesto
18. habrá, habrá habido

Crossword Puzzle 12

CHAPTER 13
Exercise Set 13-1

A.

1. entraría	=	I would enter
2. entrarías	=	you (fam. sg.) would enter
3. entraríamos	=	we would enter
4. entrarían	=	they would enter
5. entraríais	=	you (fam. pl.) would enter
6. entraría	=	you (pol. sg.) would enter

1. temería	=	I would fear
2. temeríamos	=	Raquel and I would fear
3. temerían	=	you (pol. pl.) would fear
4. temerían	=	they would fear
5. temeríais	=	you (fam. pl.) would fear
6. temerías	=	you (fam. sg.) would fear

1. descubriría	=	I would discover
2. descubrirías	=	you (fam. sg.) would discover
3. descubriríamos	=	we would discover
4. descubrirían	=	they would discover
5. descubriríais	=	you (fam. pl.) would discover
6. descubriría	=	you (pol. sg.) would discover

1. me casaría	=	I would marry
2. te casarías	=	you (fam. sg.) would marry
3. nos casaríamos	=	we would marry
4. se casarían	=	they would marry
5. os casaríais	=	you (fam. pl.) would marry
6. se casaría	=	you (pol. sg.) would marry

B.

1. Yo hablaría más español, pero debo estudiar los verbos.
2. ¿Irías aquí, por favor?
3. Ellos pagarían el café, pero no tienen el dinero.
4. ¿Dónde encontrarías una tienda abierta a esta hora?
5. ¿Quién lo vería?

6. Ellos irían a la *Reserva Natural Volcán Mombacho.*
7. Yo iría de compras, pero no tengo dinero.
8. ¿Me darías ese diario?
9. ¿Se casaría él con Carmen?
10. Me gustaría aprender más verbos españoles.

Exercise Set 13-2

A.

1. querría	=	I would want
2. querrías	=	you (fam. sg.) would want
3. querríamos	=	we would want
4. querrían	=	they would want
5. querríais	=	you (fam. pl.) would want
6. querría	=	you (pol. sg.) would want

1. cabría	=	I would fit
2. cabríamos	=	Raquel and I would fit
3. cabrían	=	you (pol. pl.) would fit
4. cabrían	=	they would fit
5. cabríais	=	you (fam. pl.) would fit
6. cabrías	=	you (fam. sg.) would fit

1. haría	=	I would do/make
2. harías	=	you (fam. sg.) would do/make
3. haríamos	=	we would do/make
4. harían	=	they would do/make
5. haríais	=	you (fam. pl.) would do/make
6. haría	=	you (pol. sg.) would do/make

1. habría	=	I would have
2. habrías	=	you (fam. sg.) would have
3. habríamos	=	we would have
4. habrían	=	they would have
5. habríais	=	you (fam. pl.) would have
6. habría	=	you (pol. sg.) would have

1. podría	=	I would be able
2. podrías	=	you (fam. sg.) would be able
3. podríamos	=	we would be able
4. podrían	=	they would be able
5. podríais	=	you (fam. pl.) would be able
6. podría	=	you (pol. sg.) would be able

1. vendría	=	I would come
2. vendrías	=	you (fam. sg.) would come
3. vendríamos	=	we would come
4. vendrían	=	they would come
5. vendríais	=	you (fam. pl.) would come
6. vendría	=	you (pol. sg.) would come

1. tendría	=	I would have
2. tendrías	=	you (fam. sg.) would have
3. tendríamos	=	we would have
4. tendrían	=	they would have

5. tendríais   =   you (fam. pl.) would have
6. tendría   =   you (pol. sg.) would have

B.

1. Yo haría los ejercicios, pero estoy muy cansado/a.
2. Ella podría hacer ese trabajo.
3. Pondríamos los platos en la mesa.
4. Yo saldría por la noche.
5. Ud. sabría la respuesta.
6. Él diría que es tarde.
7. Uds. tendrían que estar aquí a tiempo.
8. El coche valdría diez mil *córdobas*.
9. ¿Querrías ir al teatro?
10. Llovería por la noche.
11. Dirías la verdad.
12. Los libros cabrían en el estante.
13. Sabríamos conjugar el tiempo condicional.
14. Habría que levantarse temprano.

Exercise Set 13-3

A.

1. Serían las cinco de la tarde cuando Lidia llegó.
2. Habría que trabajar toda la noche.
3. ¿Qué harías durante una tormenta?
4. Costaría mucho dinero.
5. Yo compraría otro coche, pero no tengo el dinero.

B.

1. irían
2. haría
3. dirías
4. serían
5. estaría
6. cantaría
7. tendrías
8. habría
9. sabría
10. encontraría
11. podría
12. querríamos
13. haría
14. cerraría
15. valdría
16. saldrían
17. vendría
18. te afeitarías

Crossword Puzzle 13

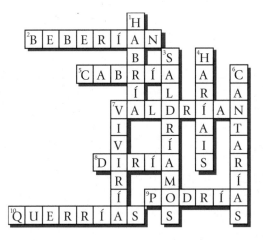

CHAPTER 14
Exercise Set 14-1

A.

1. habría llegado	=	I would have arrived
2. habrías llegado	=	you (fam. sg.) would have arrived
3. habríamos llegado	=	we would have arrived
4. habrían llegado	=	they would have arrived
5. habríais llegado	=	you (fam. pl.) would have arrived
6. habría llegado	=	you (pol. sg.) would have arrived

1. habría comprendido	=	I would have understood
2. habríamos comprendido	=	Raquel and I would have understood
3. habrían comprendido	=	you (pol. pl.) would have understood
4. habrían comprendido	=	they would have understood
5. habríais comprendido	=	you (fam. pl.) would have understood
6. habrías comprendido	=	you (fam. sg.) would have understood

1. habría discutido	=	I would have discussed
2. habrías discutido	=	you (fam. sg.) would have discussed
3. habríamos discutido	=	we would have discussed
4. habrían discutido	=	they would have discussed
5. habríais discutido	=	you (fam. pl.) would have discussed
6. habría discutido	=	you (pol. sg.) would have discussed

1. me habría quitado	=	I would have taken off
2. te habrías quitado	=	you (fam. sg.) would have taken off
3. nos habríamos quitado	=	we would have taken off
4. se habrían quitado	=	they would have taken off
5. os habríais quitado	=	you (fam. pl.) would have taken off
6. se habría quitado	=	you (pol. sg.) would have taken off

1. habría sido	=	I would have been
2. habrías sido	=	you (fam. sg.) would have been
3. habríamos sido	=	we would have been
4. habrían sido	=	they would have been
5. habríais sido	=	you (fam. pl.) would have been
6. habría sido	=	you (pol. sg.) would have been

1. habría estado	=	I would have been
2. habrías estado	=	you (fam. sg.) would have been
3. habríamos estado	=	we would have been
4. habrían estado	=	they would have been
5. habríais estado	=	you (fam. pl.) would have been
6. habría estado	=	you (pol. sg.) would have been

1. habría hecho	=	I would have done/made
2. habrías hecho	=	you (fam. sg.) would have done/made
3. habríamos hecho	=	we would have done/made
4. habrían hecho	=	they would have done/made
5. habríais hecho	=	you (fam. pl.) would have done/made
6. habría hecho	=	you (pol. sg.) would have done/made

B.

1. Yo habría ido a la fiesta, pero yo no tenía el tiempo.
2. Mis padres habrían ido a Honduras, pero ellos no tenían el dinero.
3. Yo habría ido con ellos, pero yo tenía que estudiar.
4. Ellos se habrían levantado temprano, pero durmieron tarde.
5. Él habría comprado el coche, pero costó demasiado.

C.

1. iría, habría ido
2. escribirías, habrías escrito
3. dirían, habrían dicho
4. seríais, habríais sido
5. estarían, habrían estado
6. diría, habría dicho
7. comeríamos, habríamos comido
8. viviríamos, habríamos vivido
9. te lavarías, te habrías lavado
10. tendría, habría tenido
11. morirían, habrían muerto
12. volvería, habría vuelto
13. vendrías, habrías venido
14. sabría, habría sabido
15. conocería, habría conocido
16. resolvería, habría resuelto
17. pondríamos, habríamos puesto
18. habría, habría habido

Crossword Puzzle 14

CHAPTER 15
Exercise Set 15-1

A.

1. ... mire   =   ... I look at, I am looking at, I may look at
2. ... mires   =   ... you (fam. sg.) look at, you are looking at, you may look at

3. ... miremos	=	... we look at, we are looking at, we may look at
4. ... miren	=	... they look at, they are looking at, they may look at
5. ... miréis	=	... you (fam. pl.) look at, you are looking at, you may look at
6. ... mire	=	... you (pol. sg.) look at, you are looking at, you may look at

1. ... crea	=	... I believe, I am believing, I may believe
2. ... creamos	=	... Raquel and I believe, Raquel and I are believing, Raquel and I may believe
3. ... crean	=	... you (pol. pl.) believe, you are believing, you may believe
4. ... crean	=	... they believe, they are believing, they may believe
5. ... creáis	=	... you (fam. pl.) believe, you are believing, you may believe
6. ... creas	=	... you (fam. sg.) believe, you are believing, you may believe

1. ... discuta	=	... I discuss, I am discussing, I may discuss
2. ... discutas	=	... you (fam. sg.) discuss, you are discussing, you may discuss
3. ... discutamos	=	... we discuss, we are discussing, we may discuss
4. ... discutan	=	... they discuss, they are discussing, they may discuss
5. ... discutáis	=	... you (fam. pl.) discuss, you are discussing, you may discuss
6. ... discuta	=	... you (pol. sg.) discuss, you are discussing, you may discuss

1. ... me duche	=	... I take a shower, I am taking a shower, I may take a shower
2. ... te duches	=	... you (fam. sg.) take a shower, you are taking a shower, you may take a shower
3. ... nos duchemos	=	... we take a shower, we are taking a shower, we may take a shower
4. ... se duchen	=	... they take a shower, they are taking a shower, they may take a shower
5. ... os duchéis	=	... you (fam. pl.) take a shower, you are taking a shower, you may take a shower
6. ... se duche	=	... you (pol. sg.) take a shower, you are taking a shower, you may take a shower

1. ... cuente	=	... I count, I am couting, I may count
2. ... cuentes	=	... you (fam. sg.) count, you are counting, you may count
3. ... contemos	=	... we count, we are counting, we may count
4. ... cuenten	=	... they count, they are counting, they may count
5. ... contéis	=	... you (fam. pl.) count, you are counting, you may count
6. ... cuente	=	... you (pol. sg.) count, you are counting, you may count

1. ... niegue	=	... I deny, I am denying, I may deny
2. ... niegues	=	... you (fam. sg.) deny, you are denying, you may deny
3. ... neguemos	=	... we deny, we are denying, we may deny
4. ... nieguen	=	... they deny, they are denying, they may deny
5. ... neguéis	=	... you (fam. pl.) deny, you are denying, you may deny
6. ... niegue	=	... you (pol. sg.) deny, you are denying, you may deny

1. ... muera	=	... I die, I am dying, I may die
2. ... mueras	=	... you (fam. sg.) die, you are dying, you may die
3. ... muramos	=	... we die, we are dying, we may die
4. ... mueran	=	... they die, they are dying, they may die
5. ... muráis	=	... you (fam. pl.) die, you are dying, you may die
6. ... muera	=	... you (pol. sg.) die, you are dying, you may die

1. ... consiga	=	... I get/obtain, I am getting/obtaining, I may get/obtain
2. ... consigas	=	... you (fam. sg.) get/obtain, you are getting/obtaining, you may get/obtain
3. ... consigamos	=	... we get/obtain, we are getting/obtaining, we may get/obtain

4. ... consigan	=	... they get/obtain, they are getting/obtaining, they may get/obtain
5. ... consigáis	=	... you (fam. pl.) get/obtain, you are getting/obtaining, you may get/obtain
6. ... consiga	=	... you (pol. sg.) get/obtain, you are getting/obtaining, you may get/obtain
1. ... rija	=	... I rule, I am ruling, I may rule
2. ... rijas	=	... you (fam. sg.) rule, you are ruling, you may rule
3. ... rijamos	=	... we rule, we are ruling, we may rule
4. ... rijan	=	... they rule, they are ruling, they may rule
5. ... rijáis	=	... you (fam. pl.) rule, you are ruling, you may rule
6. ... rija	=	... you (pol. sg.) rule, you are ruling, you may rule
1. ... obtenga	=	... I obtain, I am obtaining, I may obtain
2. ... obtengas	=	... you (fam. sg.) obtain, you are obtaining, you may obtain
3. ... obtengamos	=	... we obtain, we are obtaining, we may obtain
4. ... obtengan	=	... they obtain, they are obtaining, they may obtain
5. ... obtengáis	=	... you (fam. pl.) obtain, you are obtaining, you may obtain
6. ... obtenga	=	... you (pol. sg.) obtain, you are obtaining, you may obtain
1. ... componga	=	... I compose, I am composing, I may compose
2. ... compongas	=	... you (fam. sg.) compose, you are composing, you may compose
3. ... compongamos	=	... we compose, we are composing, we may compose
4. ... compongan	=	... they compose, they are composing, they may compose
5. ... compongáis	=	... you (fam. pl.) compose, you are composing, you may compose
6. ... componga	=	... you (pol. sg.) compose, you are composing, you may compose
1. ... sea	=	... I am, I may be
2. ... seas	=	... you (fam. sg.) are, you may be
3. ... seamos	=	... we are, we may be
4. ... sean	=	... they are, they may be
5. ... seáis	=	... you (fam. pl.) are, you may be
6. ... sea	=	... you (pol. sg.) are, you may be
1. ... esté	=	... I am, I may be
2. ... estés	=	... you (fam. sg.) are, you may be
3. ... estemos	=	... we are, we may be
4. ... estén	=	... they are, they may be
5. ... estéis	=	... you (fam. pl.) are, you may be
6. ... esté	=	... you (pol. sg.) are, you may be
1. ... venza	=	... I conquer, I am conquering, I may conquer
2. ... venzas	=	... you (fam. sg.) conquer, you are conquering, you may conquer
3. ... venzamos	=	... we conquer, we are conquering, we may conquer
4. ... venzan	=	... they conquer, they are conquering, they may conquer
5. ... venzáis	=	... you (fam. pl.) conquer, you are conquering, you may conquer
6. ... venza	=	... you (pol. sg.) conquer, you are conquering, you may conquer

Exercise Set 15-2

A.

1. Concepción duda que vaya a nevar.
2. Quiero que Oscar esté aquí a las nueve de la noche.
3. Sientes que el examen sea mañana.
4. A menos que trabajemos mucho, nunca terminaremos.
5. Es fácil que Rosa tenga el libro.

6. Él no cree que haya muchos estudiantes allí hoy.
7. Espero que Julio lea la novela.
8. No hay nadie que sepa usar esta computadora.
9. Ella escibirá la composición antes de que ella mire la televisión.
10. Es posible que él pague la cuenta.
11. Tan pronto como yo llegue a San Salvador, iré al *Museo Nacional de Antropología David F. Guzmán.*
12. Ellos no están seguros de que sus padres estén en El Salvador.
13. Es difícil que Laura conozca a Enrique.
14. Quiero que Salvador vea este programa.
15. Mis padres insisten en que mi hermano asista a la clase.

Exercise Set 15-3

A.

1. Es probable que ellos vayan a San Salvador.
2. Mi esposa niega que yo tenga sueño.
3. Temo que mis amigos beban mucha cerveza.
4. Espero que este libro sea muy bueno.
5. No creo que Pablo estudie demasiado.
6. Es una lástima que mis niños estén enfermos.
7. Prefiero que ellos jueguen al fútbol.
8. Tal vez Aurora venga mañana.
9. Es fácil que yo vaya a El Salvador.
10. No pienso que haga calor.

Exercise Set 15-4

A.

1. Con tal de que haga fresco, nadaremos en *La Libertad.*
2. Tal vez ellos vayan a Centroamérica. ¿Sabes?
3. Es posible que esté nublado.
4. Puede ser que ella esté cansada.
5. Iré a la biblioteca cuando Mario llegue.
6. Quiero que él escriba una carta.
7. Él no cree que haya una tormenta.
8. Temo que Esperanza no sepa la respuesta.

Exercise Set 15-5

A.

1. tenga	7. sepa	13. traigas
2. pongamos	8. conozcamos	14. te bañes
3. pidáis	9. durmamos	15. busque
4. sean	10. corrijan	16. salgan
5. estés	11. haya	17. venga
6. vayan	12. digamos	18. haga

Crossword Puzzle 15

CHAPTER 16
Exercise Set 16-1

A.

1. ... pagara	=	... I paid, I was paying, I might pay
2. ... pagaras	=	... you (fam sg.) paid, you were paying, you might pay
3. ... pagáramos	=	... we paid, we were paying, we might pay
4. ... pagaran	=	... they paid, they were paying, they might pay
5. ... pagarais	=	... you (fam. pl.) paid, you were paying, you might pay
6. ... pagara	=	... you (pol. sg.) paid, you were paying, you might pay

1. ... cometiera	=	... I committed, I was committing, I might commit
2. ... cometiéramos	=	... Raquel and I committed, Raquel and I were committing, Raquel and I might commit
3. ... cometieran	=	... you (pol. pl.) committed, you were committing, you might commit
4. ... cometieran	=	... they committed, they were committing, they might commit
5. ... cometierais	=	... you (fam. pl.) committed, you were committing, you might commit
6. ... cometieras	=	... you (fam. sg.) committed, you were committing, you might commit

1. ... permitiera	=	... I permitted, I was permitting, I might permit
2. ... permitieras	=	... you (fam sg.) permitted, you were permitting, you might permit
3. ... permitiéramos	=	... we permitted, we were permitting, we might permit
4. ... permitieran	=	... they permitted, they were permitting, they might permit
5. ... permitierais	=	... you (fam. pl.) permitted, you were permitting, you might permit
6. ... permitiera	=	... you (pol. sg.) permitted, you were permitting, you might permit

1. ... me quitara	=	... I took off, I was taking off, I might take off
2. ... te quitaras	=	... you (fam. sg.) took off, you were taking off, you might take off
3. ... nos quitáramos	=	... we took off, we were taking off, we might take off
4. ... se quitaran	=	... they took off, they were taking off, they might take off
5. ... os quitarais	=	... you (fam. pl.) took off, you were taking off, you might take off
6. ... se quitara	=	... you (pol. sg.) took off, you were taking off, you might take off

1. ... confesara	=	... I confessed, I was confessing, I might confess
2. ... confesaras	=	... you (fam. sg.) confessed, you were confessing, you might confess
3. ... confesáramos	=	... we confessed, we were confessing, we might confess
4. ... confesaran	=	... they confessed, they were confessing, they might confess
5. ... confesarais	=	... you (fam. pl.) confessed, you were confessing, you might confess
6. ... confesara	=	... you (pol. sg.) confessed, you were confessing, you might confess

1. ... volara	=	... I flew, I was flying, I might fly
2. ... volaras	=	... you (fam. sg.) flew, you were flying, you might fly
3. ... voláramos	=	... we flew, we were flying, we might fly
4. ... volaran	=	... they flew, they were flying, they might fly
5. ... volarais	=	... you (fam. pl.) flew, you were flying, you might fly
6. ... volara	=	... you (pol. sg.) flew, you were flying, you might fly

1. ... midiera	=	... I measured, I was measuring, I might measure
2. ... midieras	=	... you (fam. sg.) measured, you were measuring, you might measure
3. ... midiéramos	=	... we measured, we were measuring, we might measure
4. ... midieran	=	... they measured, they were measuring, they might measure
5. ... midierais	=	... you (fam. pl.) measured, you were measuring, you might measure
6. ... midiera	=	... you (pol. sg.) measured, you were measuring, you might measure

1. ... muriera	=	... I died, I was dying, I might die
2. ... murieras	=	... you (fam. sg.) died, you were dying, you might die
3. ... nuriéramos	=	... we died, we were dying, we might die
4. ... murieran	=	... they died, they were dying, they might die
5. ... murierais	=	... you (fam. pl.) died, you were dying, you might die
6. ... muriera	=	... you (pol. sg.) died, you were dying, you might die

1. ... fuera	=	... I was, I might be
2. ... fueras	=	... you (fam. sg.) were, you might be
3. ... fuéramos	=	... we were, we might be
4. ... fueran	=	... they were, they might be
5. ... fuerais	=	... you (fam. pl.) were, you might be
6. ... fuera	=	... you (pol. sg.) were, you might be

1. ... tuviera	=	... I had, I was having, I might have
2. ... tuvieras	=	... you (fam. sg.) had, you were having, you might have
3. ... tuviéramos	=	... we had, we were having, we might have
4. ... tuvieran	=	... they had, they were having, they might have
5. ... tuvierais	=	... you (fam. pl.) had, you were having, you might have
6. ... tuviera	=	... you (pol. sg.) had, you were having, you might have

1. ... hiciera	=	... I did/made, I was doing/making, I might do/make
2. ... hicieras	=	... you (fam. sg.) did/made, you were doing/making, you might do/make
3. ... hiciéramos	=	... we did/made, we were doing/making, we might do/make
4. ... hicieran	=	... they did/made, they were doing/making, they might do/make
5. ... hicierais	=	... you (fam. pl.) did/made, you were doing/making, you might do/make
6. ... hiciera	=	... you (pol. sg.) did/made, you were doing/making, you might do/make

1. ... fuera	=	... I went, I was going, I might go
2. ... fueras	=	... you (fam. sg.) went, you were going, you might go
3. ... fuéramos	=	... we went, we were going, we might go
4. ... fueran	=	... they went, they were going, they might go
5. ... fuerais	=	... you (fam. pl.) went, you were going, you might go
6. ... fuera	=	... you (pol. sg.) went, you were going, you might go

1. ... estuviera	=	... I was, I might be
2. ... estuvieras	=	... you (fam. sg.) were, you might be
3. ... estuviéramos	=	... we were, we might be
4. ... estuvieran	=	... they were, they might be
5. ... estuvierais	=	... you (fam. pl.) were, you might be
6. ... estuviera	=	... you (pol. sg.) were, you might be

1. ... condujera	=	... I drove, I was driving, I might drive
2. ... condujeras	=	... you (fam. sg.) drove, you were driving, you might drive
3. ... condujéramos	=	... we drove, we were driving, we might drive
4. ... condujeran	=	... they drove, they were driving, they might drive
5. ... condujerais	=	... you (fam. pl.) drove, you were driving, you might drive
6. ... condujera	=	... you (pol. sg.) drove, you were driving, you might drive

Exercise Set 16-2

A.

1. Si yo tuviera el dinero, yo compraría un boleto de lotería.
2. Yo leería *El señor presidente* de Miguel Ángel Asturias, si yo tuviera el tiempo.
3. Si no hiciera tanto calor, yo correría en el parque.
4. Si yo no estuviera tan cansado/a, yo limpiaría la casa.
5. Ella vendría si pudiera.
6. Compraríamos la casa si no fuera tan cara.
7. Iríamos a *Quetzaltenango*, si no trabajáramos.
8. Si ella estuviera aquí, ella estaría contenta.
9. Si Uds. vieran *Chichecastenango*, Uds. no se irían.
10. Si hubiera más tiempo, yo iría a Guatemala más a menudo.

B.

1. Ellos dudaban que yo empezara a estudiar.
2. Él temía que quisieras ir a Guatemala.
3. Esperábamos que no hiciera mucho frío.
4. Yo no estaba seguro/a de que Ud. tuviera razón.
5. Era increíble que ellos no miraran la televisión.
6. Ella no creía que yo supiera hablar español.
7. Era fácil que fuéramos a la capital de Guatemala.
8. Yo no pensaba que lloviera mucho.

Exercise Set 16-3

A.

1. ¿Adónde quisieras ir?
2. ¿Quisiera Ud. mostrarme la novela del nuevo escritor guatemalteco?
3. ¿Pudiera Ud. conducirme a la universidad?
4. Mi esposa quisiera ver las ruinas mayas.
5. ¿Pudiera Ud. repetir la pregunta?

Exercise Set 16-4

A.

1. Me sentí como si yo estuviera enfermo/a.
2. Toqué la guitarra como si yo fuera *Andrés Segovia*.
3. Él pinta como si fuera *Pablo Picasso*.

4. Yo escribía como si fuera *Miguel Ángel Asturias.*
5. Hablas como si fueras de Guatemala.
6. Él condujo como si él estuviera borracho.

Exercise Set 16-5

A.

1. compre, comprara
2. crean, creyeran
3. vivamos, viviéramos
4. seamos, fuéramos
5. esté, estuviera
6. vaya, fuera

7. conozca, conociera
8. sepa, supiera
9. muráis, murierais
10. digan, dijeran
11. haya, hubiera
12. corrijas, corrigieras

13. caiga, cayera
14. se duche, se duchara
15. ponga, pusiera
16. salgamos, saliéramos
17. vengas, vinieras
18. haga, hiciera

Crossword Puzzle 16

CHAPTER 17
Exercise Set 17-1

A.

1. ... haya estudiado	=	... I have studied, I may have studied
2. ... hayas estudiado	=	... you (fam. sg.) have studied, you may have studied
3. ... hayamos estudiado	=	... we have studied, we may have studied
4. ... hayan estudiado	=	... they have studied, they may have studied
5. ... hayáis estudiado	=	... you (fam. pl.) have studied, you may have studied
6. ... haya estudiado	=	... you (pol. sg.) have studied, you may have studied

1. ... haya corrido	=	... I have run, I may have run
2. ... hayamos corrido	=	... Raquel and I have run, Raquel and I may have run
3. ... hayan corrido	=	... you (pol. pl.) have run, you may have run
4. ... hayan corrido	=	... they have run, they may have run
5. ... hayáis corrido	=	... you (fam. pl.) have run, you may have run
6. ... hayas corrido	=	... you (fam. sg.) have run, you may have run

1. ... haya sufrido	=	... I have suffered, I may have suffered
2. ... hayas sufrido	=	... you (fam. sg.) have suffered, you may have suffered
3. ... hayamos sufrido	=	... we have suffered, we may have suffered
4. ... hayan sufrido	=	... they have suffered, they may have suffered
5. ... hayáis sufrido	=	... you (fam. pl.) have suffered, you may have suffered
6. ... haya sufrido	=	... you (pol. sg.) have suffered, you may have suffered

1. ... me haya afeitado	=	... I have shaved, I may have shaved
2. ... te hayas afeitado	=	... you (fam. sg.) have shaved, you may have shaved
3. ... nos hayamos afeitado	=	... we have shaved, we may have shaved
4. ... se hayan afeitado	=	... they have shaved, they may have shaved
5. ... os hayáis afeitado	=	... you (fam. pl.) have shaved, you may have shaved
6. ... se haya afeitado	=	... you (pol. sg.) have shaved, you may have shaved

B.

1. Es difícil que ella haya leído *El laberinto de la soledad* de Octavio Paz.
2. Dudo que Eulalia haya llegado.
3. Antonio no conoce a nadie que haya visto esa película.
4. En caso de que Clara haya llegado, tendré que ir al aeropuerto.
5. Temes que ella ya haya vuelto a casa.
6. Es posible que ellos hayan comido todos los dulces.
7. No creo que Benito haya hecho su tarea.
8. Ellos niegan que Blas haya ido a México.
9. Espero que Gloria no haya estado enferma.
10. César no cree que Amalia haya hecho el trabajo.

C.

1. a   2. b   3. a   4. b   5. b

Exercise Set 17-2

A.

1. Es fantástico que yo haya comenzado a estudiar.
2. Dudo que mi hermana haya llegado.
3. Temo que haya hecho mal tiempo.
4. Mi esposo niega que yo haya leído esos poemas.
5. Espero que mi amiga haya visto esa película.
6. Es posible que haya estado nublado.
7. Ella no cree que me haya divertido mucho.
8. Es increíble que mi hermano haya pagado la cuenta.
9. Es improbable que te hayas levantado muy tarde.
10. Puede ser que ellos hayan estado aquí por dos semanas.

Exercise Set 17-3

A.

1. hayamos tenido	7. hayan sabido	13. hayan traído
2. hayáis podido	8. haya conocido	14. se haya duchado
3. haya pedido	9. hayas dormido	15. haya creído
4. haya sido	10. haya roto	16. haya abierto
5. hayamos estado	11. haya habido	17. hayas cubierto
6. haya ido	12. haya dicho	18. haya hecho

Crossword Puzzle 17

CHAPTER 18
Exercise Set 18-1

A.

1. … hubiera dudado	=	… I had doubted, I might have doubted
2. … hubieras dudado	=	… you (fam. sg.) had doubted, you might have doubted
3. … hubiéramos dudado	=	… we had doubted, we might have doubted
4. … hubieran dudado	=	… they had doubted, they might have doubted
5. … hubierais dudado	=	… you (fam. pl.) had doubted, you might have doubted
6. … hubiera dudado	=	… you (pol. sg.) had doubted, you might have doubted

1. … hubiera bebido	=	… I had drunk, I might have drunk
2. … hubiéramos bebido	=	… Raquel and I had drunk, Raquel and I might have drunk
3. … hubieran bebido	=	… you (pol. pl.) had drunk, you might have drunk
4. … hubieran bebido	=	… they had drunk, they might have drunk
5. … hubierais bebido	=	… you (fam. pl.) had drunk, you might have drunk
6. … hubiera bebido	=	… you (pol. sg.) had drunk, you might have drunk

1. … hubiera escrito	=	… I had written, I might have written
2. … hubiéramos escrito	=	… Raquel and I had written, Raquel and I might have written
3. … hubieran escrito	=	… you (pol. pl.) had written, you might have written
4. … hubieran escrito	=	… they had written, they might have written
5. … hubierais escrito	=	… you (fam. pl.) had written, you might have written
6. … hubiera escrito	=	… you (pol. sg.) had written, you might have written

1. … me hubiera duchado	=	… I had showered, I might have showered
2. … te hubieras duchado	=	… you (fam. sg.) had showered, you might have showered
3. … nos hubiéramos duchado	=	… we had showered, we might have showered
4. … se hubieran duchado	=	… they had showered, they might have showered
5. … os hubierais duchado	=	… you (fam. pl.) had showered, you might have showered
6. … se hubiera duchado	=	… you (pol. sg.) had showered, you might have showered

B.

1. Yo dudaba que hubieras leído *Tres tristes tigres* de Guillermo Cabrera Infante.
2. ¿Era fácil que ellos hubieran visto a mi hermana?
3. Yo no creía que Beatriz hubiera visitado La Habana.
4. El profesor esperaba que sus estudiantes hubieran conjugado los verbos en el pluscuamperfecto del subjuntivo.

5. Negaste que yo hubiera estado en Cuba.
6. No había nadie que hubiera visto las noticias en la televisión.
7. Era difícil que Julio hubiera estado muy ocupado.
8. Era posible que mis padres hubieran llegado tarde.
9. Inés no creía que mi hermano hubiera roto los platos.
10. Era probable que hubiera habido un accidente allí.

C.

1. Si yo hubiera tenido el tiempo, yo habría ido a Cuba.
2. Bárbara habría conducido a la universidad, si ella hubiera sabido conducir.
3. Si yo hubiera sabido del examen, yo habría leído el libro.
4. Si Oscar hubiera comprado un boleto, él habría ganado la lotería.
5. Si Rosa no hubiera estado cansada, ella no habría tenido un accidente.
6. Si no hubiera llovido tanto, habríamos ido a la fiesta.
7. Si Raúl no hubiera mentido, él no habría ido a la cárcel.
8. Si me hubieras dicho la verdad, no habría estado tan enojado/a.
9. Si no hubiera habido tantos problemas, habríamos llegado a tiempo.
10. Si yo hubiera recordado mi cartera, yo habría podido pagar la cuenta.

Exercise Set 18-2

A.

1. hayáis tenido, hubierais tenido
2. haya cantado, hubiera cantado
3. haya hecho, hubiera hecho
4. hayan estado, hubieran estado
5. hayamos sido, hubiéramos sido
6. hayan ido, hubieran ido
7. haya sabido, hubiera sabido
8. haya conocido, hubiera conocido
9. hayas muerto, hubieras muerto
10. hayamos abierto, hubiéramos abierto
11. haya habido, hubiera habido
12. hayas dicho, hubieras dicho
13. haya caído, hubiera caído
14. se haya bañado, se hubiera bañado
15. haya creído, hubiera creído
16. haya abierto, hubiera abierto
17. hayan cubierto, hubieran cubierto
18. haya medido, hubiera medido

Crossword Puzzle 18

CHAPTER 19
Exercise Set 19-1

A.

1.	¡Compra!	=	Buy!
2.	¡Bebe!	=	Drink!
3.	¡Abre!	=	Open!
4.	¡Ten!	=	Have!
5.	¡Sal!	=	Leave!

B.

1.	¡No prepares!	=	Don't prepare!
2.	¡No corras!	=	Don't run!
3.	¡No cubras!	=	Don't cover!
4.	¡No hagas!	=	Don't do!
5.	¡No vengas!	=	Don't come!

C.

1.	¡Comprad!	=	Buy!
2.	¡Bebed!	=	Drink!
3.	¡Abrid!	=	Open!
4.	¡Tened!	=	Hold!
5.	¡Salid!	=	Leave!

D.

1.	¡No preparéis!	=	Don't prepare!
2.	¡No corráis!	=	Don't run!
3.	¡No cubráis!	=	Don't cover!
4.	¡No hagáis!	=	Don't do!
5.	¡No vengáis!	=	Don't come!

Exercise Set 19-2

A.

1. ¡Aféitate!
2. ¡No me lo des!
3. ¡Estúdiala!
4. ¡Léemelo!
5. ¡No te acuestes!
6. ¡ No me la digas!
7. ¡No la leas!
8. ¡Cómpralo!

Exercise Set 19-3

A.

1.	¡Cante!	=	Sing!
2.	¡Coma!	=	Eat!
3.	¡Asista!	=	Attend!
4.	¡Sea!	=	Be!
5.	¡Dé!	=	Give!

B.

1.	¡No compre!	=	Don't buy!
2.	¡No beba!	=	Don't drink!
3.	¡No viva!	=	Don't live!
4.	¡No sepa!	=	Don't know!
5.	¡No vaya!	=	Don't go!

C.

1.	¡Busquen!	=	Look for!
2.	¡Lean!	=	Read!
3.	¡Abran!	=	Open!
4.	¡Estén!	=	Be!
5.	¡Vuelvan!	=	Return!

D.

1.	¡No preparen!	=	Don't prepare!
2.	¡No crean!	=	Don't believe!
3.	¡No admitan!	=	Don't admit!
4.	¡No comiencen!	=	Don't begin!
5.	¡No protejan!	=	Don't protect!

Exercise Set 19-4

A.

1. ¡Acuéstense!
2. ¡Cómpremela!
3. ¡No se lo muestre a ella!
4. ¡Cántensela a ella!
5. ¡Levántese!
6. ¡No me miren!
7. ¡Escríbasela a ellos!
8. ¡Muéstreselos a ella!

Exercise Set 19-5

A.

1. ¡Comencemos!
2. ¡No vayamos!
3. ¡Toquemos la guitarra!
4. ¡Seamos simpáticos!
5. ¡No conjuguemos los verbos en español!

Exercise Set 19-6

A.

1. ¡Cantémosela a ella!
2. ¡No le digamos nada a él!
3. ¡Levantémonos tarde!
4. ¡Hagámoslo!
5. ¡No se lo demos a él!
6. ¡Mostrémosela a ellos!

7. ¡No nos acostemos!
8. ¡No lo bebamos!

Exercise Set 19-7

A.

1. ¡Compra!, ¡No compres!
2. ¡Bebe!, ¡No bebas!
3. ¡Vive!, ¡No vivas!
4. ¡Sé!, ¡No seas!
5. ¡Está!, ¡No estés!
6. ¡Haz!, ¡No hagas!
7. ¡Ten!, ¡No tengas!
8. ¡Dúchate!, ¡No te duches!
9. ¡Busca!, ¡No busques!
10. ¡Encuentra!, ¡No encuentres!

B.

1. ¡Compre!, ¡No compre!
2. ¡Beba!, ¡No beba!
3. ¡Viva!, ¡No viva!
4. ¡Sea!, ¡No sea!
5. ¡Esté!, ¡No esté!
6. ¡Haga!, ¡No haga!
7. ¡Tenga!, ¡No tenga!
8. ¡Dúchese!, No se duche!
9. ¡Busque!, ¡No busque!
10. ¡Encuentre!, ¡No encuentre!

C.

1. ¡Hablemos!, ¡No hablemos!
2. ¡Comamos!, ¡No comamos!
3. ¡Escribamos!, ¡No escribamos!
4. ¡Divirtámonos!, ¡No nos divirtamos!

Crossword Puzzle 19

CHAPTER 20
Exercise Set 20-1

A.

1. La casa fue construida por José.
2. Las puertas fueron abiertas por los hombres.
3. La novela será leída por Ana.
4. La canción fue cantada por los estudiantes.
5. *Don Quijote* fue escrito por Cervantes.

B.

1. La comida fue comida por los niños.
2. La casa fue construida por los obreros.
3. La ventana fue rota por los hombres.
4. La cuenta fue pagada por Carlos.
5. Los libros fueron comprados por los estudiantes.

Exercise Set 20-2

A.

1. Se habla español aquí.
2. Se dice que llueve.
3. Se venden periódicos aquí.
4. Se pagan las cuentas los viernes.
5. Se deben comer tres comidas todos los días.

Exercise Set 20-3

A.

1. Después de leer el periódico, Marisol comenzó a trabajar.
2. Caminando, vi a Pablo.
3. Terminado el partido, fuimos al restaurante.
4. Leyendo la revista, Lidia bebió café.
5. Antes de salir, Juan compró un libro.

Crossword Puzzle 20

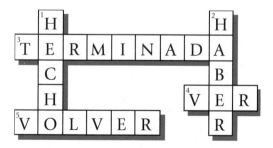

Appendix A

CONJUGATION OF REGULAR VERBS (*HABLAR, COMER, VIVIR*)

This appendix contains the complete conjugation of three regular verbs: **hablar** / *to speak;* **comer** / *to eat;* and **vivir** / *to live.*

hablar / *to speak*

Infinitive	hablar
Present Participle	hablando
Past Participle	hablado

Present Indicative	
hablo	hablamos
hablas	habláis
habla	hablan

Preterit	
hablé	hablamos
hablaste	hablasteis
habló	hablaron

Imperfect Indicative	
hablaba	hablábamos
hablabas	hablabais
hablaba	hablaban

Present Perfect Indicative	
he hablado	hemos hablado
has hablado	habéis hablado
ha hablado	han hablado

Pluperfect (Past Perfect) Indicative	
había hablado	habíamos hablado
habías hablado	habíais hablado
había hablado	habían hablado

Future	
hablaré	hablaremos
hablarás	hablaréis
hablará	hablarán

Future Perfect	
habré hablado	habremos hablado
habrás hablado	habréis hablado
habrá hablado	habrán hablado

Conditional	
hablaría	hablaríamos
hablarías	hablaríais
hablaría	hablarían

Conditional Perfect	
habría hablado	habríamos hablado
habrías hablado	habríais hablado
habría hablado	habrían hablado

Present Subjunctive	
hable	hablemos
hables	habléis
hable	hablen

Imperfect Subjunctive	
hablara	habláramos
hablaras	hablarais
hablara	hablaran

Present Perfect Subjunctive	
haya hablado	hayamos hablado
hayas hablado	hayáis hablado
haya hablado	hayan hablado

Pluperfect (Past Perfect) Subjunctive	
hubiera hablado	hubiéramos hablado
hubieras hablado	hubierais hablado
hubiera hablado	hubieran hablado

Familiar Command	
¡habla! / ¡no hables!	¡hablad! / ¡no habléis!

Polite Command	
¡hable! / ¡no hable!	¡hablen! / ¡no hablen!

comer / *to eat*

Infinitive	comer
Present Participle	comiendo
Past Participle	comido

Present Indicative	
como	comemos
comes	coméis
come	comen

Preterit	
comí	comimos
comiste	comisteis
comió	comieron

Imperfect Indicative	
comía	comíamos
comías	comíais
comía	comían

Present Perfect Indicative	
he comido	hemos comido
has comido	habéis comido
ha comido	han comido

Pluperfect (Past Perfect) Indicative	
había comido	habíamos comido
habías comido	habíais comido
había comido	habían comido

Future	
comeré	comeremos
comerás	comeréis
comerá	comerán

Future Perfect	
habré comido	habremos comido
habrás comido	habréis comido
habrá comido	habrán comido

Conditional	
comería	comeríamos
comerías	comeríais
comería	comerían

Conditional Perfect	
habría comido	habríamos comido
habrías comido	habríais comido
habría comido	habrían comido

Present Subjunctive	
coma	comamos
comas	comáis
coma	coman

Imperfect Subjunctive	
comiera	comiéramos
comieras	comierais
comiera	comieran

Present Perfect Subjunctive	
haya comido	hayamos comido
hayas comido	hayáis comido
haya comido	hayan comido

Pluperfect (Past Perfect) Subjunctive	
hubiera comido	hubiéramos comido
hubieras comido	hubierais comido
hubiera comido	hubieran comido

Familiar Command	
¡come! / ¡no comas!	¡comed! / ¡no comáis!

Polite Command	
¡coma! / ¡no coma!	¡coman! / ¡no coman!

vivir / *to live*

Infinitive	vivir
Present Participle	viviendo
Past Participle	vivido

Present Indicative	
vivo	vivimos
vives	vivís
vive	viven

Preterit	
viví	vivimos
viviste	vivisteis
vivió	vivieron

Imperfect Indicative	
vivía	vivíamos
vivías	vivíais
vivía	vivían

Present Perfect Indicative	
he vivido	hemos vivido
has vivido	habéis vivido
ha vivido	han vivido

Pluperfect (Past Perfect) Indicative	
había vivido	habíamos vivido
habías vivido	habíais vivido
había vivido	habían vivido

Future	
viviré	viviremos
vivirás	viviréis
vivirá	vivirán

Future Perfect	
habré vivido	habremos vivido
habrás vivido	habréis vivido
habrá vivido	habrán vivido

Conditional	
viviría	viviríamos
vivirías	viviríais
viviría	vivirían

Conditional Perfect	
habría vivido	habríamos vivido
habrías vivido	habríais vivido
habría vivido	habrían vivido

Present Subjunctive	
viva	vivamos
vivas	viváis
viva	vivan

Imperfect Subjunctive	
viviera	viviéramos
vivieras	vivierais
viviera	vivieran

Present Perfect Subjunctive	
haya vivido	hayamos vivido
hayas vivido	hayáis vivido
haya vivido	hayan vivido

Pluperfect (Past Perfect) Subjunctive	
hubiera vivido	hubiéramos vivido
hubieras vivido	hubierais vivido
hubiera vivido	hubieran vivido

Familiar Command	
¡vive! / ¡no vivas!	¡vivid! / ¡no viváis!

Polite Command	
¡viva! / ¡no viva!	¡vivan! / ¡no vivan!

CONJUGATION OF A REFLEXIVE VERB (*LAVARSE*)

This appendix contains the complete conjugation of the regular reflexive verb **lavarse**/*to wash oneself*.

lavarse / *to wash oneself*

Infinitive	lavarse
Present Participle	lavándose
Past Participle	lavado

Present Indicative	
me lavo	nos lavamos
te lavas	os laváis
se lava	se lavan

Preterit	
me lavé	nos lavamos
te lavaste	os lavasteis
se lavó	se lavaron

Imperfect Indicative	
me lavaba	nos lavábamos
te lavabas	os lavabais
se lavaba	se lavaban

Present Perfect Indicative	
me he lavado	nos hemos lavado
te has lavado	os habéis lavado
se ha lavado	se han lavado

Pluperfect (Past Perfect) Indicative	
me había lavado	nos habíamos lavado
te habías lavado	os habíais lavado
se había lavado	se habían lavado

Future	
me lavaré	nos lavaremos
te lavarás	os lavaréis
se lavará	se lavarán

Future Perfect	
me habré lavado	nos habremos lavado
te habrás lavado	os habréis lavado
se habrá lavado	se habrán lavado

Conditional	
me lavaría	nos lavaríamos
te lavarías	os lavaríais
se lavaría	se lavarían

Conditional Perfect	
me habría lavado	nos habríamos lavado
te habrías lavado	os habríais lavado
se habría lavado	se habrían lavado

Present Subjunctive	
me lave	nos lavemos
te laves	os lavéis
se lave	se laven

Imperfect Subjunctive	
me lavara	nos laváramos
te lavaras	os lavarais
se lavara	se lavaran

Present Perfect Subjunctive	
me haya lavado	nos hayamos lavado
te hayas lavado	os hayáis lavado
se haya lavado	se hayan lavado

Pluperfect (Past Perfect) Subjunctive	
me hubiera lavado	nos hubiéramos lavado
te hubieras lavado	os hubierais lavado
se hubiera lavado	se hubieran lavado

Familiar Command	
¡lávate! / ¡no te laves!	¡lavaos! / ¡no os lavéis!

Polite Command	
¡lávese! / ¡no se lave!	¡lávense! / ¡no se laven!

CONJUGATION OF SER, ESTAR, TENER, HACER, HABER

This appendix contains the complete conjugation of five common irregular verbs: **ser** / *to be* and **estar** / *to be*; **tener** / *to have*; **hacer** / *to do/to make*; and the auxiliary verb **haber** / *to have*.

ser / *to be*

Infinitive	ser
Present Participle	siendo
Past Participle	sido

Present Indicative	
soy	somos
eres	sois
es	son

Preterit	
fui	fuimos
fuiste	fuisteis
fue	fueron

Imperfect Indicative	
era	éramos
eras	erais
era	eran

Present Perfect Indicative	
he sido	hemos sido
has sido	habéis sido
ha sido	han sido

Pluperfect (Past Perfect) Indicative	
había sido	habíamos sido
habías sido	habíais sido
había sido	habían sido

Future	
seré	seremos
serás	seréis
será	serán

Future Perfect	
habré sido	habremos sido
habrás sido	habréis sido
habrá sido	habrán sido

Conditional	
sería	seríamos
serías	seríais
sería	serían

Conditional Perfect	
habría sido	habríamos sido
habrías sido	habríais sido
habría sido	habrían sido

Present Subjunctive	
sea	seamos
seas	seáis
sea	sean

Imperfect Subjunctive	
fuera	fuéramos
fueras	fuerais
fuera	fueran

Present Perfect Subjunctive	
haya sido	hayamos sido
hayas sido	hayáis sido
haya sido	hayan sido

Pluperfect (Past Perfect) Subjunctive	
hubiera sido	hubiéramos sido
hubieras sido	hubierais sido
hubiera sido	hubieran sido

Familiar Command	
¡sé! / ¡no seas!	¡sed! / ¡no seáis!

Polite Command	
¡sea! / ¡no sea!	¡sean! / ¡no sean!

estar / *to be*

Infinitive	estar
Present Participle	estando
Past Participle	estado

Present Indicative	
estoy	estamos
estás	estáis
está	están

Preterit	
estuve	estuvimos
estuviste	estuvisteis
estuvo	estuvieron

Imperfect Indicative	
estaba	estábamos
estabas	estabais
estaba	estaban

Present Perfect Indicative	
he estado	hemos estado
has estado	habéis estado
ha estado	han estado

Pluperfect (Past Perfect) Indicative	
había estado	habíamos estado
habías estado	habíais estado
había estado	habían estado

Future	
estaré	estaremos
estarás	estaréis
estará	estarán

Future Perfect	
habré estado	habremos estado
habrás estado	habréis estado
habrá estado	habrán estado

Conditional	
estaría	estaríamos
estarías	estaríais
estaría	estarían

Conditional Perfect	
habría estado	habríamos estado
habrías estado	habríais estado
habría estado	habrían estado

Present Subjunctive	
esté	estemos
estés	estéis
esté	estén

Imperfect Subjunctive	
estuviera	estuviéramos
estuvieras	estuvierais
estuviera	estuvieran

Present Perfect Subjunctive	
haya estado	hayamos estado
hayas estado	hayáis estado
haya estado	hayan estado

Pluperfect (Past Perfect) Subjunctive	
hubiera estado	hubiéramos estado
hubieras estado	hubierais estado
hubiera estado	hubieran estado

Familiar Command	
¡está! / ¡no estés!	¡estad! / ¡no estéis!

Polite Command	
¡esté! / ¡no esté!	¡estén! /¡no estén!

tener / *to have*

Infinitive	tener
Present Participle	teniendo
Past Participle	tenido

Present Indicative	
tengo	tenemos
tienes	tenéis
tiene	tienen

Preterit	
tuve	tuvimos
tuviste	tuvisteis
tuvo	tuvieron

Imperfect Indicative	
tenía	teníamos
tenías	teníais
tenía	tenían

Present Perfect Indicative	
he tenido	hemos tenido
has tenido	habéis tenido
ha tenido	han tenido

Pluperfect (Past Perfect) Indicative	
había tenido	habíamos tenido
habías tenido	habíais tenido
había tenido	habían tenido

Future	
tendré	tendremos
tendrás	tendréis
tendrá	tendrán

Future Perfect	
habré tenido	habremos tenido
habrás tenido	habréis tenido
habrá tenido	habrán tenido

Conditional	
tendría	tendríamos
tendrías	tendríais
tendría	tendrían

Conditional Perfect	
habría tenido	habríamos tenido
habrías tenido	habríais tenido
habría tenido	habrían tenido

Present Subjunctive	
tenga	tengamos
tengas	tengáis
tenga	tengan

Imperfect Subjunctive	
tuviera	tuviéramos
tuvieras	tuvierais
tuviera	tuvieran

Present Perfect Subjunctive	
haya tenido	hayamos tenido
hayas tenido	hayáis tenido
haya tenido	hayan tenido

Pluperfect (Past Perfect) Subjunctive	
hubiera tenido	hubiéramos tenido
hubieras tenido	hubierais tenido
hubiera tenido	hubieran tenido

Familiar Command	
¡ten! / ¡no tengas!	¡tened! / ¡no tengáis!

Polite Command	
¡tenga! / ¡no tenga!	¡tengan! / ¡no tengan!

hacer / *to do* / *to make*

Infinitive	hacer
Present Participle	haciendo
Past Participle	hecho

Present Indicative	
hago	hacemos
haces	hacéis
hace	hacen

Preterit	
hice	hicimos
hiciste	hicisteis
hizo	hicieron

Imperfect Indicative	
hacía	hacíamos
hacías	hacíais
hacía	hacían

Present Perfect Indicative	
he hecho	hemos hecho
has hecho	habéis hecho
ha hecho	han hecho

Pluperfect (Past Perfect) Indicative	
había hecho	habíamos hecho
habías hecho	habíais hecho
había hecho	habían hecho

Future	
haré	haremos
harás	haréis
hará	harán

Future Perfect	
habré hecho	habremos hecho
habrás hecho	habréis hecho
habrá hecho	habrán hecho

Conditional	
haría	haríamos
harías	haríais
haría	harían

Conditional Perfect	
habría hecho	habríamos hecho
habrías hecho	habríais hecho
habría hecho	habrían hecho

Present Subjunctive	
haga	hagamos
hagas	hagáis
haga	hagan

Imperfect Subjunctive	
hiciera	hiciéramos
hicieras	hicierais
hiciera	hicieran

Present Perfect Subjunctive	
haya hecho	hayamos hecho
hayas hecho	hayáis hecho
haya hecho	hayan hecho

Pluperfect (Past Perfect) Subjunctive	
hubiera hecho	hubiéramos hecho
hubieras hecho	hubierais hecho
hubiera hecho	hubieran hecho

Familiar Command	
¡haz! / ¡no hagas!	¡haced! / ¡no hagáis!

Polite Command	
¡haga! / ¡no haga!	¡hagan! / ¡no hagan!

haber / *to have* (Auxiliary)

Infinitive	haber
Present Participle	habiendo
Past Participle	habido

Present Indicative	
he	hemos
has	habéis
ha	han

Preterit	
hube	hubimos
hubiste	hubisteis
hubo	hubieron

Imperfect Indicative	
había	habíamos
habías	habíais
había	habían

Present Perfect Indicative	
he habido	hemos habido
has habido	habéis habido
ha habido	han habido

Pluperfect (Past Perfect) Indicative	
había habido	habíamos habido
habías habido	habíais habido
había habido	habían habido

Future	
habré	habremos
habrás	habréis
habrá	habrán

Future Perfect	
habré habido	habremos habido
habrás habido	habréis habido
habrá habido	habrán habido

Conditional	
habría	habríamos
habrías	habríais
habría	habrían

Conditional Perfect	
habría habido	habríamos habido
habrías habido	habríais habido
habría habido	habrían habido

Present Subjunctive	
haya	hayamos
hayas	hayáis
haya	hayan

Imperfect Subjunctive	
hubiera	hubiéramos
hubieras	hubierais
hubiera	hubieran

Present Perfect Subjunctive	
haya habido	hayamos habido
hayas habido	hayáis habido
haya habido	hayan habido

Pluperfect (Past Perfect) Subjunctive	
hubiera habido	hubiéramos habido
hubieras habido	hubierais habido
hubiera habido	hubieran habido

Familiar Command	
¡hé! / ¡no hayas!	¡habed! /¡no hayáis!

Polite Command	
¡haya! / ¡no haya!	¡hayan! / ¡no hayan!

Appendix B

SUMMARIES

Irregular Gerunds

Infinitive		Gerund
caer	to fall	cayendo
conseguir	to attain, to achieve	consiguiendo
construir	to construct	construyendo
corregir	to correct	corrigiendo
creer	to believe	creyendo
decir	to say, to tell	diciendo
despedirse	to say goodbye to	despidiéndose
destruir	to destroy	destruyendo
divertirse	to amuse oneself	divirtiéndose
dormir	to sleep	durmiendo
huir	to flee	huyendo
ir	to go	yendo
mentir	to lie (tell a falsehood)	mintiendo
morir	to die	muriendo
oír	to hear	oyendo
pedir	to ask for, to request	pidiendo
poder	to be able	pudiendo
reír	to laugh	riendo
repetir	to repeat	repitiendo
seguir	to follow	siguiendo
sentir	to feel	sintiendo
servir	to serve	sirviendo
traer	to bring	trayendo
venir	to come	viniendo
vestir	to dress	vistiendo
vestirse	to dress oneself	vistiéndose

Irregular Past Participles

Infinitive		Past Participle
abrir	to open	abierto
caer	to fall	caído
creer	to believe	creído
cubrir	to close	cubierto
decir	to say, to tell	dicho
descubrir	to discover	descubierto
deshacer	to undo	deshecho
devolver	to return (something)	devuelto
escribir	to write	escrito
hacer	to do, to make	hecho
imponer	to impose	impuesto
ir	to go	ido
leer	to read	leído
morir	to die	muerto
oír	to hear	oído
poner	to put, to place	puesto
rehacer	to redo, to remake	rehecho
reír	to laugh	reído
resolver	to resolve, to solve	resuelto
romper	to break	roto
sonreír	to smile	sonreído
traer	to bring	traído
ver	to see	visto
volver	to return	vuelto

SPANISH-ENGLISH VOCABULARY

A

a   at; to
a esta hora   at this time
a menos que   unless
a menudo   often
¿a qué hora?   at what time?
a tiempo   on time
abierto/-a   open
abogado (m.); abogada
   (f.)   lawyer
abrazar   to embrace; to hug
abril   April
abrir   to open
abuela (f.)   grandmother
abuelo (m.)   grandfather
aburrido/a   bored (estar);
   boring (ser)
acabar de   to have just
acabar   to complete; to finish
acaso   perhaps
accidente (m.)   accident
acción (f.)   action
aceite de olivo (m.)   olive oil
aconsejar   to advise
acordarse (ue) (de)   to
   remember
acostarse (ue)   to go to bed
activo/-a   active
adiós   good-bye
admirar   to admire
admitir   to admit
advertir (ie, i)   to notice; to
   warn
aeropuerto (m.)   airport
agosto   August
agradable   pleasant
agradar   to please
agradecer   to thank
agua (f.)   water
ahora   now
ahora mismo   right now
ajedrez (m.)   chess
alabanza (f.)   praise
alcachofa (f.)   artichoke
alcoba (f.)   bedroom
alegrarse (de)   to be glad

algo   something; somewhat
   (with an adjective)
alguien   someone
algún/-o/-a   some
allí   there
almorzar (ue)   to have lunch
alto/-a   tall
alumno (m.); alumna (f.)   pupil
amable   kind; nice
amarillo/-a   yellow
americano/-a   American
amigo (m.); amiga (f.)   friend
anaranjado/-a   orange
andar   to walk
Andes (m. pl.)   Andes
   (mountains)
animal (m.)   animal
año (m.)   year
anoche   last night
anteayer   day before yesterday
antes (de)   before; beforehand
antipático/-a   unpleasant
apetecer   to appeal to (food); to
   be appetizing to
aprender (a)   to learn
aprobar (ue)   to approve
aquel/-la   that (at a distance)
aquellos/-as   those (at a
   distance)
aquí   here
araña (f.)   spider
argentino/-a   Argentine
arqueología (f.)   archaeology
arte (m.)   art
ascensor (m.)   elevator
asistir (a)   to attend
asunto (m.)   matter; issue (as in
   business)
atractivo/-a   attractive
atraer   to attract
aula de clase (f.)   classroom
aunque   even though
aunque   although; even if
ausente   absent
autobus (m.)   bus
autor (m.); autora (f.)   author
autorizar   to authorize
avenida (f.)   avenue

avión (m.)   airplane
ayer   yesterday
ayudar   to help
azul   blue

B

bahía (f.)   bay
bailar   to dance
bajo/-a   short
ballet (m.)   ballet
baloncesto (m.)   basketball
bañarse   to bathe (oneself)
barrio (m.)   neighborhood
bastar   to be enough; to be
   sufficient
beber   to drink
béisbol (m.)   baseball
belleza (f.)   beauty
bello/-a   beautiful
besar   to kiss
biblioteca (f.)   library
bien   well
bife de costilla (m.)   rib steak
billar (m.)   pool
bistec (m.)   steak
blanco/-a   white
boleto (m.)   ticket
bolígrafo (m.)   pen
boliviano/-a   Bolivian
bolsa (f.)   purse
bonito/-a   pretty
borracho/-a   drunk
boxeador (m.)   boxer
buen tiempo (hacer)   (to be)
   good weather
buen/-o/-a   good
buscar   to look for

C

caber   to be contained; to fit
cabeza (f.)   head
cada   every
caer bien a   to create a good
   impression; to like
caer   to fall
caerse   to fall down

café (*m.*) coffee
callado/-a quiet
calle (*f.*) street
calor (*m.*) heat; warmth
cámara (*f.*) camera; bedroom
caminar to walk
canal (*m.*) canal
canción (*f.*) song
cansado/-a tired
cansarse (to get) tired
cantar to sing
capital (*f.*) capital
cárcel (*f.*) jail
caribe Caribbean
caro/a expensive
carta (*f.*) letter
cartera (*f.*) wallet
casa (*f.*) house; home
casado/-a (con) married (to)
casarse (con) to marry
cascada (*f.*) waterfall
casi almost
casino (*m.*) casino
castillo (*m.*) castle
catalán Catalan (language in Spain)
cataratas (*f. pl.*) waterfall
catorce fourteen
cena (*f.*) dinner
cenar to dine; to eat dinner
centro (*m.*) center; downtown
Centroamérica Central America
cepillarse to brush (oneself)
cerca (de) near; nearby
cerrar (ie) to close
cerveza (*f.*) beer
cesar (de) to stop
chaqueta (*f.*) jacket
charlar to chat
chileno/-a Chilean
churrasco (*m.*) barbecue (Argentina)
cien(to) hundred
ciencia ficción (*f.*) science fiction
cierto (es) certain (it's)
cinco five
cincuenta fifty
cine (*m.*) show
ciudad (*f.*) city
civil civil
¡claro que sí! of course
clase (*f.*) class
clasificar to classify

coche (*m.*) car
cocina (*f.*) kitchen
cocinar to cook
coger to grasp; to seize
colgar (ue) to hang (up)
colombiano/-a Colombian
colón (*m.*) *colon* (monetary unit in Costa Rica)
color (*m.*) color
comedor (*m.*) dining room
comenzar (ie) to begin
comer to eat
cometer to commit
cómico/-a funny
comida (*f.*) food; meal
como like
competir (i, i) to compete
completo/-a complete; exhaustive; not lacking anything
componer to compose
composición (*f.*) composition
comprar to buy
comprender to understand
computadora (*f.*) computer
con cuidado carefully
con frecuencia frequently
con tal de que provided that
concierto (*m.*) concert
concluir to conclude
condición (*f.*) condition
conducir to drive
confesar (ie) to confess
congrio (*m.*) *congrio* (local fish of Chile)
conjugación (*f.*) conjugation
conjugar to conjugate
conmigo with me
conocer to be familiar with; to know (someone)
conseguir (i, i) to get; to obtain
consentir (ie, i) to consent
constantemente constantly
construir to build
contar (ue) (con) to count (on)
contar (ue) to tell (a story)
contener to contain; to hold
contigo with you (fam. sg.)
contraer to contract
contribuir to contribute
convencer to convince

convencido/a (de) to be convinced (of)
convenir to be advisable; to be good for; to suit one's interest
convertir (ie, i) to convert
copa (*f.*) glass (wine)
corregir (i, i) to correct
correo electrónico (*m.*) e-mail
correr to run
corrida de toros (*f.*) bullfight
corvina (*f.*) *corvina* (Peruvian sea bass)
cosa (*f.*) thing
cosecha (*f.*) crop
costar (ue) to cost
costarricense Costa Rican
crear to create
crecer to grow
creer to believe
cuaderno (*m.*) notebook
cuadro (*m.*) painting
¿cuál? which one?
¿cuáles? which ones?
cuando when
¿cuándo? when?
¿cuánto tiempo hace que …? How long?
¿cuánto tiempo hacía que …? How long had …?
¿cuánto/-a? how much?
¿cuántos/-as? how many?
cuarenta forty
cuarto (*m.*) room
cuarto quarter (telling time)
cuarto de baño (*m.*) bathroom
cuatro four
cuatrocientos/-as four hundred
cubano/-a Cuban
cubierto (de) covered (with)
cubrir to cover
cuenta (*f.*) bill
cuento (*m.*) short story
cueva (*f.*) cave
cuidar to care for; to take care of
culpable guilty
cultura (*f.*) culture

D

damas (*f. pl.*) checkers
dar igual to make no difference
dar la mano to shake hands
dar saltos to jump about

dar un paseo   to take a walk
dar voces   to scream
dar   to give
darse cuenta (de)   to realize
de   by; from; of
de acuerdo con (estar)   to agree
   (with)
de buen humor (estar)   (to be)
   in a good mood
de buenas ganas   gladly
de la mañana   a.m.; in the
   morning
de la noche   p.m.; in the
   evening
de la tarde   p.m.; in the
   afternoon
de mal humor (estar)   (to be)
   in a bad mood
de niño (m.); de niña (f.)   as
   a child
de pie (estar)   (to be) standing
de vacaciones (estar)   (to be)
   on vacation
deber   should
deber   ought; should; to owe
decidir   to decide
decir (i, i)   to say; to tell
deducir   to deduce
defender (ie)   to defend
dejar   to leave (something)
delgado/-a   slender
demasiado   too much
desafortunadamente
   unfortunately
desaparecer   to disappear
desayunar   to eat breakfast
descansar   to rest
describir   to describe
descubrir   to discover
¿desde cuándo?   how long?
desear   to want
deshacer   to undo; to untie
   (a knot)
despedir (i, i)   to fire (from
   employment)
despertarse (ie)   to wake up
despierto/-a   awake; alert
después (de)   after; afterwards
destacar   to stand out
destruir   to destroy
desván (m.)   attic
desvestirse (i, i)   to get
   undressed
detener   to arrest; to detain

devolver (ue)   to return
   (something)
día (m.)   day
diciembre   December
diecinueve   nineteen
dieciocho   eighteen
dieciséis   sixteen
diecisiete   seventeen
diente (m.)   tooth
diez   ten
difícil   difficult; unlikely
dinero (m.)   money
dirección (f.)   address; direction
dirigir (i, i)   to direct
disco compacto (m.)   CD
discutir   to discuss
distraer   to distract
divertido (estar)   (to be)
   amused
divertirse (i, i)   to enjoy
   (oneself)
divertido/-a (ser)   (to be)
   entertaining
divorciado/-a   divorced
doce   twelve
doctor (m.); doctora (f.)   doctor
dólar (m.)   dollar
doler (ue)   to ache; to be
   painful
domingo   Sunday
dominicano/-a   Dominican
¿dónde?   where?
dormir (ue, u)   to sleep
dormirse (ue, u)   to fall asleep
dos   two
doscientos/-as   two hundred
ducharse   to take a shower
dudar   to doubt
dulces (m. pl.)   sweets

E

ecuatoriano/-a   Ecuadorean
eficiente   efficient
egoísta   selfish
ejercer   to exert; to exercise
el año pasado   last year
el año próximo   next year
el mes pasado   last month
elegante   elegant
elegir (i, i)   to elect
empezar (ie)   to begin
empleado (m.); empleada (f.)
   employee

en casa   at home
en caso de que   in case that
en cuanto   as soon as
en este momento   at this
   moment
en punto   exactly; sharp (time)
en voz alta   aloud
en   at; on
encantar   to delight; to be
   enchanting to
encender (ie)   to light; to turn
   on
encontrar (ue)   to find
enemigo (m.); enemiga (f.)
   enemy
enero   January
enfermarse   to get sick
enfermo/-a   sick
enojado/-a   angry
enojarse   to get angry
enorme   enormous
ensayo (m.)   essay
entregar   to hand over
entender (ie)   to understand
entrar (en)   to enter
enviar   to send
envolver (ue)   to wrap
escoger   to select
escribir   to write
escrito (m.)   writing
escritor (m.); escritora
   (f.)   writer
escuchar   to listen to
ese/-a   that (relatively far from
   the speaker and hearer)
esos/-as   those (relatively far
   from the speaker and hearer)
español   Spanish; Spaniard
esparcir   to scatter; to spread
específico/-a   specific
espejo (m.)   mirror
esperar   to hope; to wait for
esposa (f.)   wife
esposo (m.)   husband
esquiar   to ski
establecer   to establish
estante (m.)   shelf
estadounidense   U.S. citizen
estar seguro (de)   to be sure
   (of)
estar   to be (location, short
   duration)
este (m.)   East

este/-a   this (close to the speaker and hearer)
estos/-as   these (close to the speaker and hearer)
estudiante (*m.*) (*f.*)   student
estupendo/-a   stupendous
evidente   evident
examen (*m.*) exámenes (*m. pl.*) test; exam
excelente   excellent
exhibición (*f.*)   exhibition
exigir (i, i)   to demand; to require
existir   to exist

F

fácil   easy; likely
fácilmente   easily
faltar   to be lacking; to be missing to
famoso/-a   famous
fantástico/-a   fantastic
fascinar   to fascinate
favorito/-a   favorite
febrero   February
fecha (*f.*)   date
feo/-a   ugly
fiesta (*f.*)   party
fingir (i, i)   to pretend
flor (*f.*)   flower
fluir   to flow
folklórico/-a   folkloric
foto (*f.*)   photo
francés (*m.*)   French
frecuentemente   frequently
fregar (ie)   to scrub; to wash (dishes)
freír (i, i)   to fry
fresco   cool (adjective)
frijol (*m.*)   bean
frío (*m.*)   cold
frío/-a   cold
frontera (*f.*)   border
fuerza (*f.*)   force
fumar   to smoke
fútbol (*m.*)   soccer
fútbol americano (*m.*) football

G

galería (*f.*)   gallery
ganar   to win

garaje (*m.*)   garage
garganta (*f.*)   throat
gastar   to spend (money)
generalmente   generally
generoso/-a   generous
gente (*f.*)   people
gordo/-a   fat
gozar (de)   to enjoy
gracias   thanks
graduarse   to graduate
gran   great
gris   gray
gritar   to shout
guatemalteco/-a   Guatemalan
guerra (*f.*)   war
guitarra (*f.*)   guitar
gustar (a)   (to be) pleasing (to)

H

haber   to have (auxiliary)
hablar   to speak
hace   ago (with preterit)
hacer caso (a)   to pay attention (to)
hacer el papel (de)   to play the role (of)
hacer un viaje   to take a trip
hacer   to do, to make
hada (*f.*)   fairy
hallar   to find
hamburguesa (*f.*)   hamburger
hambre (*f.*)   hunger
hasta (que)   until (with clause)
hay   there is; there are
hay que   it is necessary, one must
hermana (*f.*)   sister
hermano (*m.*)   brother
hermoso/-a   beautiful
hervir (ie, i)   to boil
hija (*f.*)   daughter
hijo (*m.*)   son
histórico/-a   historic, historical
hockey (*m.*)   hockey
hombre (*m.*)   man
hora (*f.*)   hour
hotel (*m.*)   hotel
hoy en día   nowadays
hoy   today
huevo (*m.*)   egg
huir   to flee
húmedo (estar)   (to be) humid
hundureño/-a   Honduran

I

idea (*f.*)   idea
idioma (*m.*)   language
impedir (i, i)   to hinder; to impede; to prevent
importancia (*f.*)   importance
importante   important
importar   (to be) important
imposible   impossible
incásico/-a   Incan
incluir   to include
increíble   incredible
inducir   to induce; to persuade
influir   to influence
inglés (*m.*)   English
ingrediente (*m.*)   ingredient
inteligente   intelligent
interesante   interesting
interesar   (to be) interesting to
introducir   introduce
invierno (*m.*)   winter
ir (a)   to go
ir al centro   to go downtown
ir de compras   to go shopping
irresponsable   irresponsible
irse   to go away
isla (*f.*)   island
italiano (*m.*)   Italian
itinerario (*m.*)   itinerary

J

jamás   never
jardín (*m.*)   garden
joven   young
joya (*f.*)   jewel
juego (*m.*)   game
jueves   Thursday
jugar (ue) (a)   to play (game)
junio   June
justificar   to justify

L

La República Dominicana   Dominican Republic
la semana pasada   last week
la semana próxima   next week
lado (*m.*)   side
ladrillo (*m.*)   brick
lago (*m.*)   lake
lamentar   to regret
largo/-a   long

lástima (f.) pity
lavarse to wash (oneself)
lección (f.) lesson
leche (f.) milk
leer to read
lejos de far (from)
lempira (m.) lempira (monetary unit of Honduras)
lengua (f.) language
lentamente slowly
levantarse to get up
libro (m.) book
limpiar to clean
lindo/-a pretty
listo/-a clever; ready; witty (ser); to be ready (estar)
literatura (f.) literature
llamar por teléfono to phone; to telephone
llamar to call
llamarse to call (oneself); to be named
llano (m.) plain
llave (f.) key
lleno/-a full
llevar to carry
llevar to wear
llover (ue) to rain
lloviznar drizzle
lluvioso (estar) (to be) rainy
lotería (f.) lottery
lucir to display
lucir to shine
lugar (m.) place
lugar de nacimiento (m.) birthplace
lunes Monday
luz (f.) light

M

madera (f.) wood
madre (f.) mother
mal tiempo (hacer) to be bad weather
mal/-o/-a bad; evil; wicked
maleta (f.) suitcase
mañana tomorrow
mañana (f.) morning
mandar to send
manejar to drive
mano (f.) hand
mantener to maintain
mapa (m.) map
mar (m.) sea

maravilloso/-a marvelous
marrón brown
martes Tuesday
marzo March
más more
mate (m.) mate (a type of tea)
maya Mayan
mayo May
medianoche (f.) midnight
medio/-a half
mediodía (m.) noon
medir (i, i) to measure
mejor better
mentir (ie, i) to lie
mentiroso/-a lying
merecer to deserve
merecer to merit
mes (m.) month
mesa (f.) table
meter (en) to put (into)
metro (m.) subway
mexicano/-a Mexican
mi my
miedo (m.) fear
mientras while
miércoles Wednesday
mil thousand
minero/-a mining
minuto (m.) minute
mirar to look at; to watch
mirarse to look at (oneself)
mismo/-a same
molestar to annoy; to bother
momento (m.) moment
morder (ue) bite
moreno-a brunette
morir (ue, u) to die
moro/-a Moorish
mostrar (ue) to show
mover (ue) to move
muchas veces often
mucho a lot (adverb)
mucho/-a a lot
muchos/-as many
muebles (m. pl.) furniture
muerto/-a dead
mujer (f.) woman
museo (m.) museum
muy very

N

nación (f.) nation
nada nothing
nadar to swim

nadie no one
naipes (m. pl.) cards
natural natural
necesario necessary
necesitar to need
negar (ie) to deny
negro/-a black
nevar (ie) to snow
nicaragüense Nicaraguan
ningún(o)/-a no
niño (m.); niña (f.) child
no no; not
no tener razón to be wrong
noche (f.) night
norte (m.) North
noticias (f. pl.) news
novecientos/-as nine hundred
novela (f.) novel
noventa ninety
novia (f.) girlfriend
noviembre November
novio (m.) boyfriend
nublado cloudy
nuestro/-a our
nueve nine
nuevo/-a new
nunca never

O

obedecer to obey
obelisco (m.) obelisk
obrero (m.); obrera (f.) worker
obtener to get; to obtain
Océano Pacífico Pacific Ocean
ochenta eighty
ocho eight
octubre October
ocupado/-a busy
odio (m.) hate
oficina (f.) office
ofrecer to offer
oír to hear
ojalá I hope that
once eleven
oponerse (a) to oppose
organización (f.) organization
otoño (m.) fall
otro/-a another; other

P

pacífico/-a peaceful
padre (m.) father
padres (m. pl.) parents

pagar   to pay for
país (*m.*)   country
palabra (*f.*)   word
palacio (*m.*)   palace
pan (*m.*)   bread
panameño/-a   Panamanian
papel (*m.*)   paper
paquete (*m.*)   package
para   in order to
para que + clause   in order that
para   about (with estar)
para   for (see Chapter 5 for usage)
paraguas (*m.*)   umbrella
paraguayo/-a   Paraguayan
parecer   to seem
pariente (*m.*)   parent
parillada (*f.*)   mixed grill
parque (*m.*)   park
partido (*m.*)   game
partir   to leave
pasado (*m.*)   past
pasar   to spend (time)
pedir (i, i)   to ask for; to order; to request
peinarse   to comb (one's hair)
película (*f.*)   film; movie
pelirrojo/-a   red-haired
pelo (*m.*)   hair
península (*f.*)   peninsula
pensar (ie) (en)   to think (about); + infinitive = to plan, to intend
perder (ie)   to lose
perezoso/-a   lazy
perfectamente   perfectly
periódico (*m.*)   newspaper
permitir   to permit
pero   but
perro (*m.*)   dog
personas (*f. pl.*)   people
pertenecer (a)   to belong (to)
peruano/-a   Peruvian
pescado (*m.*)   fish (caught)
peso (*m.*)   *peso* (unit of money); weight
piano (*m.*)   piano
pintar   to paint
pintura (*f.*)   painting
pirámide (*f.*)   pyramid
pizarra (*f.*)   blackboard
pizza (*f.*)   pizza
plaga (*f.*)   plague
plan (*m.*)   plan

planeta (*m.*)   planet
plástico (*m.*)   plastic
plato (*m.*)   dish
playa (*f.*)   beach
plaza (*f.*)   plaza
pluscuamperfecto (*m.*)   pluperfect
probar (ue)   to prove
poco/-a   little
pocos/-as   few
poder (ue)   to be able; can
poema (*m.*)   poem
poesía (*f.*)   poetry
policía (*f.*)   police (force)
poner la mesa   to set the table
poner   to put; to place
ponerse (la ropa)   to put on (clothing)
popular   popular
por eso   for that reason, therefore
por la mañana   in the morning
por la noche   in the evening
por la tarde   in the afternoon
por   by; for (see Chapter 5 for usage)
porque   because
¿por qué?   why?
poseer   to possess
posible   possible
practicar   to practice
preferir (ie, i)   to prefer
pregunta (*f.*)   question
premio (*m.*)   prize
preocupado/-a   worried
preocuparse (por)   to worry (about)
preparar   to prepare
pretérito (*m.*)   preterit
primavera (*f.*)   spring
primero/-a   first
primo (*m.*); prima (*f.*)   cousin
prisa (*f.*)   hurry
prisa (tener)   (to be) in a hurry
probable   probable
probar (ue)   to taste
problema (*m.*)   problem
profesor (*m.*); profesora (*f.*)   professor
programa (*m.*)   program
proteger   to protect
proveer   to provide
provincia (*f.*)   province
prudentemente   prudently

puede ser   it may be
puerta (*f.*)   door
puertorriqueño/-a   Puerto Rican
puesto (*m.*)   job
punto (*m.*)   point

Q

que   that (introduces a clause)
¿qué?   what?
quedarse   to stay; to remain
¿qué hora es?   What time is it?
querer (ie)   to want; to wish; to love
querido/-a   beloved
¿quién?   who? (sg.)
¿quiénes?   who? (pl.)
quince   fifteen
quinientos/-as   five hundred
quitarse   to take off
quizá(s)   perhaps

R

radio (*f.*)   radio
rápido   fast; quickly
razón (*f.*)   reason; right
recibir   to receive
recoger   to pick up
recomendar (ie)   to recommend
reconocer   to recognize
recordar (ue)   to remember
recuerdo (*m.*)   souvenir
reducir   to reduce
regalo (*m.*)   gift
regar (ie)   to water
región (*f.*)   region
regional   regional
regla (*f.*)   rule
regresar (a)   to return
regularmente   regularly
reír (i, i)   to laugh
relampaguear   to flash (with lightning)
reloj (*m.*)   watch
repetir (i, i)   to repeat
resolver (ue)   to resolve; to solve
responsable   responsible
respuesta (*f.*)   answer
restaurante (*m.*)   restaurant
resto (*m.*)   rest

retraer   to bring back; to dissuade
revista (f.)   magazine
rezar   to pray
ridículo/-a   ridiculous
rogar (ue)   to beg; to pray; to request
rojo/-a   red
romance   romance
rompecabezas (m.)   puzzle
ropa (f.)   clothing; clothes
rosado/-a   pink
rubio/-a   blond
ruina (f.)   ruin
ruta (f.)   route
rutina (f.)   routine

S

sábado   Saturday
saber   to know (fact)
saber (+ infinitive)   to know how
sacar fotos   to take photos
sala de estar (f.)   living room
salchicha (f.)   sausage
salir (con)   to go out with
salir (de)   to leave (from a place)
salsa (f.)   salsa (music)
saludar   to greet
salvadoreño/-a   Salvadoran
SEAT (m.)   SEAT (Spanish car)
secarse   to dry (oneself)
secreto (m.)   secret
sed (f.)   thirst
seguir (i, i)   to follow
según   according to
seguro (de)   certain (of); safe; sure; sure (of)
seis   six
seiscientos/-as   six hundred
selva (f.)   jungle
semana (f.)   week
semejante (a)   similar (to)
señor (m.)   Mr.
señora (f.)   Mrs.
señorita (f.)   Miss
sentado/-a   sitting; seated
sentarse (ie)   to sit down
sentir (ie, i)   to feel sorry; to regret
sentirse (ie, i)   to feel
septiembre   September

ser   to be (enduring)
serio/-a   serious
servir (i, i)   to serve
sesenta   sixty
setecientos   seven hundred
setenta   seventy
si   if
sí   yes
siempre   always
siete   seven
silla (f.)   chair
simpático/-a   nice
sin que   without
sincero/-a   sincere
sobrar   to be in surplus; to be left over
sobre   about (concerning)
sofá (m.)   sofa
sol (hacer)   (to be) sunny
sol (m.)   sol (Peruvian monetary unit); sun
soler (ue)   to be in the habit of
sombrero (m.)   hat
soñar (ue) (con)   to dream (of)
sonar (ue)   to ring; to sound
sonido (m.)   ring; sound
sopa (f.)   soup
sostener   to support; to sustain
sótano (m.)   basement
su   her; his, their, your (pol. sg.); your (pol. pl.)
subir (a)   to climb; to go up
subjuntivo (m.)   subjunctive
Sudamérica   South America
sudamericano/-a   South American
sueño (m.)   dream; sleep
suerte (f.)   luck
sufrir   to suffer
sugerir (ie, i)   to suggest
suponer   to suppose
sur (m.)   South
surgir   to surge
suroeste (m.)   Southwest
sustituir   to substitute
sustraer   to subtract

T

tal vez   perhaps
también   also
tan pronto como   as soon as
tango (m.)   tango

tanto   so much (adverb)
tanto/-a   so much
tarde (f.)   afternoon
tarde   late
tarea (f.)   task; homework
té (m.)   tea
teléfono (m.)   phone; telephone
telenovela (f.)   soap opera
televisión (f.)   television
tema (m.)   subject; topic
temer   to fear
tempestad (f.)   storm
temprano   early
tener … años   to be … years old
tener ganas (de)   to feel like
tener que (+ infinitive)   to have to
(tener) sed   (to be) thirsty
tener   to have (possess)
tenis (m.)   tennis
terminar   to complete; to finish
terrible   terrible
tiempo (m.)   tense; time; weather
tienda (f.)   shop
tabaco (m.)   tobacco
tocar   to play (instrument); to touch
todas las semanas   every week
todas las noches   every night
todo   everything
todo/-a   all
todo el día   all day
todo los años   every year
todos los días   every day
todos los meses   every month
tomar   to take (food)
tonto/-a   foolish
tormenta (f.)   storm
tostar (ue)   to toast
trabajador/-a   hardworking
trabajar   to work
trabajo (m.)   job, work
traducir   to translate
traer   to bring
tragar   to swallow
traje de baño (m.)   bathing suit
trazar   to trace
trece   thirteen
treinta   thirty
tres   three
trescientos/-as   three hundred
tronar (ue)   to thunder

tropezar (ie) (con)   to stumble (into)
tu   your (*fam. sg.*)
tú   you (*fam. sg.*)
turista (*m./f.*)   tourist

U

Ud.   you (*pol. sg.*)
Uds.   you (*pol. pl.*)
último/-a   latest, last
un poco   a little
universidad (*f.*)   university
uno   one
uruguayo/-a   Uruguayan
usar   to use
usted   you (*pol. sg.*)
ustedes   you (*pol. pl.*)

V

vacaciones (*f. pl.*)   vacation
vagar   to wander
valer   to be worth
varios/-as   several
vaso (*m.*)   glass (drinking)
Vd.   you (*pol. sg.*)
Vds.   you (*pol. pl.*)

veinte   twenty
veinticinco   twenty-five
veinticuatro   twenty-four
veintidós   twenty-two
veintinueve   twenty-nine
veintiocho   twenty-eight
veintiséis   twenty-six
veintisiete   twenty-seven
veintitrés   twenty-three
veintiun(o)/-a   twenty-one
vencer   to conquer; to defeat
vender   to sell
venezolano/-a   Venezuelan
venir   to come
ventana (*f.*)   window
ver   to see
verano (*m.*)   summer
verbo (*m.*)   verb
¿verdad?   Aren't you?; Don't you?
verdad (*f.*)   truth
verdadero/-a   true
verde   green; unripe
verdura (*f.*)   vegetable
vergüenza (*f.*)   shame
verse   to see (oneself)
vestido/-a (de)   dressed (in)
vestirse (i, i)   to dress (oneself)
viajar   to travel

viaje (*m.*)   trip
viejo/a   old
viento (hacer)   (to be) windy
viento (*m.*)   wind
viernes   Friday
vino (*m.*)   wine
violoncelo (*m.*)   cello
visita (*f.*)   visit
visitar   to visit
vivir   to live
vivo/-a   alive; lively; bright (in color)
volar (ue)   to fly
volver (ue) (a)   return; + infinitive = to ... again
vosotros/-as   you (*fam. pl.*)
vuelo (*m.*)   flight
vuestro/-a   your (*fam. pl.*)

Y

y   and
ya   already
yacer   to lie down

Z

zurcir   to darn; to mend

ENGLISH-SPANISH VOCABULARY

A

a little bit   un poco
a lot   mucho
A.M.   de la mañana
about (concerning)   sobre
about to   para (with estar)
absent   ausente
accident   accidente (m.)
according to   según
accordion   acordeón (m.)
(to) ache   doler (ue)
action   acción (f.)
active   activo/-a
address   dirección (f.)
(to) admire   admirar
(to) admit   admitir
advisable (to be)   convenir
(to) advise   aconsejar
afraid (to be)   (tener) miedo
   (de)
after   después (de)
afternoon   tarde (f.)
afterwards   después
ago   hace
(to) agree (with)   (estar) de
   acuerdo (con)
airplane   avión (m.)
airport   aeropuerto (m.)
alert (to be)   (ser) despierto/-a
alive (to be)   (estar) vivo/-a
all   todo/-a
all day   todo el día
all night   toda la noche
almost   casi
aloud   en voz alta
already   ya
also   también
although   aunque
always   siempre
American   americano/-a
amused (to be)   (estar)
   divertido/-a
and   y
Andes   Andes (m. pl.)
angry   enojado/-a
animal   animal (m.)
(to) annoy   molestar
another   otro/-a

answer   respuesta (f.)
(to) appeal to (food)   apetecer
(to) appear   aparecer
(to) appear to   parecer
appetizing (to be)   apetecer
(to) approve   aprobar (ue)
April   abril
archaeology   arqueología (f.)
Argentinean   argentino/-a
(to) arrest   detener
(to) arrive   llegar (a)
art   arte (m.)
artichoke   alcachofa (f.)
as a child   de niño (m.); de
   niña (f.)
as soon as   en cuanto, tan
   pronto como
ashamed (to be)   (tener)
   vergüenza (de)
(to) ask for   pedir (i, i)
at   a, en
at home   en casa
at this moment   en este
   momento
at this time   a esta hora
At what time?   ¿A qué hora?
(to) attend   asistir (a)
attic   desván (m.)
(to) attract   atraer
attractive   atractivo/-a
August   agosto
author   autor (m.)
(to) authorize   autorizar
avenue   avenida (f.)
awake (to be)   (estar)
   despierto/-a

B

bad   malo/-a; mal (before m. sg.
   noun)
bad mood (to be in a)   (estar)
   de mal humor
bad weather   (hacer) mal
   tiempo
balboa   balboa (m.)
   (Panamanian unit of currency)
ballet   ballet (m.)

barbecue   churrasco (m.)
   (Argentina)
baseball   béisbol (m.)
basement   sótano (m.)
basketball   baloncesto (m.)
bathe (oneself)   bañarse
bathing suit   traje de baño (m.)
bathroom   cuarto de baño (m.)
bay   bahía (f.)
(to) be   estar (location, short
   duration)
(to) be   ser (enduring)
(to) be … years old   tener …
   años
(to) be able   poder (ue)
(to) be sufficient   bastar
(to) be sure (of)   estar seguro
   (de)
(to) be worth   valer
beach   playa (f.)
bean   frijol (m.)
beautiful   bello/-a; hermoso/-a
beauty   belleza (f.)
because   porque
bedroom   alcoba (f.); cáuara
   (f.)
beer   cerveza (f.)
before   antes (de); antes de que
   + clause
(to) beg   rogar (ue)
(to) begin   comenzar (ie);
   empezar (ie)
(to) believe   creer
(to) belong (to)   pertenecer (a)
beloved   querido/-a
better   mejor
bill   cuenta (f.)
birthplace   lugar de nacimiento
   (m.)
(to) bite   morder (ue)
black   negro/-a
blackboard   pizarra (f.)
blond   rubio/-a
blue   azul
(to) boil   hervir (ie, i)
Bolivian   boliviano/-a
book   libro (m.)
border   frontera (f.)
bored (to be)   (ser) aburrido/-a

boring (to be)   (estar) aburrido/-a
(to) bother   molestar
boxer   boxeador (*m.*)
boyfriend   novio (*m.*)
brand-new (to be)   (ser) nuevo/-a
bread   pan (*m.*)
(to) break   romper
brick   ladrillo (*m.*)
bright (in color)   (ser) vivo/-a
(to) bring   traer
(to) bring back   retraer
brother   hermano (*m.*)
brown   marrón
brunette   moreno/-a
(to) brush (oneself)   cepillarse
(to) build   construir
bullfight   corrida de toros (*f.*)
(to) burst out laughing   dar una carcajada
bus   autobús (*m.*)
busy   ocupado/-a
but   pero
(to) buy   comprar
by   por, de

C

(to) call   llamar
(to) call (oneself)   llamarse
camera   cámara (*f.*)
(to) can   poder (ue)
canal   canal (*m.*)
capital   capital (*f.*)
car   coche (*m.*)
cards   naipes (*m. pl.*)
(to) care for   cuidar
carefully   con cuidado
Caribbean   caribe
(to) carry   llevar
casino   casino (*m.*)
castle   castillo (*m.*)
Catalan   catalán
cave   cueva (*f.*)
CD   disco compacto (*m.*)
cello   violoncelo (*m.*)
center   centro (*m.*)
Central America   Centroamérica
certain   cierto/-a
chair   silla (*f.*)
chapter   capítulo (*m.*)
(to) chat   charlar
checkers   damas (*f. pl.*)

chess   ajedrez (*m.*)
child   niño (*m.*); niña (*f.*)
Chilean   chileno/-a
church   iglesia (*f.*)
city   ciudad (*f.*)
civil   civil
class   clase (*f.*)
(to) classify   clasificar
classroom   aula de clase (*f.*)
(to) clean   limpiar
clever (to be)   (ser) listo/-a
(to) climb   subir (a)
(to) close   cerrar (ie)
clothes   ropa (*f.*)
clothing   ropa (*f.*)
cloudy (to be)   (estar) nublado
coffee   café (*m.*)
cold   frío (*m.*)
cold (to be)   (tener) frío
cold (to be) (weather)   (hacer) frío
Colombian   colombiano/-a
colón   colón (*m.*) (monetary unit in Costa Rica)
color   color (*m.*)
(to) comb (one's hair)   peinarse
(to) come   venir
(to) commit   cometer
(to) compete   competir (i, i)
(to) complete   acabar, terminar
(to) compose   componer
composition   composición (*f.*)
computer   computadora (*f.*)
concert   concierto (*m.*)
(to) conclude   concluir
condition   condición (*f.*)
(to) confess   confesar (ie)
congrio   congrio (*m.*) (Chilean eel)
(to) conjugate   conjugar
conjugation   conjugación (*f.*)
(to) conquer   vencer
(to) consent   consentir (ie, i)
constantly   constantemente
(to) contain   contener
contained (to be)   caber
(to) contract   contraer
(to) contribute   contribuir
(to) convert   convertir (ie, i)
(to) convince   convencer
convinced (to be) (of)   estar convencido/-a (de que)

(to) cook   cocinar
cool (to be) (weather)   (hacer) fresco
córdoba   córdoba (*m.*) (Nicaraguan unit of currency)
(to) correct   corregir (i, i)
corvina   corvina (*f.*) (Peruvian sea bass)
(to) cost   costar (ue)
Costa Rican   costarricense
(to) count (on)   contar (con) (ue)
country   país (*m.*)
court   corte (*f.*)
cousin   primo (*m.*); prima (*f.*)
(to) cover   cubrir
covered (with)   cubierto (de)
(to) create   crear
(to) create a good impression   caer bien a
crop   cosecha (*f.*)
Cuban   cubano/-a
culture   cultura (*f.*)

D

(to) dance   bailar
(to) darn   zurcir
date   fecha (*f.*)
daughter   hija (*f.*)
day   día (*m.*)
day before yesterday   anteayer
dead   muerto/-a
December   diciembre
(to) decide   decidir
(to) deduce   deducir
(to) defeat   vencer
(to) defend   defender (ie)
(to) delight   encantar
(to) demand   exigir (i, i)
(to) deny   negar (ie)
(to) describe   describir
(to) deserve   merecer
(to) destroy   destruir
(to) detain   detener
(to) die   morir (ue, u)
difficult   difícil
dining room   comedor (*m.*)
dinner   cena (*f.*)
(to) direct   dirigir (i, i)
direction   dirección (*f.*)
(to) disappear   desaparecer
(to) discover   descubrir
(to) discuss   discutir

dish   plato (*m.*)
(to) display   lucir
(to) dissuade   retraer
(to) distract   distraer
divorced   divorciado/-a
(to) do   hacer
doctor   doctor (*m.*); doctora
   (*f.*)
dog   perro (*m.*)
dollar   dólar (*m.*)
Dominican   dominicano/-a
Dominican Republic   La
   República Dominicana
Don't you?   ¿Verdad?
door   puerta (*f.*)
(to) doubt   dudar
downtown   centro (*m.*)
dream   sueño (*m.*)
(to) dream (of)   soñar (con)
   (ue)
(to) dress (oneself)   vestirse (i,
   i)
dressed (in)   vestido/-a (de)
(to) drink   beber
(to) drive   conducir, manejar
(to) drizzle   lloviznar
drunk   borracho/-a
(to) dry (oneself)   secarse

E

e-mail   correo electrónico
   (*m.*)
early   temprano
easily   fácilmente
East   este (*m.*)
(to) eat   comer
(to) eat breakfast   desayunar
(to) eat dinner   cenar
(to) eat lunch   almorzar (ue)
Ecuadorean   ecuatoriano/-a
efficient   eficiente
egg   huevo (*m.*)
eight   ocho
eighteen   dieciocho
eighty   ochenta
(to) elect   elegir (i, i)
elegant   elegante
elevator   ascensor (*m.*)
eleven   once
(to) embrace   abrazar
employee   empleado (*m.*);
   empleada (*f.*)
enchanting to (to be)   encantar

enemy   enemigo (*m.*)
English   inglés (*m.*)
(to) enjoy   gozar (de)
(to) enjoy (oneself)   divertirse
   (i, i)
enormous   enorme
enough (to be)   bastar
(to) enter   entrar (en)
entertaining (to be)   (ser)
   divertido/-a
essay   ensayo (*m.*)
(to) establish   establecer
even if   aunque
even though   aunque
every   cada
every day   todos los días
every month   todos los meses
every night   todas las noches
every week   todas las semanas
every year   todos los años
everything   todo
evident   evidente
evil   malo/-a; mal (before *m. sg.*
   noun)
exactly   en punto (time)
exam   examen (*m.*); exámenes
   (*m. pl.*)
excellent   excelente
Excuse me   Perdón
exercise   ejercicio (*m.*)
(to) exercise   ejercer
(to) exert   ejercer
exhaustive (to be)   (ser)
   completo/-a
exhibition   exhibición (*f.*)
(to) exist   existir
expensive   caro/-a

F

fácil   easy
fairy   hada (*f.*)
fall   otoño (*m.*); caer
(to) fall asleep   dormirse (ue,
   u)
(to) fall down   caerse
familiar with (to be)   conocer
famous   famoso/-a
fantastic   fantástico/-a
far (from)   lejos de
(to) fascinate   fascinar
fast   rápido
fat   gordo/-a
father   padre (*m.*)

favorite   favorito/-a
fear   miedo (*m.*); temer
February   febrero
(to) feel   sentirse (ie, i)
(to) feel like   tener ganas (de)
(to) feel sorry   sentir (ie, i)
few   pocos/-as
fifteen   quince
fifty   cincuenta
film   película (*f.*)
(to) find   encontrar (ue); hallar
(to) finish   acabar; terminar
(to) fire   despedir (i, i)
first   primero/-a
fish (caught)   pescado (*m.*)
(to) fit   caber
five   cinco
five hundred   quinientos/-as
(to) flash (with
   lightning)   relampaguear
(to) flee   huir
flight   vuelo (*m.*)
(to) flow   fluir
flower   flor (*f.*)
(to) fly   volar (ue)
folkloric   folklórico/-a
(to) follow   seguir (i, i)
food   comida (*f.*)
foolish   tonto/-a
football   fútbol americano (*m.*)
for   para, por (see Chapter 5
   use of para and por)
for that reason   por eso
force   fuerza (*f.*)
forty   cuarenta
four   cuatro
four hundred   cuatrocientos/-as
fourteen   catorce
French   francés (*m.*)
frequently   con frecuencia,
   frecuentemente
Friday   viernes
friend   amiga (*f.*); amigo
   (*m.*)
from   de
(to) fry   freír (i, i)
full   lleno/-a
funny   cómico/-a
furniture   muebles (*m. pl.*)

G

gallery   galería (*f.*)
game   juego (*m.*); partido (*m.*)

garage   garaje (*m.*)
garden   jardin (*m.*)
generally   generalmente
generous   generoso/-a
(to) get   conseguir (i, i);
   obtener
(to) get angry   enojarse
(to) get undressed   desvestirse
   (i, i)
(to) get up   levantarse
gift   regalo (*m.*)
girlfriend   novia (*f.*)
(to) give   dar
glad (to be)   alegrarse (de)
gladly   de buenas ganas
glass   copa (*f.*) (wine); vaso
   (*m.*) (drinking)
(to) go   ir (a)
(to) go away   irse
(to) go downtown   ir al centro
(to) go out with   salir (con)
(to) go shopping   ir de compras
(to) go to bed   acostarse (ue)
(to) go up   subir
golf   golf (*m.*)
good   bueno/-a; buen (before
   m. sg. noun)
good (by nature) (to be)   (ser)
   bueno/-a
good for (to be)   convenir
good mood (to be in a)   (estar)
   de buen humor
good weather   (hacer) buen
   tiempo
good-bye   adiós
(to) graduate   graduarse
grandfather   abuelo (*m.*)
grandmother   abuela (*f.*)
(to) grasp   coger
gray   gris
great   gran
green   verde
(to) greet   saludar
(to) grow   crecer
Guarani   guaraní
Guatemalan   guatemalteco/-a
guilty   culpable
guitar   guitarra (*f.*)

H

hair   pelo (*m.*)
half   medio/-a
hamburger   hamburguesa (*f.*)

hand   mano (*f.*)
(to) hand over   entregar
(to) hang (up)   colgar (ue)
happy   alegre
hardworking   trabajador/-a
hat   sombrero (*m.*)
hatred   odio (*m.*)
(to) have   haber (auxiliary);
   tener (possess)
(to) have dinner   cenar
(to) have just   acabar de (+
   infinitive)
(to) have lunch   almorzar (ue)
(to) have to   tener que (+
   infinitive)
head   cabeza (*f.*)
(to) hear   oír
heat   calor (*m.*)
(to) help   ayudar
her   su
here   aquí
(to) hinder   impedir (i, i)
his   su
historic; historical   histórico/-a
hockey   hockey (*m.*)
(to) hold   contener
home   casa (*f.*)
homework   tarea (*f.*)
Honduran   hondureño/-a
(to) hope   esperar
hot (to be)   tener calor
hot (to be) (weather)   hacer
   calor
hotel   hotel (*m.*)
hour   hora (*f.*)
house   casa (*f.*)
How long?   ¿Cuánto tiempo
   hace que …?; ¿Desde
   cuándo?
How long had…?   ¿Cuánto
   tiempo hacía que …?; ¿Desde
   cuándo …?
How many?   ¿Cuántos/-as?
How much?   ¿Cuánto/-a?
How nice!   ¡Qué bueno!
(to) hug   abrazar
humid (to be)   (estar) húmedo
hundred   cien(to)
hunger   hambre (*f.*)
hungry (to be)   (tener) hambre
hurry   prisa (*f.*)
hurry (to be in a)   (tener) prisa
husband   esposo (*m.*)

I

I hope that …   Ojalá que …
idea   idea (*f.*)
if   si
(to) impede   impedir (i, i)
importance   importancia (*f.*)
important   importante
important (to be)   (ser)
   importante; importar
impossible   imposible
improbable   improbable
in case that   en caso de que
in good health (to be)   (estar)
   bueno/-a
in order that   para que + clause
in order to   para
in surplus (to be)   sobrar
in the afternoon   por la tarde
in the evening   por la noche
in the habit of (to be)   soler
   (ue)
in the morning   por la mañana
Incan   incásico/-a
(to) include   incluir
incredible   increíble
(to) induce   inducir
(to) infer   deducir
(to) influence   influir
ingredient   ingrediente (*m.*)
intelligent   inteligente
intend   pensar (ie) (+ infinitive)
interesting   interesante
interesting (to be)   (ser)
   interesante
(to) introduce   introducir
irresponsible   irresponsable
island   isla (*f.*)
It is necessary   Hay que …
It may be   Puede ser …
Italian   italiano (*m.*)
itinerary   itinerario (*m.*)

J

jacket   chaqueta (*f.*)
jail   cárcel (*f.*)
January   enero
jewel   joya (*f.*)
job   puesto (*m.*); trabajo (*m.*);
   empleo (*m.*)
July   julio
(to) jump about   dar saltos
June   junio

jungle   selva (f.)
(to) justify   justificar

K

key   llave (f.)
kind   amable
(to) kiss   besar
kitchen   cocina (f.)
(to) know (fact)   saber
(to) know (someone)   conocer
(to) know how   saber
   (+ infinitive)

L

lacking (to be)   faltar
lake   lago (m.)
language   idioma (m.); lengua
   (f.)
last month   el mes pasado
last night   anoche
last week   la semana pasada
last year   el año pasado
late   tarde
latest   último/-a
(to) laugh   reír (i, i)
lawyer   abogado (m.); abogada
   (f.)
lazy   perezoso/-a
(to) learn   aprender (a)
(to) leave   partir
(to) leave (from a place)   salir
   (de)
(to) leave (something)   dejar
left over (to be)   sobrar
lempira   lempira (m.)
   (monetary unit in Honduras)
lesson   lección (f.)
letter   carta (f.)
library   biblioteca (f.)
(to) lie   mentir (ie, i)
(to) lie down   yacer
lier   mentiroso/-a
light   luz (f.)
(to) light   encender (ie)
like   como; caer bien a
like new (to be)   (estar)
   nuevo/-a
likely (to be)   (ser) probable;
   (ser) fácil
(to) listen to   escuchar
literature   literatura (f.)
little   poco

(to) live   vivir
lively (to be)   (ser) vivo/-a
living room   sala de estar
   (f.)
long   largo/-a
(to) look at   mirar
(to) look at (oneself)   mirarse
(to) look for   buscar
(to) lose   perder (ie)
lottery   lotería (f.)
love   querer (ie) (a)
luck   suerte (f.)
lucky (to be)   (tener) suerte
lunch   almuerzo (m.)

M

magazine   revista (f.)
(to) maintain   mantener
(to) make   hacer
(to) make no difference   dar
   igual
makeup   maquillaje (m.)
man   hombre (m.)
many   muchos/-as
map   mapa (m.)
March   marzo
married (to)   casado/-a (con)
(to) marry   casarse (con)
marvelous   maravilloso
mate (a type of tea)   mate (m.)
matter (business)   asunto (m.)
May   mayo
Mayan   maya
meal   comida (f.)
(to) measure   medir (i, i)
(to) mend   zurcir
(to) merit   merecer
Mexican   mexicano/-a
midnight   medianoche (f.)
milk   leche (f.)
miner   minero/-a
mining   minero/-a
minute   minuto (m.)
mirror   espejo (m.)
Miss   señorita (f.)
missing (to be)   faltar
mixed grill   parrillada (f.)
moment   momento (m.)
Monday   lunes
money   dinero (m.)
month   mes (m.)
Moorish   moro/-a
more   más

morning   mañana (f.)
mother   madre (f.)
(to) move   mover (ue)
movie   película (f.)
Mr.   señor (m.)
Mrs.   señora (f.)
museum   museo (m.)
music   música (f.)
my   mi

N

named (to be)   llamarse
nation   nación (f.)
natural   natural
near   cerca de
nearby   cerca
necessary   necesario
(to) need   necesitar
neighborhood   barrio (m.)
never   jamás, nunca
new   nuevo/-a
news   noticias (f. pl.)
newspaper   periódico (m.)
next week   la semana próxima
next year   el año próximo
Nicaraguan   nicaragüense
nice   amable; simpático/-a
night   noche (f.)
nine   nueve
nine hundred   novecientos/-as
nineteen   diecinueve
ninety   noventa
no   ningún(o)/-a; before m. sg.
   noun ningún; no
no one   nadie
noon   mediodía (m.)
North   norte (m.)
not   no
notebook   cuaderno (m.)
nothing   nada
(to) notice   advertir (ie, i)
novel   novela (f.)
November   noviembre
now   ahora
nowadays   hoy en día

O

obelisk   obelisco (m.)
(to) obey   obedecer
(to) obtain   conseguir (i, i);
   obtener
obvious   obvio

October   octubre
of   de
Of course!   ¡Claro que sí!
(to) offer   ofrecer
office   oficina (f.)
often   a menudo; muchas veces
old   viejo/-a
olive oil   aceite de oliva (m.)
on   en
on call (to be)   (estar) de
   guardia
on time   a tiempo
on vacation   de vacaciones
one   uno
one must   hay que
open   abierto/-a
(to) open   abrir
(to) oppose   oponerse (a)
orange   anaranjado/-a
(to) order   pedir (i, i)
organization   organización (f.)
other   otro/-a
ought   deber
our   nuestro/-a
(to) owe   deber

P

P.M.   de la tarde, de la
   noche
Pacific Ocean   Océano Pacífico
package   paquete (m.)
painful (to be)   doler (ue)
(to) paint   pintar
painting   cuadro (m.); pintura
   (f.)
palace   palacio (m.)
Panamanian   panameño/-a
paper   papel (m.)
Paraguayan   paraguayo/-a
parents   padres (m. pl.)
park   parque (m.)
party   fiesta (f.)
past   pasado (m.)
(to) pay attention to   hacer
   caso a
(to) pay for   pagar
peaceful   pacífico/-a
pen   bolígrafo
peninsula   península (f.)
people   gente (f. sg.); personas
   (f. pl.)
perfectly   perfectamente
perhaps   acaso, quizá(s), tal vez

(to) permit   permitir
(to) persuade   inducir
Peruvian   peruano/-a
peso   peso (m.) (unit of money
   in several countries)
phone   teléfono (m.); llamar
   por teléfono
photo   foto (f.)
piano   piano (m.)
(to) pick up   recoger
pink   rosado/-a
pity   lástima (f.)
pizza   pizza (f.)
place   lugar (m.)
(to) place   poner
plague   plaga (f.)
plain   llano (m.)
plan   plan (m.)
(to) plan   pensar (ie)
   (+ infinitive)
plane   avión (m.)
planet   planeta (m.)
plastic   plástico (m.)
(to) play (game)   jugar (a) (ue)
(to) play (instrument)   tocar
(to) play the role of   hacer el
   papel de
plaza   plaza (f.)
pleasant   agradable
(to) please   agradar
pleasing to (to be)   gustar (a)
pluperfect   pluscuamperfecto
   (m.)
poem   poema (m.)
poetry   poesía (f.)
point   punto (m.)
police (force)   policía (f.)
pool   billar (m.)
popular   popular
(to) possess   poseer
possible   posible
(to) practice   practicar
praise   alabanza (f.)
(to) pray   rezar; rogar (ue)
(to) prefer   preferir (ie, i)
(to) prepare   preparar
(to) pretend   fingir
preterit   pretérito (m.)
pretty   bonito/-a; lindo/-a
(to) prevent   impedir (i, i)
prize   premio (m.)
probable   probable
problem   problema (m.)
program   programa (m.)

(to) protect   proteger
(to) prove   probar (ue)
(to) provide   proveer
provided that   con tal de que
province   provincia (f.)
prudently   prudentemente
Puerto Rican   puertorriqueño/-a
pupil   alumno (m.); alumna (f.)
purse   bolsa (f.)
(to) put   poner
(to) put (into)   meter (en)
(to) put on (clothing)   ponerse
   (la ropa)
puzzle   rompecabezas (m.)
pyramid   pirámide (f.)

Q

quarter   cuarto (telling time)
question   pregunta (f.)
quickly   rápido
quiet (to be)   (ser) callado/-a

R

radio   radio (f.)
(to) rain   llover (ue)
rainy (to be)   (estar) lluvioso
(to) read   leer
ready (to be)   (estar) listo/-a
ready to   listo/-a para
(to) realize   darse cuenta (de)
reason   razón (f.)
(to) receive   recibir
(to) recognize   reconocer
(to) recommend   recomendar
   (ie)
red   rojo/-a
red-haired   pelirrojo/-a
(to) reduce   reducir
region   región (f.)
regional   regional
(to) regret   lamentar; sentir
   (ie, i)
regularly   regularmente
relative   pariente (m.)
(to) remain   quedarse
(to) remember   recordar (ue);
   acordarse (ue) (de)
(to) repeat   repetir (i, i)
(to) request   pedir (i, i); rogar
   (ue)
(to) require   exigir (i, i)
(to) resolve   resolver (ue)

responsible responsable
(to) rest descansar; resto (*m.*)
restaurant restaurante (*m.*)
(to) return regresar (a); volver (ue) (a)
(to) return (something) devolver (ue)
rib steak bife de costilla (*m.*)
ridiculous ridículo
right (to be) tener razón
right now ahora mismo
(to) ring sonar (ue)
romance romance
room cuarto (*m.*)
route ruta (*f.*)
routine rutina (*f.*)
ruin ruina (*f.*)
rule regla (*f.*)
(to) run correr

S

safe seguro/-a
salsa (music) salsa (*f.*)
Salvadoran salvadoreño/-a
same mismo/-a
Saturday sábado
sausage salchicha (*f.*)
(to) say decir (i, i)
(to) scatter esparcir
science fiction ciencia ficción (*f.*)
(to) scream dar voces
(to) scrub fregar (ie)
sea mar (*m.*)
season estación (*f.*)
SEAT SEAT (*m.*) (Spanish car)
secret secreto (*m.*)
(to) see ver
(to) see (oneself) verse
(to) seem parecer
(to) seize coger
(to) select escoger
selfish egoísta
(to) sell vender
(to) send enviar; mandar
September septiembre
serious serio/-a
(to) serve servir (i, i)
(to) set the table poner la mesa
seven siete
seven hundred setecientos/-as
seventeen diecisiete

seventy setenta
several varios/-as
(to) shake hands dar la mano
shame vergüenza (*f.*)
sharp en punto (time)
(to) shave afeitarse
shelf estante (*m.*)
(to) shine lucir
shop tienda (*f.*)
short bajo/-a
short story cuento (*m.*)
should deber
(to) shout gritar
show espectáculo (*m.*); cine (*m.*)
(to) show mostrar (ue)
sick (to get) enfermarse; enfermo/-a; malo/-a
side lado (*m.*)
silent (to be) (estar) callado/-a
similar (to) semejante (a)
sincere sincero/-a
(to) sing cantar
sister hermana (*f.*)
(to) sit down sentarse (ie)
sitting sentado/-a
six seis
six hundred seiscientos/-as
sixteen dieciséis
sixty sesenta
(to) ski esquiar
(to) sleep dormir (ue, u); sueño (*m.*)
sleepy (to be) (tener) sueño
slender delgado/-a
slowly lentamente
(to) smoke fumar
(to) snow nevar (ie)
so much tanto/-a; tanto (adverb)
soap opera telenovela (*f.*)
soccer fútbol (*m.*)
sofa sofá (*m.*)
sol sol (*m.*) (Peruvian monetary unit)
(to) solve resolver (ue)
some algun(o)/-a
someone alguien
something algo
somewhat algo (with an adjective)
son hijo (*m.*)
song canción (*f.*)

(to) sound sonar (ue); sonido (*m.*)
soup sopa (*f.*)
South sur (*m.*)
South America Sudamérica
South American sudamericano/-a
Southwest suroeste (*m.*)
souvenir recuerdo (*m.*)
Spaniard español
Spanish español
(to) speak hablar
specific específico/-a
(to) spend (money) gastar
(to) spend (time) pasar
spider araña (*f.*)
spread esparcir
spring primavera (*f.*)
(to) spurt surgir
(to) stand out destacar
standing (to be) (estar) de pie
(to) stay quedarse
steak bistec (*m.*)
(to) stop cesar (de)
store tienda (*f.*)
storm tormenta (*f.*); tempestad (*f.*)
street calle (*f.*)
student estudiante (*m.*); estudiante (*f.*)
(to) study estudiar
(to) stumble (into) tropezar (ie) (con)
stupendous estupendo/-as
subject tema (*m.*)
subjunctive subjuntivo (*m.*)
(to) substitute sustituir
(to) subtract sustraer
subway metro (*m.*)
(to) suffer sufrir
(to) suggest sugerir (ie, i)
(to) suit one's interest convenir
suitcase maleta (*f.*)
summer verano (*m.*)
sun sol (*m.*)
Sunday domingo
sunny (weather) (to be) (hacer) sol
(to) support sostener
(to) suppose suponer
sure of (to be) (estar) seguro/-a (de)
sure to happen (to be) (ser) seguro/-a

T

table   mesa (f.)
(to) take (food)   tomar
(to) take a photo   sacar fotos
(to) take a shower   ducharse
(to) take a trip   hacer un viaje
(to) take a walk   dar un paseo
(to) take care of   cuidar
(to) take off (clothing)   quitarse
(to) take photos   sacar fotos
tall   alto/-a
tango   tango (m.)
task   tarea (f.)
(to) taste   probar (ue)
tea   té (m.)
teacher   profesor (m.);
   profesora (f.)
telephone   llamar por teléfono;
   teléono (m.)
television   televisión (f.)
(to) tell   decir (i, i)
(to) tell (a story)   contar (ue)
ten   diez
tennis   tenis (m.)
terrible   terrible
test   examen (m.) exámenes
   (m. pl.)
(to) test   probar (ue)
(to) thank   agradecer
Thank you   Gracias
that   aquel/-la (at a distance);
   ese/-a (relatively far from
   the speaker and hearer); que
   (introduces a clause)
theater   teatro (m.)
their   su
then   entonces
there   allí
there are   hay
there is   hay
therefore   por eso
these   estos/-as (close to the
   speaker and hearer)
thing   cosa (f.)

(to) think (about)   pensar (ie)
   (en)
thirst   sed (f.)
thirsty (to be)   (tener) sed
thirteen   trece
thirty   treinta
thirty-one   treinta y un/o
this   este, esta (close to the
   speaker and hearer)
those   esos/-as (relatively far
   from the speaker and hearer);
   aquellos/-as (at a distance)
thousand   mil
three   tres
three hundred   trescientos/-as
throat   garganta (f.)
(to) thunder   tronar (ue)
Thursday   jueves
ticket   boleto (m.)
time   tiempo (m.)
tired (to be)   (estar) cansado/-a
tired (to get)   cansarse
tiring (to be)   (ser) cansado/-a
(to) toast   tostar (ue)
tobacco   tabaco (m.)
today   hoy
tomorrow   mañana
too much   demasiado
tooth   diente (m.)
topic   tema (m.)
(to) touch   tocar
tourist   turista (m./f.)
(to) trace   trazar
(to) translate   traducir
(to) travel   viajar
trip   viaje (m.)
true   verdadero/-a
truth   verdad (f.)
Tuesday   martes
(to) turn on   encender (ie)
TV   telvisión (f.)
twelve   doce
twenty   veinte
twenty-eight   veintiocho
twenty-five   veinticinco
twenty-four   veinticuatro
twenty-nine   veintinueve
twenty-one   veintiun(o)/a
twenty-seven   veintisiete
twenty-six   veinteséis
twenty-three   veintitrés
twenty-two   veintidós
two   dos
two hundred   doscientos/-as

U

U.S. citizen   estadounidense
ugly   feo/-a
umbrella   paraguas (m.)
(to) understand   comprender;
   entender (ie)
(to) undo   deshacer
unfortunately
   desafortunadamente
university   universidad (f.)
unless   a menos que
unlikely   difícil
unpleasant   antipático/-a
(to) untie (knot)   deshacer
until   hasta (que, with clause)
Uruguayan   uruguayo/-a
(to) use   usar

V

vacation   vacaciones (f. pl.)
vegetable   verdura (f.)
Venezuelan   venezolano/-a
verb   verbo (m.)
very   muy
visit   visita (f.)
(to) visit   visitar

W

(to) wait for   esperar
(to) wake up   despertarse (ie)
(to) walk   andar; caminar
wallet   cartera (f.)
(to) wander   vagar
(to) want   desear; querer (ie)
war   guerra (f.)
warm (to be)   (tener) calor
warmth   calor (m.)
(to) warn   advertir (ie, i)
(to) wash (dishes)   fregar (ie)
(to) wash (oneself)   lavarse
(to) watch   mirar; reloj (m.)
water   agua (f.)
(to) water   regar (ie)
waterfall   cascada (f.); cataratas
   (f.)
(to) wear   llevar
weather   tiempo (m.)
Wednesday   miércoles
week   semana (f.)
weight   peso (m.)

(to) surge   surgir
(to) sustain   sostener
(to) swallow   tragar
sweets   dulces (m. pl.)
(to) swim   nadar
Switzerland   Suiza

well   bien
What?   ¿Qué?
What time is it?   ¿Qué hora es?
When?   ¿Cuándo?
Where?   ¿Dónde?
Which (one)?   ¿Cuál?
Which (ones)?   ¿Cuáles?
while   mientras
white   blanco/-a
Who?   ¿Quién? (sg.) ¿Quiénes?
   (pl.)
Why?   ¿Por qué?
wife   esposa (f.)
(to) win   ganar
wind   viento (m.)
window   ventana (f.)
windy (to be)   (hacer) viento
wine   vino (m.)
winter   invierno (m.)

(to) wish   querer (ie)
with me   conmigo
with you (fam. sg.)   contigo
without   sin que
witty (to be)   (ser) listo/-a
woman   mujer (f.)
wood   madera (f.)
word   palabra (f.)
work   puesto (m.); trabajo
   (m.)
(to) work   trabajar
worker   obrero (m.); obrera (f.)
worried   preocupado/-a
(to) worry (about)   preocuparse
   (por)
(to) wrap (up)   envolver (ue)
(to) write   escribir
writer   escritor (m.); escritora
   (f.)

writing   escrito (m.)
wrong (to be)   no tener razón

Y

year   año (m.)
yellow   amarillo/-a
yes   sí
yesterday   ayer
you (fam. pl.)   vosotros/-as
you (fam. sg.)   tú
you (pol. pl.)   ustedes; Uds.
you (pol. sg.)   usted; Ud.
young   joven
your (fam. pl.)   vuestro/-a
your (fam. sg.)   tu
your (pol. pl.)   su
your (pol. sg.)   su

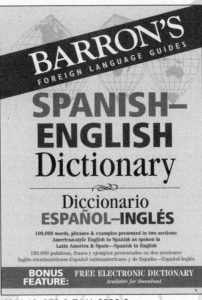

BONUS!

FREE AUDIO LESSONS GIVE YOU EVEN MORE SPANISH VERB PRACTICE!

Take your Spanish language skills even further with a special bonus from Barron's. Free audio lessons — included with your purchase of *Spanish Verb Tenses* — will give you extra instruction for mastering the language's verb forms and their uses. Simply download your free content and increase your fluency even more with:

- **90 Minutes of Audio** — supplemental instruction to reinforce workbook lessons

- **Repetition Exercises** — listen to and repeat verb forms for maximum retention

- **Knowledge Exercises** — test your knowledge of verb conjugations

To access your **FREE** bonus audio content, visit:

www.barronsbooks.com/practice-fs/